THE ILLIMITABLE FREEDOM
of the HUMAN MIND

THE ILLIMITABLE FREEDOM
of the
HUMAN MIND

THOMAS JEFFERSON'S IDEA
OF A UNIVERSITY

ANDREW J. O'SHAUGHNESSY

UNIVERSITY OF VIRGINIA PRESS

CHARLOTTESVILLE AND LONDON

University of Virginia Press
© 2021 by Andrew J. O'Shaughnessy
All rights reserved
Printed in the United States of America on acid-free paper

First published 2021

1 3 5 7 9 8 6 4 2

Library of Congress Cataloging-in-Publication Data
Names: O'Shaughnessy, Andrew Jackson, author.
Title: The illimitable freedom of the human mind: Thomas Jefferson's idea of a
university / Andrew J. O'Shaughnessy.
Description: Charlottesville: University of Virginia Press, [2021] | Includes
bibliographical references and index.
Identifiers: LCCN 2020053650 (print) | LCCN 2020053651 (ebook) |
ISBN 9780813946481 (hardcover) | ISBN 9780813946498 (ebook)
Subjects: LCSH: University of Virginia—History. | Jefferson, Thomas, 1743–1826. |
Public universities and colleges—Virginia—History—19th century. | Education,
Higher—United States—History—19th century.
Classification: LCC LD5678.3 .O84 2021 (print) | LCC LD5678.3 (ebook) |
DDC 378.755/482—dc23
LC record available at https://lccn.loc.gov/2020053650
LC ebook record available at https://lccn.loc.gov/2020053651

Cover art: "Thomas Jefferson" by Thomas Sully, 1821, oil on canvas (American
Philosophical Society) and "Jefferson's elevation and floor plan for a typical pavilion
and dormitories at Albemarle Academy," A Calendar of the Jefferson Papers of the
University of Virginia, Jefferson Papers, 1814 (Courtesy of Albert and Shirley Small
Special Collections Library, University of Virginia)

To Peter S. Onuf,
friend and mentor

Contents

Illustration gallery appears following page 174

FOREWORD

The University of Virginia has always seemed in between. It was born in the vast space between the visions of the ancient philosophers and a worn field in the Piedmont of Virginia, between the ideals of the Enlightenment and the dominion of evangelical Christianity, between a Roman temple and bricks formed from local clay by the hands of enslaved people.

Thomas Jefferson's university embodied many of the puzzles of Thomas Jefferson himself. He too was a paragon of Enlightenment dependent on the labor of enslaved people, a global visionary sometimes given to parochial concerns. And just as his words in the Declaration of Independence came to be embraced by people denied political voice in his time, so did his university eventually welcome people excluded from education for generations.

After two centuries of change, the institution remains, with its complications intact, "Mr. Jefferson's University." Jefferson's vision of the Academical Village remains as evocative as ever, his Rotunda as beautiful and graceful. Meanwhile, the university struggles, as it has from its origins, to serve its home state while priding itself on its place among elite institutions and with national reach. The university reckons with a past whose shape and meaning change with the passage of time and has made its fair share of contributions to that past.

This eloquent book helps us understand how such a university came to be, to change, and to endure. Andrew O'Shaughnessy's thoughtful study offers the deeply researched exploration the university needs and deserves, positioning it in the context of American higher education, allowing us to see how emblematic and influential the institution has been since its inception, revealing the University of Virginia to be as complex and compelling as the man whose vision it embodies.

EDWARD L. AYERS

Acknowledgments

It has been a pleasure and an education to write this book. I was especially fortunate in doing so at the Robert H. Smith International Center for Jefferson Studies at Monticello, whose activities include the editing of the retirement correspondence and many of the manuscripts relating to the early history of the university, as part of *The Papers of Thomas Jefferson*, published by Princeton University Press. First begun under the editorship of Julian P. Boyd in 1943, the series was split in 1998 when the Thomas Jefferson Foundation, which owns and operates Monticello, agreed to publish the Retirement Series, whose first volume appeared in 2005. I am much indebted to the staff of the Retirement Series for their assistance and support, especially to J. Jefferson Looney, the Daniel P. Jordan Editor, who read, corrected, and commented in detail on an early draft. Jeff insisted that the quotes should be exact transcriptions that include Jefferson's idiosyncratic spellings and no capitals at the beginnings of sentences. Lisa A. Francavilla, the senior managing editor, read and offered corrections, in addition to providing references and access to unpublished archives. Ellen Hickman shared copies of unpublished papers and alerted me to the importance of the hitherto unknown drafts of Jefferson's Rockfish Gap Commission.

The Robert H. Smith International Center for Jefferson Studies arranges conferences, both international and domestic, including a 2018 conference on the early history of the University of Virginia. Thanks to the alacrity and persistence of my colleague John Ragosta, the conference papers were published as a volume by the University of Virginia Press in 2019, coedited by him, Peter S. Onuf, and myself, entitled *The Founding of Thomas Jefferson's University*. The conference was entirely funded by the Thomas Jefferson Foundation, thanks to the generosity of trustee J. F. Bryan and his wife, Peggy Bryan. The work of our research scholars, along with that of the archaeology and curatorial departments, has transformed the interpretation of Monticello, especially in the study of slavery and the lives of the descendants of enslaved families in the *Getting Word* African American Oral History Project. My thinking was also stimulated by the visiting fellowship program at the center, in which some thirty recipients give talks about their works in progress.

The research for this book was conducted at the center through the Jefferson Library, which holds copies of the relevant documents, including digital duplicates of manuscripts in the Albert and Shirley Small Special Collections Library at the University of Virginia. Jack Robertson, the Fiske and Marie Kimball Librarian, along with his colleagues, Endrina Tay and Anna Berkes, helped check the endnotes, pursued references, and arranged numerous interlibrary loans. In addition to carefully reading and annotating the manuscript, Endrina Tay provided information about Jefferson's book purchases on educational topics after the sale to the Library of Congress. Fraser Neiman, the director of archaeology, reviewed the manuscript and assisted with the tables relating to students in chapter 9. Senior Fellow Gaye Wilson took notes from the first manuscript workshop on my behalf and helped with the illustrations. As scholarly programs coordinator, Whitney Pippin arranged the illustrations permissions, checked notes, set up the manuscript workshops, and helped in myriad ways, supported by interns Christian Guynn and Bolling Izard. As president of the Thomas Jefferson Foundation, Leslie Greene Bowman was unflinching in her encouragement and support of this project. It is additionally a pleasure to acknowledge the remarkable commitment to research by the foundation's Board of Trustees; their chairman, Jon Meacham; and his predecessor, Don King.

The process of writing this book was facilitated by a 2019 Miegunyah Distinguished Visiting Fellowship at the University of Melbourne (Australia), thanks to the sponsorship and generous hospitality of Jennifer Milam in the School of Culture and Communication and Trevor Burnard in the School of Historical and Philosophical Studies. Alan Taylor generously shared much of his then-unpublished manuscript and later the full proofs of his book *Thomas Jefferson's Education*. Others kindly answered questions, sent references, and shared unpublished papers, including Jeremy Adams, Melissa Adler, Brian Alexander, Jonathon Awtrey, Coy Barefoot, Robert Battle, Bruce Boucher, George Boudreau, Jane Calvert, Jeremy Catto, Elizabeth V. Chew, Stephen Conway, William J. Courtenay, Robert Rhodes Crout, Rebecca Dillingham, Gerald Donowitz, Dennis Dutterer, William Ferraro, Sandy Gilliam, Andrea R. Gray, Adam Griffin, Kevin Gutzman, Robert F. Haggard, Gardiner Hallock, Scott Harrop, Andrew Holowchak, Arthur Kiron, David Konig, Elizabeth Jones, David McCormick, Christine McDonald, Holly Mayer, David Moltke-Hansen, Kenneth Morgan, Johann Neem, Mark Peterson, Eric Proebsting, Sandra Rebok, Nicholas Richardson, Lyndsey Robertson, Chris Rogers, Simon Sun, Elizabeth Dowling Taylor, John Charles Thomas, Peter Thompson, John C. Van Horne, Paula Viterbo, David Wang, Gaye Wilson, and Richard Guy Wilson. Daniel

Keith Addison gave me access to his extensive archive of photographs of the University of Virginia, and Travis McDonald provided photographs of Poplar Forest, where he is the director of architectural restoration. Eduardo Montes-Bradley filmed a pilot documentary about this book that featured an interview with me at Kenwood. Andrew Mullen translated Maria Cosway's songs and *Jours Heureux*, which he also performed and recorded, along with Theresa Goble, Bradley Lehman, and David Sariti, at a concert in the Rotunda in 2008.

I received useful feedback in the course of writing the book from lecture audiences and hosts. It was a privilege to give the first Masaryk Day Lecture at the University of Masaryk at Brno in the Czech Republic, in honor of Tomáš Garrigue Masaryk, regarded as both a founder of the country and of the university, during which I was warmly hosted by University Vice-Rector Břetislav Dančák. After many years of teaching in Wisconsin, it was an honor to deliver the James Madison Lecture at both the University of Wisconsin–Madison and the University of Wisconsin–Milwaukee, where I was kindly hosted at both events by Matt Blessing, the state archivist and division administrator at the Wisconsin Historical Society. It was also a pleasure to deliver the Miegunyah Distinguished Visiting Fellowship Lecture at the University of Melbourne (Australia) hosted by Kathleen Fitzpatrick, and the keynote lecture at the National Constitution Center in Philadelphia for a conference on "The Spirit of Inquiry in the Age of Jefferson," held by the American Philosophical Society and hosted by their library director, Patrick Spero. Other venues included the Centre for the Study of International Slavery at University Liverpool and the International Slavery Museum (England), hosted by Laura Sandy; the University of Potsdam (Germany), hosted by Hannah Spahn; the Summer Academy of Atlantic History in Bernried, Upper Bavaria (Germany), hosted by Susanne Lachenicht; the Revolutionary Age Seminar at Kylemore Abbey (Ireland), sponsored by the University of Notre Dame and hosted by Patrick Griffin; the South Carolina Historical Society, hosted by Virginia DeWitt Zemp; the College of Charleston, hosted by Trisha H. Folds-Bennett and John and Dianne Culhane; the Charlottesville branch of the English-Speaking Union, hosted by Phil Williams; the Treasure Coast UVA Club in Vero Beach, Florida, hosted by Guy Fritz; and the University of Virginia Lifetime Learning Programs' UVA at Oxford Seminar and the Summer Jefferson Symposium, both graciously directed by Althea Brooks. I presented a paper on the origins of the University of Virginia to the Virginia Forum. Finally, I spoke to UVA faculty in talks for the Colonnade Club, hosted by Don E. Detmer, and the Eighteenth-Century Study Group, hosted by David T. Gies and Cynthia Wall.

I am especially grateful to those readers who reviewed the entire manuscript at various stages, sending their corrections and thoughts, including Cameron Addis, Andrew Burstein, Vincent Cahill, Christa Dierksheide, Diane Ehrenpreis, Lisa Francavilla, Robert S. Gibson, Nancy Isenberg, Brenda LaClair, Joseph Michael Lasala, Ann Lucas, Christine McDonald, Robert McDonald, Andrew Miles, Fraser Neiman, Peter S. Onuf, John Ragosta, Robert Self, James R. Sofka, Hannah Spahn, Susan Stein, James Stoner, Claudia Strawderman, and Endrina Tay. John Thelin and Robert D. Anderson read and reviewed the manuscript for the University of Virginia Press. They corresponded with me and shared their respective expertise on the histories of higher education in the United States and Europe. My thanks are also due to those who read and discussed the manuscript in three workshops beginning with Frank Cogliano, Christine McDonald, Robert McDonald, Barbara Oberg, Peter S. Onuf, John Ragosta, Annette Gordon-Reed, Susan Stein, John Thelin, Gaye Wilson, and Nadine Zimmerli. In a follow-up session, the participants included Cameron Addis, Bill Barker, Andrew Burstein, Diane Ehrenpreis, Lily Fox-Bruguiere, Lisa Francavilla, Robert Gibson, Nancy Isenberg, Brenda LaClair, Joseph Michael Lasala, J. Jefferson Looney, Ann Lucas, Andrew Miles, Robert Self, Tasha Stanton, Claudia Strawderman, and Endrina Tay. Arranged by Ann Lucas, the third workshop consisted of Vincent ("Biff") Cahill, Bob DeMento, Peter Grant, Brenda LaClair, Paula Newcomb, Oliver and Ana Schwab, and Chip Stokes.

The revised manuscript was read and commented on by Antoinette White, my childhood friend and former editor at Knopf; Jeanie Grant Moore, a dear friend, ally, and esteemed former colleague; and John Kaminski, who was always the most accessible faculty member during my time in Wisconsin where he was director of the Center for the Study of the American Constitution. Finally, I am grateful to those who read back chapters of the manuscript to me and offered comments: Robert Almanza, Ariel Armenta, Bob DeMento, Richard Douglas, Ann Lucas, Paula Newcomb, Whitney Pippin, Tasha Stanton, and Elizabeth Willingham. As my editor at the University of Virginia Press, Nadine Zimmerli participated in the various workshops, made excellent textual suggestions, and has been a pleasure to work with. The opinions expressed in this book are entirely those of the author and do not reflect those of the readers nor affiliated organizations.

My father, John O'Shaughnessy, reviewed the manuscript as one of my toughest critics and strongest supporters. He first introduced me to the world of American universities during the tumultuous year of 1968 when we sat with my brother for a photograph in front of the Alma Mater statue at Columbia University. He inculcated in me a respect for the academic profession, often prefacing the names of colleagues with "the great," especially members of the philosophy department, such as Ernest Nagel and Sidney Morgenbesser. He also recognized the limitations of universities, saying that they all too frequently merely rationalize prejudices and delighting in Sean O'Casey's definition of a university as "a place where they polish pebbles and dim diamonds." My brother, Nicholas, a professor at Queen Mary College, London University, was the most important early influence in my enjoyment of history and inspired my interest in the history of universities with his 1992 book, co-authored with Cambridge economist Nigel Allington, *Light, Liberty, and Learning: The Idea of a University Revisited.* Just as Jefferson credited the formative influence of his early teachers, I am indebted to those such as Ronald ("Ron") Dalzell, an art teacher, who first introduced me in a slide lecture to the University of Virginia when I was ten years old at Bedford School in England. It transpired later that he was a friend of Frederick ("Freddie") D. Nichols, who was responsible for the renovation of the Rotunda in the 1970s. Jeremy Catto, my undergraduate tutor, was an authority on early scholasticism and the editor of the second of eight volumes that represented the most ambitious history of any university, *The History of the University of Oxford,* published by Oxford University Press. He lived long enough to suggest readings and to answer some of my questions for this book.

Simon Sibelman, a valued friend and former colleague, was responsible for my first visit to the University of Virginia in 1992, when he introduced me to his beloved native state in a whirlwind spring break tour that encompassed Monticello, Williamsburg, and Yorktown. I have dedicated this book to Peter S. Onuf, who is the most prolific, nuanced, and thoughtful interpreter of Jefferson. My endnotes only list those works directly cited in this book, but the larger corpus of his writings has greatly influenced my understanding and analysis. He has been a mentor to me, as well as students and even colleagues. He has an unparalleled gift in my experience to help others better articulate and develop their ideas without imposing his own views. I shall always be indebted to him for reading my doctoral thesis and writing a multipage, single-spaced, typed letter about how to turn it into a book. Since my appointment as the Saunders Director of the Robert H.

Smith International Center for Jefferson Studies in 2003, Peter has given unstintingly of his time and advice in his capacity as the Thomas Jefferson Memorial Foundation Professor at the University of Virginia. He is more importantly a true friend, along with his wife, Kristin, and his daughter, Rachel.

Chip Stokes generously donated money to cover the cost of the color illustrations on behalf of the Jefferson Legacy Foundation.

THE ILLIMITABLE FREEDOM
of the HUMAN MIND

Introduction

As one of the most persuasive and poetic writers of his generation, Thomas Jefferson's writings are still inspirational, most notably the famous passage inscribed on the marble walls of the Jefferson Memorial in Washington, D.C., "if a nation expects to be ignorant and free, in a state of civilization, it expects what never was and never will be."[1] As compared to some of the most eminent educators of his day in the United States, Jefferson had an inspiring and clear-sighted vision for what a university could and should be, as well as the political and practical skills that were so essential to its implementation.[2] He was intimately involved with every aspect of creating the University of Virginia. Along with his authorship of the Declaration of Independence and the Virginia Statute for Religious Freedom, the founding of the university was the third great achievement he wanted acknowledged on his tombstone. It represented the apex of a much broader educational vision that distinguishes Jefferson as one of the earliest advocates of a public education system. Better known for his belief in limited government, his paradoxical emphasis on public schools and universities raised the potential of a major extension of local and state government into the social sphere.

While heads of state have founded universities and acted as patrons, Jefferson's ubiquitous role in every detail of creating the University of Virginia is unparalleled. His vision and its execution reveal his multiple talents as a lawyer who drafted the legislation and the deeds to purchase the property; as a politician who cajoled the state legislature into supporting him against furious opposition; as a surveyor who measured and mapped the grounds; as an architect who designed the layout, chose the building materials, managed the construction, and corresponded with the artisans; and as an intellectual who developed an innovative curriculum, suggested books for the library, and devised the criteria for selecting faculty. Jefferson maintained a firsthand connection with the university even after its completion, making certain that he knew each student individually by inviting them to dinners at Monticello. His intense involvement in the university displayed his political skill in marketing his ideas, obtaining favorable publicity, overcoming opposition, influencing the Virginia Assembly through intermediaries into accepting his vision—including his controversial exclusion of a chapel and a theology department—and not least in persuading the legislature to situate the university in Charlottesville.

Although he relied on others to assist him, seeking the best advice at home and abroad, it was his own ideas that ultimately prevailed to such an extent that contemporaries began calling it "Mr. Jefferson's University."[3] In the words of a former governor of the state to Jefferson, "Your College is made the University of Virginia. I call it yours, as you are the real founder, its commencement can only be ascribed to you, to your exertions & influence its being adopted can only be attributed."[4] George Tucker, the first chairman of the faculty, described how the trustees, known as the Board of Visitors, left the matter of "the regulations entirely to Mr. Jefferson; not merely from a regard to his superior competence, but because he was regarded as its founder, the responsibility for its success would principally fall on him."[5] Describing it as "somewhat of an experimental institution," James Madison similarly wrote that he and fellow members of the Board of Visitors deferred to Jefferson as "it was but fair to let him execute it in his own way."[6]

Jefferson was fanatical in his determination to found a university in Virginia, convinced as he was that the state was the last preserve of the unadulterated republican ideas of 1776. Seeing the legacy of the American Revolution imperiled by northern Federalists, he regarded his home state as having a unique responsibility to sustain the revolutionary flame. He aimed to create an institution that would be "the future bulwark of the human mind in this hemisphere," producing students who replicated his values.[7] There is an inescapable suspicion that he thought only he could create an institution that could replicate in its students his own role carrying the torch of freedom and acting as beacons to the rest of world. A critic of organized religion, he nevertheless spoke of republicanism as if it were a holy creed, dismissing opponents as "apostates" and "heretics." In this respect, he was always a true revolutionary in his conviction that his cause was right and that each successive generation would undergo a continuing struggle to inculcate correct values and beliefs in its children. Acknowledging that his ideas were utopian, he regarded himself as an idealist who wanted to benefit humankind, improve society, and offer a happier life.

JUST AS MEMBERS of the founding generation spent more time examining the origins of government and the creation of constitutions than any other, they were also interested in the advancement of education as essential for maintaining the republican system of government and the idea of government by the people. Apart from Jefferson, none of the other so-called founding fathers actually founded a university, but they did help to encourage and foster colleges. Benjamin Franklin came closer than any of the leading revolutionaries as a cofounder of the University of Pennsylvania. As early as 1749, Franklin published *Proposals Relating to the Education of Youth in Philadelphia* and wrote anonymously about the lack of educational institutions in Philadelphia in the *Pennsylvania Gazette*. He wanted to establish an English-language academy to teach modern languages, history, and science with a view to preparing students for citizenship, business, and the professions. He wanted poor children to be admitted free of charge, once the endowment was large enough, to enable them to become schoolteachers. He was outvoted by the other trustees and lost control during his absence in Europe, where he wrote an indictment of his fellow trustees titled *Observations Relating to the Intentions of the Original Founders of the Academy in Philadelphia* (1789). Nevertheless, Franklin's ideas and energy played a critical role in the origins and later development of the University of Pennsylvania.[8]

The American Revolution proved to be a catalyst with the number of colleges in America doubling before 1800. John Adams reformed Harvard into a republican university in the Massachusetts Constitution of 1780, which contained a separate, innovative fifth chapter titled "The University of Cambridge and Encouragement of Literature, &c."[9] Benjamin Rush helped to found Dickinson College (then called Carlisle College), which he regarded as the "best bulwark of the blessings obtained by the Revolution."[10] Alexander Hamilton devised a scheme for the University of New York State. Although Noah Webster resigned from the board of trustees before it became a degree-granting institution, he founded Amherst Academy. Like Jefferson, he regarded it as a child of his old age and the climax of a career devoted to the spread of republican principles, but neither he nor any of the other revolutionary leaders matched Jefferson's zeal in the cause of education.

Jefferson was concerned with the perennial issue of the role of higher ed-ucation in the success of the republican democratic experiment. As business models increasingly gain hold of higher education and public universities enjoy less state support, his vision is still compelling and worth revisiting. It invites us to engage in discussing the purpose of a university, the concept of a university as a community, and the importance of an outstanding full-time professional faculty. His ideas were innovative, whether in terms of the architectural layout of the university or its broader curriculum. In contrast to the bland mission statements of the majority of modern universities, his concept of the role of universities was poetic, emotionally engaging, and still resonant. He believed the university should enshrine "the illimitable free-dom of the human mind. for here we are not afraid to follow truth wherever it may lead, nor to tolerate any error so long as reason is left free to combat it."[11] Jefferson regarded intellectual freedom as the most important of all liberties but realized that its full expression was dependent on political and religious freedom. He looked beyond the classroom to a university that con-tained museums, art galleries, and botanical gardens open to a wider public. While his educational ideas reflect the elitist and racist assumptions of his generation, they are worth interrogating because the creativity of his vision still has the potential to stimulate discussion about the role of universities today.

Like other members of the revolutionary generation, Jefferson believed in the civic value of education and saw it as vital to the survival of a repre-sentative system of government. Also like them, he believed that history was the most critical of all subjects: students needed to learn why past re-publics had failed; why they will always be susceptible to demagoguery—what we call populism—that descends into tyranny; and why the electorate needs to be vigilant against the abuses of executive power. Jefferson's fear still remains pertinent in the era of "fake news," with what the *New Yorker* journalist Evan Osnos calls the "embarrassing insight into America life" that "large numbers of Americans are ill-equipped to assess the creditably of the things they read," or the warning of Chief Justice John Roberts that "in our age, when social media can instantly spread rumor and false information on a grand scale, the public's need to understand our government, and the protections it provides, is ever more vital."[12] Jefferson looked to education to teach the people to hold government accountable. In this, his vision was very different from that of contemporary Prussian elites, such as Wilhelm von Humboldt, who helped pioneer the first state public school system, with a view to strengthening central government by providing trained administrators and bureaucrats.

ALTHOUGH CONCEIVED as a bulwark against tyranny of one kind, the university was blemished by its own promotion of another tyranny in the form of slavery. Like the Declaration of Independence, Jefferson's university was tainted by the presence of slavery. It would become the premier university of the South and therefore implicated in "the peculiar institution." Although his university, like his home, was built primarily by enslaved labor, Jefferson had hoped that slavery would gradually erode as the population spread westward and that a future generation of graduates would solve what he called a "deplorable entanglement."[13] Instead, slavery remained a constant and ubiquitous feature of the university until the Civil War. Jefferson wanted to train leaders who best represented the values and ethos of the American Revolution in contrast to what he regarded as the heretical Federalist colleges of the north like Yale and Princeton. Instead, the university would educate a high proportion of the leaders of the Confederacy.

Just as the ideals of equality expressed in the Declaration of Independence were not fulfilled in practice, the loftier aspirations of Jefferson's vision for the university were not fully realized. He had hoped that it might offer merit-based scholarships to some impoverished students but no such assistance occurred until twenty years after his death and then on a very limited basis. When it opened in 1825, the university had the highest tuition costs in America. Jefferson's more recent critics question whether he was sincere about his plans for universal public education because he ultimately gave priority to the university. Despite his belief in the "illimitable freedom of the human mind," Jefferson insisted that the professors and their curricula in law and politics conform to Republican and not Federalist doctrines. He did not have a vision for the education of women, beyond their attending primary schools and preparing for domestic roles in life. In his impressive history of American higher education before World War II, Roger L. Geiger encapsulates the unfavorable verdict of modern historians when he argues that the University of Virginia was essentially an irrelevant model for other institutions, as it was "functioning at once as finishing school of southern aristocrats and the academic beacon of the South."[14]

INTENDED AS A CRITICAL and nuanced study, this book considers such limitations but argues that Jefferson's vision represented a major personal achievement and the brilliant culmination of a career dedicated to republicanism. Existing biographies treat Jefferson's founding of the university as merely an epilogue, while institutional histories give little consideration to the biographical context. This book contends that a knowledge of his philosophical, political, and religious beliefs is vital to understanding the unique character of the university at the time of its founding. During his retirement, Jefferson sought the best advice about the curriculum, selection of faculty, and choice of books in the library through his vast network of intellectuals both at home and abroad. Beginning at the age of seventy-three—having lived already far beyond the average life expectancy of the period—he spent the last decade of his life preoccupied with the quest to establish the University of Virginia. He wrote out the minutes of the Board of Visitors, estimated the number of bricks required for each building, and on his last visit to the university even unpacked boxes of books intended for the library. Despite ill health and excruciating pain in his right hand, he produced architectural drawings and drafted legislation. Ignoring his impending bankruptcy, he donated his own money to begin a fundraising campaign and hosted dinners for members of the university community. Because the university was so much of his making, its history is inseparable from Thomas Jefferson's life.

This book claims that Jefferson's educational vision was as revolutionary as the other achievements listed on his tombstone, anticipating many of the key features of the modern secular university. It also contends that the university had an important influence on higher education in America. This insight is often unappreciated because Jefferson's innovations were eventually so widely copied elsewhere that they are no longer distinctive, while some were abandoned at the University of Virginia. Like his political ideas, they have become so commonplace that it is easy to take them for granted. Herbert Baxter Adams, the late nineteenth-century educator and historian, wrote that "there is scarcely any college in the South which has not to a greater or lesser extent modelled its system of teaching after that of the University of Virginia."[15] Some of the most significant reformers in American higher education, such as Harvard presidents Charles William Eliot and James Bryant Conant, invoked the educational vision of Thomas Jefferson.

The biographical approach used here aims at engaging general readers. It begins by introducing the intellectual interests, education, and later years of the life of Thomas Jefferson during which he founded the University of Virginia. Each chapter starts with a narrative account that opens the subject

and theme to be subsequently developed. The book is arranged chronolog-
ically and thematically, with the first half devoted to Jefferson's educational
objective, the origins of his interest, the influences, and the stages leading
up to the opening of the university. It reveals the political skills of Jefferson, who in a five-year period transformed the moribund Albemarle Academy into Central College (1816) and finally into the University of Virginia
(1819). The second half concerns all aspects of the life of the university and
Jefferson's involvement, including the faculty, curriculum, religion, enslaved
laborers, and students. The final chapter discusses the impact of the university on higher education in America.

This study departs from the vogue of recent bicentennial histories that
ascribe all characteristics of the University of Virginia to slavery.[16] These
works are laudable in addressing a virtually ignored subject in previous
scholarship and in reinforcing current efforts by the university to address
its history of slavery and legacy of racial discrimination. They provide much
good information that has proved useful in the writing of this book, which
incorporates their important insights, but it also recovers the vision, curriculum, faculty, and academic departments in a holistic and contextual
manner. Unlike other studies, it compares the university to other colleges
in America and Europe, thereby highlighting the distinctiveness of Jefferson's contribution. This book seeks to provide a more balanced and deeply
contextualized approach to Thomas Jefferson's vision for the University of
Virginia.

Historians of the university have neglected religion as a key to understanding Jefferson's motivation in founding the university, his proposed
curriculum, his criteria for selecting faculty, and even his cataloging of the
books in the library.[17] His views about the separation of church and state
were a major reason why he opposed other plans for public education, why
he wanted the university in the nonsectarian town of Charlottesville, and
why he was so opposed to southern students going to northern colleges
dominated by Presbyterians and Congregationalists. Jefferson's views on religion also factored into his abandoning his original aim of reforming the
College of William and Mary, which he thought too tied to the Episcopal
church. His anticlerical views helped undermine his own attempts at creating a public school system and nearly wrecked the prospects of the University of Virginia. His religious views remain almost as controversial today as
his relationship to slavery. The curriculum of the university did not include
theology and privileged the findings of scientific inquiry over the claims

of direct revelation. Ignoring precedents in Napoleonic Europe, the *North American Review* described it as the only university in the world to exclude religion from its curriculum and its premises.[18]

Previous accounts similarly do not adequately address the political context of the founding of the University of Virginia. Jefferson demonstrated his supreme political skills in what he compared to forcing a dose of medicine down the throat of an unwilling patient. He was determined to rescue higher education from the dominance of Federalists, who he regarded as bigoted, antediluvian, and anti-science. Jefferson envisaged the University of Virginia as the last best hope of transmitting the untainted legacy of the American Revolution to future generations. He wanted the university to be what he called "a bulwark of liberty." If he seemed histrionic, he knew that most revolutions fail, ending in civil war and military coups, and that earlier republics had not survived. America was still a fragile experiment with its proclaimed object of government by the people. Jefferson was one of the few revolutionary leaders to keep the faith and not become disenchanted. He is so often dismissed today as a hypocrite that it is easy to forget that he was an idealist who wanted to make the world better for future generations.

Jefferson revealed much about himself in his preoccupation with founding the University of Virginia. It indicated his values, his objectives, and his political skills. He was a pragmatist who wrote that "he who would do the country the most good he can, must go quietly with the prejudices of the majority till he can lead them into reason."[19] For him, politics was the art of the possible and a tradeoff between conflicting objectives. He regarded the creation and maintenance of the republic as the first and foremost goal, without which other objectives and improvements could not be achieved.

Jefferson's achievement was all the more remarkable in what Richard Hofstadter called "the age of the great retrogression," when the country was retreating from the values and rational emphasis of the Enlightenment with the rise of evangelicalism and the Romantic movement.[20] Jefferson's emphasis on a broad curriculum that would teach science and vocational subjects was in marked contrast to the continued focus elsewhere on a traditional education in the classics, which gained renewed vigor with the defense of the traditional classical curriculum in the influential Yale Report of 1828. The issue still raged in the late nineteenth century in a famous debate between the cultural critic Matthew Arnold and the scientist Thomas Henry Huxley. Jefferson's vision looked back to the height of the Enlightenment and the American Revolution. It embodied beliefs championed by Jefferson in secularism, republicanism, and useful knowledge. Even its neoclassical architecture was increasingly old-fashioned in the age of the Greek Revival. Although formally inaugurated in 1819, his ideas of a university were inspired by the ideals of 1776 and the Enlightenment.

WHILE SOME HISTORIANS argue that we should stop writing about the founders and dismiss the never-ending literature on the subject as mere chic, Jefferson and other revolutionary leaders remain important, beyond the symbols they have become, among large swaths of the American public.[21] In a country that pays homage to the idea of the original intent of the Constitution, it is necessary to understand the beliefs and worldviews of those who wrote the founding documents of the nation. In the U.S. Congress, Jefferson is the second-most-cited former president after George Washington.[22] Furthermore, politicians quote him for his words, rather than merely invoking him as an icon, in contrast to Washington. Jefferson has attracted more biographies than any other American but Abraham Lincoln. Of Jefferson, Lincoln famously said, "All honor to Jefferson—to the man who, in the concrete pressure of a struggle for national independence by a single people, had the coolness, forecast, and capacity to introduce into a merely revolutionary document, an abstract truth, applicable to all men and all times, and so to embalm it there, that to-day, and in all coming days, it shall be a rebuke and a stumbling-block to the very harbingers of re-appearing tyranny and oppression."[23]

Franklin Roosevelt commemorated the bicentenary of Jefferson's birth by building the Jefferson Memorial. In his speech at the opening ceremony on April 13, 1943, Roosevelt declared, "Today, in the midst of a great war for freedom, we dedicate a shrine of freedom. To Thomas Jefferson, Apostle of Freedom, we are paying a debt long overdue."[24] During Roosevelt's administration, the nickel began to feature Jefferson's profile by Jean Antoine Houdon, along with the west-lawn view of Monticello. Ronald Reagan said that every American should pluck a flower from Thomas Jefferson's life, and Bill Clinton began the day of his first inauguration as president at Monticello. Barack Obama was the only president to have visited Monticello with another head of state, French president François Hollande, in 2014. Jefferson has been similarly invoked by global leaders such as Václav Havel and Mikhail Gorbachev.[25] Andrew Burstein aptly describes the pervasive modern influence of Jefferson in his hilariously titled book *Democracy's Muse: How Thomas Jefferson Became an FDR Liberal, a Reagan Republican, and a Tea Party Fanatic, All the While Being Dead* (2015).

Yet apart from a brief period between the 1930s and the 1960s, when the need for national unity and consensus was at a premium, Jefferson has never been uncritically venerated. His reputation has ebbed and waned among succeeding generations.[26] Nevertheless, different groups have continued to claim him to give historical legitimacy to their divergent and sometimes clashing causes. In her article "Why Jefferson Matters," Annette Gordon-Reed highlights the remarkable symbolism of counter-protesters attempting to prevent white supremacists from surrounding the statue of Thomas Jefferson at the University of Virginia during the notorious Unite the Right Rally on August 11, 2017. In a moving and personal account, she recounts how she "knew instantly why the men holding tiki torches felt the need to make their case for white supremacy by walking toward the statue," and equally why the protesters surrounded the statute "to keep the tiki torchers from reaching it, staking a defiant claim, in the face of superior numbers, to ideas about human equality and progress that they correctly perceived were under siege that night." From the perspective of the protesters, Gordon-Reed explains, "It was not necessarily the man himself, but the ideas associated with him that mattered and warranted forming a protective barrier around the statue."[27]

Just as the nation was a laboratory for what became the republican and later democratic systems, so the university was an experiment that is still ongoing in an unfinished revolution. Jefferson understood that the limitations of his own generation would be apparent to posterity, in the same way that his contemporaries were wiser than their witch-burning ancestors. He believed that each generation should be free of the restraints of tradition and the dead hand of the past to chart a new path to improve the happiness and prosperity of the people. He declared that "the earth belongs in usufruct to the living," a legal term suggestive of a temporary right, as if each generation were passing on the baton to the next.[28] In establishing the university, Jefferson provided a way for future generations to think for themselves and foster progress. Meredith Jung-En Woo, president of Sweet Briar College and former dean of the College of Letters and Science at the University of Virginia, observes that "among the many wonders of the mind of Thomas Jefferson, one is not mentioned: his vision for his university remains as vital in the 21st century as it was in the 18th century."[29] His example and his vision challenge us to ask ourselves how far we have progressed and whether we have helped pave the way for those who succeed us.

1

Feast of Reason

E ACH SUNDAY, to avoid interfering with regular weekday lectures,
Thomas Jefferson invited a group of four or more students to dine at
Monticello. The setting was reminiscent of his own experiences as the guest
of his professors at the College of William and Mary and his later dinners
at the White House, then known as the Executive Mansion. He characteristically invited the students in alphabetical order to avoid any appearance of preference or hierarchy. According to the oldest living alumnus in
1894, Burwell Stark, all the students dined at Monticello at least once, and
often like himself two or three times.[1] When students declined the invitation owing to religious convictions, Jefferson invited them during the week.
About a fifth of the students were aged between sixteen and eighteen and
were therefore not even alive when Jefferson had retired as president of the
United States in 1809. Ellen Randolph Coolidge, Jefferson's favorite granddaughter, described the conversations at such dinner parties as "completely
the feast of reason," which was an allusion to a line by the English poet
Alexander Pope, "The Feast of Reason and the Flow of the Soul," from the
Imitations of Horace.[2]

Understanding the creation of the university requires an understanding
of the personal side of Jefferson, which is inextricably connected to his political, philosophical, and educational beliefs. His literal "feasts of reason" offered students insights into his mind and character, while their accounts of
these dinners offer us glimpses of the man and his values at the time of his
creation of the university. These dinner parties were opportunities for Jefferson to become acquainted with the students and to model the discourse
of the "feast of reason" that he hoped to foster at the University of Virginia.
As later described by Henry Tutwiler, one of the students to attend these
dinners, Jefferson sometimes pushed his chair back during the course of the
party because he was going deaf and "could not hear well amidst the clat-

ter of knives and the chat of a merry company." With "an unselfish regard for the comfort of others," Jefferson did not want his hearing impediment to deter their conversation and enjoyment. He always "received them with great kindness, entertained them with rare tact, and never failed to impress them deeply with the elevation of his character and the tender kindness of his heart."[3]

Professor George Long, one of the first faculty, remembered that some of the students misspelled the word "Republic" as "Rebublic," yet Jefferson ignored their shortcomings, with what Tutwiler described as "a wonderful tact in interesting his youthful visitors, and making even the most diffident feel at ease in his company." Jefferson was careful to pay attention to each individual student during the dinner parties. Knowing where their families lived, he would draw the students out by asking questions about their homes and any remarkable events or people in their locality. He would alternatively ask them about their studies or comment on the professors, for whom he showed the highest admiration. Despite probing the students, he still managed to create the impression that he was giving rather than receiving information.[4]

At these weekly Sunday dinners, over which his daughter Martha Randolph presided, Jefferson related anecdotes about famous people whom he had known abroad, such as Madame de Staël, an author and historian whose salon he had attended in Paris. On one occasion, during a discussion about novels of which her father disapproved, Martha described how "she induced him to read" Sir Walter Scott's recently published *Ivanhoe* (1819) in the hope it might change his opinion. Jefferson "smiled and said, yes, he had tried to read it at her urgent request, but he had found it the dullest and hardest task of the kind he had ever undertaken." To the amazement of the students listening, she continued this playful banter with her father, saying that she found the legal works of Sir William Blackstone "as interesting as a novel," which was particularly mischievous because Jefferson did not want Blackstone taught in the introductory law classes for fear that Blackstone's seductively simplified synthesis and defense of monarchy might turn the students into Tories. After dinner, Jefferson talked about the paintings on the walls and pointed to one of George Washington, remarking that "though not a handsome man, he presented on horseback the most splendid figure he had ever seen."[5]

FIFTY-SEVEN YEARS after Henry Tutwiler of Alabama arrived as one of the first students at the newly opened university, he described it as having become "part and parcel of my entire being. Pleasant and profitable in themselves, they have left their impress upon the whole of my life." On June 29, 1882, he rose to address the alumni society of the University of Virginia. Time had not "effaced those precious memories," which provided an abundance of material for his speech but also evoked feelings that he could not put into words, in which "silence is more expressive." Tutwiler had subsequently become a professor at the University of Alabama. He had been invited by the alumni society's secretary to recollect "the historic days of our *alma mater*, when Mr. JEFFERSON was a living presence among us, and when the high scholastic attainments and lofty erudition of the first professors began the new creation of Virginia's high culture."[6] Conscious that he was one of the last surviving members of the first generation to attend the university, Tutwiler sought out information from others including George Long, his former professor of ancient languages with whom he had a lifelong correspondence and who was then living in Brighton, England.

In his address to the alumni and their wives, Tutwiler thanked God "for directing my youthful steps to this seat of learning." He then thanked "its illustrious founder for providing us such teachers as we then had." Listing the names of the eight first professors and two of their successors, he said that they "are all too well known to need any eulogium from me." He had been privileged to attend the lectures of all of them except Dr. Robley Dunglison in medicine and Dr. Gessner Harrison, a former student who later replaced Long as professor of ancient languages. Tutwiler fondly recollected the friendship and hospitality of both professors and their families over the course of his five years at the university. He described how Harrison, a friend and companion of Tutwiler's boyhood years, had "occupied the same room, and were class-mates in every study but one."[7]

Tutwiler dwelt mostly on the founder, Thomas Jefferson: "Foreign Universities boast of *Royal* founders—their Alfred and Elizabeth, their Henrys and Jameses—but we claim one who derives his title, not from accident or birth, but from his own inherent greatness." Tutwiler recalled that when Jefferson was about "to close his eyes to all earthly scenes, he asked, as is well known, to be remembered for three things: *Author of the Declaration of Independence, of the Act establishing Religious Freedom*, and last, but not least, *Father of the University of Virginia*." The speaker added that Jefferson well understood that "without education, political and religious freedom would have no firm basis upon which to rest." After a political career of almost sixty years, virtually without intermission, when he might simply have rested on his well-earned laurels, he "felt that he had another duty to perform, the highest of all," and despite his great age "he entered upon the work with all the ardor of youth, sparing neither time, labor, nor expense with no hope of remuneration" while exposing himself to "the certainty of incurring the enmity and ill-will of many." His only reward would be "the gratitude of those who were to reap the benefit of these sacrifices." According to Tutwiler, this entitled Jefferson "to our love and admiration, and these are enhanced when we consider the difficulties he had to surmount, and the patience and perseverance with which he overcame them." Tutwiler acknowledged that Jefferson had some "noble coadjutors, and among them we must not omit the name of his 'fidus Achates' [devoted friend] Joseph C. Cabell, who well deserves a monument at this University."[8]

Tutwiler reminded his audience that it was "almost impossible at this day to form an adequate idea of the obstacles" that Jefferson had to overcome of which "the greatest and most serious was that of a large and respectable portion of the religious community." With distrust still lingering from the intense and bitter partisan party politics of Jefferson's presidency, "Many good people sincerely believed that he was about to establish a school for the purpose of promulgating infidelity." They argued that the university did not teach religion, "therefore they teach no religion, therefore they teach infidelity." Tutwiler recollected a clergyman saying to someone who was about to send his son to the university, "'Much as I love your son,' who had been a favorite pupil, 'I would this day, rather follow him to the grave than see him enter the University.'"[9]

Tutwiler recalled the first time that he saw "Mr. Jefferson." It was in the office of the proctor, Arthur S. Brockenbrough, where Tutwiler had gone with some other students on business when "a tall, venerable gentleman, in plain but neat attire, entered the room and, bowing to the students, took his seat quietly in one corner." Upon being told by another student that it was Jefferson, Tutwiler was "struck by his plain appearance, and simple unassuming manners," waiting for the students to finish their business before greeting the proctor. He and his fellow students used to see him afterward, as he passed their rooms on the Eastern Range, "in his almost daily visits to the University." Aged eighty-three, Jefferson would ride the five-mile distance between Monticello and the Grounds, as the campus is still called, "on horseback over rough mountain-road," which showed "the deep interest with which he watched over this *child of his old age*, and why he preferred the more endearing title of *Father* to that of Founder."[10]

The alumni association invited Tutwiler because he was one of the few living graduates who had attended during the university's first year of operation. He was also one of the most academically distinguished former students. As a southerner, it was noteworthy that he was an opponent of slavery throughout his adult life. Even so, he did not mention the subject in his speech and did not allude to the fact that these "feasts of reason" took place on an eight-square-mile plantation in Virginia's Piedmont, the home of Jefferson's family and of 140 enslaved persons. At the time that Jefferson wrote the Declaration of Independence, he had owned over 175 enslaved persons on five plantations comprising a total of some 14,000 acres, with 5,000 acres at Monticello and the rest at his plantations at Elk Hill, Willis Creek, and Poplar Forest. Jefferson's very first childhood memory was of a slave adjusting his pillow.[11] By the time of the construction of the University of Virginia in 1817, the number of men, women, and children that he held in bondage on all his plantations had actually increased to over 240. Margaret Bayard Smith, the novelist and commentator, described how the quarters for enslaved persons appeared poor, with their cabins forming "a most unpleasant contrast" to the Monticello edifice.[12] Over the course of his life, Jefferson owned at least 607 enslaved African Americans. He sold some of them for profit and gave others away as gifts. He liked to pride himself on treating his slaves benignly, avoiding the use of the whip, keeping families together, and hiring them out rather than selling them when possible. However, in practice, economic self-interest compromised his ideals when he looked to maximize profits and when he delegated supervision to sometimes harsh overseers. The ideal of enlightened management was always illusory when the essence of slavery was aimed at denying the identity and autonomy of individuals, subjecting them to the whims of a master without any legal rights or redress.[13]

Despite his antislavery beliefs, it is understandable that Tutwiler would have avoided the subject of slavery in a speech given so soon after the Civil War. Instead he focused on Jefferson. Tutwiler's recollections of his student days offer us a picture of Jefferson as almost a personification of the Enlightenment, with his broad range of intellectual interests and desire to impart knowledge to others, traits that were fundamental to his concerns about education and founding of the University of Virginia. Described by one visitor as "having a philosophic turn of mind," Jefferson was an intellectual who declared that "nature intended me for the tranquil pursuit of science, by rendering them my supreme delight. but enormities of the times in which I have lived, have forced me to take a part in resisting them, and to commit myself on the boisterous ocean of political passions."[14] He was interested not only in collecting information but in educating his guests, a passion reflected in the decor and objects displayed throughout his home.

Regarded as his architectural autobiography, Monticello is still the closest that a modern visitor can come to having a conversation with Thomas Jefferson.[15] It exudes the mindset of the founder of the university in all its complexity. Constructed with a view to shaping the experience of the visitor, guests approached the house along circular roads and so-called roundabouts that encircled the mountainside at a gentle gradient leading to the top. He regarded it as idyllic, writing that "there is no quarter of the globe so desirable as America, no state in America so desirable as Virginia, no county in Virginia equal to Albemarle, and no spot in Albemarle to compare to Monticello."[16] Jefferson was a natural teacher and enjoyed sharing and displaying his knowledge at Monticello. Like modern visitors, the students and faculty entered the house through the East Portico into what Jefferson variously described as the Entrance Hall, known at the time simply as the Hall and sometimes as the Indian Hall because it displayed objects from the Lewis and Clark expedition. This was the most public room in the house, which acted as a museum aimed at instructing visitors. The contents attested to the intellectual breadth, the inquisitiveness, and the variety of interests of their owner. They showed him to be simultaneously cosmopolitan and patriotic.

Visiting Monticello in 1824, Auguste Levasseur, the secretary to the Marquis de Lafayette, wrote that "what especially excites the curiosity of visitors is the rich museum situated at the entrance of the house." He called it an "extensive and excellent collection."[17] Like the parlor and the dining room, the two-story Entrance Hall contained a blend of objects from the Old World and New, aiming to educate both his family and guests about the best of Europe and the potential greatness of the Americas. Upon entering the main door, visitors saw busts of Jefferson and his political nemesis Alexander Hamilton, of whom Jefferson sometimes joked, "with a pensive smile," that they were still "opposed in death as in life." He found it amusing that his own bust was much larger than the life-size statue of Hamilton.[18] They flanked busts, created by Jean Antoine Houdon, of two great Enlightenment French thinkers—the writer Voltaire and the economist Turgot—with two Meso-American Native stone carvings positioned in between them. Maps hanging from the walls of the Entrance Hall showed the Louisiana Purchase and South America, as well as an Indian map on a buffalo hide depicting "the southern waters of the Missouri, and an Indian representation of a bloody battle, handed down in their traditions."[19] The

Entrance Hall contained fossils, objects, and specimens that encouraged the visitor to equate the ancient history and origins of both Europe and the Americas, such as dinosaur bones from Big Lick, Kentucky, and representations of Egypt, with a cork model of the pyramid of Cheops at Giza given to Jefferson by the French philosopher and politician the Comte de Volney. The Hall contained what Jefferson thought was a marble statue of Cleopatra but was in fact a modern reproduction of the reclining Ariadne at the Vatican. There were many Native American objects and artifacts from the Lewis and Clark Expedition (1804–6). These included painted skins, weapons, clothing, ornaments, utensils, pipes, and the horns of an elk, a deer, and a buffalo.[20] Religious paintings included one of the *Repentance of Saint Peter.*

Jefferson demonstrated in the Entrance Hall that he was very much a product of the Enlightenment. Like most historical labels, the term does not do justice to the range of competing beliefs and different shades of opinion that it encapsulates, but it remains useful for describing a fundamental shift in Western thought during the eighteenth century. Through the double doors from the Entrance Hall, the parlor contained portraits of three men whom Jefferson called "my trinity of the three greatest men the world has ever produced," Sir Francis Bacon, Sir Isaac Newton, and John Locke. Jefferson used to tell how he once showed them to Alexander Hamilton, who dismissed his choice and after a pause responded, "The greatest man . . . that ever lived was Julius Caesar."[21]

Jefferson's selection of great men is the same as some historians of ideas who see the trio as the foundational thinkers of the Enlightenment.[22] He several times repeated Bacon's famous adage that "knowledge itself is power," as well as other phrases such as "advancement of learning," "diffusion of knowledge," and "useful knowledge." Sharing Bacon's belief in the scientific method, Jefferson thought that knowledge was not static but constantly evolving and expanding. Newton continues to be revered as one of the most influential scientists of all time, a pioneer in physics, optics, and mathematical rationalism; the father of calculus; and a leading figure in the late seventeenth-century scientific revolution that helped give birth to the Enlightenment. Influenced by Locke's political thought in his *Two Treatises on Government* (1689), Jefferson was also well aware of his *Some Thoughts Concerning Education* (1693), the reading of which the Virginia politician recommended to a correspondent as early as 1771.[23] Locke not only made the case for the formative power of education on children but also its political importance in creating an informed citizenry. He argued that education was more effective by means of persuasion than by authoritarian methods of teaching.

Jefferson's vision for the University of Virginia reflected the thinking of the Enlightenment. In a letter of advice about religion and education to his nephew Peter Carr, he wrote what might be regarded as the mantra of the Enlightenment: "You must lay aside prejudice . . . neither believe nor reject anything, because other persons . . . have rejected or believed it. your own reason is the only oracle."[24] This flow of ideas was coterminous with the eighteenth century, often called the age of reason because of its emphasis on facts and empirical evidence, scientific method, and a desire to establish objective truth. Enlightenment thought variously promoted a benign and optimistic view of human nature as capable of progress and improvement through science and rational thought. It emphasized liberty as necessary for the free exchange of ideas and education as essential for progress. It embraced the concept of natural rights that lawful governments could not breach. It espoused religious toleration. In contrast to the traditional religious view of the fall of man, it promoted the belief that humans could improve their destiny through rational thought and the pursuit of happiness, meaning the public good as well as individual self-fulfillment. In a summary of his political testament, Jefferson wrote to a correspondent, "we believed that man was a rational animal . . . that men habituated to think for themselves and to follow their reason as their guide, would be more easily and safely governed than with minds nourished in error, and vitiated and debased, as in Europe, by ignorance, indigence and oppression."[25] Jefferson never lost faith in the possibilities of human progress through science and reason. He was an extreme empiricist who believed that intellectual progress could only be achieved through experiment, study, and reason to challenge preconceptions and inherited beliefs. It is now difficult to convey the novelty of these ideas, which have become second nature to the modern world and easy to take for granted because they are so familiar.

Published as a book, Jefferson's *Notes on the State of Virginia* (1787) represented one of the most brilliant intellectual achievements of the American Enlightenment. Intended initially for private circulation, he tellingly sent ten copies to close friends and thirty-seven copies to be distributed at the discretion of his former tutor, George Wythe, to students at William and Mary. He eventually wanted it given "to every young man at the College."[26] The gesture betokened his desire to influence and impart knowledge to the rising generation. In his *Notes*, Jefferson wrote that "reason and free enquiry are the only effectual agents against error."[27] Completed in the last years of the Revolutionary War, the work was a response to a questionnaire sent to every state by François Barbé-Marbois, then secretary of the French delegation in Philadelphia. Refuting European arguments asserting the inferiority of America, Jefferson challenged what now seems the farcical claim of some leading European intellectuals that animals and people physically degenerated and became smaller in the New World relative to Europe. Tracing the argument back to the Abbé Raynal, Jefferson specifically repudiated the leading exponent of the theory, George Louis Leclerc, Comte de Buffon, whom James Madison described as "the best informed of any naturalist who has ever written."[28] Jefferson even pursued the argument beyond the book by having physical specimens, including the bones and skin of a moose, sent from America to Buffon in France.

In addition, Jefferson's *Notes* contained some of his most quotable and memorable writings on liberty, the principles of government, education, religion, and slavery, as well as his notorious discussion of racial differences. He famously denounced slavery as "a perpetual exercise in the most boisterous passions, the most unremitting despotism."[29] The *Notes* included information on topics ranging from botany and geology to agriculture and climate, reflecting the increased demand for collating and classifying knowledge in single works of reference, such as dictionaries and encyclopedias. In general, he used the opportunity of his book to articulate one of the most outspoken critiques of the social, economic, religious, political, and cultural features of his native Virginia.[30] The book acted as a manifesto of his political beliefs and a rallying call for future reform within the state, including his pending bill for religious freedom, a plan for the emancipation of slaves, and a proposal for a public school system. He was dismissive of the architecture, religious bigotry, poverty of public education, and constitution of the state, but the *Notes* was at the same time celebratory. Although scathing about many aspects of his native state, Jefferson took pride in the mixed agricultural economy with its wide variety of crops and the impressive landscape.

Born a provincial colonial subject on the frontiers of an expanding empire, he looked to Europe for examples of refinement and art, and, more importantly for our purposes, for superior models of education and universities, while eschewing the inequality and tyrannical political systems in Europe. The *Notes* reminds us that Jefferson was first and foremost a Virginian. His formative years were shaped by the plantation economy, the system of slavery, and the cultural values of Virginia. While rightly regarded as a pioneer of nationalism in America, Jefferson gave his primary attention to the reform of Virginia, not least in the belief that his improved state would both act as an example and provide the leadership for the rest of America.[31] This was why it was so important to him that his native state should have a public education system and one of the best universities in the country.

The breadth of Jefferson's intellectual interests and his desire to disseminate knowledge, later realized in his university, was further apparent through his forty-six-year involvement with the American Philosophical Society (APS), of which he became a member in 1780.[32] Founded in 1743 by Benjamin Franklin and others, its mission was to promote useful knowledge. Like the Royal Society in London, such scientific societies often acted as the principal conduits for research and inquiry, rather than universities and colleges, whose primary focus at the time was teaching. When Jefferson was vice president, the society held an essay competition "for the best system of liberal education and literary instruction . . . comprehending also a plan for instituting and conducting public schools in this country."[33] In 1797, Jefferson became president of the APS, which he described as "the most flattering incident of my life."[34] As its president until 1814, Jefferson still holds the record for the longest tenure in this office. While the society's president, he presented his own scholarly papers, including one in 1797 on the bones of a large animal recently excavated in western Virginia, which he called a Megalonyx, and another paper the following year in which he discussed his own design for a moldboard plough.[35] He influenced the APS's research and collecting agenda by encouraging the library to gather information about the past and present state of the country, showing a particular interest in artifacts and information relating to Native Americans. As secretary of state and later vice president of the United States, Jefferson continued to attend the society's meetings, usually held at least once a month and often lasting several hours. He donated books, manuscripts, and artifacts to the APS, including the journals of Lewis and Clark, having encouraged Meriwether Lewis to consult with the society in 1803 in preparation for their transcontinental journey.

The French soldier and author the Marquis de Chastellux described Jefferson as "at once a musician, skilled in drawing, a geometrician, an astronomer, a natural philosopher, legislator and statesman."[36] Jefferson's library reflected his breadth of interest: it was the largest and most expensive private collection in the country with some 6,500 volumes, until sold in 1815, when it became the core collection of the resurrected Library of Congress.[37] His library was twice the size of the original three thousand volumes destroyed by what Jefferson called "the devastations of British Vandalism at Washington" during the War of 1812.[38] His collection included many books purchased while in Europe, with one of the finest collections of books and manuscripts of Americana, relating not just to the United States but also to all of the Americas and especially Spanish America. Within Monticello, Jefferson had a private suite of rooms, like an apartment, with a study (called his Cabinet), library, greenhouse, and bedroom (known as his Chamber). Margaret Bayard Smith described this secluded place as Jefferson's *Sanctum Sanctorum*, where he did the majority of his writing and reading, kept scientific equipment for observations, filing presses, bookshelves, and an architect's table.[39] He even had plans to build a laboratory at Monticello.

Jefferson classified his library according to Sir Francis Bacon's system, based on the three faculties of Memory (History), Reason (Philosophy), and Imagination (Poetry). There were odd choices, such as the classification of books on religion under the heading of jurisprudence. After the 1815 sale of his library, Jefferson declared to John Adams, "I cannot live without books; but fewer will suffice where amusement, and not use, is the only future object." Within an eleven-year period, he managed to collect another 1,600 volumes, covering a broad range of subjects that included new publications on education.[40] Jefferson understood the importance of libraries, once suggesting that every county should have a small circulating library with a few well-chosen books.[41]

Jefferson's concern with knowledge and facts was apparent in his obsessive recordkeeping. From the time that he wrote the Declaration of Independence, he kept a continuous meteorological diary in which he recorded the temperatures and levels of precipitation when he rose at dawn in the morning and again during the midafternoon. It also included observations about the flowering of trees; the appearance of birds; and the incidence of frosts, snow, rain, hail, and fair or cloudy weather. He likewise tried to collect data on winds and humidity. He encouraged others to copy him in the hope that it would become possible to discern national weather patterns. Jefferson variously kept a Farm Book, a Garden Book, a Memorandum Book, and three different Commonplace Books. After 1783, he kept a daily list of his correspondence, both incoming and outgoing, which amounted to 656 pages by the time of his death.[42] Typical of his meticulousness was his creation of a visual diagram, while president, showing the dates when particular vegetables were in season in Washington, D.C.[43] At Monticello, his filing system enabled him to locate a document among the thousands he retained within minutes.[44] He commissioned customized furniture to assist in his work, including a filing press and an octagonal writing table with alphabetically labeled file drawers. He loved gadgets like the revolving cube-shaped stand, sized for paper and pamphlets, in his Cabinet, where he also kept a polygraph machine in which he made copies of the vast majority of his outgoing correspondence.

Jefferson was fortunate in his own education, which in many ways he sought to replicate in his plans for the University of Virginia. He was initially educated at a school on a plantation called Tuckahoe, managed by his father, Peter Jefferson, acting as guardian to a deceased friend's family. Peter Jefferson was an important influence, with a library of four hundred books and a practical ability as a surveyor, who in collaboration with Joshua Fry produced the most celebrated map of early Virginia (1753). When Thomas's father returned to his family home at Shadwell, near Charlottesville, Jefferson studied at what he called a Latin school with the Reverend William Douglas, a Scottish tutor whom Jefferson disparaged in his memoirs but who taught him at least rudimentary Greek, Latin, and French. After losing his father at the age of fourteen, Jefferson attended the Reverend James Maury's school for boys in Albemarle. Maury also taught James Madison, James Monroe, and four other signers of the Declaration of Independence. Maury was an independent thinker who believed in a rational approach to religion, in which individuals questioned beliefs and accepted only what they found credible. He was an advocate of baptizing enslaved children and religious toleration.[45] Jefferson had fond memories of his time at Maury's school, where he received a good classics background enabling him to read original texts in Greek and Latin.

In January 1760, at the age of sixteen, Jefferson wrote to his father's executor seeking permission to attend the College of William and Mary in Williamsburg, the capital of Virginia, where he said he would "make a more universal acquaintance which may hereafter be serviceable to me; and I suppose I can pursue my Studies in Greek and Latin as well there as here, and likewise learn something of the Mathematics."[46] The College of William and Mary was the only college in the South before 1775 and the second oldest college in British America. It was founded by the Anglican church, which required the faculty to subscribe to its doctrines and rules as encoded in what is known as the Thirty-Nine Articles. Like other colleges, it required students to attend chapel twice a day, a tradition continued until well into the nineteenth century. They had to learn the catechism and dine together with the faculty in the college dining hall, known as "Commons." In America, the College of William and Mary was the first to have a professorship of mathematics and would later be the first to allow students to choose courses in an elective system, the first to teach modern languages, and the first to appoint a law professor. When Jefferson was a student, the college president was associated with a remarkable experiment in establishing the first school for free and enslaved Black children. Founded in 1760 at the initiative of Benjamin Franklin and a London-based charity called the Associates of Dr. Bray, the Bray School was located in a small house on Prince George Street. Operating until 1774, it was attended by at least thirty Black children, with a primary emphasis on instruction in religion.[47]

Once referring to Williamsburg as "Devilsburg," Jefferson later reminisced to his grandson, "[when] I recollect the various sorts of bad company with which I associated from time to time, I am astonished I did not turn off with some of them, & become as worthless to society as they were."[48] Nevertheless, his self-restraint prevailed, with a friend describing Jefferson as a model student who was able "to tear himself away from his dearest friends, to fly to his studies," sometimes for as much as fifteen hours in a day, working until two o'clock in the morning and getting up at dawn, with his "only recreation being a run at twilight to a certain stone which stood at a point a mile beyond the limits of the town."[49]

In his vision for the University of Virginia, Jefferson tried to recreate the learning environment that he experienced at the College of William and Mary. His time at the college had introduced him to the ideas of the Scottish Enlightenment through the only lay professor among the six faculty members, Dr. William Small. With Small, Jefferson studied mathematics, rhetoric, modern languages, poetry, and science. He later wrote that their relationship was one of his greatest fortunes, and "what probably fixed the destinies of my life." He described his professor as "a man profound in most of the useful branches of science, with a happy talent of communication, correct and gentlemanly manners, & an enlarged & liberal mind." He especially valued their friendship and conversation, during which they became daily companions and through which he gained his "first views of the expansion of science & of the system of things in which we are placed."[50] Possibly because of the influence of Small, who left the university soon afterward, Jefferson became skeptical about organized religion during the 1760s. Studying both modern and ancient languages, he grew conversant in French, Spanish, and Italian, with a reading knowledge of Ancient Greek, Latin, and Anglo-Saxon. It was this intimacy and the rich intellectual culture of his student years that he tried to reproduce at his own university. Jefferson so valued his education that he said later that if he were asked to choose between "the classical education that his father had given him and the estate he had left him, he would decide in favor of the former."[51]

After spending less than two years at the College of William and Mary, Jefferson studied law under the tutelage of Small's friend George Wythe, who would later tutor Chief Justice John Marshall and Henry Clay. Thanks partly to his ability to play the violin, Jefferson, along with Small and Wythe, attended dinners and musical events at the residence of the colonial lieutenant-governor Francis Fauquier, a natural philosopher and fellow of the Royal Society. These men were his role models, of whom he wrote, "Under temptations & difficulties, I would ask myself what would Dr. Small, Mr. Wythe, Peyton Randolph [a cousin who served prominently in the Virginia House of Burgesses] do in this situation? what course in it will ensure me their approbation? I am certain that this mode of deciding on my conduct tended more to its correctness than any reasoning powers I possessed."[52] At these parties of Lieutenant-Governor Fauquier, Jefferson wrote that he "heard more good sense, more rational & philosophical conversations than in all my life besides."[53] He would try to incorporate this type of intellectual community into his vision of an "Academical Village" for the University of Virginia.

Throughout his adult life, Jefferson was able to discuss his ideas on education and to keep informed about educational institutions elsewhere through his transatlantic network of fellow intellectuals, what he called "a great fraternity spreading over the whole earth" whose correspondence "is never interrupted by any civilized nation." He elsewhere referred to them as "one great commonwealth, in which no geographical divisions are acknowledged," in what contemporaries dubbed a "republic of letters."[54] He variously consulted some of the great luminaries of the period about their preferred curricula, systems of education, and more specifically views on universities. His circle included John Witherspoon, the president of Princeton (then the College of New Jersey); the British theologian and scientist Joseph Priestley and his protégé Thomas Cooper; William Richardson Davie, the politician and cofounder of the University of North Carolina; Bishop James Madison, the geologist president of the College of William and Mary and cousin of President James Madison; Samuel Knox, who wrote a prize-winning essay on public education for the American Philosophical Society; Antoine Louis Claude Destutt de Tracy, the French *philosophe*; George Pictet, a Swiss scientist; and Alexander von Humboldt, the celebrated German naturalist whose brother Wilhelm played a major role in creating the public school system in Prussia and the University of Berlin.

During his retirement at Monticello, Jefferson personally met with others who were involved with creating and administering universities, such as Dr. Charles Caldwell, the founder of the innovative medical school at Transylvania University in Kentucky; Horace Holley, Transylvania's Unitarian president; Pierre Samuel du Pont de Nemours, the French economist and educationalist; and José Corrêia da Serra, known as the Abbé Corrêia, the Portuguese philosopher, politician, diplomat, and scientist who cofounded the Academy of Science in Lisbon. He corresponded with George Ticknor of Harvard, who twice visited him at Monticello, along with Edward Everett. Ticknor and Everett were among the first Americans to do postgraduate work in Germany, at the universities of Göttingen and Berlin. Jefferson collected information about "the best seminaries" or universities including Harvard, Yale, Princeton, Pennsylvania, South Carolina, Geneva, Oxford, Cambridge, Edinburgh, Paris, Rome, Naples, Turin, and Göttingen. Always *au courant* as to the relative status of universities in America and Europe, he regarded Edinburgh University, especially its medical school, and the University of Geneva, as the great exemplars in the 1790s. By the time of the founding of the University of Virginia, he thought Edinburgh had declined and, thanks in part to reports from George Ticknor, he was aware of the rise to preeminence of the German universities.

HENRY TUTWILER'S SPEECH to the alumni association revealed not only the intellectual culture of his host but also the domestic life and character of Jefferson during the years that he oversaw the university's creation. Jefferson was involved with every aspect of it, in what he called the "hobby of my old age," during the last decade of his life from the age of seventy-three until his death ten years later in 1826. Other than an occasional trip for a few weeks to his tobacco plantation at Poplar Forest in Bedford County, near Lynchburg, or when making the thirty-mile journey to James and Dolley Madison at Montpelier, near Orange Court House, he remained where, he once wrote, "all my wishes end, where I hope my days will end, at Monticello."[55] Known affectionately as "The Sage of Monticello," once a phrase of derision by his political opponents, Jefferson was already the object of pilgrimages in which "his mountain" was "made a sort of Mecca."[56] His Cabinet had interior shutters, a large portable screen, two layers of curtains on the windows, exterior louvered blinds, and internal locks on his bedchamber door, indicative of his desire for privacy and his need to shield himself from the prying eyes of curious strangers who often visited his mountain on a whim. The arrangement also enabled him to watch his enslaved laborers while remaining unseen, functioning like a panopticon, a circular prison in which inmates were observed through hidden blinds, modeled on a design by the English philosopher and social theorist Jeremy Bentham.[57]

Jefferson's founding of the university coincided with an active retirement in which he was deluged with visitors. Ellen Coolidge later recounted the constant stream: "We had persons from abroad, from all the states of the Union, from every part of the State—men, women, and children." Almost every day, "for at least eight months of the year," a contingent of guests visited: politicians, wealthy people, professionals, lawyers, doctors, clergymen, military men, tourists, travelers, artists, strangers, and friends.[58] They began to throng in June with people passing through Charlottesville on visits to the fashionable warm springs in Bath County, about ninety miles west of Monticello. Arriving at all hours and in all seasons, wanting to "catch a glimpse of him," some strangers would beg "to be allowed to sit in the hall . . . waiting until the dinner-hour arrived" to see "him as he passed through from his private apartments to his dining-room." On one occasion, a woman "who was peering around the house, punched her parasol through a window-pane to get a better view of him."[59] Jefferson's daughter Martha, when asked the largest number of unexpected overnight guests that she had entertained in the house, "replied *fifty!*"[60] They not only fed and entertained the guests but also provided stables and fodder for their horses. Some guests stayed for weeks; two of the rooms at Monticello were named after the two most regular guests: "Mr. Madison's Room" and the "Abbé Corrêia Room."

During his retirement when he was creating the university, Jefferson kept a regular daily routine. Congressman Daniel Webster described how Jefferson arose at dawn, "as soon as he can see the hands of his clock, which is directly opposite his bed," claiming that the "sun had not caught him in bed for fifty years."[61] After taking the temperature, entering the results in his diary, and then bathing his feet in cold water, he began his morning working on his correspondence and reading. He remained in his Cabinet until 8 o'clock when the first bell rang in the Entrance Hall, at which time he joined his guests and family for a breakfast of coffee or tea, along with some fresh oven-baked bread and occasionally some cold meats. After breakfast, he often strolled around his garden looking at the flowerbeds. Jefferson could identify every plant and tree throughout the gardens and grounds, where he liked to grow vegetables and fruits. Following his walk, he returned to his rooms to read, write, and look over papers until about 1 p.m. Believing in the importance of exercise for mental activity, he would go out riding daily, usually in the early afternoon, between 1 and 3 p.m. During hot days in the summer, Jefferson waited until the early evening, preferring always to be alone, as he was "fond of solitary rides and musing" over a distance of between seven and fourteen miles to one of his farms or to his mill. He was known for "his bold and graceful horsemanship," using only the best Arab thoroughbreds.[62] As he grew older, an enslaved man accompanied him, carrying a stool for him to sit on when he dismounted.

Following a second chime of the bell in the Entrance Hall at about 3:30 p.m., Jefferson's enslaved butler Burwell Colbert would lead Jefferson, his family, and their guests from the parlor into the dining room for dinner, after which Jefferson "returned for a while to his room" until sunset when he would walk on the wooden terraces or the lawn.[63] A light tea and refreshments were served at 7 p.m. As it became dark, Jefferson returned to sit by candlelight with his daughter and grandchildren in the dining room until about 10 p.m. He had his own chair and his own candle "a little apart from the rest, where he sat reading, if there were no guests to require his attention, but often laying his book on his little round table or his knee, while he talked" to his daughter or to one of the grandchildren who was old enough to stay up.[64] Before going to sleep, he would read for about thirty minutes or an hour something that he found morally uplifting "whereon to ruminate in the intervals of sleep."[65]

Isaac Granger Jefferson, an enslaved blacksmith, recollected seeing Jefferson with as many as twenty books sprawled across the floor, which he would read one after another.[66] Since his retirement, Jefferson claimed only to read for pleasure, especially the classics; to peruse only one newspaper, the *Richmond Enquirer*; but never to miss an issue of his favorite journal, the *Edinburgh Review*. His library purchases indicate that he continued to read new works on education. He withheld a few books relating to general and popular education from the sale of his library to Congress in 1815, such as those of James Ogilvie, the orator and local teacher; Antoine Destutt de Tracy; Joseph Lancaster; and Pierre Samuel du Pont de Nemours.[67] Jefferson's later acquisitions included books of the statutes at other universities like that of South Carolina College, of which he had a copy annotated by its president, Thomas Cooper.

The many firsthand accounts of personal meetings with Jefferson are remarkably consistent in describing him. He impressed visitors by his physical height at six feet two-and-a-half inches with a thin and gangly body. They noticed the effects of aging as he became stooped and his once-red hair turned a sandy white, but he still seemed robust, spry, and physically energetic for much of the remainder of his life. His guests found him initially shy, diffident, slightly awkward, and even grave, but he would soon warm to reveal an easy, mild, amiable, and pleasant manner with a "sweet, winning smile" and benign countenance.[68] According to Margaret Bayard Smith, he had "a manner and voice almost femininely soft and gentle."[69] She and others were soon put at ease by his obligingness, his seeming intimacy, and his ingratiating personality. As he was to do with young students, Jefferson encouraged his guests to speak about their interests and about subjects with which they were familiar, regardless of whether he was speaking to a laborer or a mechanic.[70] They in turn delighted in his "unabated flow of conversation" in which he avoided any controversial subjects or differences of opinion, being averse to direct conflict and confrontations.[71] Visitors warmed to the simplicity of his manner and plain dress; he seemed devoid of pomp and affectation yet dignified. They found him to be courteous, gracious, and very correct, with one commentator likening him to the "old colonial school" of manners and another referring to him as "a perfect gentleman" in his house.[72] Although his complexion was sallow, it did not detract from the charm of the intelligence and expressiveness of his face, captured in one of the last portraits of Jefferson in 1821, when he was seventy-eight years old, by the artist Thomas Sully.[73]

At Jefferson's dinner parties, as experienced by both students and faculty, "the table was plainly, but genteely & plentifully spread," with a hint of "European elegance," indicative of his projecting an unpretentious image while also wishing to be the consummate southern host.[74] The congressional representative and orator Daniel Webster described the meals as "half Virginian, half French style, in good taste and abundance."[75] The table would offer a wide variety of dishes of roasted poultry, meats, fish, soup, and vegetables, followed by a dessert course consisting of cakes, biscuits, custards, puddings, and jellies. Jefferson was unusual among his contemporaries in believing that it was healthier to eat only small amounts of meat and large portions of vegetables. During the course of a dinner, the enslaved staff regularly changed the plates and utensils of the guests, which was not customary. The guests drank beer or cider during the dinner, some of it pressed and brewed at Monticello. After the clearing of the tablecloth, Jefferson served "his immense and costly variety of French and Italian wines," followed by dessert wines and Madeira.[76]

Jefferson never drank spirits, partly because they adversely affected his stomach, and he generally only had a single glass of wine, at most three. He did keep some of the best old Antigua rum for guests. He discouraged toasts because they might lead to excessive drinking. He preferred small gatherings and an intimate atmosphere. According to Margaret Bayard Smith, in order to enjoy "a free and unrestricted flow of conversation," he placed a dumbwaiter next to his guests, "containing everything necessary for the progress of the dinner from beginning to end," so as to make the attendance of servants less essential. He had a revolving service door that enabled all the dishes to be transferred from the kitchen with the least interruption, and another type of dumbwaiter that allowed wine to be brought up on a pulley from the cellar, enabling guests to serve themselves in the informal style he had encountered in Paris. Martha Jefferson Randolph presided; the surviving tablecloths and napkins are monogrammed with her name. According to George Ticknor, the women in the household were "obviously accustomed to join the conversation, however high the topic may be."[77]

Like the Entrance Hall, the dinner parties offered an educational experience for guests in which they might taste French food for the first time, along with the wines, while simultaneously learning from the paintings and engravings on the walls. Jefferson owned primarily European paintings, including a copy of Raphael's *Holy Family*, along with an engraving of Natural Bridge, in Rockbridge County, Virginia, side by side with one of England's famous Ironbridge, in Coalbrookdale, contrasting the wonders of nature with the achievements of science. While displaying the best of Europe, Jefferson also collected artworks portraying America. In the dining room, with its brilliant and exorbitantly expensive chrome-yellow painted walls, he had two engravings of Niagara Falls, a picture of George Washington's Mount Vernon, and *A View of New Orleans Taken from the Plantation of Marigny*. In the adjoining Tea Room were the busts of American revolutionary heroes, plaster copies of originals by the great French sculptor Houdon.

More than the works of art, the brilliance and range of Jefferson's conversation captivated his guests. He was humorous and loved to dwell on irony, although often given to embellishment and hyperbole in the view of John Quincy Adams. Jefferson would pepper his conversations and tours of the house with anecdotes of the American Revolution, relating tales of its long-dead great men, most notably Benjamin Franklin and George Washington, to guests who were generally too young to remember them. When not deferring to the choice and interests of his guests, according to Daniel Webster, Jefferson particularly enjoyed talking about "science and letters, and especially the University of Virginia, which is coming into existence almost entirely from his exertions, and will rise, it is to be hoped, to usefulness and credit under his continued care."[78]

Jefferson presented himself as a patriarch and a patriot, albeit one in the midst of a plantation populated by some 140 enslaved people.[79] He enjoyed, in his own words, living "like a patriarch of old" with his daughter, his sister, eleven grandchildren, and half a dozen great-grandchildren.[80] He used the term "family" in its oldest sense to embrace all subordinates, including his enslaved laborers, artisans, and domestics. Although occasionally resenting all the visitors and the amount of time he spent on the university, his grand-children described an almost idyllic childhood at Monticello. In her private travel diary in England in 1839, Ellen Randolph Coolidge wrote a moving testimonial about her grandfather, saying that "his domestic character was the most perfect that I have ever known," an opinion in which she had be-come more confirmed with the passage of time and her own experiences as a mother "of the qualities necessary to make the happiness of family life." She remembered him as a devoted grandfather who was "equaled by few, surpassed by none in all the virtues that command reverence and love."[81] He played with his white grandchildren in the garden, and after 1816, he took his granddaughters in pairs to Poplar Forest. Jefferson's desire to play the role of patriarch may explain why he wished to be known as the fa-ther, rather than the founder, of the University of Virginia. He often used the metaphor of a family to describe the academic community, invoking fatherhood as the ideal metaphor for the relationship between professors and students.

Tensions, however, rose beneath the surface of this seemingly idyllic fam-ily life. In his retirement, Jefferson persuaded Martha Randolph, then his only surviving child by his marriage to Martha Wayles Skelton, who had died in 1782, to move close to him with her husband and later to bring her family to live with him at Monticello. Ellen, Martha's daughter, wrote of her mother that her personality "seemed to have the sunshine of heaven in it," since "nothing ever wearied my mother's patience, or exhausted what was inexhaustible, her sweetness, her kindness, [and] indulgence." Mar-tha Randolph similarly impressed visitors with her intelligence and good nature. Margaret Bayard Smith described her as one of the most lovely women that she had ever met and wrote effusively of her "intelligence, be-nevolence, and sensibility" and her "interesting conversation." Yet Martha's marriage to her cousin Thomas Mann Randolph became strained, and he began to spend the night at his own home at Edgehill while she and the rest of the family lived at Monticello. The couple separated after Jefferson's death. Some historians have blamed Jefferson for the split because he was so dependent on Martha's assistance. Randolph was a considerable figure in his own right, serving variously as a U.S. representative and two-term governor of Virginia. Rejected by his own father, who did not bequeath him the family home at Tuckahoe, giving it instead to a son from a second marriage, Randolph initially idolized Jefferson and treated him as a surrogate father. Martha's biographer Cynthia A. Kierner argues that "their marital problems owed at least as much to personal feuds and financial problems that plagued" the Randolphs as to Jefferson.[82] Thomas Mann Randolph had drinking problems that dated back to at least the early 1800s, while his financial affairs were even more precarious than Jefferson's.

Also, beneath the surface appearance of domestic tranquility, Jefferson had a shadow family of six children by his enslaved servant Sally (Sarah) Hemings, who is thought to have been the half-sister of his wife, Martha. The case for his fathering her children is compelling, based on multiple sources and a variety of evidence. Jefferson was always resident at the plantation at exactly the right moment for conception for each of Heming's six documented children, even while president of the United States. The statistical probability of this being a coincidence is negligible. Later DNA tests have corroborated other sources by disproving the much-later claim that the children were fathered by Jefferson's nephews; the tests further confirmed that Sally Heming's son Eston was descended through the male line of the Jeffersons.[83]

The Hemingses enjoyed a special status at Monticello. Unlike most other enslaved servants, Jefferson acknowledged their surnames while their first names were those of family members and friends of Jefferson. Many others mentioned the connection besides the disgruntled journalist who first made the story public, James T. Callender. The connection was portrayed in an engraving and the subject of a satirical poem by John Quincy Adams. A few visitors and friends alluded to it, such as John Hartwell Cocke, a particularly credible source as a member of the governing board of the university and an evangelical, who commented that it was not surprising that there were thousands of mixed-race children in the state, "when Mr. Jefferson's notorious example is considered."[84] John Adams predicted that "Callendar and Sally will be remembered as long as Jefferson as blotts on his Character."[85]

The children of Sally Hemings identified Jefferson as their father, with the most detailed account given by Madison Hemings, named after President James Madison, whom even Thomas Jefferson Randolph, the oldest of the white male grandchildren, acknowledged looked like Jefferson. In a memoir published in the *Pike County Republican* (Ohio) in 1873, Madison Hemings said that his mother was an enslaved "concubine" of Jefferson from the time she was a teenage girl with him in Paris, where she had begun "to understand the French language well" and where she initially refused to return to Virginia because she knew she could be legally free in France. In order to persuade her to return with him to America, Jefferson "promised her extraordinary privileges, and made a solemn pledge that her children should be free at the age of twenty-one years," which he did indeed honor. Madison Hemings remembered his father as a mild man who was slow to anger and who was "uniformly kind to all about him." Unlike other enslaved children, Madison and his siblings "were always permitted to be with our mother" and "were measurably happy" because they "were free of the dread of having to be slaves all our lives long." Nevertheless, Jefferson "was very undemonstrative" to them and "was not in the habit of showing partiality or fatherly affection to us children," but "he was affectionate toward his white grandchildren."[86]

In addition to domestic issues, Jefferson's debt problems became an increasing source of anxiety. This situation during his retirement was mortifying to a man who had a terror of both public and personal debt, which he saw as destructive of independence.[87] He had always championed balancing the budget and opposed the idea of a national debt, which he associated with Alexander Hamilton and the influence of Britain. Jefferson did not want the country to be in the thrall of bankers and creditors holding it ransom. Beginning with his pending retirement from the presidency, he wrote to his daughter that he had "the gloomy prospect of retiring from office loaded with serious debts, which will materially affect the tranquility of my retirement."[88] He had spent much of his life away from his plantation, which overseers managed in his absence, and in retirement he handed over the management of all his farms to his oldest grandson, Thomas Jefferson Randolph, in 1815.

Jefferson's difficulties were due partly to the poor quality of his land, which one of his overseers described as "too uneven and hard to work" with its clay soil, in addition to the effects of soil erosion.[89] His extravagant lifestyle did not help his financial situation either, nor did the loss of a very costly legal case over land in the nearby town of Milton. He also had to support his daughter Martha and her children because of Thomas Mann Randolph's financial problems. During Jefferson's time in office, his income from the government often did not cover his expenses. He spent more equipping himself as an ambassador than the equivalent of a year's salary, and after his presidency, he received no government pension. He felt obligated to entertain his numerous guests at great cost, not just in feeding them but also in providing stables and food for their horses. His problems escalated when a friend defaulted on a major loan for which he had acted as a guarantor. Jefferson never fully appreciated the extent of the crisis of his finances until 1818. He later wrote that this was the year he would have preferred to have died, an odd statement given that he enjoyed good health until virtually the last three months of his life and delighted in the company of his family. If he had died in 1818, he would not have achieved his vision to create the University of Virginia. Nevertheless, it would have saved him from the remorse of knowing that he was leaving his family in penury.

While subject to momentary periods of doubt and pessimism as he contemplated his financial problem, Jefferson still remained stubbornly optimistic about his finances almost until the end.[90] Although he kept detailed records of all his financial transactions, he seems to have thought that these were a sufficient substitute for making calculations as to his actual financial status. Always fond of nautical metaphors, he likened the various blows to waves striking a boat but soon passing. George Ticknor described being with Jefferson when he lost a mill in which he had invested a major sum of money, swept away in a flood after a dam burst. Ticknor said that "from his manner, I supposed it an affair of small consequence, but at Charlottesville, on my way to Richmond, I found the country ringing with it" and that "it would cost $30,000 to rebuild."[91] The same naive optimism informed much of Jefferson's other thinking, including the belief that slavery would somehow disappear. Despite occasional flashes of a potentially horrific future, his sanguine personality also gave him faith in republican government based on consent and a belief in the transforming potential of his university. Although a shrewd political operator and often a pragmatic individual, he was also an idealist and incessant optimist.

THIS OPTIMISM WAS especially evident in his interest in education and desire to share his knowledge. Jefferson not only advised younger people about their education, often providing them with reading lists, but he formally taught members of his own extended family and unrelated young men who sought his help. Early in his retirement, he wrote to the Polish revolutionary war hero Thaddeus Kosciusko that "part of my occupation, & by no means the least pleasing, is the direction of the studies of such young men as ask it. They place themselves in the neighboring village, and have use of my library and counsel, and make part of my society." In advising their course of reading, he always endeavored "to keep their attention fixed on the main objects of all science, the freedom & happiness of man," in the hope that when they

reached positions of authority, they would ever have "in view the sole objects of all legitimate government."[92] He wrote to the governor of Virginia
in 1810, "I still lend my counsel & books to such young students as will fix
themselves in the neighborhood."[93] He would encourage his students to
study in the pavilions at Monticello.

Jefferson had advised both his future sons-in-law, Thomas Mann Randolph and John Wayles Eppes, on their education. In the case of the former,
he asked Randolph to correspond weekly and read Randolph's extensive
notes of the medical lectures at Edinburgh University. After attending West
Point, Nicholas Philip Trist studied law with Jefferson and later married
his granddaughter Virginia Randolph. Jefferson variously mentored Francis
Walker Gilmer, whom he regarded as one of the most brilliant young men
of his generation and whom he later invited to be the first law professor
at the university; Archibald Stuart, who studied law under Jefferson; Carter H. Harrison; William Short, whom Jefferson likened to his "adoptive
son" and who acted as secretary to Jefferson in Paris; and his nephew Peter
Carr. In mentoring his own students, he was replicating his education under William Small, George Wythe, and Francis Fauquier at Williamsburg.
He recognized the value of students' supplementing their study and reading
by conversation with sophisticated, knowledgeable, experienced, and exem-
plary individuals.

While he believed that women should principally be educated with a view
to their future domestic and household responsibilities, Jefferson gave his
own daughters a much broader education, fearing that the chances were
fourteen to one that they might marry a "blockhead" and that they would
need to be responsible for the education of their own family. He therefore
included some "reading in the graver sciences."[94] In Philadelphia, he hired
some outstanding tutors to teach Martha, including Francis Hopkinson,
regarded as one of the first composers in America. In France, he sent both
his daughters to the Abbaye Royale de Penthemont, conducted by nuns of
the Order of Saint Bernard, because it was the "best" school for girls, with
the "best" teachers."[95] He had Maria read Don Quixote and Edward Gibbon.
While he would tell his daughters that needlework was the most important
skill they could acquire, he never attempted to have anyone instruct them in
that craft. Martha had to acquire her knowledge of household management
as an adult, learning by trial and error. She taught her own children, usually during the mornings while Jefferson was reading and writing. Granddaughter Ellen later reflected on how she would study for seven or eight
hours while she was with her grandfather at Poplar Forest. She wrote that

she had often thought "that the life of a student must be the most happy and innocent in the world." She regretted that she had never had the opportunity because "being a woman and not a rich woman, I must be content with peeping every now and then into a region too blissful for my inheritance."[96]

Jefferson revealed his academic values when he told his daughter Maria that she would be more respected and valued in the world if she appeared well educated.[97] To John Banister Jr., he wrote, "Cast your eye over America: who are the men of most learning, of most eloquence, most beloved by their country and most trusted and promoted by them? They are those who have been educated among them, and whose manners, morals and habits are perfectly homogeneous with those of the country."[98] Jefferson believed that it was the duty of the living generation to educate the "rising generation" to whom he looked to produce "great reformations" in government and society, including the end of slavery.[99] He saw it as essential that they should not be fettered by the superstitions and traditions of past errors, which could only be corrected through reason and education. In what could be the credo of the Enlightenment, Jefferson believed that with education would come progress and happiness: "When I contemplate the immense advances in science and discoveries in the arts which have been made within the period of my life, I look forward with confidence to equal advances by the present generation, and I have no doubt they will consequently be as much wiser than we have been," just as his generation had been wiser than their witch-burning fathers.[100]

2

Enlighten the People

W HILE JEFFERSON'S OWN education and his Enlightenment values might have predisposed him to be interested in public education, the catalyst was the American Revolution. The revolution was a subject to which he and John Adams frequently alluded in their retirement correspondence, which commenced in 1811 and continued until their deaths in 1826.

Shortly after Jefferson retired as U.S. president in 1809, Benjamin Rush wrote to former president John Adams claiming that he had recently had a dream in which Rush found his son reading a future history of the United States.[1] A signer of the Declaration of Independence, Rush described how, in his dream, he started to read the future history of the coming year and that "among the most extraordinary events of this year was the renewal of the friendship & intercourse between Mr. John Adams and Mr. Jefferson, the two ex-presidents of the United States." According to this vision, Adams had revived their old friendship by writing a conciliatory note to Jefferson congratulating him "upon his escape to the shades of retirement and domestic happiness," concluding with regards and "good wishes for his Welfare."[2]

The history book in Rush's dream recounted how Adams's overture to Jefferson initiated "a correspondence of several years, in which they mutually reviewed the Scenes of business in which they had been engaged." They acknowledged "to each other all the errors of Opinion & conduct into which they had fallen during the time they filled the same stations in the Service of their country." Their letters were filled with observations, experiences, and "profound reflection," which would hopefully one day be published. According to the dream, they would both go to the grave "nearly at the same time, full of years, and rich in the gratitude and praises of their country," and they would outlive their opponents. "To their numerous merits and honors," posterity would record that they became "rival friends."[3] Rush regarded the two men "as the North and South poles of the American Revolution." Writing to Adams, he observed, "Some talked, some wrote—and some fought to promote & establish it, but you, and Mr. Jefferson *thought* for us all."[4]

For Rush, the breach between Adams and Jefferson was a personal and national misfortune. He had first known them when they were allies and friends serving in the Continental Congress in 1775. The two ex-presidents were both lawyers by training who had played prominent roles in the patriot cause, representing the two largest colonies in British America. They would serve as diplomats for the new republic, Jefferson in France and Adams in Britain. During their time in Europe, they would help one another not only in their diplomatic negotiations but in personal matters, such as Jefferson's buying the linens and table settings with which Abigail Adams equipped their home in London's Grosvenor Square. After an unsatisfactory attempt to seek a new treaty with Britain in June 1786, John and Thomas traveled together for six weeks around England during which they anticipated the path of many later American tourists with visits to such sites as Shakespeare's birthplace at Stratford-upon-Avon. Jefferson even commissioned portraits of them both by the American artist Mather Brown. The portrait of Adams depicted him next to the leather-bound volumes of Jefferson's *Notes on the State of Virginia*. Jefferson and Adams served in George Washington's first administration with Adams as vice president and Jefferson as secretary of state. Subsequently, they ran against one another in the presidential contest of 1796. Adams was the winner, but since Jefferson received the second greatest number of votes, he became vice president, a procedure used for the last time in the election of 1800. Their friendship did not survive the rancor of party politics and especially the venomous negative campaigning of the presidential election of 1800 in which Jefferson defeated Adams.

Adams replied to Rush that he had "no objection to your Dream, but that is not History. It may be Prophesy."[5] Regardless, the dream did not sufficiently motivate Adams to write to Jefferson. Rush was undeterred and wrote a long letter to Jefferson requesting, in consideration of his affection for Adams and of "how much the liberties & Independance of the United States owe to the Concert of your principles and labors," that "a friendly and epistolary intercourse might be revived between you before you take a final leave of the Common Object of your Affections." The resumption of their correspondence would be "highly useful to the cause of republicanism not only in the United States but all over the world."[6]

During the summer of 1811, two young neighbors of Jefferson, Edward Coles and his brother John, spent a couple of days with Adams in Quincy. According to Edward Coles, who was then serving as the private secretary of President James Madison, upon hearing that Jefferson had been debating about the appropriate moment to contact his former friend, Adams exclaimed, "I always loved Jefferson and still love him."[7] The Coles brothers' visit provided the necessary spur to reignite Adams's contact with Jefferson.

Rush's dream was prophetic. Throughout the time that Jefferson was overseeing the creation of the University of Virginia, he was engaged in one of the most remarkable correspondences, likened by one scholar to a "ceaseless symposium," amounting to 158 letters exchanged between the two great statesmen of the American Revolution.[8] At the start of the New Year in 1812, the seventy-seven-year-old Adams initiated the first of these exchanges with the sixty-nine-year-old Jefferson. There was a playful banter in their correspondence and an occasional jibe. In 1819, the year of the bill creating the University of Virginia, Adams humorously began giving his address as "Montezillo Alias the little House."[9] Over a period of fourteen years, up until their deaths on the same day, the fiftieth anniversary of the Declaration of Independence, their correspondence traversed an expansive array of intellectual, personal, and mutual interests, ranging from science to foreign affairs, theology, history, political science, education, languages, literature, morality, Native peoples, religion, aging, and death. "We ought not to die," wrote Jefferson, "before we have explained ourselves to each other."[10]

Jefferson and Adams were both acutely aware that they had outlived most of the revolutionary generation and become icons among their contemporaries. Writing an average of three letters for every letter that he received from Jefferson, Adams envied the acclaim that Jefferson received as author of the Declaration of Independence. Having personally penned so many of the earlier grievance petitions, Adams argued that Independence Day should be celebrated on July 2, which would have put the emphasis on the day that the Continental Congress voted for independence rather than on the document that was ratified and published on July 4. He implied that Jefferson's fame was a historical accident since it was only because he was a Virginian that he was selected to draft the Declaration.[11] It was almost by chance that Jefferson was still in Philadelphia since, at the time, he wanted to return to his wife, Martha, at Monticello. Adams and his contemporaries in 1776 never realized that the document and the date would be so significant in later celebrations of the American Revolution. Between April and July 1776, there were some ninety comparable declarations by towns, patriotic groups, and colonies. It was only during the party strife of the 1790s that it even became public knowledge in America that Jefferson had composed the Declaration of Independence.[12] As Adams remarked to Rush, he had always considered the Declaration "a Theatrical Show" in which "Jefferson ran away with the Stage Effect of that, ie. all the Glory of it."[13]

As the last two survivors of the five-member committee for drafting the Declaration, Adams and Jefferson differed in their recollection of the event. In a letter to fellow Federalist Timothy Pickering, Adams took some credit for the document by claiming that he and Jefferson had been a subcommittee in which he had nominated Jefferson to write the first draft of the Declaration.[14] When Pickering repeated the substance of the letter from Adams in a Fourth of July Address of 1823, Jefferson indignantly denied to Madison the existence of any such subcommittee and bristled at the charge that the text "contained no new ideas, that it is a commonplace compilation, it's sentiments hacknied in Congress for two years before, and it's essence contained" in a pamphlet of the deranged Boston patriot James Otis, "as I suppose-in one of his lucid intervals." Recalling a similar charge from fellow Virginian Richard Henry Lee, that Jefferson had copied from John Locke's *Second Treatise on Government* (1689), Jefferson protested to Madison that he had not considered it "as any part of my charge to invent new ideas altogether," and that he had not meant the Declaration to be original but "intended [it] to be an expression of the american mind."[15] Adams could not resist openly taunting Jefferson with news of the discovery of a rumored declaration of independence by militia companies in Mecklenburg County, North Carolina, which had allegedly been written "fifteen months before your Declaration of Independence." "And you seem to think it genuine," wrote Jefferson and then added, in a verdict supported by subsequent research, "I believe it spurious."[16]

JEFFERSON REPEATEDLY SOUGHT advice from Adams about founding the University of Virginia, a natural expectation given that the latter had played a major role in the reform of Harvard. If Jefferson had hoped to engage more interest, however, he must have been disappointed by the rather tepid, short responses. Adams only professed his admiration for the project and gave some encouragement, even recommending books for the library, but he did not reveal much enthusiasm. Upon hearing of the laying of the foundation stone by the three presidents, Adams wrote discouragingly that if the university "contains anything quite original, and very excellent, I fear the prejudices are too deeply rooted to Suffer it to last long. It will not always have three Such colossal reputations to Support it."[17] Adams had ceased to believe in the transformative power of education and its potential to provide a panacea for the ailments of the republican system of government. It had not always been so. During the American Revolution, Adams contributed a section on education to the Massachusetts Constitution (1780), asserting that "wisdom and knowledge, as well as virtue, diffused generally among the body of the people [were] necessary for the preservation of their rights and liberties." Adams, thereafter, no longer thought that all men were created equal but rather that an aristocracy of wealth was inevitable and all the more insidious in the pretended egalitarianism of America. He did not have the same faith in the virtue of the people or democracy as the ultimate form of government. Unlike Jefferson, who increasingly regarded his country as the torchbearer of liberty throughout the world, Adams thought the United States would probably be no better long-term than Europe. Jefferson never lost faith in the ideals of the American Revolution, which provided the impetus for his educational initiatives and ultimately for his creation of the University of Virginia.[18]

LIKE BENJAMIN FRANKLIN, one of the founders of the University of Pennsylvania, Thomas Jefferson might well have pursued educational reform and founded a university even if America had remained British, but the American Revolution provided the impetus that led him to propose a public school system and craft a distinctly republican conception of a university whose foundations lay in "the spirit of 1776." More than any other event of his subsequent political career, Jefferson was defined by both his role in and experience of the American Revolution. Indeed, his later political life was dedicated to protecting and perpetuating what he regarded as the true ideals of the Revolution as enshrined in his Republican Party and his electoral victory as president in 1800, which he dubbed the Second American Revolution.

Jefferson sought constantly to commemorate the American Revolution.[19] It was the source of his fame, and its republican philosophy became the credo of his life. He saw himself as the most reliable guardian of its ideals and values, writing of the "republican principles to which my whole life has been devoted."[20] He had an almost religious zeal in promoting his own interpretation of its meaning while regarding critics and opponents as heretics and even traitors. The survival of the republic would determine his own legacy, but his concern with the future was more than a vanity project. He *believed* in what was still an experiment that had the potential to create a more rational system of government and to make happier the lives of the great majority of the population. And he regarded public education as necessary for securing the achievements of the American Revolution.

Jefferson was acutely aware that the new republican system of government was experimental and fragile. He knew that republics failed historically. In common with many others of the revolutionary generation, including Benjamin Rush, John Adams, Samuel Knox, and Noah Webster,
Jefferson regarded the education of the electorate as one of the best safe-
guards against tyranny and as essential for the survival of the republic. As
he observed in *Notes on the State of Virginia*, "Every government degenerates
when trusted to the rulers of the people alone. The people themselves therefore are its only safe repositories. And to render them safe their minds must
be improved to a certain degree."[21] Writing to his friend and mentor George
Wythe in Williamsburg in 1786, he dismissed the taxes that would be necessary to pay for a public-education system as incidental, just "one thousandth
part of what will be paid to kings, priests and nobles who would rise up
among us if the population was kept in ignorance."[22] In a letter from Paris
in December 1787, reacting to the proposed Constitution for the United
States, Jefferson wrote to Madison that "above all things I hope the education of the common people will be attended to," since he was convinced "that
on their good sense we may rely with the most security for the preservation
of a due degree of liberty."[23] Since the republican system was based on opinion, he thought it important that voters be able to read newspapers and be
fully informed about their government.[24] In his retirement, he was much
impressed by a provision to prohibit illiterate citizens from voting in Spain's
new constitution.[25]

Jefferson and other founders thought they were beginning the world
anew with the American Revolution. They believed the political revolution
would be succeeded by a moral revolution in which education would constitute a major component. As Benjamin Rush wrote after the Revolutionary War, "We have only finished the first act of the drama . . . it remains
yet to effect a revolution in our principles, opinions, and manners so as to
accommodate them to the forms of government we have adopted."[26] In his
pamphlet *Thoughts upon the Mode of Education Proper in a Republic* (1786),
Rush argued that "the business of education has acquired a new complexion
by the independence of our country. The form of government that we have
assumed has created a new class of duties to every American. It becomes
us, therefore, to examine our former habits upon this subject, and in laying
the foundations for nurseries of wise and good men, to adapt our modes
of teaching to the peculiar form of our government."[27] In *On the Education
of Youth in America* (1788), Noah Webster, the lexicographer and reformer,
noted that the new constitutions were republican but complained that the

laws governing education were monarchical.[28] Echoing a theme of the popular pseudonymous *Cato's Letters* (1720–24), Simeon Doggett voiced the beliefs of many of the revolutionary generation when he asserted that "the throne of tyranny is founded on ignorance. Literature and liberty go hand in hand."[29] Similarly, John Adams thought the way to end tyranny was to ensure that "no human being shall grow up in ignorance."[30] Robert Coram, the librarian of the Library Company of Wilmington, Delaware, called on his contemporaries to perfect "the system of education as a property whereon to erect a temple to liberty."[31] Like Jefferson, other reformers had various motives for championing public education beyond the primary object of ensuring the survival of republican government. They were concerned that the new nation should be civilized and compare favorably with Europe. They believed that education would be a source of happiness, virtue, stability, harmony, employability, improvement, and progress. "If all the sovereigns of Europe were to set themselves to work, to emancipate the minds of their subjects from their present ignorance and prejudices, and that as zealously as they now endeavor the contrary," wrote Jefferson, "a thousand years would not place them on that high ground, on which our common people are now setting out."[32]

Although college graduates represented less than 1 percent of the white male population, and fewer than a hundred students graduated from nine colonial colleges annually before the American Revolution, they made up a third of the signers of the Declaration of Independence and of the delegates to the Philadelphia Convention that wrote the Constitution.[33] In addition to providing a basic level of education to create a vigilant citizenry, Jefferson thought it important that the future leaders of the republic be distinguished by their virtue and talents, traits to be nurtured and developed in public universities. For Jefferson, an educated elite would constitute a "natural aristocracy" based on virtue and merit in America as opposed to the "artificial aristocracy" based on wealth and birth that held sway in Europe. Beginning with the Romans and running through the Renaissance, the term "virtue" was used not only in the modern sense of being moral and ethical but also in denoting a willingness to set aside personal interest and ambition to serve the public good.[34] It was the antithesis of "corruption," in which leaders sought public office to satisfy personal ambition and, once in office, abused their powers, leading ultimately to tyranny.

Keenly aware of the temptations of power, Jefferson believed that power corrupts and that absolute power degenerates into tyranny. As a result, he thought it most important that the future generations of leaders be educated to act wisely for the sake of the common good, to be self-sacrificing, and to seek public office out of a sense of responsibility, rather than self-interest. It was the role of the natural aristocracy to liberate the living generation from the dead hand of the past through reason and education in contrast to pseudo-aristocrats who manipulated the masses through superstition and asserted traditions. Jefferson was always something of a class rebel, seeking to undermine the inherited privileges of his own class by removing primogeniture (in which the oldest son inherited an unequal share of the estate) and entail (which acted like a trust to keep family lands undivided over several generations), and by disestablishing the Anglican church from state support. He simultaneously sought a state constitution that would provide up to fifty acres of land to each adult freeman who either owned no land or less than fifty acres. Jefferson told his overseer Edmund Bacon that laborers and journeymen would replace those expecting to live without work and industry.[35] He always identified more with his self-made surveyor-father than his mother and her better-connected family.

DISTRUSTFUL OF THE ABILITY of a well-educated elite to resist the temptations of power, Jefferson thought it even more important to educate the masses to hold those in power accountable. He looked to an independent and industrious yeomen class of small landowners to be the bedrock of the republican system. At the time of the American Revolution, there were only a few private academies and charity schools in Virginia. It was an elitist system of education with the result that illiteracy rates were much higher in the state than in New England. Unlike Puritans and Congregationalists in colonial New England, the planter elites showed little interest in educating the population. In 1671, William Berkeley, the royalist governor of Virginia, wrote, "I thank God that there are no free schools nor printing, and I hope we shall have none of these [for a] hundred years; for learning has brought disobedience, and heresy, and sects into the world, and printing has divulged them, and libels against the best of government. God keep us from both!"[36] The inequalities of wealth distribution, even among the white population, helped perpetuate discrepancies in education.

Jefferson's support of public education was not just rhetorical and philosophical. He stood out as a champion of education and proposed one of the earliest plans for an integrated public education system. In 1779, he chaired a committee of the General Assembly to revise the entire legal code of Virginia. As part of his lifelong quest to improve the state, he personally drafted a series of bills to conform with republican principles, including his celebrated bill for religious freedom, bills revising inheritance laws, and a bill to reform the criminal code. He regarded his education bill, "A Bill for the More General Diffusion of Knowledge," as by far the most important of all the laws reviewed, "since no other sure foundation can be devised for the preservation of freedom, and happiness."[37] Describing the bill almost a quarter of a century later to John Adams, Jefferson wrote that it "would have raised the mass of the people to the high ground of moral respectability necessary to their own safety, and to orderly government; and would have completed the great object of qualifying them" to select representatives from the natural aristocracy rather than the pseudo-aristocracy of wealth. While his education bill did not pass, he remained hopeful that "some patriotic spirit will, at a favorable moment, call it up, and make it the key-stone of the arch of our government."[38] The bill represented an objective that Jefferson continued to pursue for the rest of his life, helping to initiate similar legislation as late as 1817 and 1821.

The 1779 bill envisaged a competitive three-tier system in which both boys and girls received a basic three-year education with a sliding scale of tuition fees, exempting poor children who could attend at no charge. Based on a public oral examination, the more academically gifted boys would advance to a grammar school where the very best pupil from each school would then go on, at public expense with a scholarship that included the cost of clothing and boarding, to the College of William and Mary. With echoes of the French philosopher Montesquieu, the preamble of the bill warned that even the best system of government was likely to degenerate into tyranny: "The most effectual means of preventing this would be, to illuminate the minds of the people at large, as far as is practicable, and more especially to give them knowledge of those facts, which history exhibiteth." Once possessed of knowledge of the history of other ages and countries, the people "may be enabled to know ambition under all its shapes" and prompted "to exert their natural powers to defeat its purposes."[39] The bill's comprehensive vision of a state system of education detailed the buildings, the location of schools, staffing arrangements, administration, maintenance, examinations, supervisors (called overseers), and external visitors. Jefferson wanted the elementary schools administered and funded at the local level with counties subdivided into hundreds of wards, what he later dubbed "ward republics." The idea was to ensure local support, which was consistent with his belief in the necessity of engaging and empowering the people. The bill represented a coherent and systematic plan in a period that showed little appreciation for the roles of different levels of education.

In his *Notes on the State of Virginia*, Jefferson included a summary of his education bill in which he elaborated on his preferred curriculum, which aimed "to provide an education adapted to the years, to the capacity, and to the condition of every one, and directed to their freedom and happiness." He observed that the first stage of education was the most critical because this was where "the great mass of the people will receive their instruction." It would be "the principal foundation of the future order," since the primary purpose of education was "rendering the people safe, as they are the ultimate guardians of their own liberty." He envisaged that the basic elementary education would consist of reading, writing, and arithmetic, but that the most important subject would "be chiefly historical." Eschewing the tradition of children learning to read the Bible "at an age when their judgments were not sufficiently matured for religious enquiries," he proposed that they should instead become familiar with texts "from Grecian, Roman, European and American history." As he wrote in the *Notes*, "History by apprising them of the past will enable them to judge of the future; it will avail them of the experience of other times and other nations; it will qualify them as judges of the actions and designs of men; it will enable them to know ambition under every disguise it may assume; and knowing it, to defeat its views." The second-tier grammar schools were to prepare students to enter the professions and to prepare a select few to enter the university. The bill recommended that these students be taught Greek, Latin, geography, and "the higher branches of numerical arithmetic." Although he acknowledged that Greek and Latin were "going into disuse in Europe," Jefferson still thought it important that children learn both ancient and modern languages at an age when their minds were most supple and best able to retain the vocabulary, "the learning of languages being chiefly a work of memory." [40]

Jefferson's attempt to create a public education system was far ahead of its time. In contrast to John Locke and Benjamin Franklin, he wanted poor children to receive a free education at state schools, not private academies. His bill represented what would have been the first state-supported school system in the United States. Thanks to the emphasis of Puritan Congregationalists and Presbyterians on the need for everyone to be able to read the Bible, there were high levels of literacy and numerous schools in New England and Scotland. Although laws passed in 1645 and 1647 by the Massachusetts General Court had attempted to require towns to build schools in the Massachusetts Bay Colony, they were never fully implemented. It was not until the 1830s through the 1860s that the northern states incrementally began to develop public school systems in the United States—a development associated with the work of Horace Mann as the first secretary of the Board of Education in Massachusetts. Before the Civil War, the South lagged far behind the North in literacy levels and state education. The defeat of Jefferson's education bill was therefore a major lost opportunity for the advancement of Virginia. Not until 1870 did the Virginia Constitution require the establishment of a "uniform system of free public schools" with an "Act to Establish and Maintain a System of Public Free Schools." Even then, it was not only segregated but the funding arrangements discriminated against Catholics. Furthermore, not until 1906 did the legislature vote sufficient funds for a public school system in Virginia.[41]

Ironically, the most authoritarian, autocratic regimes in Europe took the initiative in setting up a state school system, beginning with Russia under Tsar Peter the Great, who called for the creation of state schools, and later Catherine II (the Great), who ordered in 1786 the setting up of government primary schools in district and provincial towns. However, although they were forerunners, they achieved little in the short term. Prussia was the first country to create a state system but only after many false starts. As early as 1717, Elector Frederick William I ordered all children to attend primary school, and he later issued edicts for the construction of schools in underserved areas. In his General School Regulations (General-Landschul-Reglement) of 1763, Frederick II (the Great) made school attendance for children mandatory, with fines for absences. In Austria in 1774, Empress Maria Theresa also introduced compulsory schooling throughout the Habsburg Empire. Frederick V of Denmark, Louis XV of France, Joseph II of Austria, and Carlos III of Spain each introduced educational initiatives during the Enlightenment.

The requirement of these autocratic rulers that children attend schools remained largely unrealized in the eighteenth century because their governments failed to provide funding. Unlike Jefferson, who later famously declared, "Enlighten the people generally, and tyranny and oppressions of the body & mind will vanish like evil spirits at the dawn of the day," public education in these monarchies aimed to inculcate obedience and strengthen the state by training bureaucrats and professionals, rather than encourage a vigilant citizenry, free thought, and cultural enrichment.[42] These autocratic regimes did not aim to promote social mobility but instead expected that individuals would receive educations appropriate to their particular social stations and class. Not until the early nineteenth century did these embryonic national education systems begin to be fully realized in Prussia and France.

In contrast to these educational initiatives in Europe, Jefferson's 1779 bill stipulated that merit rather than wealth should be the criterion for selection. The best pupils would attend the College of William and Mary, chosen *"without regard to wealth, birth or other accidental condition or circumstance."* Recognizing that "the indigence of the greater number" of people disabled them from obtaining an education "at their own expence," the bill declared that "it is better that such should be sought for and educated at the common expense of all, than that the happiness of all should be confided to the weak or wicked." The college was to train "persons whom nature endowed with genius and virtue" to be the future leaders responsible for guarding "the sacred deposit of the rights and liberties of their fellow citizens."[43] In a summary of the bill published in his *Notes on the State of Virginia,* Jefferson wrote that "by that part of our plan which prescribes the selection of the youths of genius from among the classes of the poor, we hope to avail the state of those talents which nature has sown as liberally among the poor as the rich, but which perish without use, if not sought for and cultivated."[44]

Modern detractors of the bill stress the very limited opportunities it made available to the poor. It provided annually for the state to fund only one student from each elementary school to continue on to the grammar school level, with seven state-funded pupils at each of the twenty proposed grammar schools, where they would study alongside regular fee-paying students.[45] After a year, at least a third of those receiving state scholarships would be weeded out. In their second year, only one of the state-sponsored students at each grammar school would continue on to complete the rest of the four years of schooling. Jefferson himself wrote of a selection process in which "twenty of the best geniuses will be raked from the rubbish annually" to go to the grammar schools, followed by a further process of winnowing over six years, after which only ten publicly funded students would continue annually to the College of William and Mary. While the opportunities represented were limited in comparison to today, they were expansive for their time. Furthermore, the number of scholarships may well have reflected what he thought practical to obtain from a stingy legislature rather than his aspirations for a more mobile society.

Jefferson's 1779 education bill was also innovative in providing girls with a basic education, though not beyond the elementary school level. Like Benjamin Rush, the few advocates of education for women were largely concerned with their domestic roles and educating them as "republican mothers" to inculcate the next generation with republican values. Only about a dozen specialist female academies were established at the time of the passage of the bill founding the University of Virginia. In 1820, John Hartwell Cocke, a collaborator in the founding of the university, proposed a female academy. The same year a group of fathers set up the Charlottesville Female Academy and two other female academies began operating on Vinegar Hill in Charlottesville in the 1820s.[46] It was only in the next two decades that momentum for reform and improvement of education for women occurred, resulting from the advocacy of pioneers such as Catharine E. Beecher, Hannah Croker, Sarah and Angelina Grimké, the Reverend Thomas Hopkins Gallaudet, Sarah Josepha Hale, and Theodore Weld. Mary and Cornelia Jefferson Randolph, Jefferson's granddaughters, ran their own female academies in the 1830s and 1840s. Other initiatives included those of Emma Willard, who founded Troy Academy in New York in 1814, and Mary Lyon, who established Mount Holyoke Seminary in 1837.

In the 1830s, a few pioneer colleges experimented with coeducation, such as Oberlin in Ohio and Berea in Kentucky. In Europe, other than a few isolated earlier examples, it was not until the second half of the nineteenth century that women gained admission to universities, beginning with schools in France and Switzerland in the 1860s. Germany and Prussia held out until 1908.[47] Jefferson looked to colleges primarily to train elite politicians, which was a male preserve. He thought women should be strangers to political rancor.[48] When asked to provide a plan of female education in 1818, Jefferson admitted that this was never "a subject of systematic contemplation" for him, and that "it has occupied my attention so far only as the education of my own daughters occasionally required, considering that they would be placed in a country situation, where little aid could be obtained from abroad, I thought it essential to give them a solid education which might enable them, when they become mothers, to educate their own daughters and even direct the course for their sons."[49]

After coming before the House of Delegates in 1779 and 1780, Jefferson's education bill was finally passed by the house in 1785. However, it failed in the state senate. Writing from Paris, Jefferson urged George Wythe to revive the bill: "Preach, my dear Sir, a crusade against ignorance: establish and improve the law for educating the common people."[50] The following year, it was again rejected, this time by the house. In 1796, the state legislature approved a truncated version of the bill that applied only to elementary education. Jefferson blamed the legislature for the failure of his plan of public education. He specifically criticized a clause in the amended bill that made it optional for counties to implement the scheme and dependent on the decision of unelected magistrates, who resented a plan to educate the poor at the expense of the rich. Of ninety-two counties in Virginia, only Norfolk attempted to implement the bill and then only for three years before giving up. Jefferson's efforts were ultimately undermined by the unwillingness of taxpayers to fund schools, a reluctance that similarly thwarted constitutional mandates for public education in Pennsylvania, North Carolina, Georgia, Vermont, and Massachusetts. Beyond the cost, a major obstacle to gaining support for the education bill was the absence of mandated teaching of religion, which gave rise to opposition among all religious denominations and which doomed all of Jefferson's later proposals for a public school system. Modern-day critics argue that Jefferson has received undue acclamation for what amounted to nothing more than a failed proposal, but his genuine passion for public education should be acknowledged, along with his principled but unpopular exclusion of government-sanctioned religion in schools.[51]

In addition to his "Bill for the More General Diffusion of Knowledge" in 1779, Jefferson drafted "A Bill for Amending the Constitution of the College of William and Mary, and Substituting More Certain Revenues for Its Support," which contained elements of his later vision for the University of Virginia. Despite being "amply endowed by the public," Jefferson thought that his alma mater had "not answered their expectations."[52] He was particularly unhappy with the religious establishment of the college and the influence of the Episcopal church, which appointed the Board of Visitors. Jefferson was critical of the quality of the faculty, the hierarchical system of administration, and what he regarded as an outdated curriculum. He also disliked the fact that the college was combined with the Brafferton School, which taught adolescents.

In order to remedy what he perceived as the deficiencies of the college and to make it "more useful," Jefferson's bill represented his first efforts to legislate his vision of a university and is noteworthy for anticipating many of the future features of the University of Virginia. His reform bill dealt with all aspects of the college, including governance, the curriculum, salaries, the library, and finances. The bill aimed to revise the curriculum so as to offer "all the useful sciences," with the expectation that students would spend "three years in the study of such sciences as they shall chuse." It provided for chairs in law, medicine, anatomy, and modern languages, all of which were still novel disciplines when most colleges were emphasizing theology and the classics. Also in anticipation of his vision for the University of Virginia, he critically sought to secularize the college by abolishing theology and giving the legislature more control over the Board of Visitors. Departing from the mission to convert Native Americans to Christianity, the bill required the college to conduct research into the laws, customs, religions, traditions, and particularly languages of "the several tribes of Indians." Additionally, Jefferson wanted the college to buy a "mechanical representation, or model of the solar system, conceived and executed by that greatest of astronomers," David Rittenhouse in Philadelphia.[53] In the Notes, Jefferson mentioned his desire to begin a public library and an art gallery.[54]

Jefferson later attributed the failure of his college reform bill in the state legislature to "religious jealousies," when other denominations "took alarm lest this might give an ascendancy to the Anglican sect" who had hitherto dominated the College of William and Mary.[55] As governor of Virginia and a member of the college's Board of Visitors, Jefferson succeeded in implementing some of his desired changes to the college, even without a reform bill, such as the closure of the junior school. Although he wanted to expand faculty from six to eight, he was only able to reassign existing positions. In order to introduce professorships in law and government, anatomy and medicine, chemistry, and modern languages, he succeeded in removing the professorships in divinity, Greek, Latin, and Oriental languages. These reforms indicated his pedagogical priorities at the university level by giving emphasis to subjects that were "useful," vocational, and secular. His old mentor George Wythe became the first professor of law and politics to be appointed in the United States.

As part of his series of bills to improve education in the state in 1779, Jefferson also proposed "A Bill for Establishing a Public Library." Although he would later encourage the idea of circulating libraries in every county for the general public, this library was to be a specialist book and map collection aimed at "indulging the researches of the learned and curious without fee . . . or reward," implying that it would be aimed at scholars, legislators, and members of the elite.[56] The scheme is a reminder of Jefferson's broader vision of educational institutions, which encompassed libraries and galleries. In retirement in 1823, he was involved in the creation of a public library in Charlottesville, located on the eastern side of Court Square.[57] While he made the case for the public provision of education in exclusively political terms, his later statements indicate that he believed education was also important economically to the state, for it could make individuals more self-sufficient through vocational training. Jefferson likewise regarded education as a path to greater happiness and to progress though scientific discoveries.

JEFFERSON'S ADVOCACY OF public education was not limited to Virginia. In his draft of a Northwest Ordinance (1784), he included a provision for each town to devote a centrally located space for a school, a policy adopted in the Northwest Ordinance of 1787. Jefferson's interest in education persisted while he was a diplomat in France. In 1787–88, he was initially sympathetic to a scheme of the Chevalier Quesnay de Beaurepaire, a former captain in the Continental Army under Lafayette, to create an Academy of Sciences and Fine Arts of the United States of America, to be headquartered in Richmond. In a highly ambitious plan, Quesnay envisaged a federal academy with other branches in Baltimore, Philadelphia, and New York, spanning the Atlantic with locations in London and Paris. Its supporters included the radical pamphleteer Thomas Paine, the playwright Pierre Beaumarchais, the scientist Pierre Lavoisier, and the philosopher La Rochefoucauld. Quesnay's major aim was to advance science through academic journals and scientific knowledge. His proposal for separate schools (departments) within each academy would later be features of the University of Virginia. He succeeded in raising 60,000 francs and building an academy in Richmond, but the French Revolution led to the project's abandonment. Jefferson thought that Quesnay's scheme had been "too expensive for the poverty of the country (the United States)."[58]

After his return to the United States to serve as secretary of state in the first cabinet, Jefferson nominally supported George Washington's idea for a national university but never with as much enthusiasm as James Madison or later John Quincy Adams. Holding a stricter constructionist view than even Madison, Jefferson claimed that the creation of a national university would require an amendment to the Constitution. In addition, his minimal support may have been due to what one scholar suggests was his "hidden agenda" of locating the national university in Virginia.[59]

When the impact of the French Revolution disrupted Switzerland, Jefferson was interested in the idea of transplanting the entire faculty of the University of Geneva to Virginia. He regarded it as one of the outstanding universities in Europe, rivaling the University of Edinburgh, describing them collectively as the two "eyes of Europe."[60] He thought that the Geneva school could be bought for a reasonable price. In November 1794, he asked a delegate in the Virginia legislature to see if the idea would gain any traction with other members. Only after receiving a discouraging reply did he suggest to George Washington that this might be an opportunity to establish a national university. Washington objected, not least because the faculty spoke French.[61]

The date of Jefferson's initiative to bring the University of Geneva to Virginia is important since it represented his first attempt to bypass the College of William and Mary and create a separate University of Virginia. He even acknowledged that he would have considered overseeing the project, "procuring a residence in its neighborhood."[62] It is also significant since it came less than a year after he had resigned from the cabinet, following his differences with Alexander Hamilton and others who wanted a more powerful central government. They became members of what is known as the Federalist Party. Jefferson believed that the party of government—the Federalists—was subverting the spirit of 1776. This gave added urgency to his vision of educating a future generation of Republican Party leaders to return the nation and the state to the true republican ideology of the American Revolution.

At the height of his fears about what he regarded as the tyrannical direction of the country in the hands of his opponents toward the end of the eighteenth century, Vice President Jefferson asked Pierre Samuel du Pont de Nemours to write a proposal for a public education system. Published in 1800 under the title *Sur l'education nationale dans les États-Units* (National Education in the United States of America), it appeared in the year of one of the most bitter presidential campaigns in the nation's history. A protégé of Quesnay, Du Pont had previously designed a system of national education for Poland and served as an educational commissioner in France. As with Jefferson's "Bill for the More General Diffusion of Knowledge," the book divided education into the three levels: primary schools, secondary schools, and a university. Du Pont proposed a national university with a federated structure of specialist branches in eighteen states, which together would constitute the University of the United States. The different branches would be combined with museums, botanical gardens, public libraries, philosophical societies, and a governing council. The plan provided for just ten students annually to attend the university from Virginia.[63]

As president in 1802, Jefferson drafted and signed into law a bill to create the U.S. Military Academy at West Point, which historians Robert McDonald and Christine McDonald have argued was intended to become part of a national university based in Washington.[64] In his sixth annual message to Congress in 1806, Jefferson recommended a constitutional amendment to enable budget surpluses to be distributed among the states for education and infrastructure. He urged the members to take up the issue of a national university for which he also recommended an amendment. While conceding that private enterprise "manages so much better all the concerns to which it is equal," he was insistent that "only a public institution can supply those sciences which though rarely called for are yet necessary to complete the circle, all parts of which contribute to the improvement of the country, and some of them to its perseverance."⁶⁵ As president of the United States, Jefferson even served on the Board of Education for the District of Columbia. He encouraged Joel Barlow to write a plan for a national university that was published as a *Prospectus of a National Institution to Be Established in the United States* (1806). It advocated a national academy and a university in Washington similar to Napoleon's National Institute. Jefferson consulted with his treasury secretary, Albert Gallatin, about the feasibility of funding the national university. Interestingly, Jefferson specified to Barlow that only a public, rather than a private, institution would be of real benefit.⁶⁶ In 1806, he told one of his sons-in-law that a national establishment for education was "one of the ardent goals of [my] Presidency."⁶⁷

In January 1800, Jefferson first broached the subject of creating the University of Virginia as a replacement for the College of William and Mary in a letter to Joseph Priestley, the scientist, theologian, and political refugee from Britain. Jefferson wrote to Priestley that the College of William and Mary was "just well enough endowed to draw out the miserable existence to which a miserable constitution has doomed it." He was critical of its location in an unhealthy and increasingly depopulated area. He described a general desire "among the ablest and highest characters of our state" to establish a public university in a more healthy and central location "on a plan so broad & liberal & *modern*, as to be worth patronising with the public support." Jefferson foresaw that the faculty would need to be small and that it would be difficult to appoint professors with sufficient range to cover the desired subjects. He was determined that they should be professionals and that the university should "draw from Europe the first characters in science" by offering considerable incentives.⁶⁸

There is great significance to the date of Jefferson's first letter proposing the University of Virginia. It was the same year as the infamous presidential election of 1800 between the Republican Jefferson and the Federalist John Adams. The rhetoric of the election was particularly vitriolic since both sides regarded themselves as fighting to preserve the legacy and soul of the American Revolution. Jefferson believed that the Federalists would revive monarchy and aristocracy while making the United States a satellite of Britain. Using a language normally reserved for religious conformity, he regarded his political opponents as apostates whose government would ultimately end in tyranny. The Federalists accused Jefferson of atheism and of being an apostle of the Jacobins of the French Revolution. Jefferson and his allies associated the Federalists with their stronghold in New England and regarded Virginia as the home of Republicanism. It was Jefferson's fear of the Federalists that gave added urgency to his plan for a university. His worry about the dominance of Federalists became clear when he used the founding of the military academy at West Point as an opportunity to create a Republican officer corps in an army dominated by Federalists. The emphasis on science and engineering was weak in the early years of the school's existence, suggesting Jefferson's priority of making West Point part of a broader plan to republicanize institutions of government, hitherto dominated by Federalists. He wanted to break the upper-class monopoly of education and by the same token the officer corps of the army.[69]

The division between the parties was not confined to policy issues but also reflected their different views of education. Federalist intellectuals were more skeptical about the ability of human reason to make improvements and regarded their Republican counterparts as seeking knowledge that lacked virtue or social value. The split was even mirrored in scholarly institutions with the American Philosophical Society becoming increasingly Republican and Boston's American Academy of Arts and Sciences more Federalist. The former emphasized natural history (especially botany, geology, and paleontology) and the latter natural philosophy (particularly astronomy and mathematics). Federalists distrusted "French" science that threatened to displace revealed religion, while Jefferson's views on geology caused him to dismiss the story of Noah and the biblical Flood. Federalist critic Clement Clark Moore accused Jefferson, with some justice, of according Jewish history, Grecian stories, and classical works equal authority with the Bible. Federalist Edmund Quincy scathingly wrote that the *Transactions* of the American Philosophical Society were bulkier than the journal of the American Academy in order to give the impression of substance but that in reality the former were little better than three-penny pamphlets given to children. Federalists were suspicious of plans for universal education and the idea of a national university, associating them with the influence of Napoleonic France. They distrusted the emphasis on a professional education and science rather than the traditional classics.[70]

Writing again to Joseph Priestley in 1801, Jefferson accused the Federalists of being barbarians who wanted to return to the age of Vandalism, "when ignorance put every thing in the hands of power and priestcraft." According to Jefferson, the Federalists "pretended to praise & encourage education, but it was to be in vain the education of our ancestors, we were to look backwards not forwards for improvement."[71] He claimed that Adams himself had declared the present age would never surpass their ancestors in real science. To Jefferson's embarrassment, this letter was published during his retirement, causing John Adams to write to him denying ever having made such a statement.[72] Jefferson believed that the parties vied for competing visions of the future of education, with his opponents looking nostalgically to the past, to aristocracy, tradition, and the Old World, as opposed to a future age of improvement in which the country could become a beacon of enlightenment. In the generational view that was so central to his thinking about education, he saw himself as responsible for liberating the living generation from the past, with its unquestioned and unverified beliefs, while his contemporaries would pass on discoveries to the next generation.

As the political battles between the parties escalated, most colleges supported the Federalist Party. With the notable exception of the College of William and Mary, the majority of colleges were hostile to Jefferson, who they associated with the radical ideas of William Godwin and Thomas Paine and the excesses of the French Revolution. During the 1795 commencement at Dickinson College, orators attacked the French Revolution and its Republican supporters with topics like "The Necessity of Moral Virtue" and "The Necessity of Religion for the Support of Civil Government." According to one of his students at Union College, John Blair Smith lectured in support of the Federalists in his philosophy classes during the presidential election of 1796.[73] When celebrating George Washington's birthday in 1798, the Hasty Pudding Club at Harvard drank two toasts, followed in each case by three cheers, in honor of George Washington and President John Adams. Afterward they drank a third toast, without cheers, to Jefferson saying, "May he exercise his elegant literary talents for the benefit of the world, in some retreat, secure from the troubles and dangers of political life," adding, "May the government of *our own choice*, never be assailed by *Jacobinism*."[74] Although Joseph Pulitzer donated a bronze statue of Jefferson to stand outside the Graduate School of Journalism at Columbia University in 1914, the trustees of the university were all Federalists in the 1790s. It was the alma mater of some of the most prominent Federalist leaders, such as Alexander Hamilton and John Jay.[75]

In 1800, the majority of college presidents, trustees, and faculty, in both the North and the South, supported the election of John Adams against Jefferson, whom they associated with French Jacobins. These leaders included David Caldwell at the University of North Carolina, Joseph McKeen at Bowdoin College, and Theodore Sedgwick and Ebenezer Fitch at Williams College. Reverend Timothy Dwight, president of Yale, helped lead the Fed-

eralist attack on Jefferson's supposed atheism and asked students the following year to take an oath never to vote for Jefferson.[76] In the event of his election, Dwight warned that Bibles would be burned; innocent children would
be terrified into singing "Ça Ira," the French revolutionary anthem; and their
wives and daughters would be forced into legal prostitution.[77] Known as
the "Pope of Connecticut," Dwight was the most influential leader in the
Presbyterian movement. Reverend William Linn, the former president of
Queen's College (later Rutgers University), wrote a pamphlet warning that
"the election of any man avowing the principles of Mr. Jefferson would . . .
destroy religion, introduce immorality and loosen all the bonds of society."[78]
After a student riot in 1802, even the president of the College of William
and Mary banned the writings of philosophers like Claude Adrien Helvé-
tius and the English radical William Godwin.[79] Writing in 1800 to Jeremiah Moore, an ally in the bill to separate religion and the state in Virginia,
Jefferson expressed alarm at "the general political dispositions of those to
whom is confided the education of the rising generation."[80]

After becoming president of the United States in what he dubbed the
"Revolution of 1800," Jefferson became more optimistic, writing to Joseph
Priestley of the dawn of a new era in which "the storm is now subsiding
& the horizon becoming serene." With echoes of the book of Ecclesiastes,
he observed, "We can no longer say that there is nothing new under the
sun. for this whole chapter in the history of man is new. the great extent
of our republic is new." In contrast to the backward direction of what he
called "times of vandalism" under the previous administration, Jefferson anticipated an era of progress. The "momentous crisis which lately arose" had
demonstrated a "strength of character in our nation which augurs well for
the duration of the republic" and had made him more confident of its future
stability.[81] In a continued mood of optimism in 1803, President Jefferson
wrote to the Swiss scientist George Pictet that he "still had constantly in
view to propose" to the state assembly the establishment of a university "on
as large a scale as our present circumstances would require or bear." Despite
his responsibilities as president, Jefferson still sought advice from Pictet
about the teaching of science at the proposed University of Virginia.[82]

In 1805, the movement to create a university in Virginia gained momentum. St. George Tucker, a professor at the College of William and Mary,
drew up a plan for a state college to be built in Virginia's Piedmont that
he envisaged would replace the College of William and Mary. In January,
rejoicing at the news that "the legislature of Virginia are likely at length to

institute an University on a liberal plan," Jefferson wrote to Littleton Waller Tazewell, a member of the Virginia House of Delegates, describing his own vision for a future university. Complaining of constant interruptions that prevented him from writing more than three lines at a time, Jefferson outlined the purpose of the university, its location, funding, faculty, buildings, and administration. Since he was "convinced that the people are the only safe depositories of their own liberty, & that they are not safe unless enlightened to a certain degree," he believed there should be two levels of education that trained both a governing elite and the people in general. At the most advanced level, an institution should provide those few individuals "to whom nature has given minds of the first order" an education to "the highest degree to which the human mind has carried it." For the majority of the population, both free men and women, local schools should be available "as will enable him to read, to judge & to vote understandingly on what is passing." Aware that only the university was at present in contemplation, Jefferson enjoined his correspondent to "receive with contentment what the legislature is now ready to give" until the day when mass education would "be incorporated into the system at some more favorable moment."[83] The comment both indicated his continued support for a public school system and his recognition of the reality in which politicians have to accept tradeoffs.

Jefferson wanted the Virginia legislature to create a broad charter without prescribing too many details, especially decisions regarding the curriculum and selection of faculty, which he believed should be delegated to a nonsalaried board of no more than five people. This number derived from Jefferson's impression that no more than five men in any state were sufficiently knowledgeable about the current progress of the sciences. Jefferson recognized that knowledge evolved and "what is now deemed useful will in some of its parts become useless in another century." He thought half the professorships at his alma mater were outdated and that everyone knew "that Oxford, Cambridge, the Sorbonne, etc. are now a century or two behind the science of the age." He recommended high salaries for professors to attract a faculty composed of "the first names of Europe . . . in order to give it a celebrity in the outset, which will draw to it the youth of all the states, and make Virginia their cherished & beloved Alma mater."[84] If the university went ahead in a way that met with his approval, he offered to bequeath his library, the worth of which he estimated at a minimum of $15,000. To Tazewell, he proposed a layout of the university, with small clusters of buildings connected by covered walks, rather than one large central building, foreshadowing many of the architectural features of his future Academical Village.

President Jefferson's vision in 1805 was consistent with what he had written five years earlier to Priestley. And it dovetailed with what essentially became the ultimate blueprint for the University of Virginia. Indeed, it could be traced back to his plans to reform the College of William and Mary in 1779 and was thus derived from what he saw as the essential imperatives of the American Revolution forty years before the bill establishing the University of Virginia in 1819. His goals were reinvigorated by party conflict and the need to educate a rising generation in what he regarded as the pure republican philosophy of the Revolution exclusively embodied by his own party. Given these earlier articulations, his vision for the University of Virginia did not originate in the sectional crisis between the North and the South over slavery as an attempt to create "a southern pro-slavery Ivy League school."[85] The cotton boom was still in its infancy in 1805, and other issues in the 1790s played a larger role than slavery in dividing North and South. In the election of 1800, Jefferson had won by a narrow margin and then only because of a split within the Federalist Party, with Alexander Hamilton supporting Charles Cotesworth Pinckney against John Adams. Jefferson believed he had saved his country from what he called "the reign of witches" by Anglomen (Anglophiles) and Monocrats (monarchists and pseudo-aristocrats).[86]

Reacting to the Alien and Sedition Acts (1798), Jefferson regarded the Federalists as hostile to basic liberties. By their antagonism to France, he thought that Federalists were making the United States a satellite of Britain. He feared that they were creating a large standing army and that they were enlarging federal government power in an unconstitutional manner with such Hamiltonian economic reforms as the establishment of a national bank. Even after Jefferson's party seized the executive and legislative branches of government in the election of 1800, the federal judiciary continued to be dominated by Federalists, not least thanks to the appointment of the so-called midnight judges by the outgoing President John Adams. Under the leadership of Chief Justice John Marshall, the federal justices strengthened central government by their broad interpretation of the Constitution.

Consequently, far from thinking the country safe under his presidency, Jefferson regarded "our present state of liberty as a short-lived possession unless the mass of people could be informed to a certain degree."[87] Unlike Adams, who regarded the perils of liberty as the inevitable result of human nature and subversion by an aristocracy of wealth, Jefferson was optimistic that the threat of tyranny could be contained by education. He therefore agitated all the more for a republican university in his own state of Virginia that could save the nation from what he saw as the heresies of the Federalists and their undermining of the true ideals of the American Revolution.

3

My Single Anxiety in the World

Located twenty miles west of Charlottesville, along what had been the main pass for wagons and carriages crossing the Blue Ridge Mountains, a dramatic opening at the top of Rockfish Gap enables travelers to contemplate sweeping vistas of the Shenandoah Valley and vast expanses of the state of Virginia. At an elevation of over 1,900 feet, the rugged terrain was the result of violent tectonic clashes, the last occurring over 300 million years ago, with North Africa in the Paleozoic Alleghenian orogeny, when the mountains were situated nearer to Richmond with altitudes that were probably comparable to the Rockies. The first paths were created by elk and buffalo, which were later hunted by Monocan Indians, who settled in villages along the floodplains of the James River and its tributaries flowing from the Blue Ridge into the Piedmont. From the 1730s, British settlers crossed over to cultivate small farms in the Shenandoah Valley. Eager to sell produce in the eastern part of the state in the 1750s, they began to clear a road to avoid the alternative route through the valley to Philadelphia or Baltimore. Subject to high winds and sometimes engulfed in fog, Rockfish Gap was named after a river below. Its western edge was the site of a tavern called Rockfish Inn, later renamed Mountain Top Inn. Built in the 1770s, the inn offered the only accommodations for many miles along the often appalling road that served travelers between the Piedmont and western Virginia. Like a forced spiritual experience, the view of far-off horizons invites meditation and expansive thoughts.[1]

At the beginning of August 1818, a group of twenty-one commissioners selected by the governor met at the Mountain Top Inn to create the blueprint for the future University of Virginia, in what became known as the Rockfish Gap Commission. They were instructed to decide on the location of the university and recommend a plan for its buildings, curriculum, faculty, and any general provisions to be enacted by the legislature "for the better organizing and governing of the University." Kept by Samuel Leake and his son Walter, the Mountain Top Inn was a "modest country inn, unpretending in appearance, but offering an abundant and well-served table, far from the turmoil of the cities and excitement of politics." In a whitewashed room, with a low ceiling, simple dining-room table, and crude homemade "split-bottom" chairs, sat the president of the United States, James Monroe, and his two immediate predecessors, James Madison and Thomas Jefferson. Over half of the commissioners were judges and lawyers. Besides Jefferson, four of the commissioners had served or would serve in the U.S. Congress, along with a former and future governor of Virginia. Others had served in the state legislature. According to a later account, "it was remarked by the lookers-on that Mr. Jefferson was the principal object of regard, both to the members and spectators; that he seemed to be the chief mover of the body—the soul that animated it; and some who were present, struck by these manifestations of deference, conceived a more exalted idea of him, on this simple and unpretending occasion than they had ever previously entertained."[2] In fact, Jefferson essentially choreographed the entire gathering. In advance of the meeting at Rockfish Gap, while still at Monticello, he wrote the substance of the report of the commissioners. His strategy revealed the political skills that had enabled him to mastermind the creation of what became the most successful political party in American history.

Before the meeting at Rockfish Gap, Jefferson had sent James Madison a draft copy of what essentially became the final report.[3] Worried that he might be a political liability, Jefferson was keen to downplay his own role, partly out of concern about the likely opposition to the proposed location of the new university at Charlottesville. He asked Madison to write the report for the commissioners. Jefferson's trepidation was well founded. The site of Rockfish Gap straddled the geographical, political, and cultural divide between the eastern Piedmont and the Shenandoah Valley. The latter contained a predominantly Presbyterian Scots-Irish population and the largest concentration of Federalists in Virginia who supported either the building of the state university in Staunton or the candidacy of Washington College (later known as Washington and Lee University) in Lexington.[4] On the eve of his departure for Rockfish Gap, Jefferson had requested a "secret" meeting at Monticello of a subcommittee "to advise what will be proposed." Despite having sent a full draft of the report to Madison, Jefferson claimed to one of the commissioners that he had merely sketched his thoughts before the meeting. In reality, he had written at least two successive fifteen-page drafts in which he had refined his arguments in favor of Charlottesville.[5]

On Saturday, August 1, the Board of Commissioners convened and unanimously elected Jefferson as their president. The first order of business was to "enquire & report on a proper site" for the university, whereupon there were proposals for Lexington, Staunton, and Charlottesville. "After some time spent in debate," Archibald Rutherford, a prominent politician and gunsmith from the Shenandoah Valley, made a resolution to postpone consideration of the location for the present, in order to "ascertain the sense of the board on the question." William A. Dade, a lawyer, proposed that the board might visit the various sites beginning with Lexington. His resolution was unanimously defeated. With their selection based on the unrepresentative distribution of senate districts, the majority of commissioners were from the eastern counties of the Piedmont. Comprising Jefferson's allies, they did not favor locating the university in Lexington. The absence of four commissioners from the eastern districts, two of whom excused themselves on the grounds of illness, essentially removed the College of William and Mary from consideration as the future University of Virginia.[6] The board then voted on a select committee of six members to consider all matters except the site of the university. This resulted in the appointment of Jefferson, along with Madison and Spencer Roane, all of whom had attended the secret meeting to discuss strategy at Monticello; Archibald Stuart, who had suggested that Jefferson write the report in advance; James Breckenridge, a former Federalist U.S. congressman who had represented western Virginia and who would later serve on the university's Board of Visitors; and William A. Dade, who was later invited to be professor of law at the University of Virginia.[7]

The full Board of Commissioners reconvened the following Monday morning. Throughout much of the preceding discussion, Jefferson had been silent and waited till the last to speak. In his earlier drafts of the report, he argued that Charlottesville was the healthiest place in the state, but he ultimately focused on demonstrating that it was the most central location relative to the white population of Virginia. He presented a cardboard cutout map and a chart to demonstrate the geographic and demographic centrality of Charlottesville, telling his fellow commissioners: "Run your lines in what direction you please, they will pass close to Charlottesville."[8] In order to prove that it was the center of the white population of the state, he massaged the evidence by including the free Black population in his count. After this demonstration, Jefferson's ally Spencer Roane then moved that the board decide which of the three places proposed was the most convenient and proper site for the university. The sixteen commissioners from the eastern part of the state voted for Charlottesville, while the five western members split their votes with two for Staunton and three for Lexington. The board then asked the subcommittee to present its report. After making a few minor amendments, the board unanimously adopted the report and asked the secretary to make a fair copy for each house of the legislature. The group met again the following day, signed the copies of the report, and unanimously resolved "that the thanks of this board be given to Thomas Jefferson Esq for the great ability, impartiality & dignity, with which he has presided over its' deliberations."[9]

A pioneer in the history of education and one of the early exponents of the tradition in America of the German research seminar, Herbert Baxter Adams thought that Jefferson's statement of the role and purpose of a university in the Rockfish Gap Report "has never been better formulated by any professional educator."[10] The report did not simply repeat the civic benefits of higher education in forming "statesmen, legislators & judges, on whom public prosperity, & individual happiness are so much to depend," to which Jefferson had given such emphasis in his education bill in 1779. The Rockfish Gap Report also discussed the economic benefit of university graduates in promoting and improving agriculture, manufacturing, and commerce in the state, as well as improving medicine and the "comforts of human life." Furthermore, it addressed the innate value of education in forming those "habits of reflection, and correct action" that make graduates "examples of virtue to others," as well as giving them "happiness within themselves." In addition to outlining the specific features of the university, such as the curriculum and structure, the report was a marketing document that promoted not only the objectives of a university but also its advantages both for the state and the individual. It asserted that "education generates habits of application, of order and love of virtue." It dismissed the idea that individual character was fixed by the laws of nature, saying that it was delusive to think that humanity cannot be improved beyond the condition of their forefathers. On the contrary, education "engrafts a new man on the native stock, & improves what in his nature was vicious & perverse, into qualities of virtue & social worth."[11]

The Rockfish Gap Report contended that, by adding new discoveries and accumulating knowledge, education would continue to enrich succeeding generations indefinitely. In a passage that read like the later work of the eminent British Whig historian Thomas Babington Macaulay, the report invited readers to look back only half a century and reflect on the intervening progress, improvement, and "wonderful advances in the sciences and arts." Far from being "vain dreams of sanguine hope, we have before our eyes

real & living examples" of the benefits of education. The report argued that
education alone was responsible for the better conditions of Virginians in
relation to Native Americans. It added that education offered a more encouraging idea of the possibilities of the future "than the desponding view
that the condition of man cannot be ameliorated, that what has been, must
ever be, and that to secure ourselves where we are, we must tread with aw-
full reverence in the footsteps of our fathers."[12]

In order to cover the expenses to attend the meeting at Rockfish Gap,
Jefferson borrowed one hundred dollars from the Charlottesville merchant
James Leitch. Jefferson had received a letter the previous week from the
Bank of Virginia in Richmond demanding that he begin repaying a loan
and arranging a settlement schedule. It was an indication of his declining
financial situation, which was soon to become dire. Upon leaving the meeting on August 4, Jefferson joined James Breckenridge, a Federalist who had
supported the site of Lexington against Charlottesville, on a ride to Warm
Springs. It was a smart maneuver to win over a political adversary and to
attend to his own health problems. Seventy-five years old, Jefferson had suffered "troublesome attacks of rheumatism for some winters past" and had
decided to take advantage of the opportunity to visit the hot springs, which
had become a popular resort, known for their healing powers. Suffering
from an inflamed knee, he found it difficult to walk and tried "the delicious
bath" for a cure, resolving to go twice a day. He soon increased his visits to
three times a day for a quarter of an hour each. Although feeling much re-
covered after a week, Jefferson was so determined to prevent a return of his
symptoms that he accepted advice to remain another three weeks for a full
treatment. He toured other local springs but found the company dull and
complained of unprecedented boredom. Unfortunately, during these baths
at Warm Springs, he contracted a fever and what he described as large boils
and swellings on his buttocks that medical experts now think was probably
a staph infection (staphylococcus aureus). Suffering great pain during the
hundred-mile return journey over rocks and mountains, he arrived home
utterly exhausted and reduced to the extremity of lying down throughout
the day for several months, making it difficult for him to write. Looking
back on his treatment at this time of mercury and sulfur, he wrote that it
should have occurred to him that the "medicine which makes the sick well,
may make the well sick."[13]

JEFFERSON'S SUCCESS AT Rockfish Gap did not guarantee the creation of
the University of Virginia. The report would still need to be endorsed by

the state legislature and—more critically—be publicly funded. Neverthe-less, it was auspicious that, in the four preceding years, he had managed to transform the moribund Albemarle Academy, whose board he joined in 1814, into Central College (1816) and subsequently into the University of Virginia (1819). Four years before the Rockfish Gap Commission, Jefferson had first started to seriously engage in his project of creating a university by improbably joining the board of a local academy that had neither students nor buildings. Known as the Albemarle Academy, it existed only on paper, but he turned this unpromising shell into what was soon regarded as the premiere university in the South. The story of how he achieved his objec-tives offers one of the most illuminating examples of his political skills and ability to implement a vision.

In January 1814, Jefferson informed Thomas Cooper, a protégé of Joseph Priestley and like Priestley a political exile from England, that he "long had under contemplation, and been collecting materials for the plan of an uni-versity in Virginia which should comprehend all the sciences useful to us, & none others." Jefferson added that the university he had in mind "would probably absorb the functions" of the College of William and Mary "and transfer them to a healthier and more Central position . . . perhaps to the neighborhood of this place." He complained of the "long & lingering de-cline" of his alma mater, made worse by the death of its capable president Bishop James Madison, the cousin of President James Madison. Jefferson argued that these factors, combined with its unhealthy location and climate, "force on us the wish for a new institution more convenient to our country generally and better adapted to the present state of science." He had heard of a possible effort in the current legislature to establish such an institution. Admitting that he had little confidence it would happen, he told Cooper that if the legislature did go ahead, the new university would be worthy of his employment.[14]

According to a popular oral tradition, Jefferson was supposedly on busi-ness in Charlottesville's Court Square on March 25, 1814, and happened to stumble on the meeting of the board of the Albemarle Academy at the Stone Tavern along East Market Street. Since it had been established by a law of the Virginia General Assembly in January 1803, the Albemarle Academy had only existed on paper. The trustees included Jefferson's nephews Peter and Dabney Carr, his son-in-law Thomas Mann Randolph, and his friend Wilson Cary Nicholas. In the twenty-year period after the American Rev-olution, more academies were founded in Virginia than in any other state, while private academies were the dominant form of schooling throughout

America until the Civil War. Outnumbering university students by ten to one, the academies might cover the modern equivalent of an elementary school curriculum up to the first year of junior college.[15] Jefferson dismissed these "petty *academies*, as they call themselves, which are starting up in every neighborhood," for their limited classical curriculums and production of pupils "with just taste enough of learning to be alienated from industrious pursuits, and not enough to do service in the ranks of science."[16] At the meeting on March 25, 1814, five of the surviving trustees of the Albemarle Academy had convened to revive plans for establishing the academy and to elect new members, including Jefferson.

A much later, rather embellished account described seeing "the tall form of a horseman rapidly coming down the public road that led from the eminence called Carter's Mountain." Superbly mounted on a thoroughbred horse, Jefferson rode with the consummate skill of one "who had been familiar with horseback exercise from childhood up." As he neared the tavern, "the stately proportions of his frame became more and more distinct," together with the brilliance of his clear blue eyes, which "could be discerned under his broad-brimmed hat." Dressed from head to foot in a dark gray "homely-cut" broadcloth, with an immense white cravat swathed around his neck, his noble open countenance and poised, firm expression became visible. As he entered the village of Charlottesville, nothing escaped his attention as he "cast a searching glance" at a leaking gutter or a broken fence while courteously returning the greetings of the young and old. As they watched him approach, an "expression of welcome relief rose on every countenance" of the trustees of the Albemarle Academy; one of them said, "Let us consult Mr. Jefferson." After dismounting with the alacrity of a young man and carefully fastening his horse to the railing, Jefferson unscrewed the top of his cane and pulled out three legs to form a stool upon which "ingenious contrivance" he sat down. Having politely acknowledged the honor done him by his friends and neighbors, he "listened attentively to their arguments, now and then throwing in a judicious question as to elicit facts."[17]

Even if we accept the improbable story that his appearance at the Stone Tavern was "wholly accidental and unexpected," Jefferson's actions thereafter were clearly premeditated and revealed his wish to establish a state university in Charlottesville.[18] At the request of the Board of Trustees, on September 7, in what has long been regarded as one of the foundational documents of the University of Virginia, Jefferson wrote a long letter to his nephew Peter Carr, one of the founding trustees, outlining the future of the Albemarle Academy. Jefferson had previously advised his nephew on his own education and accommodated Carr at Monticello. Four years before the meeting of the board to revive the academy, Carr had set up a short-lived academy of his own at his plantation home at Carrsbrook. In April 1814, he had been selected to be president of the Albemarle Academy. Jefferson submitted his plan to Carr during the most intense stage of the War of 1812 with Britain, two weeks after the burning of the White House and a few days after the surrender of Alexandria to the British fleet, which had destroyed the batteries at Fort Belvoir on the Potomac. Jefferson's own male relatives were away on guard duty in Richmond, leaving only what he called "silver grays" in Albemarle County.[19]

Written "on the subject of the academy or college proposed to be established in our neighborhood," Jefferson's plan was too elaborate for an academy or grammar school. Instead, he set out a more general vision of education at various levels similar to his 1779 education bill. He repeated his wish that his native state would take up the subject of education and that it would establish an institution that covered "every branch of science deemed useful at this day," which should be "taught in its highest degree." He gave a summary of how he had attempted to acquaint himself with institutions elsewhere and to obtain the advice of those most knowledgeable. He reflected that none of the existing systems and institutions were exactly alike and argued that none of them could simply be transplanted, since whatever was adopted needed to be adjusted to local circumstances. Thinking it necessary to begin by defining "our institution" within the context of a general system of education, Jefferson proceeded to address three levels of education: elementary schools, general schools, and professional schools.[20]

Jefferson asserted that every citizen should receive an education but that it should be tailored to their "condition and pursuits in life." Influenced by the work of the French philosopher Destutt de Tracy, he divided the mass of citizens into two classes—the laboring and the learned—with the laboring classes needing only an elementary education. He hoped that the state would "someday resume ... in a more promising form" his education bill. At the more advanced level, Jefferson subdivided the "learned" class into those who were independently wealthy and those seeking a professional career. He thought both would require "instruction in the higher branches of science," which would qualify the wealthy for public office or a more useful life and would provide the others with a foundation in their future professions. He thought that the former only needed to attend the general schools, while the latter would need additional training at a professional school. Jefferson's creativity was apparent in his curriculum suggestions, with a professional school that would have a department of fine arts including architecture, gardening, painting, and musical theory. The departments would offer ag- riculture, military science, and a course in "technical philosophy" to attract carpenters, clockmakers, distillers, vintners, millwrights, mariners, and tan- ners, all of whom would receive a background in relevant disciplines such as geometry, hydraulics, astronomy, botany, chemistry, and natural history. Jefferson argued that this technical department should be "wholly at the public expense" and that the lectures should be offered at night "so as not to interrupt the labors of the day." It is interesting that he saw no difficulty in mixing technical training with professional law and medical schools. As his later plans evolved for the University of Virginia, he wanted to encourage the presence of artisans among the students to help them acquire practical skills that he himself possessed and valued.[21]

Jefferson concluded his letter to Carr by attempting to define the role of the Albemarle Academy, asking what portion of this educational system should "we mark out for the occupation of our institution." He answered that in regard to the first grade or elementary schools, "we shall have noth- ing to do." The main object should be the general schools for both the wealthy and career professionals. However, his plan was ambiguous as to whether the general schools were the equivalent of grammar schools, offer- ing secondary-level education, or whether they and the professional schools would be incorporated into a university. His prescribed syllabus was far too elaborate for a grammar school where he additionally envisaged a faculty of at least four "professors." He repeated in the letter that the plan could be enlarged and adjusted. In the words of historian Harold Hellenbrand, the proposal was "awkward because it attempted too much." Jefferson had essentially "grafted onto a grammar school a departmentalized university."[22]

In addition to the outline that he wrote to Carr for the Board of Trust- ees, Jefferson's aim to establish a college was apparent in his architectural drawing for the school, which envisaged an institution far more ambitious than an academy. Based on earlier suggestions he had made for East Ten- nessee College (1810), the plan for the academy resembled many of the fea- tures he incorporated into the University of Virginia. Following a decision of the board to choose a location about a quarter of a mile outside of Char- lottesville, his drawing showed a group of buildings and enclosed walkways surmounted by railings and arranged around three sides of a square. They included pavilions to accommodate faculty members with classrooms, liv- ing quarters, and gardens.[23]

By November, Jefferson had drafted a petition and an associated bill on behalf of the academy's trustees for the Virginia General Assembly. The petition requested funds arising from the sale of land (glebes) in the local parishes of St. Anne and Fredericksville that had been confiscated as part of the disestablishment of the Anglican church. The bill sought changes in governance procedures, including reducing the size of the board and changing its method of appointment. In addition, Jefferson requested an annual appropriation from the state Literary Fund and the renaming of the Albemarle Academy as Central College.[24] The name was significant because Jefferson's case for locating the leading state university in Charlottesville rested primarily on the alleged centrality of the location within the state of Virginia. Preferring to adopt what amounted to a campaign slogan, he rejected a proposition that the institution be named after himself and insisted on calling it Central College. Although the term "college" was used permissively, it was suggestive of a higher level of education than that offered by an academy.

In the fall of 1814, Carr forwarded the petition of the Board of Trustees and the accompanying bill, together with the written plan and architectural drawing from Jefferson, to David C. Watson, a delegate of neighboring Louisa County, for presentation to the General Assembly. A lawyer and contributor to literary anthologies, Watson was remembered by U.S. Attorney General William Wirt for relieving the tedium of military camp by quoting Shakespeare during the War of 1812. He later became a member of the first Board of Visitors of Central College before it became the University of Virginia.[25] Having taken the lead in the campaign to establish the main state university in Charlottesville, Peter Carr died in February 1815. In the meantime, the petition and bill arrived too late in the legislative season for presentation and were consequently not debated until the following year's session in December 1815.

A month before Carr's death, Jefferson had written to Joseph Carrington Cabell regretting that the petition had not been presented to the General Assembly. Afterward, Cabell became Jefferson's front man in the state senate, in much the same way that James Madison had led the opposition Republicans as a proxy for Jefferson during the presidency of John Adams. Jefferson thought that the trustees had missed an opportunity to obtain a small appropriation, in addition to the funds requested, which would have enabled them to build in Charlottesville what he said would be "the best seminary" in the United States. Calling Cabell "the main pillar of their support," Jefferson sent Cabell written copies of his plan, together with another letter he had written on the subject, the original petition, and his draft bill, "as we shall probably return to the charge at the next session." If he could raise sufficient funds, he thought he could recruit "three of the ablest characters in the world to fill the higher professors," a trio unequaled in any university in Europe. He hoped that the sciences might be taught "more profoundly" in Charlottesville than in any institution in America. Thirty-five years his junior, Cabell was first introduced to Jefferson by the physician and botanist Benjamin Smith Barton during Jefferson's second term as president. Cabell had presented Jefferson with a whalebone and ivory walking stick upon his retirement from the presidency, which was engraved, "T.J. Joseph Cabell to his friend Christmas 1809."[26]

Later considered second only to Jefferson in the founding of the University of Virginia, Cabell shared with Jefferson a passion for education and for improving his native state of Virginia. While in his mid-twenties in 1803, he undertook a grand tour of almost four years throughout Europe. Unusual for an American, not least because of the prohibitive cost, he visited France, Italy, England, Switzerland, Belgium, and Holland. In Naples, he met his fellow countryman Washington Irving, with whom he spent considerable time in Rome, and in England he met William Godwin, the radical thinker and writer and the husband of the feminist author Mary Wollstonecraft, by whom he fathered Mary Shelley. During his tour of Europe, Cabell studied botany at the University of Montpellier in France, one of the oldest universities in Europe, dating to 1289. He visited the universities of Leyden, Oxford, and Cambridge. After seeing the famous primary school in Yverdon in Switzerland, founded by Johann Heinrich Pestalozzi, Cabell became an advocate of Pestalozzi's fashionable educational philosophy, a nurturing approach to teaching that developed the innate capacity of children. Cabell returned from Europe convinced that education was central to the future of Virginia. Along with canal building and infrastructure projects, education would be his leading passion and sustained his alliance with Jefferson.

Married to the wealthy stepdaughter of St. George Tucker, his professor at the College of William and Mary, Cabell would be a member of the first Board of Visitors for Central College and would remain involved with the administration of the University of Virginia until his death in 1856. Throughout the rest of his life, he would also continue to lobby for public education, later developing an interest in the Lancastrian school system originated by Joseph Lancaster in England.[27] Telling Jefferson that his "greatest happiness" was "to give you pleasure upon any and upon all occasions," Cabell worked tirelessly, despite ill health, to obtain support for the college and later the university from the state legislature.[28] He described himself as one of the "steadfast patriots engaged in the holy cause of the University."[29] Cabell was otherwise very different from Jefferson. He identified with the elite planter class and did not approve of extending the franchise. Unlike Jefferson, he had little interest in revising the state constitution or allocating more seats in the legislature to western counties. Nevertheless, he proved an invaluable ally thanks to his connections and his membership in the Virginia Senate.

On February 14, 1816, Cabell proved his skills as a negotiator and legislator in managing to persuade the General Assembly to pass a bill approving the establishment of Central College. To Jefferson's chagrin, Cabell encountered opposition to some features that forced him to relinquish the request for annual grants from the Literary Fund. Established in 1810 at the recommendation of Governor John Tyler, the Literary Fund was set up for educational purposes with money accrued from state escheats, penalties, and forfeitures.[30] In order to appease local opposition, Cabell also had to abandon the provision in the bill shifting responsibility for the policing of students from local magistrates to a university provost, despite Jefferson's plea that this system prevailed in every great European seat of learning. In the passage of the bill, Cabell managed to deflect a rival bill for a lottery to buy the old Stone Tavern to be the main premises of Central College or the Albemarle Academy. The petitioners for a lottery represented overly enthusiastic customers of the tavern, who were fond of its keeper, Triplett Estes. Their scheme had the potential to undermine the grand plans for Central College and simultaneously perpetuate the Albemarle Academy. Referring to northern states as "foreign countries," this other petition for a lottery amusingly reflected the differences between the ambitious vision of Jefferson and the lesser expectations of the leading citizenry of Albemarle County.[31]

Jefferson was determined to make Central College the premier institution of higher education in Virginia. One of his first coups was persuading Albemarle Academy's trustees to agree to their own replacement by a smaller board of seven men of higher stature and greater political influence. Jefferson wanted to divest the college "of all local character" and place "it under the will of those who represented the Legislature." He alone continued as a member of the new Board of Visitors for Central College, while his preferred slate of candidates for the new board was adopted by Virginia governor Wilson Cary Nicholas, a political ally and fellow planter in the county. Nicholas appointed Jefferson, James Madison, James Monroe, Joseph C. Cabell, John Hartwell Cocke, James Breckenridge, Chapman Johnson, and David Watson. Jefferson was again astute in keeping the group much smaller than other university governing boards. It made the board more manageable, less likely to become unwieldly and factional. However, even with so many friends and allies, the members were not all malleable and pliant. James Breckenridge was a former Federalist, and Chapman Johnson, a representative of the rival western part of the state at Staunton, was a self-made man who grew up in poverty and hired himself out as a farm laborer. Nevertheless, with the support of a brother-in-law, Johnson devoted his time to reading and attended the College of William and Mary, where he studied under St. George Tucker.[32] Jefferson would face dissent from Johnson, Breckenridge, and Cocke, especially regarding the extravagant costs of the building of the university and the secular religious arrangements.

Yet Jefferson was still able to play a major role in the governance of the university because his friends formed a majority and only the local members were able to meet regularly. Joseph Cabell additionally proved a useful intermediary with the more recalcitrant members, especially his close friend John Hartwell Cocke, who shared Cabell's belief in the importance of education and internal improvements in Virginia. The board did not change when Central College became the University of Virginia.

Because only a bare quorum of three members appeared for the first meeting on April 18, 1817, the board confined itself to visiting possible sites for the college. On May 5, Jefferson, Madison, Monroe, and Cocke convened a follow-up meeting in which they agreed to both the site and the purchase of land near Charlottesville. Eager to appoint the first professors, they agreed to the construction of the first pavilion and dormitories, pending the availability of funds. After discussing strategies to finance the project, they launched a fundraising campaign to raise private donations.

On July 18, 1817, Jefferson personally surveyed the site for Central College. Edmund Bacon, his overseer at Monticello, recalled that the board chose the cheapest of three alternative sites offered by their owners, "a poor turned-out field, though it was finely situated." Located along Three Notched Road (the main western road between Richmond and the Shenandoah Valley), the forty acres were purchased at twelve dollars per acre from one John M. Perry. Once belonging to James Monroe, the land was deceptively cheap since the agreement required the board to offer construction projects to Perry. Bacon accompanied Jefferson, along with ten "able-bodied" hands, presumably enslaved laborers, and James Dinsmore, the Irish master carpenter at Monticello, to the location of what would become the Lawn of the University of Virginia. Along the way, Bacon picked up a ball of twine from "old Davy Isaac's store." Dinsmore brought some shingles and pegs. Upon arrival, Jefferson "looked over the ground some time, and then stuck down a peg" and directed the placement of the other pegs. It was the first groundbreaking of the university. Using a little ruler that he always carried with him in his pocket, Jefferson "measured off the ground and laid off the foundation" before assigning the enslaved work crew to level the surface.[33]

To INCREASE THE CHANCES of obtaining public funding for Central College and adopting it as the University of Virginia, Jefferson wanted to finish building the first pavilion before the end of 1817. He was similarly keen to start recruiting faculty. In May, the board voted to authorize the first faculty appointment and the hiring of stonecutters from Italy.[34] During July, Jefferson, Madison, Monroe, Cocke, and Cabell each subscribed $1,000 to Central College. Having helped to kick off what amounted to a professional fundraising campaign, with personal donations of the board, the members agreed to ask their friends to assist. With a flair that typified the enterprise, Jefferson and other members circulated printed forms to which they continuously added the names and amounts pledged, indicating the success of the fundraising campaign. While some were cash gifts, they also accepted gifts in kind and donations spread over time. Jefferson attempted to bolster the campaign for Central College with an article in the *Richmond Enquirer*.[35]

Jefferson and Cabell saw the salvation of the college in the state Literary Fund, which was indeed the only viable prospect for financing their ambitious plans. In a bid the previous year to capture the Literary Fund, Cabell had arranged for Jefferson's letter to Peter Carr to be published in the sympathetic *Richmond Enquirer*. This announcement in the press was possibly one of their few tactical errors, since it may have inspired the governor to issue a circular letter seeking ideas on public education, making it easier for other institutions to apply for money from the Literary Fund.[36] In any case, another competitive proposal was submitted.

In January 1817, Charles Fenton Mercer, the leader of the Virginia Federalist Party and an Episcopalian from Loudoun County in northern Virginia, proposed his own education bill that would set up elementary schools and create twenty-four banks aimed at increasing the wealth of the Literary Fund. Educated at Princeton, Mercer was a leading advocate of public education in the South. He not only helped to create the Literary Fund but was principally responsible for increasing its size by $1.2 million with money from the federal government in the form of reparation payments for costs and damages suffered by the state of Virginia during the British invasion in the War of 1812. Unlike Jefferson, Mercer's fondness for popular education was motivated less by an idealistic belief in the people than by a fear of extending the franchise to illiterate men. Having personally witnessed the industrial working class in Birmingham, England, he believed that with increasing social inequality, much worse was to come from the people he called "the rabble." Filled "with a school boy parade of details," Mercer thought that the Declaration of Independence "utters at the start an untruth that 'all men are equal and of right ought to be.'" Rather, he believed that "man neither is equal, can be equal, or ought to be equal."[37] He advocated military training to teach the children of the poor docility, obedience, and industry.[38] He ideally wanted the federal government to embrace education at all levels, requiring all children to attend school with the threat to resistant parents of denying them voting rights and the right to hold office. A generation younger than Jefferson, he thought that creating elementary schools should take precedence over a state university.

On February 18, 1817, Mercer's first education bill passed by a great majority in the House of Delegates. It sought not only to finance primary schools throughout the state but also to support as many as fifty-one academies, four colleges, and a university. It was the first bill to refer to the University of Virginia. However, the bill gave priority to the funding of primary schools, with any remaining surplus money to "be applied to found and support the University of Virginia."[39] Whether a compliment or an insult, one of the second-rank colleges, to be built in central Virginia, was to be called Jefferson. Like Jefferson, Mercer had an integrated vision of an interdependent system of education. In contrast to Jefferson's plan, however, Mercer's bill did not outline the academic curriculum to be followed at the various levels. Whereas Jefferson had only prescribed three years of education for girls, Mercer's bill allowed for the support of up to three female academies, beginning with the Anne Smith Academy in Lexington. Undaunted by the defeat of his first bill in the senate, Mercer introduced a second bill in February called the "General Education Bill," which gave priority to primary schools, support for existing denominational colleges (William and Mary, Hamden-Sydney, and Washington), and a public university located in the western part of the state, not Charlottesville.

Unlike Jefferson, Mercer wanted a highly centralized system under the control of a Board of Public Instruction. In the first iteration of the bill, the General Assembly would appoint the members of this state education board but thereafter would have no explicit control over it. Four of the ten members of this central board were to be appointed from the western half of the state, including two from west of the Allegheny Mountains. Mercer's education bill was also to be partly financed by the state from the Literary Fund. The primary schools were to be a mixture of "those able to pay" and state-funded pupils.[40] With a view to gaining western support, his bill provided for the university to be located near "the geographical centre of the commonwealth," by which he intended Staunton or Lexington, where westerners also wanted to locate the state capital. In advocating this, Mercer made a major tactical error by awakening eastern fears of western ambitions, which he further inflamed by planning to establish two new banks in the west to fund the schools, arousing the consternation of Richmond financiers.[41] Following a tie vote in the senate, Mercer's bill was essentially killed by Cabell and the Republican Party. They were encouraged to defeat the bill by Jefferson, who perceived it as a sinister ploy of Federalists and Presbyterians, whom he regarded as interchangeable because Presbyterians were a mainstay of the Federalist Party in New England. Furthermore, the Presbyterians posed a greater threat because they were then the most successful religious denomination in setting up schools and colleges throughout the United States.

With construction already begun at Central College in the fall of 1817, Jefferson responded to Mercer with his own "Bill for Establishing a System of Public Education." Like that of his rival, it contained a formal proposal to establish a University of Virginia while aiming to be "more within the compass of our funds."[42] Drafting his bill proved to be slow and painful, owing to a stiffening wrist that Jefferson had injured long before in Paris. Writing to the Abbé José Corrêia da Serra from his retreat at Poplar Forest, Jefferson described his proposal as offering three years of elementary schooling free of charge and a system of nine district colleges and a university "in a healthy and central situation," incorporating the lands, buildings, and funds of Central College. The obvious inference was that the university would be located in Charlottesville, replacing Central College. In an effort to reward merit and ability, he wanted gifted pupils at the elementary schools "whose parents are too poor to give them further education" to be eligible to receive a free education up to and including the university level. He explained that "the object is to bring into action that mass of talents which lies buried in poverty in every country, for want of the means of developement." He added that it would double or triple the proportion of highly educated citizens relative to most countries.[43] In his bill, he wrote of enriching the commonwealth of Virginia with "those talents and virtues which nature has sown as liberally among the poor as rich, and which are lost to their country by the want of means for their cultivation."[44]

Jefferson was quite hopeful of the likely success of his own bill, given that Mercer's "less practicable and boundlessly expensive" bill had passed in the House of Delegates. "Mine, after all may be an Utopian dream," he declared, "but being innocent, I thought I might indulge in it till I go to the land of dreams, and sleep there with the dreamers of all past and future times."[45] Unwilling to make the elementary schools compulsory, Jefferson instead wanted to follow Spain's requirement that made literacy a necessary qualification for citizenship. Still, his allies in the legislature removed this clause and another that debarred the clergy from serving as teachers. In any case, his bill was overwhelmingly defeated the following February.

JEFFERSON THEREAFTER FOCUSED primarily on the founding of the University of Virginia. Historians accuse him of sacrificing a public education system for an elite university.[46] Yet, for the rest of his life, he insisted that the first priority of government should be to educate the majority of citizens, on the grounds that "it is safer to have the whole people respectably enlightened, than a few in a high state of science, and the many in ignorance."[47] His own bill for establishing Central College in 1814 had also aimed to "Amend the 1796 Public Schools Act" so as to divide Albemarle County into wards, with a view to extending education to all citizens and transferring superintendence of future schools in the country from the magistrates to the Board of Visitors of Central College. The provision would have enabled Jefferson to create a prototype of the system that he wanted for the rest of the state, but it had to be discarded owing to opposition from the local representatives.

Jefferson argued that the primary schools alone in Mercer's bill would exceed the capacity of the Literary Fund. He feared that the ambitious scheme for several colleges would deplete available resources, leaving no possibility of funding an elite university.[48] His opposition to Mercer's bill was also ideological. Jefferson feared that allowing the central state government to run the public school system would lead to the "consolidation" of authority. It was a mantra for him that the concentration of power had destroyed liberty and the rights of man in every government "which has ever existed under the sun."[49] He wanted to see schools locally managed and funded through his favorite scheme of ward republics as a means to ensure local support and involvement in a public school system. In common with the later argument of Alexis de Tocqueville, Jefferson was concerned that ordinary citizens would feel alienated and marginalized by remote governments, even at the state level.

Jefferson's preference for local control became more pronounced in his retirement, when he wanted to see counties divided into "hundreds," or what he increasingly preferred to call "ward republics," which would fund a local primary school, care for the poor, and organize a company of militia. He saw such a division "as the most fundamental measure for securing good government, and for instilling the principles & exercise of self government into every fibre of every member of our commonwealth."[50] Based on Aristotelian ideas about keeping democracies small and a largely mythical historical image of the grassroots democracy of Anglo-Saxon England, Jefferson wanted to see wards elect their own judges, sheriffs, and juries, in order to give each citizen a part in the administration of public affairs.[51] Regarding each ward as a republic within a republic, he later wanted the wards to elect the visitors to the schools in order to prevent the system from being subjected to the control of "fantasizing preachers" and thus making it less likely that schools throughout the state could be controlled by the Presbyterians and Federalists who supported Mercer's bill.[52] "The only pure republic," he argued, "is impractical beyond the limits of a town."[53] He regarded his proposed ward system in Virginia as being analogous to the town government system he so admired in New England.[54] Emulating town governments in Connecticut and Massachusetts, Jefferson wanted the parents of each ward to be the judges of their children's education, not politicians whom he claimed would next presume to manage the farms, mills, and stores of the people if permitted.[55]

Jefferson's arguments in favor of local funding of schools at the ward level tend now to be dismissed as a ploy to give primacy to the state university. Yet he deserves more credit for recognizing the problem of popular alienation from central governments and the need to make ordinary citizens feel empowered. Hannah Arendt, the twentieth-century philosopher and political theorist, argued that Jefferson's idea about ward republics was one of the most creative and fundamental parts of his political philosophy.[56] Former presidential candidate Gary Hart regarded ward republics as Jefferson's most original thought in later life and recommended revisiting it as an antidote to the problems of democracy in the twenty-first century.[57] A more serious charge against his proposed scheme is that a local system of funding, rather than a central state system, has led to massive inequality between districts, with schools in poorer communities receiving less support.

Jefferson's willingness to sacrifice the elementary schools did not result from any change in his attitude about the importance of primary education for the survival of the republic. He was painfully aware that the existing schools could not supply well-prepared students for the university and that their inadequacy posed a major obstacle to its success. The draft Rockfish Gap Report included a discussion of the objectives of elementary schools, adding that it might "become perhaps a subject of future, and further attention for the legislature."[58] As late as February 1825, he wrote of the need for reports on each primary school in the state, including the regulations under which they operated, their funding sources, and their curricula.[59] In the last year of his life, he wrote yet another education bill and attempted to revive interest in a public school system. In addition to his unrealistic scheme of funding without state aid, he undermined his own proposal by insisting that such a system should not only promote republican values but also exclude the influence of any religious denomination and not employ clergy on the faculty. Unable to win support for a broader network of schools, he became more determined to ensure that, at a minimum, future leaders would receive a college education that was republican and free of religious dogma. He went ahead with the university project as the only attainable option due to the limited state funds then available. Nevertheless, he remained committed to the creation of a public school system and warned of the dangers of not pursuing his original objective.

In Jefferson's eyes, even the universities and colleges in his native state taught the antirepublican and authoritarian "heresies" of both his political and religious opponents. Mercer's bill had enjoyed support from the Shenandoah Valley, which Jefferson labeled "Tory" due to its large contingent of Presbyterians and Federalists. Furthermore, Mercer's proposal invited both Hampden-Sydney and Washington Colleges to be incorporated within the public system, which was anathema to Jefferson, since both were Presbyterian with close links to Princeton.[60] The bill would have extended the same courtesy to the College of William and Mary, dominated by Episcopalians. Jefferson's modern-day critics underestimate the role of religion in his objections and his plausible fear that locating the University of Virginia in the Shenandoah Valley would essentially have meant control by Presbyterians. It was precisely to combat what he regarded as their nefarious influence that he wanted to found the University of Virginia with the mission to inculcate the values of republicanism and the spirit of 1776. As Cameron Addis astutely observes, "Like the clergy, Jefferson knew the most direct and immediate impact on society resulted from control of higher education," not elementary schools, in a hierarchical society.[61] John Locke had similarly observed that "if those of that Rank are by their Education once set right, they will quickly bring all the rest into Order."[62] This was still the era of what Richard Hofstadter called the "gentleman politician" in America. Jefferson also opposed the rival claims of other colleges for a still more fundamental reason besides religion: if the state funds were divided among several institutions, his own ambitious plans for a top university might never be realized.

In order to try to compensate for the absence of public secondary schools, Jefferson set up a grammar school called the Charlottesville Academy. Hoping that it might provide as many as fifty to a hundred students annually for the university, he appointed Gerard E. Stack as its headmaster. He had been recommended by Thomas Cooper, with whom he had taught at Carlisle College in Pennsylvania. Educated at Trinity College Dublin, Stack appealed to Jefferson on account of his classical knowledge and style of teaching "beyond any example I have known in this state, and indeed in the US."[63] As with all his educational projects, Jefferson planned the school with meticulous detail. Rehearsing an idea for the university, Jefferson hired a Frenchman to run a boardinghouse so that pupils would be forced to speak French. Again anticipating his plans for the university, Jefferson did not allow any vacations other than a six-week break in the winter. He visited the school regularly and examined the pupils. Opened in May 1818, the academy closed after only fifteen months due largely to indiscipline among the students, a problem that would also haunt the University of Virginia. Historian Alan Taylor attributes the failure of the school to Jefferson's "dogmatic assurance" and "authoritative meddling," along with his "pet theories" and intimidation of Stack, who was apparently too frightened of Jefferson to accept an invitation to dinner at Monticello. Historian John Hammond Moore places the blame on Stack's lack of disciplinary skills.[64] Regardless of responsibility, the academy was replaced by a series of schools that similarly failed, including that of George Carr, an assistant master at the Charlottesville Academy who had immediately opened his own school on East Main Street after the other academy's demise. John Hartwell Cocke similarly fared no better with a school that he established at his plantation home of Bremo.

EVEN AS HE TRIED to fend off competitors, Jefferson's own efforts to obtain state funding for a university remained stalled. In February 1818, seeing an opportunity in a bill to create charity schools for boys from poor families,

Joseph Cabell added an amendment in the state senate to establish a state university and create the board of commissioners that gathered at Rock-fish Gap, where their meeting was so successfully orchestrated by Jefferson. With members selected by the governor from each electoral district of the senate, the commission was tasked with selecting the location of the university and making recommendations regarding its construction, curriculum, faculty, organization, and governance. The final bill provided annual payments of $45,000 to charity schools and $15,000 for a state university from the Literary Fund.

Since, as previously noted, the senatorial districts were disproportionately representative of the eastern and central areas of Virginia, the membership of the Rockfish Gap Commission favored Jefferson and Central College. However, the commission could only make recommendations to the General Assembly. On behalf of Jefferson, Cabell worked to ensure the election of sympathetic members to the legislature and to persuade others to remain. Friends wrote articles in support of the selection of Central College. To John Adams, Jefferson wrote just before the final vote, "We are all a-tip-toe here in the hourly expectation of hearing what our legislature decides on the Report. Being a good piece of a century behind the age they live in, we are not without fear as to their conclusions."[65] On January 25, 1819, the senate formally chartered the University of Virginia. Carrying overwhelming majorities in both houses, the act incorporated essentially all the recommendations of the Rockfish Gap Report. Although a jubilant Jefferson hoped to place newspaper advertisements for students as early as June, any celebrations were to prove premature, since the university did not begin classes until March 1825. The creation of the university would continue to be challenged. As Jefferson recognized, the act in practice had fallen "miserably short in the execution" of the Rockfish Gap Report.[66] Still, Cabell reassured him later in the year, "we have got possession of the ground, and it will never be taken from us."[67]

JEFFERSON WAS SHREWD to call the new institution the *University* of Virginia. Although other terms like "college" and "academy" were often used interchangeably, the use of the name "university" distinguished his new venture as the only university in the state. The ambiguity of the various designations reflected a lack of distinctions in the levels of education for different age groups and the rather haphazard arrangements that existed. With an average age of fourteen at Columbia College and the University of Pennsylvania, many so-called colleges were little more than secondary grammar schools, and indeed many originated as academies, such as the University of Pennsylvania.[68] As Du Pont de Nemours explained in his book *National Education in the United States of America*, "The term university comes from Europe and implies the claim of our great institutions of learning, that they introduce students to the universality of knowledge."[69] In 1818, Noah Webster defined "university" first as an assembly of colleges with legal power to confer degrees and next as a "universal school" with graduate schools "in which are taught all branches of learning, or the four faculties of theology, medicine, law, and the sciences and arts."[70] As with Harvard, Oxford, and Cambridge, a university might contain a college or several colleges. Harvard maintained a legal and functional difference between its college and university. The college was the residential and functional unit but did not have the power to award degrees and did not teach law or medicine. The university taught the "higher" branches, such as law and medicine at a graduate level, not just the "philosophical" faculty or what would now be called the Faculty of Arts and Sciences.[71]

In his "Bill for the More General Diffusion of Knowledge" (1779), Jefferson complained that the College of William and Mary had failed to develop into a university. In his draft report for the Rockfish Gap Commission, he wrote, "The term university comprehends the whole circle of the arts and sciences and extends to the utmost boundaries of human knowledge." Jared Sparks, who was later president of Harvard, thought "the title served merely to inflate the importance of an institution in the eyes of the clientele." Writing in 1829, he considered "it a great mistake . . . to call any of our institutions by the name of Universities. They are mere schools," and he did "not believe that a university can be engrafted on any of our old colleges."[72] Although established in 1636, Harvard did not become a university until 1780, the College of Philadelphia became the University of Pennsylvania in 1779, the College of New Jersey did not become Princeton University until 1896, and Columbia College did not change to Columbia University until 1912.[73] Jefferson was making a statement in his use of the word at a time when only nine other American institutions identified themselves as universities.

When the University of Virginia was created in 1819, the distinction between private and public was still ambiguous. States had traditionally helped fund private colleges, some of which later became public and others of which remained private. The University of Virginia and South Carolina College (University of South Carolina) were the first public colleges to receive annual funding from the state, thus pioneering a new model of public higher education in the United States.[74] Although in 1795 North Carolina became the first to be formally chartered as a public university in America, it did not receive annual income from the state. Just as Jefferson had tried to reform the College of William and Mary in 1779, John Adams succeeded in imposing a new constitution on Harvard in 1780. In the landmark case of *Dartmouth College v. Woodward* in 1819, the Supreme Court provided some clarification in ruling in favor of Dartmouth College as a private institution established before the creation of the state, against the legislature of the state of New Hampshire. Nevertheless, the differences between private and public continued to be blurred. Even though Daniel Webster argued the case for Dartmouth College's private status, he thought that Harvard should be considered a public university subject to the control of the Massachusetts General Court. Between 1814 and 1823, the state contributed $10,000 per annum or the equivalent of a quarter of the operating costs of Harvard. As late as 1849, Edward Everett, the former president of Harvard, spoke in favor of state financial support for Williams, Amherst, and Harvard. Harvard did not formally declare itself a private university until 1851 and continued to have state government-appointed trustees, known as overseers, through 1865. Public officials continued to have the right to sit on the governing boards of Yale until 1872 and Dartmouth until 1898.[75]

In reference to South Carolina and Virginia, Richard Hofstadter observed the irony that it was "the centers of aristocratic culture" which were "far more generous in fostering higher education than were the regions in which popular democracy enjoyed a more unqualified reign."[76] Indeed, Stanford historian Caroline Winterer suggests that the early republican experiment was "only partially successful" in its attempt to prove its superiority over monarchies and to claim to be the only path toward an enlightened future. In what she calls "a massive propaganda campaign," republicans dismissed monarchies as "peddlers of ignorance," seemingly oblivious to the pioneering role they played in public education and the miserliness of republics toward the funding of state schools.[77] James Madison condemned "the hardheartedness of the Legislature towards what ought to be the favorite offspring of the State," deplorable and reproachable treatment of the "university, as the Temple thro' which alone lies the road to that of Liberty."[78]

Less than five months before his death in July 1826, Jefferson proclaimed to Madison, "It is in our Seminary that the Vestal flame is to be kept alive. it is thence to spread anew over our own and the sister states. if we are true and vigilant in our trust, within a dozen or 20. years, a majority of our own legislature, will be from our school, & many disciples will have carried its doctrines home with them to their several states, and have leavened thus the whole mass."[79] Jefferson hoped that his university would improve Virginia and the rest of the United States by educating the future governing elite in Enlightenment and Republican principles. It was integral to his view of education that hope lay with future generations who would not be tied by tradition. He told Cabell that "nobody, more strongly than myself, advocates the right of every generation to legislate for itself, and the advantages which each succeeding generation has over the preceding one from the constant progress of science and the arts."[80] Jefferson had conceived his idealist vision of a university some forty years before the passage of the act establishing the University of Virginia (1819), whose name he first proposed in 1800. As he wrote to Cabell from Poplar Forest at the end of 1817, "I have only this single anxiety in this world. it is a bantling of 40. years birth & nursing, & if I can once see it on its legs, I will sing with sincerity & pleasure my nunc demittas (now lettest thou thy servant depart)."[81]

Jefferson had started to raise funds for the university and to plan its architecture four years before the Missouri Crisis (1819–20), which split the North and South over the question of whether slavery should be permitted in the new state of Missouri. Far from receiving the support of a united front of proslavery planters and legislators, Jefferson's vision for the university would be contested at every stage and fought against a background of one of the worst economic depressions suffered by Virginia. Although achieving an important milestone in 1819, Jefferson thereafter faced constant opposition within the state, which continued even beyond the opening of the university in March 1825.

4

We Shall Have Every Religious Man in Virginia against Us

O N THE MORNING of Monday, October 6, 1817, much of the population of Albemarle County gathered to watch the ceremonial laying of the cornerstone for the first building of Central College. Clouds soon threatened the fair and mild start to the day, but fine weather returned before the start of a procession from Charlottesville. Beginning at Court Square and the nearby Stone Tavern, the procession consisted of judges, lawyers, court officials, "respectable" citizens, and Freemasons from the Widow's Son's Lodge No. 60 and the Charlottesville Lodge No. 9. The judges descended from their benches, people left the courts, private houses shut, and the businesses suspended operations while "in one rolling tide the multitude pressed to the spot where the first twig of Science was to be planted."[1] After a one-and-three-quarter-mile journey to the groundbreaking celebration, they arrived at "the old field," which "was covered with carriages and people."[2]

The great object of interest was the presence of three presidents of the United States: the seventy-four-year-old Thomas Jefferson, the tallest of the three at six feet two inches; the sixty-six-year-old James Madison, the shortest at five feet four inches; and finally the six-foot tall, fifty-nine-year-old incumbent James Monroe. In front of the barely visible foundations of what became Pavilion VII, the three presidents lined up beside three members of the Board of Visitors (Joseph Cabell, David Watson, and John Hartwell Cocke). Edmund Bacon later recalled, "Mr. Jefferson—poor old man!—I can see his white head just as he stood there and looked on."[3]

In July 1817, construction had begun with the leveling of the ground and laying of the foundations for the first faculty house, which would become Pavilion VII. Acting as a committee of the Board of Visitors, Thomas Jefferson, Joseph Cabell, and John Hartwell Cocke had chosen an appropriate site outside of Charlottesville. It was a forty-four-acre location near Three Notched Road (now University Avenue). Ten enslaved men "had leveled the ground with hoe and spade."[4] The board had launched an ambitious fundraising campaign, enabling them to recruit faculty, purchase the site, and even arrange to hire stonecutters from Italy. Jefferson had already consulted with William Thornton and Benjamin Henry Latrobe, the two leading architects of Washington, D.C. On the day of the cornerstone-laying ceremony, Jefferson received another roll of drawings of two more pavilions from Latrobe.

Jefferson had been keen to grant the request of Albemarle's two Masonic lodges to participate in the cornerstone laying for the college.[5] He even loaned them three of his famous silver cups for use in the ceremony. The presence of Freemasons was a longstanding tradition at such occasions for the dedication of public, private, or religious buildings. The fraternal brotherhood claimed descent from the guild of stonemasons in Britain. Despite their quasi-mystical rituals and secrecy, they had a positive reputation for spreading the ideals of republican government, Enlightenment virtue, and benevolence. Their symbols, such as the pyramid, were widely adopted. The organization expanded its membership in the United States faster than that of the population overall by broadening beyond colonial elites to include professionals and tradesmen. Although there is no evidence that Jefferson was ever one of them, several of his family members were, including his son-in-law Thomas Mann Randolph and his favorite grandson, Thomas Jefferson Randolph. While a student at the College of William and Mary in 1775, James Monroe had joined Williamsburg Lodge No. 6.

At 1 p.m., the event began with the Masons forming a line at an arch erected near the foundations of Pavilion VII. Wearing his full regalia, Alexander Garrett, the grandmaster and also the college bursar (treasurer), led a parade of the chaplain, Masons, and bearers of corn and oil, followed by the orator, supervisor of construction, a band of musicians, judges, and the massed spectators. After reviewing the procession, the board members divided into two groups to follow the grandmaster to the site of the cornerstone, led by Jefferson, Madison, and Monroe. Beginning with a prayer given by the Episcopalian chaplain, the Reverend William King, the grandmaster requested the visitors allow the presidents to proceed: "Gent[lemen]: You have been pleased to grant us the masonic order, the high privilege of laying the corner stone of this building, will you further indulge us in your aid and participation [on this] interesting occasion." After receiving nods of assent, he then delivered a prayer: "May almighty God, without invocation to whom no work of importance should be begun, bless this undertaking and enable us to carry it on with success. protect this college the object of which institution is to instill in the minds of Y[o]uth principles of sound knowledge, to inspire them with the love of religion & virtue, and preparing them for filling the various situations in this society with credit to themselves and benefits to their country."[6]

As the former owner of the land and supervisor of construction, John Perry, with the assistance of a Mason, then placed the stone in its bed, to which was added a vial containing a piece of parchment with the words, "Laid by Lodges Nos. 60. and 90 on the 6th day of October AL 5817 AD 1817. Alex Garrett, R.W.G. Master Allen Dawson Deputy Grandmaster and substitute the Revd. William King Chaplain and John Perry Architect." President James Monroe applied the square, plumb, and level to check that the stone was fit. After the grandmaster confirmed the stone, the crowd gave three huzzahs, at which point the band played "Hail Columbia," a tune composed for the inaugural of George Washington and used as a national anthem until 1931:

> Hail Columbia, happy land!
> Hail, ye heroes, heav'n-born band,
> Who fought and bled in freedom's cause,
> Who fought and bled in freedom's cause,
> And when the storm of war was gone
> Enjoy'd the peace your valor won.
> Let independence be our boast,
> Ever mindful what it cost;
> Ever grateful for the prize,
> Let its altar reach the skies.

The ceremony continued with the scattering of corn and the pouring of wine and oil over the cornerstone, followed by a blessing and confirmation that the stone was "true and trusty," at which point the band played "Yankee Doodle" before another speech by the orator, Freemason Valentine W. Southall. After final blessings for the completion of the buildings and future of the institution, the band struck up the "Jefferson March," composed for Jefferson's inaugural in 1801, at which point sword bearers faced each other to create an arch of crossed swords through which the board members, the judges, and the lawyers then departed. Accompanied by a final rendition of "Madison's March," they headed for the Stone Tavern, off Court Square, sitting "down to a dinner prepared for the occasion where reigned an undisturbed feeling of pl[ea]sure and [harm]ony that welcomed in the approaching evening." The memory of the day would "long live in the recollection of those who witnessed it."[7]

THE FANFARE OF the stone-laying ceremony was a political gambit to persuade the Virginia legislature to transform Central College into a state university, thereby achieving Jefferson's ultimate goal of locating the future University of Virginia in Charlottesville. It was a testament to his successful campaign to achieve this desired outcome. The presence of a sitting president and the two most recent former presidents was a very effective way to promote the candidacy of Central College, winning the admiration of John Adams, who called them "a noble Triumvirate" from whom "the World will expect something very great and very new."[8] Jefferson simultaneously arranged a three-day meeting of the Central College board. Desiring maximum public visibility, Jefferson chose to hold the stone-laying ceremony on court day. These days were among the most important and busiest in the social calendar, with not only the judges, lawyers, and clerks congregating but also throngs of onlookers who wanted to see the spectacle, watch the court sessions, hear stump speeches, listen to itinerant preachers, transact business, and engage in commerce. On such occasions, there was always a procession, which ritualistically upheld local order and hierarchy by celebrating the legal system and observing rules of precedence according to social rank.[9]

Jefferson demonstrated his political skill in overcoming opposition, not only through the orchestration of the splendid, star-studded ceremony but also through his command of persuasive rhetoric in his writing and conversation. As one who had always appreciated the influence of public media and newspapers, Jefferson and Cabell planted articles of support in the *Richmond Enquirer,* a Democratic-Republican paper edited by the sympathetic Thomas Ritchie and regarded by Jefferson as "the best that is published or ever been published in America."[10] Posing in one letter as a tourist who had passed through Charlottesville, Jefferson wrote of the benefits of the location for a university, including "its fertility, its central position with respect to the population of the state, and other advantages," such as its altitude, healthiness, and "good water."[11] He had key documents printed to raise interest and awareness, such as the Rockfish Gap Report. It was typical of his behind-the-scenes method of operating. Jefferson thought his public involvement might prove a liability and wished the public to understand that he was not interested in meddling with state politics other than in matters relating to education.[12] He was so diffident that he feared that he was doing more harm than good by playing the leading role.[13]

Along with Madison, Jefferson sought to persuade potential political allies of the university to run for or remain in the General Assembly. This
was essential for obtaining support for funding and overcoming considerable legislative opposition. He therefore surrounded himself with capable
people, such as Joseph C. Cabell in the state senate, who acted as a proxy
through whom Jefferson could influence elections, votes, and debates. Always seeming to remain aloof and avoiding direct confrontation, Jefferson
encouraged others to do his bidding. His clear vision, determination, and
persistence kept them active on his behalf. Owing to the difficulty of con-
vening meetings of the Board of Visitors, he had to act on his own initiative.[14] Despite his increasing difficulty in writing, he drafted all the necessary bills for the legislature and even the legal document of purchase for the
land. He disliked what he called the "verbose and intricate style" of modern
statutes in Britain and the revised code in the United States. He wrote ironically that Cabell should feel free to change his bills to make them incomprehensible to anyone outside the legal profession.[15] As he had with the
Declaration of Independence, Jefferson wrote bills with a view to instruct,
explain, and persuade, beginning with a preamble introducing the purpose,
objectives, and principles of the proposed legislation. He similarly undertook the seemingly dull task of writing the minutes of the Board of Visitors.
This ensured that his version became the final record of their meetings. He
produced the annual reports that detailed for the legislature the progress
of construction and related costs. Writing of the political acumen of her
grandfather, Ellen Coolidge thought that he must be "acknowledged as one
of the great leaders of public opinion. No man of his times produced on his
contemporaries an effect so marked and so likely to be lasting."[16]

Although not as active as Cabell, James Madison was another important
ally in founding and building the university. He was a luminary repeatedly
willing to hold his own light under a bushel in his veneration for Jefferson. Having met in 1776, they remained lifelong friends and political allies
who shared similar intellectual interests and political views, including the
importance of public education. They particularly bonded over their joint
fight against state-supported religion. In the post-independence revision
of the Virginia laws, Madison assisted Jefferson and played a critical role
in the passage of the Virginia Statute for Religious Freedom in the mid-
1780s when Jefferson was in Paris. In 1791, they traveled to New England to
study botany and the Hessian fly for the American Philosophical Society.
Believing it necessary to promote a degree of uniformity in political principles across the nation, Madison was more committed than Jefferson to a

national rather than just a state system of education. At the Constitutional Convention of 1787, he proposed a clause permitting the establishment of a national university. As president of the United States, Madison similarly urged the creation of such an institution in three annual addresses to Congress. In retirement, Jefferson urged Madison to become a neighbor in Albemarle County. Although he never took that offer, Madison and his wife, Dolley, regularly traveled the thirty miles to Monticello, and Jefferson visited their home at Montpelier in Orange County.[17]

Influenced by Jefferson, Madison believed that representative government, in the absence of an educated public, would end in farce and tragedy. He warned that "knowledge will for ever govern ignorance: and a people who mean to be their own Governours, must arm themselves with the power that knowledge gives." He dismissed those who argued that ordinary people did not have an interest in paying taxes in support of universities, on the erroneous assumption that they merely benefited the elite and those most able to afford private fees. Citing Jefferson's "Bill for the General Diffusion of Knowledge," Madison asserted that every class ought to have an interest in all levels of public education, "which give to the human mind its highest improvements, and to every Country its truest and most durable celebrity." Referring specifically to universities, he wrote, "Learned institutions ought to be favorite objects of every free people." They help enlighten the populace generally "against crafty & dangerous encroachments on the public liberty." They "are nurseries of skilful Teachers for schools distributed throughout the Community." They nurture the talents of those destined for public office, "on the able execution of which the welfare of the people depends." According to Madison, universities multiply the number of educated people qualified for public office, thereby expanding the choice of candidates.[18]

Madison was concerned that without state funding, only the very wealthy would be able to afford to go to college, giving them a monopoly of higher education. In contrast, at a public university, talented individuals of "slender incomes" would be on the same level as "the sons of the richest." It was in the interests of both rich and poor to support public funding, "not merely for the existing generation, but for succeeding ones also." Because of the rotation of property, in which the children of the rich might one day be poor and vice-versa, "the rich man when contributing to the permanent plan of education for the poor ought to reflect that he is providing for that of his own descendants." Madison thought nothing more edifying than the spectacle of "Liberty & Learning, each leaning on the other for mutual support."[19]

Jefferson thought it "most important" that Madison serve as one of the commissioners at Rockfish Gap.[20] Subsequently, Jefferson consulted with Madison to provide lists of books for the university library and to discuss the recruitment of faculty. Madison held some of the meetings of the Board of Visitors at Montpelier and later succeeded Jefferson as rector, in which capacity he served until 1834 when he was eighty-three years old. He was one of the most regular attendees of the board meetings. Writing shortly before Jefferson's death, Madison assured him that "you do not overrate the interest I feel in the University, as the Temple thro' which alone lies the road to that of Liberty."[21]

As governor of Virginia in 1801, James Monroe had also championed public education, telling legislators that "in a government founded on the sovereignty of the people . . . knowledge should be diffused through the whole society and for that purpose the means of acquiring it made not only practicable but easy to every citizen."[22] Before Jefferson retired as president, he wrote to Monroe that he "viewed Mr. Madison and yourself as the two principal pillars of my happiness," and that "were either to be withdrawn, I should consider it as among the greatest calamities which could assail my future peace of mind."[23] Later, as president of the United States, Monroe urged the creation of "seminaries of learning" by Congress, and when Jefferson died, Monroe replaced him on the Board of Visitors, having always taken a deep interest in the success of the University of Virginia.

After reading an account of the opening ceremony, the architect William Thornton wrote of his admiration of this gathering of "three Presidents of the United States on so praise worthy an Occasion," which was so "different to the meeting of the three Emperors on the Continent of Europe, after a bloody Battle!"[24] Yet, despite Thornton's praise, the endeavor was far from a guaranteed success. Jefferson may have won the first round at the Rockfish Gap Commission, but he and his allies still had to persuade the General Assembly to adopt the report and its recommendation that Central College in Charlottesville become the new University of Virginia. Bitter opposition to Jefferson's plan for the university soon emerged and continued for the rest of his life. Although funding would be the perennial obstacle, religious objections nearly wrecked the whole endeavor from the start.

THE DAY AFTER the ceremonial laying of the foundation stone, in a decision that nearly proved disastrous, Jefferson invited Thomas Cooper to become the first faculty member. Regarded by Jefferson as "one of the ablest men in America," Cooper was the son-in-law, intellectual disciple, and fellow radical British émigré of the scientist and theologian Joseph Priestley. Known as Old Coot, Cooper was less than five feet tall and plump, looking like "a wedge with a head on it."[25] He was an advocate for science, education, and freedom of speech. Like Priestley, Cooper was a polymath and a prolific writer on subjects ranging from economics and law to chemistry, geology, and medicine. A former state judge in Pennsylvania, he presented papers to the American Philosophical Society and taught for a while at Dickinson (then called Carlisle) College before becoming professor of chemistry and mineralogy at the University of Pennsylvania. He was a pioneer in the study of Roman law and translated one of the key texts, the *Institutes of Justinian* (1812).

Other than George Tucker, Thomas Cooper came to be regarded as the finest political economist in the South. Herbert Baxter Adams called him "one of the greatest and most influential teachers of his time," while Dumas Malone, who wrote his biography, "thought that no man of his generation in America had read more widely or could make greater display of erudition," calling his energy incredible and remarking that "few of his contemporaries could compare with him either in intellectual acquirements or in prophetic insight into the future course of thought."[26] In England, he had sparred with Edmund Burke over the French Revolution, writing a *Reply to Burke's Invective* (1792). After moving to America and meeting Jefferson in 1794, Cooper endeared himself by publishing political tracts for which he was imprisoned under the Sedition Act. He thereafter became something of an apologist in the press and in pamphlets for the Republican Party, leading to a close friendship that grew while Jefferson was president. As early as 1814, Jefferson tried to recruit Cooper to teach at the Albemarle Academy. He was undoubtedly Jefferson's first choice, but it was also his most politically naive decision, given its effect on his campaign to gain public support for locating the state university in Charlottesville.

One complication was that the Board of Visitors had already offered the first professorship at Central College to the esteemed Irish-born scholar the Reverend Samuel Knox of Baltimore. Knox had been one of two winners of the American Philosophical Society's 1796 essay contest on public education and later wrote an essay defending Jefferson's religious views during the election of 1800. Jefferson claimed that Knox had turned down the offer; Knox denied ever receiving it. Jefferson extended the offer instead to Cooper and renewed it in March 1819 with the chartering of the University of Virginia. Faculty appointments in a private college were of little consequence to the electorate, but it was another matter at a public state institution. Cabell denied even knowing about Cooper's appointment and warned Madison that it would "cause the entire overthrow of the institution" at a time when the university desperately needed additional public funding. Because of Cooper's radicalism and unorthodox religious views, Cabell feared that the appointment was "excessively unpopular" among nine-tenths of the state and had united different religious groups. He claimed that "even all the free thinkers of my acquaintance about Richmond protest against his being made a Professor of the University; all on the ground of policy, & some on the ground of principle."[27] The opposition extended to other members of the Board of Visitors. John Hartwell Cocke, who had become an evangelical after the death of his wife, similarly opposed Cooper's appointment.

John Holt Rice, a writer, editor, teacher, and clergyman, spearheaded the opposition. The founder of the First Presbyterian Church in Richmond and founding editor of the popular monthly *Virginia Evangelical and Literary Magazine*, Rice led the Presbyterian interest in Virginia. Like Jefferson, he wanted a public education system in the state at both primary and college levels. Recognizing that the powers of the whole state were necessary for the creation of a public school system, he had supported the 1817 bill of Charles Fenton Mercer. Turning down in 1822 the presidency of Princeton (then the College of New Jersey), which had given him an honorary doctorate, Rice was equally committed to focusing his energy and public funding on education in the South. Writing under the name of "Crito," he supported the idea of a state university by providing estimates of the loss of revenue from students going to northern colleges. Joseph Cabell and Jefferson used these same figures. Rice even invited Francis Walker Gilmer, a young lawyer who was a friend of Jefferson, to write an article on the "Necessity of a Better System of Instruction in Virginia."[28]

Pressured by fellow Presbyterians in the Shenandoah Valley to oppose Cooper's appointment, Rice ran excerpts in his magazine from the 1805 London edition of Priestley's *Memoirs*, in which Cooper declared that a man might be a good citizen regardless of whether he believed "in three Gods, in thirty thousand Gods or in no God." Rice also condemned Cooper's belief that the soul did not exist before birth or after death. Invoking the specter of Jacobinism and the extremism of the French Revolution, Rice asked whether the pious could "send their children to a place where they would be taught that an Atheist may be as good a man as a Christian."[29] In an earlier booklet distributed to the General Assembly, he had expressed concern for the future of Christianity. In deference to the Virginia Statute for Religious Freedom, Rice was willing to countenance a nominally nonsectarian university that made provision for other religions, including Judaism, but he believed that the students should be required to engage in regular worship and instruction in the Bible. He later devoted himself to founding the Union Theological Seminary, first located at Hampden-Sydney College and moved to Richmond in 1898.

Jefferson blamed opposition to Cooper on the Presbyterian clergy alone, whom he thought "bitterly federal and malcontent." He regarded them as "violent, ambitious of power and intolerant in politics as in religion," wanting nothing but "licence from the laws to kindle again the fires of their leader John Knox, and to give us a 2nd blast of his trumpet," a reference to the Scottish Calvinist reformer's 1558 pamphlet *The First Blast of the Trumpet against the Monstrous Regiment of Women*. Jefferson had especially resented the invective of the Presbyterian clergy against him during the election of 1800, such as that espoused by New York pastors William Linn and John Mitchell Mason in their *Serious Considerations on the Election of a President* (1800). Twenty years later, Jefferson continued to fulminate against the clergy, who "having a little more monkish learning than the clergy of the other sects, they are jealous of the general diffusion of science, and therefore hostile to our Seminary, lest it should qualify their Antagonists of the other sects to meet them in equal combat." Showing himself to be unaware of the growing evangelical fervor within the state, Jefferson dismissed "the snarle of Mr. Rice" resulting "from the spirit of *his priesthood*," wrongly claiming that only "a dozen or two fanatics or bigots of his sect in this state may read his Evangelical magazine." The subscription numbers were closer to a thousand.[30] Equating Presbyterianism with Calvinism and Federalism, Jefferson viewed it as an inherently authoritarian religion with its doctrine of the elect and its belief in predestination.

Jefferson was wrong to assume that all Presbyterian clergy were Federalists.[31] He never showed similar prejudice to the Baptists and Methodists, whom he regarded as "sound republicans" since they had supported him during the passage of the Virginia Statute for Religious Freedom and in the 1800 presidential contest.[32] Although growing at a faster pace than the Presbyterians, the Baptists and Methodists were less interested in education at this stage, partly because they did not require college-trained ministers and were therefore not competitors for state funds. Joseph Cabell initially took the same view as Jefferson, believing Presbyterians to be "an artful, able, aspiring sect, who have contrived to monopolize in a great degree the education of the country," and that they were alarmed "at the prospect of its being taken out of their hands."[33] Cabell later changed his mind, realizing that it was both possible and essential to work with the Presbyterians. Knowing that the rest of the Board of Visitors supported him, he approached Madison to persuade Jefferson that he must terminate Cooper's contract. Rice's campaign against Cooper succeeded: Jefferson was put in the embarrassing situation of accepting Cooper's resignation. Never having taught at the University of Virginia, Cooper soon went on to become president of South Carolina College. Jefferson made sure that Cooper received a good financial settlement in ending his contract and continued to correspond with him for the rest of his life.

JEFFERSON AND HIS ALLIES were more successful in combating intense demands to locate the university elsewhere in the state. "The subject of controversy," according to contemporary writers on education, was "whether a large city or a country village is the most eligible situation for a college or university." European universities were all located in cities and increasingly in national capitals. Admitting that a major objection to public education was the fear that city locations would be a source of corruption, vice, and debauchery, the Reverend Samuel Knox countered that "the most dangerous temptations to vice" came in private domestic settings and in "retired shades," rather than in bustling crowds and public assemblies.[34] Benjamin Franklin had wanted to locate the University of Pennsylvania in a village, while Benjamin Rush favored having a major university in Philadelphia.[35] Noah Webster thought that the arguments in favor of a village were the most compelling, since "large cities are always the scene of dissipation and amusement, which have a tendency to corrupt the hearts of youth and divert their minds from their literary pursuits. Reason teaches this doctrine, and experience has uniformly confirmed the truth of it."[36]

Jefferson's long-held distrust of cities and belief in the superiority of rural settings manifested itself in his preference for Charlottesville. The countryside was more likely to inculcate moral virtue in his mind, thanks to the presence of independent yeomen farmers over financiers and industrialists. He associated cities with corruption, describing New York, "like London," as being "a Cloacina [the Roman goddess who presided over the great sewer] of all the depravities of the human nature," while here "crime is scarcely heard of, breaches of order rare, and our societies, if not refined, rational moral and affectionate at least."[37] He was also influenced by health considerations and the threat of disease in overcrowded cities. Nevertheless, he was not totally committed to the idea that a university should be in the countryside. While in Paris in 1785, Jefferson wrote that the move-ment of the Virginia state capital to Richmond left Williamsburg "a mere academical village" whose isolation was exacerbated by the destruction of many of its former buildings, such as the Governor's Palace. This was the first occasion in which he used the expression "academical village," a phrase that was to later feature prominently in his thinking about the University of Virginia.[38] As late as 1816, he wrote that he preferred the University of Pennsylvania because Philadelphia "is a great city while Williamsburg is but an academical village."[39] In selecting Charlottesville, he may have been mo-tivated by little more than a desire to keep the university under his personal control and supervision and out of the control of the Presbyterians and Federalists in Staunton.

Established in 1762 in the name of Queen Charlotte, the wife of George III, Charlottesville was still little more than a village, with only three hun-dred residents, by 1815. It contained just a few houses and two or three busi-nesses, while the main street was so rough that it stalled wagons. Char-lottesville was so remote that it sometimes did not receive mail for three weeks. Although little more than seventy miles away from the state capital of Richmond, it took a stagecoach about twenty-eight hours to travel the distance, owing to the primitive roads, which northern and foreign visitors thought some of the worst they had ever encountered. Connecting Char-lottesville to Richmond, the Rivanna River was only navigable for eight months a year and the James River was obstructed by rocks.[40]

Charlottesville partly appealed to Jefferson because of the absence of a dominant religious organization. Until the Episcopalians built Christ Church in 1824, it lacked "a house of worship in the village or its immedi-ate vicinity," and preachers of different denominations rotated services in the courthouse. Reverend William S. White, the pastor of the Presbyterian Church in Lexington, described Charlottesville as a place that "from time immemorial" had been "not only irreligious as any community, but anti-religious as any community in the State." While "the number of professing Christians was very small," White claimed that "dissipation of a certain gen-teel sort was very common" and "deistical sentiments were widely diffused and unblushingly avowed." In 1818, Dr. Conrad Speece attempted to preach one night in the courthouse but "well-nigh failed because of the insufficient light and the rudeness of the boys." When he then spent the night at a hotel, "such were the sentiments uttered in his hearing by prominent gentlemen, and such the ill-conduct of the young men frequenting the tavern," that he said afterward, "When Satan promised all the kingdoms of the world to Christ, he laid his thumb on Charlottesville, and whispered, 'Except this place, which I reserve for my own special use.'"[41]

Three of the four competing locations in Virginia—Staunton, Lexington, and Richmond—were associated with what Jefferson regarded as the twin evils of Presbyterianism and Federalism. The three existing colleges and a fourth projected college in Staunton each sought to become the leading university in Virginia. Through the influence of their alumni, they vied to divert public funds for themselves. Two of the three existing colleges were Presbyterian: Washington College (renamed Washington and Lee University in 1870) and Hampden-Sydney College. Indeed, Presbyterians were a dominant force in higher education throughout the United States. Founded in 1749 as the Augusta Academy, becoming Liberty Hall Academy in 1776 and Washington Academy in 1798, Washington College in Lexington was the best endowed of the colleges in Virginia. It had received a major gift of shares in the James River Company from President George Washington in 1796 and another from the Virginia Chapter of the Society of the Cincinnati in 1802. Despite his initial opposition to the creation of the Society of the Cincinnati, Jefferson had also tried to obtain funding from the same source, even offering to name a chair at his school in gunnery and fortifications the Cincinnati Professor.[42]

John Robinson, a whiskey distiller, promised a fortune of $100,000 if the state chose Lexington as the location of the University of Virginia. Changing its name from Washington Academy in 1813, Washington College sought state funding both before and after the creation of the University of Virginia. It had over three hundred acres and held in bondage fifty-seven enslaved laborers. Cabell heard that the friends of what he continued to call Washington Academy were "using great exertions to defeat the claims of Central College" and "were as much excited as if we had attempted to pull down their college."[43] In 1817, he feared that they had majority support in the House of Delegates. According to an alumnus, Jefferson's supporters then resorted to a smear campaign against Washington College.[44]

Founded as the Prince Edward Academy near Farmville in 1776 and renamed in 1777, Hampden-Sydney College had a governing board of trustees that included Patrick Henry and James Madison. While never formally affiliated with any sect, it was established by Scots-Irish Presbyterians and the first president of the college was a Presbyterian minister, Samuel Stanhope Smith, who later became a celebrated president of Princeton. Receiving a state grant in 1784, the legislature attempted to turn it into a public college in 1796. As late as 1821, Hampden-Sydney College sought funding from the state in competition with the University of Virginia.

The College of William and Mary represented the greatest political threat and competition. As a private institution, the college remained Episcopalian in ethos and leadership, making it unacceptable to western Presbyterians and to Jefferson. In the aftermath of the Revolutionary War, the college was weakened by the state's confiscation of Episcopal church property, which deprived the college of three-fourths of its funds, and the removal of the capital from Williamsburg to Richmond. During the early nineteenth century, the college's reputation suffered in the wake of student riots. After the death in 1812 of Bishop James Madison, its much-respected president, the Board of Visitors appointed a Federalist clergyman, the Reverend John Bracken, who had been a leading opponent of Jefferson's attempted reform of the college in 1779. Regarding Bracken as a simpleton and a Tory, Jefferson nevertheless dissuaded Cabell from trying to oust Bracken as president in favor of Jefferson's nephew Peter Carr. Jefferson saw no hope for the college, while the appointment of Bracken may have been the catalyst for his wish to create a separate state university. Under Bracken's leadership, the college went into decline with only twenty-one students in 1814, fewer than Hampden-Sydney.[45] Following Bracken's forced resignation in 1814 and his replacement by the more dynamic Dr. John Augustine Smith, a former medical professor in New York, the College of William and Mary started to prosper: enrollment began to climb and there was a concerted effort to improve the facilities, including the scientific apparatus. Revitalized by Smith, the college represented a threat to Jefferson's desire to create a new state university. Even after creation of the University of Virginia in 1819, William and Mary had ambitious plans to add a medical school and move to Richmond, which had the benefit of a local hospital in contrast to Charlottesville.

The College of William and Mary had powerful support among its alumni and members of the General Assembly from the eastern shore. In the Virginia House of Delegates, 50 percent of the members had attended college and three-quarters were alumni of William and Mary; some 67 percent of all the delegates were Episcopalians.[46] Having once considered an invitation to join its faculty, even Jefferson's ally Joseph Cabell admitted that he would feel "delicately situated" in opposing the interests of his old college and thereby also his "nearest and dearest relatives and friends."[47] Before the legislative session of 1824–25, William and Mary attempted to obtain funding for its proposed move to Richmond. Jefferson was adamant that all available state funding go exclusively to the University of Virginia. He saw no point in having "two institutions crippling one another," instead of one college offering the "highest grade of instruction," which was impossible with divided support.[48] Few states could afford to fund one university, let alone two.[49] Jefferson's willingness to undermine the requests of the other colleges ran so deep that he suggested to Cabell that their allies support William and Mary's request to move to Richmond. Revealing the extent of his political cunning, he wrote, "Let them get the old structure completely on wheels and not till then put in our claim" to dissolve the college and transfer its considerable endowment to the University of Virginia.[50] He fortunately did not succeed in attempting to eliminate the College of William and Mary.

ALTHOUGH THE REPUBLICAN PARTY dominated Virginia, Jefferson was far from enjoying unquestioned support, especially in the House of Delegates. He relied on Joseph Cabell to orchestrate support in alliance with the leading Republicans who represented the eastern Tidewater of Virginia. Dubbed by a political adversary the "Richmond Junto" in 1824, they were an informal group of about twenty leading planters, lawyers, judges, and bankers who coalesced on some issues.[51] The *Richmond Enquirer*, the leading state newspaper, acted as their mouthpiece through its editor, Thomas Ritchie. Ritchie was the cousin of the Junto's most important member, Spencer Roane, himself a successful lawyer and judge and the son-in-law of Patrick Henry. Like Jefferson, Ritchie was opposed to clergymen teaching in public schools and believed in the importance of public education, lamenting that the state had too "long suffered the geniuses to wither or run wild in the streets."[52] Ritchie was active in the movement to create the Richmond Academy, and in 1816 he founded the Richmond Lancastrian School, based on the popular educational ideas of Joseph Lancaster in England. A fellow member of the Richmond Junto and a cousin of Spencer Roane, Dr. John Brockenbrough was the president of the Bank of Virginia and the brother-in-law of Andrew Stevenson, the speaker of the House of Delegates (1819–21) and a U.S. congressman (1821–34). A "cofounder" of the Richmond Junto with Roane, Wilson Cary Nicholas was a former governor of the state (1814–16). Thanks to its assistance, Cabell was able to obtain generous and extended loans from the state banks for the University of Virginia.

Despite the Junto's support, the views of some of its members diverged widely from Jefferson on other issues. Unlike Jefferson, the members mostly opposed the ambitions of the western settlers, whom they regarded as "pot-

boilers and mechanics . . . the peasantry of the west," a threat to the traditional planter elite of the Old Dominion.[53] They were not in favor of
expanding the franchise or revising the state constitution of 1776. They
disliked some of the major platforms of western delegates, such as state-
funded internal improvements in infrastructure and the expansion of banks
westward that threatened their own financial control. The colonial-era politics of deference continued in eastern districts, where elections were more
likely to be uncontested, consequently returning members of the mostly
Episcopalian planter elite. Although the representatives of the Piedmont
(the region between the Tidewater and the Blue Ridge Mountains) often
voted with the Junto, Cabell could not totally rely on united eastern support, since some of their representatives were frequently absent and others
were sympathetic to the College of William and Mary. Nevertheless, sharing some of their conservatism on issues like the franchise, he was able to
operate as a successful intermediary between them and Jefferson.

What Cabell called "the hostile party" to Charlottesville largely consisted
of representatives of the western districts of Virginia. Settled primarily by
Scots-Irish Presbyterians and Germans, the number of western representatives was less and less proportionate to the growing population in the
Shenandoah Valley and the trans-Allegheny region. The imbalance was
particularly egregious in the state senate, which was able to obstruct legislation passed in the House of Delegates. The western parts of the state
had a more diversified economy, dominated by small farms less dependent
on slavery. Its delegates sought to reform the state constitution, expand the
franchise, improve transportation, obtain greater access to the justice system, and build public schools. Despite their inability to obtain a new constitutional convention until 1829, their increasing numbers in the House of
Delegates made it harder for Cabell to obtain favorable votes in the later
stages of the building of the University of Virginia.[54] Even with the support of the Richmond Junto, Cabell needed some votes from the western
districts of the state and the southern Piedmont. Jefferson was fortunate
that the western delegates split between those supporting the founding of
the university in Staunton, where they also wanted to move the state capital,
and those championing Washington College in Lexington.

Virginia's Republicans were also divided. Some argued against any public
funding of education. William Branch Giles had opposed the education
bills of both Charles Fenton Mercer and Thomas Jefferson in 1817. Writing
a series of seven articles under the name "A Constituent" in the *Richmond
Enquirer*, Giles mocked the "prince of philosophers," alluding to Jefferson.[55]

Beginning his publications in January 1818, with dense articles that occupied three to five columns, Giles thought it unjust for one man to be taxed to educate the children of another and claimed that teachers would become a special-interest group who would always vote for higher taxes. Echoing his attacks on Federalists in the 1790s, Giles employed similar language against his erstwhile ally Jefferson. Embarrassed, Thomas Ritchie distanced himself and the newspaper with an editorial disclaimer that Giles's views did not represent those of the *Richmond Enquirer.*[56] Still the potential for damage remained. Others regarded the university as an elitist project and questioned whether the university should be given priority over educating the poor. Fortunately for Cabell and Jefferson, the two most vigorous opponents of the University of Virginia left Richmond: Mercer joined the U.S. House of Representatives in 1817, and Rice moved to Farmville to become a professor at the Union Presbyterian Seminary in 1821.

Even after the successful passage of the bill creating the University of Virginia in January 1819, Jefferson faced a potentially devastating development when Joseph Cabell decided not to run again for his seat in the state senate. Cabell had been so ill that he was spitting blood on the senate floor. As his health declined, his wife and friends urged him to withdraw from politics.[57] With another election approaching and the seemingly unquenchable need for additional funding, Cabell expressed greater resolve to resign in January 1821. His letters were full of gloom about the prospects for support of the university in the recently elected legislature. He suffered exhaustion from tirelessly working to reconcile colleagues in the legislature, speaking at courthouses in all seasons and traveling throughout the state to rally support for the university. Demonstrating his political and manipulative abilities, Jefferson sought to assuage and cajole Cabell to continue in the senate. He first appealed to Cabell's sympathy. Wondering how the university could proceed in the absence of Cabell, Jefferson exclaimed, "I perceive that I am not to live to see it opened." Having assumed that his allies would "stand at your posts in the legislature, until every thing was effected, and the institution opened," Jefferson now appealed to Cabell's sense of duty and to his foresight into the calamities that might lie ahead, asking him, "What service can we ever render [our country] equal to this? what object of our lives can we propose so important? what interest of our own, which ought not to be postponed to this? health, time, labor, on what in the single life which nature has given us, can these be better bestowed than on this immortal boon to our country? the exertions and the mortifications are temporary; the benefit eternal." In closing, he appealed to Cabell's loyalty to himself, reminding Cabell,

> If any member of our College of Visitors could justifiably withdraw from this sacred duty, it would be my self, who "quadragenis stipendiis jam-dudum peractis" [having already completed forty years of service] have neither vigor of body or mind left to keep the field. but I will die in the last ditch. and so, I hope, you will, my friend. . . . nature will not give you a second life wherein to atone for the omissions of this. pray then, dear and very dear Sir, do not think of deserting us; but view the sacrifices which seem to stand in your way, as the lesser duties, and such as ought to be postponed to this, the greatest of all. continue with us in these holy labors, until, having seen their accomplishment, we may say with old Simeon, "nunc dimittis, Domine" [Now lettest thy servant depart, O Lord].[58]

In regard to this manipulative appeal, Cabell wrote to John Hartwell Cocke, "If you can stand such a letter you must be made of steel."[59] Cabell was clearly not made of such metal to defy Jefferson because he not only remained in the legislature until 1835 but continued on the Board of Visitors, twice serving as rector of the university, until his death in 1856.

AFTER THE ESTABLISHMENT of the University of Virginia in 1819, a major financial obstacle remained, owing to the escalating and unparalleled costs of the building program. This endeavor represented one of the largest government-funded works projects at the time, other than the construction of Washington, D.C., and the Erie Canal. The total cost of opening the university in 1825 was $308,673, with the Rotunda alone costing over $60,000.[60] Virginia was simultaneously facing one of the worst economic and financial crises in its history owing to the financial crash of 1819 and a parallel depression in the main export market of Europe. Even friends and allies balked at the expensive, ornate buildings, which far exceeded the cost of any of the other universities in the United States. Whereas most universities, such as the University of North Carolina and Transylvania University, began with the construction of one building, Jefferson insisted that his university would not open until his entire architectural plan for dormitories, hotels, and faculty pavilions was in place. In 1822, Cabell warned him that the charge of extravagance was now on the lips of even the "intelligent circle of society."[61] The *Niles Register* in 1826, in an article published soon after the opening of the university, charged that the goodwill of the state "had been frittered away by the extravagant demands."[62]

Dismissing what he characterized as the "ignorance, malice, egoism, fanaticism, religious, political & local perversities" of his opponents, Jefferson and his allies managed to overcome the financial obstacles, even though many of the original donations and pledges, some of them in kind as services or goods, did not materialize in the wake of the economic slump.[63] For each building, Jefferson personally submitted all the cost estimates, which were always well below the actual amounts eventually required. He was intent on completing the buildings of the university before the arrival of the first students, submitting cost estimates piecemeal and keeping back the most expensive building, the Rotunda, until the very end. An anonymous author, writing under the pseudonym of an "American Citizen" in the *Richmond Enquirer*, described a visit to Monticello where he found Jefferson gloating over his deception of the General Assembly. According to the author of the article, Jefferson indiscreetly admitted that he had "teased" the legislature by seeking financial aid for six or seven successive sessions. When asked "why he did not apply for as much at once as was required, so as to give the government no further trouble," Jefferson replied jocosely, "*no one liked to have more than one hot potato at a time crammed down his throat.*"[64] Less than five months before his death, Jefferson did not deny the meeting but privately expressed "the pain which this unfaithful version and betrayment of private conversation has given me."[65]

Jefferson and the Board of Visitors were reduced to accepting three bank loans of $60,000 each in 1820, 1821, and 1823, all authorized by the legislature on the surety of the annual $15,000 from the Literary Fund. With the prospect of needing sixteen years to pay off the total loans of $180,000, the board hoped that the state would forgive the loans so that the university could open sooner. Jefferson braced Cabell not to give up "this important idea" when they were so near to success, "to stop where we are is to abandon our high hopes and to become suitors to Yale and Harvard for their secondary characters [faculty] to become our first." He asked rhetorically, "Have we been laboring then merely to get up another Hampden-Sydney or Lexington?"[66] By January 1823, Jefferson thought that the university was "advanced to the point, from which it must and will carry itself through; and it will strengthen daily."[67] By December, their efforts were not only crowned with success, but they obtained an additional $50,000 for library books and scientific equipment.

Just months before his death, Jefferson was widely criticized for recruiting the majority of the university faculty from Britain. He complained that he had been "squibbed for this" by disappointed applicants in America.[68] Indignant newspaper articles argued that he could have found professors at half the trouble and cost in New England or at an even shorter distance in Pennsylvania. "Mr. Jefferson," wrote one, "might as well have said that his taverns and dormitories should not be built with American bricks." An-other article asserted that "this sending of a commission to Europe to en-gage professors for a new university is, we think, one of the greatest insults the American people have received." It was likened to taking coals to New-castle. An article appeared in the *Central Gazette* in Charlottesville titled "Imported Professors." It quoted northern newspapers "expressing indigna-tion at what they term the 'importation of professors'" but went on to lam-poon this sudden abhorrence by "the patriotic editors of New England" for importations from Old England. The *Central Gazette* reminded its readers that during the Embargo of 1814 and Hartford Convention, the northern press "would not only have freely imported professors, but also English leg-islators, governors and rulers." It associated their newfound distrust of Brit-ain with their fondness for high tariff duties against British imports, which worked to the detriment of Virginia.[69]

THE QUESTION REMAINS, why did it become so urgent for Jefferson in his retirement to found and build the University of Virginia? When he first be-came involved with the project in 1814, he was seventy-one years old and well aware that he had little time to achieve the educational vision he thought so essential to the survival of the republic. He worried about the quality of political leadership at both the state and federal levels, fearing "that there was some fatal flaw in the system of representation, since it failed to bring the wisdom of the country into its councils."[70] At the height of the Missouri Crisis in 1820, he claimed that he now believed the "useless sacrifice of them-selves, by the generation of '76. to acquire self government and happiness to their country, is to be thrown away by the unwise and unworthy passions of their sons," calling it an act of "treason against the hopes of the world."[71] The Missouri Crisis was one of the first major sectional divisions over slavery that polarized politics between the North and South.

Jefferson thought that the state of Virginia had fallen far behind in ed-ucation in relation to other states, which had progressed since the revolu-tion: "What is her education now? where is it? the little we have we import, like beggars, from other states; or import their beggars to bestow on us their miserable crumbs." With a total of only about 150 students annually attending the three colleges in the state, he thought it imperative that the Old Dominion be saved "from the degradation of becoming the Barbary of the union."[72] Thanks to the establishment of Transylvania University, Jefferson protested that even Kentucky, "our daughter, planted since Virginia was a distinguished state," had a university with fourteen professors and upwards of two hundred students.[73] Repeating Bacon's dictum that "knowledge is power," he warned that Virginians were "sinking into the Barbarism of our Indian aborigines, and expect like them to oppose by ignorance the overwhelming mass of sciences by which we shall be surrounded." In relation to the public school initiatives in New York, he lamented, "What a pygmy to this Virginia is become!"[74]

In Virginia, population growth had slowed while western migration accelerated after the War of 1812. Seeking better economic opportunities, some of Jefferson's own grandchildren contemplated moving west with their families, including his namesake Thomas Jefferson Randolph.[75] The War of 1812 dramatically demonstrated the weakness of Virginia in relation to New England in terms of their relative lobbying power for troops and resources from Washington. Despite the fact that a Virginian, James Madison, was in the White House, the federal government concerned itself much more with the defense of New England than that of Virginia. The commonwealth was additionally being eclipsed demographically by New York and Pennsylvania, with a resulting shift in the balance of power in favor of the North in the U.S. Congress. Furthermore, the state was less economically vibrant and prosperous than either New York or Pennsylvania. Jefferson's native state achieved nothing comparable to the Erie Canal (1825), whose opening coincided with the end of an era of the "Virginia Dynasty" and the ascent of John Quincy Adams of Massachusetts to the White House. Jefferson found it galling to receive a letter from his favorite granddaughter, Ellen Coolidge, a newlywed living in Boston, that "the southern states could not begin to match the prosperity and the improvement" of the northern states.[76] Furthermore, the elite of the younger generation were going to colleges in the northeastern states, especially Princeton and Yale, where Jefferson feared they would be contaminated by religious fanatics and Federalists.

Before 1821, even when the construction of the university was already well along, Jefferson made no mention of any concern about the influence of radical northern abolitionists on southern students. Instead, he associated northern colleges with religious indoctrination and Federalism. In the election of 1800, Massachusetts and Connecticut still had a religious establishment, with state support for the Congregational church. The clergymen

teaching at northern universities were among the most vociferous opponents of Jefferson. In his *Remarks on the Review of Inchiquin's Letters* (1815),
the Reverend Timothy Dwight, president of Yale, identified Jeffersonians
as one of the three greatest dangers to the country, along with Napoleon
and British Jacobins. Dedicating his *Remarks* to British conservative George
Canning, Dwight wrote, "There is not, I presume, an Englishman, who regards the character and politics, of *Mr. Jefferson* and *Mr. Madison*, with less
approbation than myself."[77] Like many Federalists, he opposed the War of
1812 against Britain. In a brief "essay on New England's religious intolerance" (1816), anonymously published in the *Richmond Enquirer*, Jefferson
denounced the "pious young monks from Harvard and Yale." He revealingly
referred to northern colleges as seminaries, a word more commonly applied
to divinity and theological training schools.[78]

Jefferson also used economic arguments on behalf of the university in a
period when the northern economy was booming in relation to the South.
Despite being a Federalist, Joseph Caldwell, president of the University of
North Carolina, complained that "forcing our citizens to send their sons
to Northern Colleges sends out streams of wealth, and increases the advantages they already have over us."[79] Jefferson and other southern leaders deployed many of the same arguments against studying in the North
that the revolutionary generation had made against American students attending colleges in Britain. Citing personal experience, John Holt Rice, educated at Yale and Princeton, wrote that southern students conceived "an
incurable disgust at all that was Virginian, and nothing could be heard from
them but censures of the laws, the politics, the manners and the customs of
Virginia."[80]

Only in the aftermath of the Missouri Compromise, in what he dramatically likened to a terrifying "fire bell in the night," did Jefferson write a series of letters warning of the dangers of southern students being exposed
to radical abolitionists in northern colleges.[81] These letters are now cited
as evidence that he founded the university to protect and expand slavery.
The Missouri Compromise allowed slavery to expand into Missouri, but it
excluded slavery from Maine and the northern territory obtained west of
the Mississippi in the Louisiana Purchase. Jefferson admitted that "in the
gloomiest moment of revolutionary war I never had any apprehension equal
to what I feel from this source."[82] In February 1821, he wrote to James Breckenridge, with somewhat inflated figures, inferring that "we send 300,000.D.
a year to Northern seminaries for instruction of our sons imbibing opinions
and principles in discord with those of their own country, this canker is eat-

ing on the vitals of our existence, and if not arrested at once will be beyond remedy."[83] He similarly wrote to fellow Virginian John Taylor of Caroline, a pioneer theorist of southern states' rights, that "these [northern] seminaries are no longer proper for Southern and Western students. the signs of the times admonish us to call them home."[84] Jefferson's panicked response to the debates over the Missouri Compromise seems to accord with the view that he was becoming more reactionary and provincial in old age.

Yet the argument that Jefferson was founding the university to defend and even expand slavery is at odds with his proclaimed views in favor of emancipation against a system that he had called an abomination. He had always believed that the Revolution would only be secure if followed by a moral revolution which included the elimination of slavery. Historian Stuart Leibiger suggests that Jefferson's impassioned letters about the influence of northern abolitionists on southern students was an attempt to exploit the hysteria surrounding the Missouri Compromise. According to Leibiger, his real aim was to secure the support of three representatives, including James Breckenridge, to vote to approve $60,000 to complete the building of the University of Virginia.[85] A Federalist, Breckenridge was a political opponent whose support Jefferson had courted following the meeting of the commissioners at Rockfish Gap. When the state legislature approved the loan and later converted it into a gift, Jefferson not coincidentally became less alarmed about the compromise. Cameron Addis additionally suggests that Jefferson "used sectionalism to deflect from religious opposition" as a "strategy that resonated in the Virginia legislature."[86] Just before his excited letters to Breckenridge and Taylor, Jefferson told Albert Gallatin, his former secretary of the treasury, that the Missouri issue might even prove beneficial by bringing "the necessity of some plan of general emancipation and deportation more home to the minds of the people than it ever has been before."[87] During the Missouri Crisis, Jefferson's often hyperbolic language was consistent with his responses to earlier national crises that threatened the union. His impassioned style reflected his strong emotional evaluations, which he had demonstrated in response to the Alien and Sedition Acts by the secessionist tone of his Kentucky Resolutions (1798).

STUDYING IN THE NORTH may actually have had little impact on the views of young southerners about slavery, since northern universities were all too often beneficiaries of slavery and hardly bastions of antislavery sentiments.[88] John C. Calhoun, the leading proponent of nullification and secession, had graduated from Yale. Historian Samuel Eliot Morison likened the treatment of abolitionists before the 1840s at Harvard to that of communists in the 1950s. Appointed professor of divinity at Harvard in 1829, the Reverend Henry Ware was attacked in the Boston press for founding an antislavery society in Cambridge. After fleeing the Prussian government, who demanded his extradition from the University of Basel, Professor Karl Follen was not renewed as professor of German at Harvard, a rejection his friends attributed to his antislavery stance, espoused in his "Address to the People of the United States" (1834).[89] Under the presidency of Timothy Dwight (1795–1817), a recent university report finds that Yale produced more proslavery clergy than any other college in the nation. Although equivocal on the subject of slavery, Dwight wrote in 1815 that the southern planter "who receives his slaves from his parents by inheritance, certainly deserves no censure for holding them. He has no agency in procuring them: and the law does not permit him to set them free."[90] Southerners continued to attend northern colleges and universities until well into the 1850s. At the opening of Princeton's 1860–61 term, they represented a third of the student body.[91]

As long as slavery continued to exist in some northern states, Jefferson regarded slavery as a national problem and resented the imputation that the South was purely to blame. He opposed the means rather than the ends of northern abolitionists, fearing they would dangerously divide the states and jeopardize the future of the union. In his mind, the radicalism of northern abolitionists represented a "treason against the hopes of the world" by undermining the republican system of government and the achievements of 1776.[92] Jefferson thought them a front for vestigial Tories seeking to unite the North and revive the fortunes of the Federalist Party. "Despairing of ever rising again under the old division of whig and tory," they had artificially divided slaveholding and non-slaveholding states. He saw the issue as a question of power rather than morality. Indeed, he told Gallatin, if there was any morality in the Missouri Crisis, it lay with the South. That said, since the abolition of the Atlantic slave trade in 1808, Virginia had become the leading exporter of slaves to the West and Deep South. The profits from slavery helped offset losses from soil exhaustion and a volatile export market. By appealing to the fear that northern abolitionists would indoctrinate southern students and by siding with opponents of the Missouri Compromise, Jefferson had allowed himself to become complicit with the proslavery South.

During his retirement years, Jefferson was becoming more fearful about the future of republican government and less utopian. Like Francis Fukuyama, who in 1992 proclaimed the end of history and the ultimate triumph of western liberal democracy, Jefferson had similarly thought that the American Revolution would be the catalyst for republican revolutions throughout the world and that the rest of the world would eventually become like the United States. After 1815, such optimism seemed naive. He observed instead counterrevolutions in which monarchies reappeared throughout Europe. Even Jefferson conceded that the French Revolution had failed with the rise of Napoleon. Britain was ascendant, not France. Its empire encompassed a fifth of the global population. In light of these developments, the survival of the republican system became all the more vital to Jefferson. He looked to Virginia to preserve its true ideology from contamination by pseudo-aristocrats, bankers, moneyed corporations, and religious fanatics. Virginia had led the South, and its revitalization was essential for the future of republicanism throughout the world and the survival of "the spirit of 1776."

Long after the Hartford Convention (December 15, 1814–January 5, 1815), the last hurrah of the New England Federalists, Jefferson continued to believe that the Federalists represented a threat to the union and that they were actually gaining a "vast accession of strength from their younger recruits," who had "nothing in them of the feelings or principles of '76." As late as 1825, he argued that the Federalists aimed to create government by aristocracy, "founded on banking institutions and monied in corporations . . . riding and ruling over the plundered ploughman and beggared yeomanry" as a steppingstone toward monarchy.[93] Jefferson's fears of the Federalists were not unfounded. Unlike the North, their support continued unabated among a minority in Virginia and elsewhere in the South who opposed the War of 1812. They made up a third of the voters in the western districts.[94] At the national level, Jefferson saw the work of the Federalists in the contemporary federal judicial judgments, enlarging central government power. He was especially alarmed by the decisions of Chief Justice John Marshall, such as *McCulloch v. Maryland* (1819), a landmark case that prohibited the state of Maryland from taxing the Bank of the United States.[95] This ruling coincided with the Missouri Crisis. Fearing that the Federalists were rewriting and twisting the history of the American Revolution, Jefferson began to draft his autobiography to give his own version of the events of the 1790s.[96]

As we have seen, Jefferson regarded Presbyterians as interchangeable with Federalists. Charles Fenton Mercer, the author of the alternative education bill for Virginia, represented everything that Jefferson despised: a graduate of Princeton, a Presbyterian, and a Federalist. Mercer championed government-funded infrastructure projects, roads, canals, and banks.

Even as a Federalist in Virginia, he was still able to win an election to the U.S. House of Representatives in 1816. Furthermore, although the Federalist Party was in reality heading toward extinction, Presbyterianism was expanding its influence over higher education in the South. Beginning in the 1790s, the religious revivals in the Northeast had made slower progress in the South. At this time, the Northeast was the "Bible Belt," not the South. This situation was rapidly changing in the early nineteenth century, however, with almost half the white population regularly seeking out evangelical preachers by the 1830s.[97] Although the real growth was among the Methodists and Baptists, Jefferson was more worried about the Presbyterians because of their influence over education in the South. He believed that Presbyterians would spread antirepublican and authoritarian ideas that might undermine the achievements of the American Revolution.

Although Jefferson's mantra of states' rights would become little more than a cover for slavery by 1860, this was not the case in 1819 when other issues besides slavery divided the South and North. These included the high tariff levels charged on imported goods from Europe, reaching their highest levels in the 1820s, which benefited manufacturers in the North to the disadvantage of the agrarian South, where planters relied on cheaper manufactured goods imported from Britain. It was tariffs that were the primary cause of the nullification crisis in South Carolina (1832–33). Between 1818 and 1821, owing to a simultaneous recession in Europe and the impact of British Corn Laws, the value of Virginian exports fell 36.8 percent compared to an average of a 15.7 percent decline nationally. The financial crisis heightened southern fears about northern domination and intensified their resentment of tariffs. In his presidential campaign in 1860, Abraham Lincoln threatened to raise the tariff but it was then not such a critical cause of sectionalism.

Finally, compounding their problems and coinciding with the Missouri Crisis, Virginians experienced one of the worst financial crashes in their history in 1819. Jefferson blamed the depression on the northern Federalist Hamiltonian system of paper money, credit, and the Bank of the United States.[98] To a fellow planter, a rising politician in Albemarle, he wrote on "the distresses of our country" in 1819, blaming the flood and then ebb of bank paper.[99] After several years of poor harvests, the crash was devastating for Jefferson's personal finances and doomed him to bankruptcy. The ultimate blow for Jefferson came when his friend and political ally Wilson Cary Nicholas defaulted on a loan for which Jefferson had acted as guarantor; as a result, Jefferson became liable for a significant portion of the money owed. He had to mortgage essentially all his property to cover it. Sharing in the losses caused by the financial crisis, James Madison was simultaneously unable to secure a loan from the Bank of the United States. Their fellow member of the Board of Visitors, John Hartwell Cocke, had trouble paying for the building of his neoclassical plantation house at Bremo.

THE 1819 CRASH was one of the worst depressions in the history of the state, but Jefferson still overcame financial obstacles and all other hurdles to build the University of Virginia.[100] It gave "employment to my remaining years, and quite enough for my senile faculties," in what he regarded as his "last act of usefulness."[101] Jefferson likened himself to "discharging the odious function of a physician pouring medecine down the throat of a patient insensible of needing it." He was confident "of the future approbation of posterity, and of the inestimable effect we shall have produced in the elevation of our country, by what we have done."[102] He was proud of having helped to create an institution that would "raise its youth to an order of science unequalled in any other state," whose superiority would be all "the greater from the free range of mind encoraged there, and the restraint imposed at other seminaries by the shackles of a domineering hierarchy, and a bigoted adhesion to antient habits."[103] He did not doubt that its "reputation once established will maintain itself for ages."[104] As he reflected on the prospects of the university, less than a year before it opened, Cabell was jubilant, asking Jefferson, "How can this State and nation ever repay you, my dear sir, for this great and good work! What must be your feelings in contemplating this precious work of your hands!"[105] For the past several years, Jefferson had only wanted to see it open and would then "not ask an hour more of life."[106]

5

The Academical Village

"Jour Heureux" (Happy Day) is an aria from the opera *Dardanus* by Antonio Sacchini, first performed in Paris in October 1786. That same month, Thomas Jefferson gave a copy to Maria Cosway, adding, "I send you the song I promised. bring me in return its subject, *Jours Heureux!* were I a songster I should sing it to all these words 'Dans ces lieux qu'elle tarde a rendre?'[In these places that it takes so long to return]." He asked her to learn it and to "sing it with feeling." The aria had a refrain,

> Happy Day(s), enchanting hope! Charming prize
> of so tender a love.
> I will see it, hear it,
> I will find happiness again.
> In this spacious scene, where she tarries to show herself,
> by what new ill do I feel bothered?
> Moment that I've so much desired! Ah wait no longer.[1]

The two had first met in early August when they were introduced by the American artist John Trumbull in the Paris grain market at the Halle aux Blé, where Jefferson had gone to examine the architecture as a possible model for a proposed market in Richmond.[2] A widower of four years and serving as the U.S. minister plenipotentiary to France, Jefferson was then forty-three and she a twenty-seven-year-old Anglo-Italian artist. She was accompanied by Richard Cosway, her British husband, an artist known for his miniatures who enjoyed the patronage of the Prince of Wales.

Upon meeting Maria Cosway, Jefferson immediately claimed urgent business and canceled his appointment with a duchess, and Cosway similarly dispatched "lying messengers" to her friends in order that they might spend the remaining hours of the day together in a whirlwind sightseeing tour.

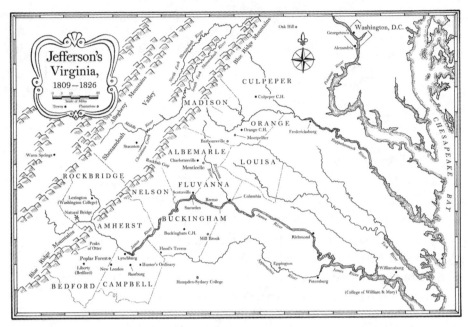

Jefferson's Virginia, 1809–1826. (Courtesy of the Thomas Jefferson Foundation at Monticello)

Jefferson later described this first encounter "as long as a Lapland summer day," in which his rapture at her company was mixed with the excitement of seeing the "wonderful piece of architecture" represented by the Halle aux Blé, which vied with Maria Cosway herself as "the most superb thing on earth!" and was worth more than all that he had seen until then in Paris.[3] Fascinated by neoclassical domes and aware of the problems of their construction in general, he was especially transported by the distinctive dome, whose method of building he would later adopt for the Rotunda: the jewel in the crown of his architectural masterpiece at the University of Virginia, based on the Pantheon in Rome.[4]

Completed just four years earlier, the Halle aux Blé was used for celebrations, including both festivities marking the signing of the Treaty of Paris that ended the American Revolution in 1783 and a commemoration of Benjamin Franklin. Arthur Young, a British writer on agriculture and economics, described it as "by far the finest thing" in Paris, "a vast rotunda, the roof entirely of wood, upon a new principle of carpentry . . . so well planned and so admirably executed that I know of no public building that exceeds it in either France or England."[5] Located on land owned by the city of Paris near the site of the Church of Saint-Eustache, the 130-foot-wide dome was designed by the architects J. G. Legrand and Jacques Molinos to cover the circular building, using laminated wood held together by mortise and tenon, a method of construction introduced by the Renaissance architect Philibert Delorme. They adapted Delorme's lightweight wooden-frame structure by adding ribs supporting glass spaces in a pattern that Jefferson described as honeycombed, permitting natural light to radiate and flood the interior, as it would do through an oculus in his design for the Rotunda at the University of Virginia.

Obsessed over the course of forty years with this dome, Jefferson would propose a version of it for the building of the President's House in Philadelphia (1792), together with a barrel-vaulted roof proposal for a naval drydock (1802) and the U.S. Capitol's House of Representatives (1804). He possessed a copy of Delorme's *Inventions pour bien bastir et a petits fraiz* (New Inventions for Building Well and at Small Expense) in his library and included the book in his recommendations for works on architecture for the university library. When the architect Benjamin Henry Latrobe advised against adopting the Delorme method for the U.S. Capitol, Jefferson wrote, "I cannot express to you the regret I feel on the subject of renouncing of the Halle au bled lights of the capitol dome. that single circumstance was to constitute the distinguishing merit of the room, & would solely have made it the handsomest room in the world without a single exception."[6] Substituting nails to hold together the laminations, Jefferson adapted the Delorme method in the building of the domes at Monticello and the Rotunda.

Corresponding with Maria Cosway intermittently until his death, Jefferson outlined his architectural plans for the university, in which he wrote of his vision of "an academical village." The subject was of mutual interest since she had founded a school for girls in Lyon in 1803 and, at the behest of Napoleon's uncle Cardinal Joseph Fesch, another in Paris in 1809. Afterward, she founded yet another school for girls, aged between six and twelve, within a convent at Lodi in Italy. Like Jefferson, Cosway's pedagogical method emphasized the individual and was indebted to the child-centric thinking of the Swiss education reformer Johann Heinrich Pestalozzi.

In April 1819, the same year as the bill creating the University of Virginia, Maria Cosway wrote of her everlasting esteem, admiration, friendship, and gratitude for Jefferson. She wrote of her schools and the consolation that she found in the convent at Lodi while acknowledging, "OH! how often have I thought of America!" She had returned to England to nurse her estranged husband, who was suffering after two paralytic strokes, admitting that her head told her correspondence with Jefferson was enough but that her heart wished for more.[7]

For his part, in October 1822, Jefferson had written to Cosway that their "sympathies of our earlier days harmonise" and that he hoped the university he was constructing would repay the generosity of Virginia's "legislature by improving the virtue and science of their country, already blest with a soil and climate emulating those of your favorite Lodi." He explained that he had designed its buildings and the system of instruction. Under construction for the previous four years, he assured her that "it would be thought a handsome & classical thing in Italy." He had preferred "the plan of an Academical village rather than that of a single, massive structure." The plurality of buildings allowed for diversity and "varieties of the finest samples of architecture," which made the university "a model of beauty, original and unique." Furthermore, his ability to view it from Monticello meant that this "splendid object" was "a constant gratification to my sight." There was "still one building to erect," he told her, noting that it would be constructed "on the principle of your Pantheon, a Rotunda like that, but of half its diameter and height only." He wished she "could recall some of your by-past years and seal it with your approbation."[8]

Upon learning from Jefferson about the building of the University of Virginia, she replied, "The work is worthy of you" and you are "worthy of such enjoyment. Nothing, I think, is more useful to Mankind than a good Education," adding that she wished she could come and learn from him.[9] The walls of the grand salon at Lodi were decorated with scenes from the four corners of the globe, but one wall was incomplete with just the portrayal of a hill on which she intended to display Monticello and the University of Virginia. She died twelve years after Jefferson.

IN A NOVEL, based on firsthand acquaintance, Margaret Bayard Smith portrayed Jefferson as saying that "architecture is my delight, and putting up, and pulling down, one of my favourite amusements."[10] He was a self-taught architect whose interest stemmed from his student days, when he made a chance purchase of a treatise on classical architecture from a drunken cabinet-maker whose premises were near the college gate at William and Mary.[11] Jefferson rejected earlier styles of colonial and Georgian architecture, which were only loosely based on classical sources and thought by him to lack proportion. He preferred neoclassical designs that represented a system of architecture more strictly based on sources from antiquity, attracted by the mathematical precision of the proportions, their elegance and coherence. He relied on books to inform him of classical designs, most notably those of Andrea Palladio, the sixteenth-century Italian architect whose four-volume work, first published in 1570, illustrated and described the five orders of classical architecture of ancient Greece and Rome. Between 1784 and 1789, Jefferson's travels in Europe took him not only throughout France but also to northeastern Italy, where he was able to see firsthand examples of the ruins of Roman buildings. As the social reformer the Duke de Rochefoucauld-Liancourt observed in 1796, "Jefferson had studied taste and the fine arts in books only. His travels in Europe have supplied him with models."[12]

Jefferson regarded antiquity as furnishing the "finest models for imitation; and he who studies and imitates them most nearly, will nearest approach the perfection of the art."[13] The elegant simplicity of neoclassical architecture well represented republican values, in contrast to the self-conscious grandeur of monarchical and aristocratic Europe. During his time in France, he described how he had gazed "whole hours . . . like a lover at his mistress" at the Maison Carrée, or "square house," the ancient Roman Temple in Nîmes, which would be the model for his design of the Capitol Building in Richmond. He wrote of being "violently smitten with the Hôtel de Salm," with its impressive dome, going daily to watch it being built from the Tuileries Garden. From Lyon to Nîmes, he was "nourished with the Remains of Roman grandeur" and "immersed in antiquities from morning to night," to the extent that he felt as if Roman society was still "existing in all the spendour of its empire" and was "filled with alarms" at the prospect of tribal invasions returning "us to our original barbarism."[14] As he wrote to Maria Cosway, he "took a peep into Elysium" when he visited northeastern Italy, seeing Turin, Milan, and Genoa but not getting as far as Vicenza, Venice, or Rome.[15]

Jefferson wanted the new nation to possess examples of fine architecture like those in Europe. He wished to shape and improve the artistic taste of fellow Americans, writing to James Madison from France that "you see that I am an enthusiast on the subject of the arts but it is an enthusiasm of which I am not ashamed as its object is to improve the taste of my countrymen, to increase their reputation, to reconcile them to the respect of the world & procure them its praise."[16] Born a member of the provincial elite on the peripheries of the British Empire, Jefferson was very sensitive to the alleged inferiority of America to Europe; it motivated him to write the *Notes on the State of Virginia*. In that work, he was overly critical of the architecture of his native state, describing the buildings of his own alma mater as "rude, mis-shapen piles, which, but they have roofs, would be taken for brick-kilns," referring to the rather attractive Wren building at the College of William and Mary and the similarly aesthetically pleasing mental hospital in Williamsburg.[17] Indeed, he regarded the architecture of Virginia as the worst in America.[18]

Despite being self-taught, Jefferson was one of the earliest and finest architects in America. When he sold his library to Congress in 1815, he owned some forty-nine books on architecture. He had a multipurpose drafting table, which he used for his architectural drawings, located in his library at Monticello.[19] From England, he purchased drafting instruments that he used to make hundreds of architectural drawings, often using "drawing paper" (graph paper) which he explained, "being laid off in squares . . . saves the necessity of using the rule and dividers in all rectangular draughts."[20] He designed several public buildings besides the University of Virginia. As early as 1771–72, Jefferson drew a plan, although never adopted, for an extension to the College of William and Mary. He designed the Virginia State Capitol in Richmond (1785), for which he commissioned Jean-Pierre Fouquet to create the first documented architectural model in the United States. With the design of the state capitol, Jefferson began the tradition of designing American public buildings in the neoclassical style based on the best models from antiquity. Jefferson submitted his own anonymous plans for the President's House (White House) and for the U.S. Capitol. He designed the houses of other planters, such as Barboursville, and his own octagonal home at Poplar Forest, which he began working on in 1806. Much smaller than Monticello, he thought that some might prefer it as "more proportioned to the faculties of a private citizen."[21] Jefferson's contributions as an architect only began to receive posthumous recognition with the publication of a limited edition, folio-sized volume by Fiske Kimball, *Thomas Jefferson, Architect* (1916). Before its publication, it was not even widely known that Jefferson had indeed been the architect of the University of Virginia.

BY THE TIME he began building the future university, Jefferson had over forty years of experience designing, remodeling, enlarging, and overseeing the construction of what he called his "essay in architecture" at Monticello.[22] He had begun building his first home there before the American Revolution, with work commencing on leveling the site in 1768. The interior was still incomplete when he departed for France in 1784. After returning from Europe, Jefferson demolished much of the first house and started to rebuild.

Between 1797 and 1809, he enlarged the rooms for comfort and convenience, increasing the natural light and ventilation by adding French doors, skylights, triple-hung sashed windows, alcove beds, and indoor privies. Monticello included many elements that Jefferson repeated in his design for the university. His use of different classical orders in each room at Monticello corresponded to the different designs of the pavilions for the professors in the center of the university, known as the Lawn. He added a dome at his house using the Delorme building technique, which he replicated in the building of the Rotunda. Even Monticello's layout, with the terraces and house flanked by service buildings in L shapes, influenced by Palladio's Villa Saraceno, resonated with his later plans for the Lawn.[23]

Even after the laying of the foundation stone in 1817, Jefferson's thinking about the architecture of a university continued to change. The layout today is not what he originally envisaged. He accepted suggestions, worked with other architects, improvised, and made changes even during the construction process. Nevertheless, Jefferson's various architectural plans for a university are linked by his core concept of an "academic village." As early as 1771, his unsigned plan for the College of William and Mary included a scheme to complete the unfinished quadrangle by adding an arcaded corridor (loggia) around an open courtyard and six faculty apartments of two rooms each, reflecting his idea of a residential university for both faculty and undergraduates.[24] This early plan involved extending the main building, an approach that became anathema to him later. When discussing ideas for a university in Virginia with state representative Littleton W. Tazewell in 1805, Jefferson cautioned against building a single large building "sufficient to contain the whole institution," since such structures "are always ugly, inconvenient, exposed to the accident of fire, and bad in cases of infection." He advised instead a series of buildings for faculty residences and student dormitories "connected by covered ways of which the rooms of students should open," concluding that "in fact a University should not be an house but a village."[25]

When advising on the architecture of East Tennessee College in 1810, Jefferson similarly wrote that he considered "the plan followed in this country, but not in others, of making one large & expensive building, as unfortunately erroneous." Nassau Hall at the College of New Jersey (Princeton) was the largest building in America in 1756. It contained the chapel, library, dining hall, kitchen, and dormitory rooms. The Wren building fulfilled similar functions at William and Mary. Jefferson proposed instead that each professor be given a small and separate lodge, containing a hall below for his class and two chambers above for himself: "The whole of these arranged around an open square would make it what it should be in fact, an academical village." Such an arrangement would be preferable to the common dens "of noise, of filth, & of fetid air," instead affording "that quiet retirement so friendly to study." Using the term "academical village," Jefferson envisaged a community dispersed among small buildings in which professors lived among and even dined with the students, an enlightened model of intergenerational relations. He aimed to create a familial setting to enhance the role of the professors as mentors of the students. His plan recreated his own college experience with William Small, George Wythe, and Governor Francis Fauquier. It also reflected his dream of having some of the most brilliant of his friends living around him at Monticello, for their conversational skills and company, including James Monroe, James Madison, and William Short. Jefferson was additionally very much attracted to the health benefits of students living in the countryside in separate smaller buildings, less prone to the "dangers of fire, infection & tumult."[26]

In the summer of 1814, Jefferson's plan for building the Albemarle Academy contained many of the key principles that would later be enshrined in the layout of the Lawn. The design for the academy was so elaborate that it defies credulity that it was intended for a mere grammar school, and indeed he emphasized that it could be enlarged. As with the plan for a state university that he outlined to Tazewell, he proposed nine pavilions (houses for professors) flanked by ten dormitories on each side, with covered walkways surrounding a square with one side open, symbolically distinguishing the design from the enclosed quadrangles of religious institutions and medieval colleges.

Following the decision to begin construction of Central College but lacking the copies of Palladio that he had sold to the Library of Congress, Jefferson wrote for advice to Dr. William Thornton, the architect who had won the design competition for the U.S. Capitol. He enclosed a rough sketch of the proposed layout of the university. When Thornton submitted a uniform design for the pavilions, Jefferson wrote to the other chief architect of Washington, D.C., the English-born Benjamin Henry Latrobe, who had modified Thornton's plan for the Capitol and designed the porticos at the President's House. Latrobe paid homage to the plan from Jefferson, claiming to "have derived important professional improvement from the entirely novel plan of an Academy suggested by you." He had "long considered the common plan of a College as most radically defective.—In your design the principal evils of the usual *barrack* arrangement appear to be avoided."[27]

Receiving drawings from Latrobe, Jefferson in turn adopted his idea of a principal building at the top of the Lawn, which would become the Rotunda.

As with his political ideas, Jefferson's architectural designs were not derivative of any one model but represented an assimilation of various archetypes. The three-sided square was similar to the ground plan of the College of William and Mary. Other influences included the French royal chateau and gardens at Marly, where six pavilions flanked this residence on either side of a wide expanse of grass; the ground plan of the Hôtel de Salm (now the Palais de la Légion d'Honneur); and the ancient Carthusian monastery of Certosa di Pavia, which Jefferson visited in Italy in 1787. Architectural historian Bruce Boucher has also proposed that Palladio's reconstruction of the Baths of Agrippa "played a decisive role in Jefferson's design for the Lawn."[28] Herbert Baxter Adams regarded the university as a neoclassical version of a medieval monastery in which the arcades reminded him of the cloistered corridors of some of the colleges of Oxford and Cambridge. Jefferson shared a guidebook of Oxford and Cambridge with Joseph C. Cabell and had an illustrative set of plates of the two English universities at Poplar Forest.[29] However, in contrast to monasteries and medieval colleges, he did not fully enclose the university, possibly symbolic of his concept of an open forum of ideas. Although the view is now obscured by Cabell Hall, the university looked out southward toward the mountains, the frontier, and the future. Jefferson had to modify his original square design owing to the unsuitability of the site, which was a runner-up to the location that he had originally planned further east (near the modern intersection of Rugby Road and Preston Avenue). The new site had a rocky ridge at the top whose peak became the site of the Rotunda. The ridge necessitated laying out the Lawn from north to south in three terraces, which he intended to be 255 feet long and 240 feet wide, but inaccurate digging and leveling by the workers caused the lengths to vary. He had to regroup the pavilions to create parallel rows of buildings in what are now the East and West Ranges.

Jefferson intended the university to provide a living education in classical architecture. They would introduce students to the five orders: Tuscan, Doric, Ionic, Corinthian, and Composite. A professor could take his students and "explain to them successively these samples of the several orders, their varieties, peculiarities, and accessory circumstances."[30] To the untutored eye, at first glance the university is a symmetric arrangement with parallel rows of five two-story pavilions facing each other on the east and west side of the Lawn, connected by one-story colonnades and student rooms. Its appearance is an optical illusion: each pavilion is different, varying in size, with unequal distances between them and distinctive facades that each represent one of the classical orders. As Jefferson explained to Thornton and Latrobe, the residences for the faculty should be "models of taste & good architecture, & of a variety of appearance, no two alike, so as to serve as specimens for the Architectural lectures."[31]

Although the styles of the pavilions intermingled on both sides of the Lawn, those designed in a pure classical form face pavilions embodying the more modern neoclassical features.[32] This opposition of ancient and neo-classical architectural styles is suggestive of a dialogue between the past and present, analogous to Jefferson's larger educational mission. However, the juxtaposition may have been due to accident, rather than design, because Jefferson only had access to Madison's copy of Palladio when he drew the plans for Pavilions VII, III, and V.[33] The pavilions were all identified by a Roman numeral, with even numbers on the east and odd on the west side of the Lawn. Pavilion I, on the west side, adjacent to the Rotunda, imitated the Doric design of Diocletian's baths in Rome. The pavilions appear to be two-story buildings, but they are in fact three levels, with a kitchen cellar. The top two rooms functioned as living quarters for the faculty, and the ground floor had a classroom. Distributed among the professors by lot, the pavilions additionally served as schools or departments, according to the subject of the professor in residence, with their students living in the adjoining dormitory rooms. The professors each had a yard providing workspace for enslaved laborers, whose inadequate living spaces were often in small, windowless rooms adjacent to the kitchen.[34]

Jefferson regarded the pavilions as both a recruitment and retention tool for faculty "in the hope of attaching them to the comforts of their situation and by that means prevent their being seduced from us by other institutions."[35] He seems to have assumed that the faculty would be bachelors and therefore did not provide sufficient living space for families, which the young Edward Everett, later president of Harvard University and governor of Massachusetts, criticized anonymously in the North American Review. Robley Dunglison, the first professor of medicine, who lived with his wife in Pavilion X, lamented that the pavilions would have been "more commodious had Mr. Jefferson consulted his excellent and competent daughter, Mrs Randolph, instead of planning the architectural exterior first, and leaving the interior to shift for itself." Dunglison complained that closets "would have interfered with the symmetry of the rooms or passages and hence there were none in most of the houses," which mirrored a longstanding argument of Martha Randolph with her father about the second floor of Monticello.

Dunglison told an amusing anecdote in which Jefferson, upon leaving one of the few pavilions that had a closet, unsuspectingly opened the door and walked into it.[36] The lecture halls were so inappropriate for science experiments and medicine that Dunglison successfully insisted Jefferson add an anatomical theater for dissecting cadavers. Contrary to Jefferson's plan of a resident faculty, John P. Emmet became the first professor to leave his pavilion, moving out with his wife, Mary Byrd, in 1834 to a home they built on nearby land.

As part of his concept of a village, containing smaller communities of students, Jefferson built six dining halls, which he called hotels, labeled by alphabetical capitals A through F. Uniformly designed in the Tuscan order, interconnected by brick arcades rather than colonnades, he located the hotels behind the pavilions, with three on the East Range and three on the West. He outsourced their operation by leasing them to independent contractors who acted as hotelkeepers, competing with one another, with responsibility for a minimum of twenty-five students each, among whom they lived with their own families and their enslaved servants. In contrast, the kitchen at Harvard fed two hundred students, making it the largest dining hall in New England.[37] Jefferson had wanted the first hotel to be managed by "some French family of good character, wherein it is proposed that the boarders shall be permitted to speak French only, with a view to their becoming familiarised to conversation in that language," anticipating the idea of a Maison Française.[38] Because of topological problems at the site and his desire to maintain aesthetic harmony, the hotels proved insufficient to accommodate the enslaved labor, who consequently lived in cramped and often unlit spaces.

The hotelkeepers were responsible for providing students with three meals a day, with a minimum of two different choices of meat and four vegetables at dinner. They were required to supply bedding and furniture in student rooms, which had at most two occupants, in contrast to the four or five students to each room in the dormitories at Hampden-Sydney, which were located in one building, Stewart Hall.[39] The managers of the hotels were required to maintain order among the students and report bad behavior. All domestic tasks were performed by enslaved servants: cleaning student rooms, lighting their fires, doing their laundry, bringing shaving water, polishing boots, making the beds, and running errands. The hotelkeepers could not charge more than one hundred dollars for ten and a half months of student board and lodgings. Owing to fewer students than expected enrolling in the early years and some failing to pay, the hotelkeepers found it difficult to make ends meet. The professors occasionally accused hotel-keepers of permitting gambling and drinking, probably for extra income. Indeed, in addition to being dining halls, these buildings also acted as societies, clubs, and assembly places for students.

Within a year, the board withdrew the right of students to select their preferred hotelkeeper. Thereafter, the proctor allocated them. As the sister of the proctor and mother of seven children, a Mrs. Carter Gray ran one of the most successful refectories at Hotel E, remaining the keeper until 1845. Known as "Mrs. Gray's Hotel," her husband, John Gray Jr., originally bought the lease as early as 1824. Known to drink and gamble with the students, he disappeared to Florida. By about 1830, a high proportion of students were living outside the university, and boardinghouses began to appear beyond its precincts in areas on Carr's Hill, named after one of the more successful such establishments run by Dabney S. Carr.

THOMAS JEFFERSON WAS omnipresent throughout the construction of the university. After building commenced in 1817, he rode every other day the five-mile distance to the site, usually via Secretary's Ford, crossing the Rivanna River at Moore's Creek, and continuing through what is now called Belmont. In 1819, at the age of seventy-five, he began making daily visits when John Hartwell Cocke joined him as a two-man subcommittee to oversee the building activities on behalf of the Board of Visitors. Jefferson initially sought to expedite construction because he wanted some buildings completed to help persuade the legislature to adopt what was still technically Central College as the University of Virginia. He wished to ensure that legislators provided the necessary funding by impressing them with "the prospect of its immediate operation."[40] From March 29 on, he was able to delegate some of the tasks of supervision to the newly appointed proctor, an experienced builder from Richmond named Arthur Spicer Brockenbrough, who had an office in the still-vacant Hotel D. Brockenbrough, however, preferred to operate out of the Monroe House, a former law office of James Monroe, who had once owned some eighty-eight acres of the university's site, now known as Monroe Hill.

With much of the university built by 1822, Jefferson commissioned Peter Maverick in New York to engrave 250 copies of a ground-plan of the university. Two years later, in anticipation of the opening of the university and with virtually all of the buildings complete, Jefferson ordered a revised version, accompanied by "An explanation of the ground plan of the University of Virginia," from Maverick. The engraving was part of his marketing

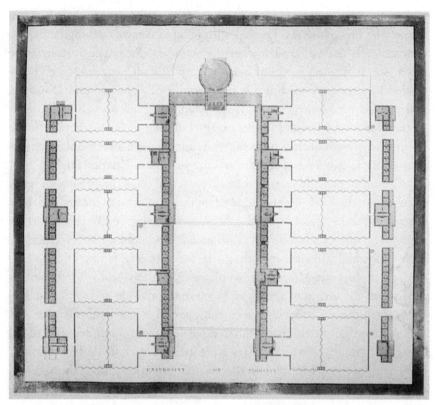

University of Virginia, engraved by Peter Maverick, 1825. (Courtesy of the Albert and Shirley Small Special Collection Library, University of Virginia)

strategy, giving the public its first visual impression of the university, selling copies to prospective students for fifty cents, and distributing it among members of the Virginia General Assembly. Parallel with his commissioning the revised ground-plan, Jefferson encouraged William Goodacre, a visiting Englishman who dined with him at Monticello, to do a drawing of the Lawn.[41]

In October 1822, Jefferson described the university as his "sole occupation." His ambitious architectural designs required the best skilled artisans; he regarded "ignorant workmen" as "always the dearest."[42] As soon as he had received permission from his board to begin construction in 1817, Jefferson hired two of the best workmen he had employed at Monticello: James Dinsmore and John Neilson, both of whom he regarded as "of the very first order both in their knolege in architecture, and in their practical abilities."[43] He had first encountered the Irishman James Dinsmore in Philadelphia in 1798 and subsequently employed him as a joiner for ten years at Monticello. This meant that Dinsmore was familiar with Jefferson's favorite design motifs as they appeared in Pavilion III, where he was the principal builder. Jefferson lured John Neilson, a native of Ireland, from Philadelphia in 1804 and contracted him to work for him for four years. Both Neilson and Dinsmore had worked on Montpelier for James Madison. Neilson had additionally worked for John Hartwell Cocke on the building of his plantation house, Bremo. Neilson's contract with the university proved so remunerative that he was able to buy several acres near Vinegar Hill in Charlottesville.[44]

Jefferson personally recruited bricklayers and sometimes went so far as to supervise the brick-making himself, in order to achieve the effect that he desired in the facades. He wrote and placed newspaper advertisements for carpenters and joiners in Richmond and Philadelphia. He corresponded with individual artisans, including the woodworker James Oldham, his former employee at Monticello, who worked on Pavilion I.[45] Jefferson arranged for the hiring of sculptors to carve the marble and stone, such as the Raggi brothers from Italy, who complained of the food provided and, in a rebuke that would have embarrassed Jefferson, reminded him of the superior manner in which artists were treated in Italy. When the local stone quarry proved inferior to the task, Jefferson organized the shipping of twenty-four Carrara marble capitols, each weighing between three to five tons, from Italy via New York to Richmond. The marbles were then transported by bateau along the James River to Scottsville, where they were unloaded and carried by oxcarts to Charlottesville. Jefferson introduced novel construction techniques, such as the iron suspension rods that supported the balconies in seven of the pavilions. Other innovations included ornaments cast from terracotta, tin-coated iron roof shingles, and wood-fired drying kilns for lumber.[46] He suggested the serpentine walls in the pavilion gardens, which he probably saw in England during his visit in 1786. They were one brick thick, requiring alternative curves to give them stability. In brief, Jefferson proposed creative solutions and improvised.

His detailed understanding of the process of building is reflected in his two notebooks relating to the design and construction of Monticello. Taught by his father, he revealed his own craftsmanship, his knowledge of how to use tools, and his practical skills. With meticulous detail, he calculated measurements to tens of thousandths of an inch, far beyond tolerances achievable at the time. He owned his own personal "gentleman's" tool kit, which he had purchased in London in 1786 from ironmonger Thomas

Robinson.[47] According to the formerly enslaved Isaac Granger Jefferson, "My Old Master was neat a hand as ever you see to make keys and locks and small chains, iron and brass. He kept all kinds of blacksmith and carpenter tools in a great case with shelves to it."[48] Madison Hemings recalled that his father was more interested in skilled trades like carpentry, joinery, and forging than in agriculture.[49] The Marquis de Chastellux described him as having been "often one of the workmen" at Monticello.[50] A visitor to the university in 1822 encountered Jefferson "taking the chisel from the hand of an Italian sculptor and showing him how to turn a volute of the capital on which he is engaged."[51]

Up to 1826, the university was one of the largest public works projects undertaken in North America, requiring bricklayers, brick makers, lime burners, carpenters, joiners, plasterers, painters, blacksmiths, masons, stonecutters, tinners, sawyers, glaziers, and laborers. Thanks to the depression of 1819, some of the best skilled tradesmen from Baltimore, New York, and Philadelphia were available. With incomplete drawings for the buildings, the builders themselves enjoyed discretion in the decorative features and motifs, which they obtained from books other than those used by Jefferson. While some were skilled white and free Black artisans, the majority were enslaved laborers contracted by their owners to the university through the proctor. They leveled the ground in preparation for the construction and they quarried the stone. They acted as carpenters, bricklayers, painters, stonemasons, boatmen, and blacksmiths. Jefferson set up a brick-making plant in which fifteen enslaved laborers made as many as 900,000 bricks in one season in 1825. He substituted hired slave labor for white workmen to cut costs, saying bluntly on one occasion that covering the roofs with tin could be performed "perfectly by a common negro man whose labor is not worth more than half a dollar a day."[52]

Rather than work, on constructing the University of Virginia, a skilled enslaved worker named Winsten ran away to the northern states. Described in a runaway advertisement in the Central Gazette for May 21, 1821, as a well-clothed, "first-rate House joiner" who was "apt to smile at people when spoken to," Winsten was twenty-two years old and five-feet-eight-inches tall. Like all the enslaved workmen involved with the university buildings, he was employed by a private contractor who either owned or hired his workforce from local plantations. Winsten was employed by John M. Perry, who had earlier sold the university the land on which it was located. Perry also sold lumber, flour, and cornmeal to the proctor and provided brick for the serpentine walls and for the Rotunda. In the runaway advertisement, Perry wrote that he understood that Winsten had "obtained free papers," and he offered a one-hundred-dollar reward for Winsten's capture.[53]

The construction workforce at the university also included some enslaved boys who were so small that the proctor, fearing they would not be able to stand the work of the season, asked that they be replaced by John Hartwell Cocke, who was their owner and a member of the Board of Visitors.[54] The enslaved workmen at the university included some who had formerly worked for Jefferson at Monticello, such as Thrimston Hern. Believed to have been one of those who surveyed the site of the university, Hern installed the slate paving stones and the bases of the columns of the West Portico at Monticello and completed the stonework at the Rotunda.

EVEN JEFFERSON'S MOST faithful adherents criticized aspects of his design for the university and especially the rising costs. In March 1819, David Watson, a member of the state legislature from Louisa and a member of the Board of Visitors for Central College, wrote to fellow board member John Hartwell Cocke that he was ashamed he had not visited the university since the laying of the foundation stone until a recent trip. He now regretted his absence all the more because "the buildings are not upon a plan to meet my notions of convenience & utility." He felt that convenience and appropriateness should be the first objectives, without which the buildings' architectural merits would be "thrown away." Of Pavilion VII, Watson wrote, it was "altogether unfit for the residence of a professor who has a family," with only two rooms and no storage space. The cellar was insufficient for a kitchen, lacking enough space to keep food. Of Pavilion III, the second pavilion built, he conceded that it was "less objectionable" but still thought it inconvenient. He felt the interiors of the pavilions too lavish and the floors too expensive when, not being private property, they would be subject to being mistreated and poorly maintained. He was even more critical of the student rooms. He considered them too small and too public for study, which would be impossible with the distraction of "idle fellow students walking & talking & sporting" within arms length. He also thought them insecure. Fearful that the serrated, almost flat, tin roofs would leak, Watson admitted to being an "ignoramus" about architecture but feared that "Mr. J. is sacrificing every thing to Attic & Corinthian order & chastity; about which I know nothing, & care almost as little." He urged his fellow board members to appoint someone with experience in managing large building projects.[55]

After Jefferson's death, William Short was scathing, having always believed that once the "master & creating spirit was gone, it would languish dwindle & decay." He thought that "the Institution was got up against the grain, & grew much more by the personal influence of one man than by public feeling in its favor." Furthermore, he felt that Jefferson's influence did more to "check than excite public feeling—I mean that of the great & disproportionate expenditure on its buildings," a sum of more than $300,000. Short claimed that the public would never understand the intention of instructing the rising generation in architecture.[56]

Other than the Rotunda, much of the construction was finished by 1822, but Jefferson was adamant that it had been their intention "from the beginning never to open the institution until the buildings shall be compleat."[57] He had earlier teased the legislature with the prospect of an immediate opening. To William Short in October, he wrote that "our University still wants the key-stone of its arch the Rotunda; but even in its present state it is worth a visit, a specimen of classical architecture which would be remarked [on] in Europe."[58] He warned Joseph Cabell that the "opening of the institution in a half-state of readiness would be the most fatal step which could be adopted," and that it would be self-defeating to begin with an inferior appearance, "which never would be shaken off." Jefferson felt that "opening largely and in full system, taking our standing on commanding ground at once," would create the impression that he desired, one that would "beckon everything to it." He did not doubt that "a reputation once established will maintain itself for ages."[59] He believed that the momentum of the building project would "force itself through" the legislature to pay for the most expensive building, the Rotunda.[60]

The rising costs of construction impeded progress. When James Dinsmore sent a local state representative an estimate of $70,000 for the Rotunda, Joseph Cabell persuaded the recipient to throw it in the fire to avoid "the event of its being seen by our enemies."[61] Opposition came not only from outside but also from within the Board of Visitors, where some of the dissenting voices opposed the rising costs and secular religious arrangements for the university. A member of the board from Staunton, Chapman Johnson—appointed to appease opponents of the university in the Shenandoah Valley—even moved in the General Assembly that no money be given for another building. Writing to John Hartwell Cocke, Johnson feared "that the old chief has us bound beyond our power of extrication" and that the public disapproved of the building.[62] Cabell warned that his friends in the legislature would not sanction funding of more than $50,000 for the Rotunda, which ultimately did prove more expensive than all the pavilions taken together, with a total cost of $57,749 by 1828.[63] Yet in February 1823, Cabell informed Jefferson that the legislature would grant the loan of $60,000 for construction, to which he reacted with the "joy of a father on the birth of a first and long-wished son." Riding the next day to the university for the first time since breaking his left arm after a fall from the steps of one of the terraces at Monticello, Jefferson directed the workmen to begin the Rotunda.[64]

As revealed by architectural historian Joseph Michael Lasala, Jefferson erased the name of Benjamin Henry Latrobe not only from the original drawing of the Rotunda but also from his notes, where he had originally written "Latrobe's Rotunda."[65] This may have been a political decision to appease the Board of Visitors because Latrobe had been fired from further work on the U.S. Capitol. Jefferson may even have felt that he amended the plans sufficiently to consider them his own. While regarding the Pantheon as the most perfect specimen of spherical architecture, he made several modifications, including adding windows and changing the portico from eight to six columns. Jefferson may simply have wanted to take credit for a building that is superior to his other work.[66]

The quality of the Rotunda certainly suggests the influence of Latrobe, one of the first professional architects in North America. Latrobe had originally suggested the idea of a central domed building. Instead of the narrow staircases at Monticello and in the faculty pavilions, the Rotunda had two elegant, double-curved staircases. Unlike the Halle aux Blé in Paris, Jefferson did not use ribbed glass skylights but achieved a similar effect with a single oculus that filled the upper room with natural light on the third floor. Like the doors at Monticello, the pine entrance doors were painted to look like grained mahogany. A miniature fireplace on a small landing on one staircase enabled students to warm themselves on the way up to the library. With convenience subordinated to aesthetic appearance, the hidden chimneys did not obtrude, but the fireplaces never drew well. Like Monticello, the Rotunda originally had a bell and a clock that could be heard from a mile away. Finally having all arrived from Italy by the spring of 1826, the installation of the Carrara marble capitals on the south portico completed the building.

Jefferson demonstrated his Enlightenment vision of the university by placing the library, rather than a chapel, at the head of the Lawn in the Rotunda. The Pantheon was originally the site of a pagan temple, while domes often represented heaven in some of the great Christian buildings like Michelangelo's dome in the center of Vatican City. The Rotunda therefore represented a secular temple of reason that replaced revelation with empiricism. Richard Guy Wilson suggests that the circle was a perfect form to Jefferson. Its symbolism as a representation of man gained currency with the Vitruvian belief that "the human form could be inscribed in a circle," in which everything connects to everything else, as in Leonardo da Vinci's drawing of Vitruvian Man. According to Wilson, this matches Jefferson's scheme in which "the human is at the center, and the library is the mind of the University—the repository of wisdom, knowledge of the past, and ideas for the future."[67]

Between June and September 1824, Jefferson prepared a handwritten desiderata list of 6,860 books for the library valued at $24,076.[68] His list included details of the size, cost, and place of publication of each volume. He thereafter continued to revise the list, seeking advice from others, including former presidents James Madison and John Adams. He later consulted with the professors about their preferences. Jefferson added requests by the faculty and books purchased by Francis Walker Gilmer from John Bohn, a dealer in London. On the recommendation of his son-in-law Joseph Coolidge, he arranged for the Boston firm of Cummings, Hilliard & Company, one of the main suppliers of classical books to Harvard University, to purchase items. Jefferson instructed them to buy the latest and best editions, which "for the most part" would be German for classical language texts.[69] He persuaded the firm to establish a bookstore in Charlottesville. Within five years the library contained some 8,000 volumes, more than any other college in the United States, except Harvard with a collection of 8,500 and Yale with 8,000.[70] This was a remarkable accomplishment given the earlier founding dates of many other colleges. Founded in 1764, Brown University had a library of 3,500 books, less than half the number of the University of Virginia in 1828.[71]

Jefferson also appointed the first two librarians and wrote the first library regulations. Although he wanted a faculty member to undertake the role of librarian, he eventually resorted to using students. In January 1826, he appointed student William Wertenbaker to be the librarian with an annual salary of $150. He instructed Wertenbaker "to keep the books in a state of sound preservation, undefaced, and free from injury by moisture or other accident, and in their stated arrangement on the shelves according to the method and order of their catalogue."[72] Apart from an intermission between 1831 and 1835, Wertenbaker remained librarian up until 1857. The library was initially open only on weekdays for an hour, and students were only permitted to borrow books one day per week with the written permission of their professors.[73]

The creativity of Jefferson's vision for the university was apparent in his plans for the dome room located on the third floor of the Rotunda. He envisaged using the ceiling of the library as a planetarium, in which an astronomy professor mounted on a saddle with stirrups could be elevated thirty feet to the concave ceiling by a mechanical boom, guided by a student operator.[74] The professor would thereby have the ultimate visual aid to illustrate the constellations of the northern hemisphere, by placing gilded representations of the stars and planets onto a grid chart, with longitudinal and latitudinal lines painted on the interior plaster face of the dome. Jefferson considered astronomy to be the most sublime of the sciences and a high point of an Enlightenment education, which is why he was willing to give it pride of place in the Rotunda. It was a practical way for students to appreciate the physical laws of the universe and its infinite dimensions, and thus they could gain a rational appreciation of the divine. He drafted a diagram of the wood-laminated dome, built using the framing assembly of Delorme. He characteristically intended the building to be multifunctional with other purposes besides the library. On the second floor, one of the large oval rooms was to be used for annual examinations and for lectures that were too large to be held in the pavilions. The other oval would be devoted to teaching the arts, including drawing and music, by instructors approved and licensed by the faculty. The basement was to contain a chemistry laboratory. Jefferson also envisaged a museum in which he may well have intended to house some of the fossils and artwork from Monticello.[75] While sick in bed in 1824 with a fever and so weak that he could not sit up, it occurred to him to extend the arcade along the front of the Rotunda terraces for use as a year-round gymnasium. He immediately sent off a note to the proctor who incorporated it into the building plan.[76] Other ancillary rooms were to be offered for rent to artisans to demonstrate their skills to students, who would be permitted use of the tools at their own risk.

IN NOVEMBER 1824, Jefferson achieved a publicity coup for the university by dining with the Revolutionary War hero the Marquis de Lafayette in the unfinished Rotunda. First visiting Monticello, Lafayette's return was part of an extended farewell tour of the United States. Heralded by the sound of a bugle at 2:00 p.m. as they ascended the roundabouts of the mountain up to Monticello, Lafayette was escorted by a cavalcade of forty or fifty cavalry, along with the Jefferson Guards and the Virginia militia, with "all the military show of gay scarfs and prancing horses, whose glittering accoutrements flashed in the sunshine." Outside the entrance on the northeast portico, Jefferson, his daughter Martha, James and Dolley Madison, and a crowd of four hundred onlookers who had begun assembling in the early hours awaited the "Nation's Guest."[77]

As the carriages drew up in front of Monticello, Jefferson appeared feeble and tottering, and Lafayette lame and "ruined," in part from his long imprisonment in an Austrian dungeon at Olmûtz. Jefferson walked down the steps of the portico and the two approached each other, with their uncertain gaits quickening into a shuffling run, greeting one another saying, "My dear Mr. Jefferson!" and "My dear Lafayette!" and "God Bless you General" and "Bless you my dear Jefferson."[78] They burst into tears as they fell into one another's arms, repeatedly embracing and kissing. There was scarcely a dry eye in the crowd, which remained silent, apart from the audible sobs of those who could not suppress their emotions.[79] According to Peter Fossett, who was an enslaved nine-year-old boy at the time, "even the slaves wept."[80] The few surviving recollections of enslaved persons from the period mention this event and the known antislavery views of Lafayette.

On the following day, Lafayette rode in a carriage with Jefferson, accompanied by forty cavalrymen wearing blue sashes, as the first official guest of the University of Virginia. Fossett remembered that everyone received a day off and that a grand procession left the house preceded by the Jefferson Guards, with the first carriage carrying Jefferson with Lafayette on his right, opposite Madison and Monroe. Another member of the party was Frances "Fanny" Wright, the Scottish writer and early feminist. After hundreds gathered on the Lawn to hear a speech welcoming the honored guest, the party climbed the steps to dine at around 3:00 p.m. in the half-finished dome of the Rotunda. During a long dinner, some four hundred male guests sat in three circles inside, while the women sat outside on the Lawn. The two revolutionary heroes became so animated and eloquent in recalling the stirring scenes of their early lives that the rest of the company left their seats at the table and gathered around the two sages, to avoid missing a word.[81] Lafayette thought Jefferson much aged, and his private secretary seemed most impressed by Madison, who "distinguished himself to all by the originality of his mind and the subtlety of his allusions."[82]

For the dinner in honor of Lafayette, Jefferson had prepared some written remarks that were read aloud on his behalf. They paid tribute to Lafayette, acknowledging that he "only held the nail" which Lafayette "drove in." Turning from the past to the future and to the university, Jefferson acknowledged that he was "old, long in disuse of making speeches and without voice to utter them." His "feeble state, the exhausted powers of life," had left him little within his competence to be of public service. If, with the help of younger allies, he could "still contribute any thing to advance the institution within whose walls we are now mingling manifestations of our affection to this our guest, it will be as it ever has been chearfully and zealously bestowed." If he could "live to see it once enjoy the patronage & cherishment of our public authorities with undivided voice I should die without a doubt of the future fortunes of my native state, and in consoling contemplation of the happy influence of this institution on its character, its virtue, its prosperity and safety."[83] The company drank thirteen toasts, including one to "Thomas Jefferson and the Declaration of Independence—alike identified with the cause of Liberty." Toward the end of the dinner, the master builder James Dinsmore offered a toast to "Thomas Jefferson. Founder of the University of Virginia." Lafayette and his entourage afterward toured the Grounds, where his private secretary was impressed that "the construction had been managed by Mr. Jefferson himself, who took pleasure in spending several hours each day, sometimes in the midst of the workers, sometimes in the midst of the students and professors, all of whom felt all the better for his wise counsel."[84]

As EARLY AS JUNE 1820, Jefferson had written to John Wayles Eppes, his son-in-law, that "our University is now so far advanced as to be worth seeing. it exhibits already the appearance of a beautiful Academical village, of the finest models of building and of classical architecture, in the U.S." It was "much visited by strangers and admired by all for its beauty, originality, and convenience of the plan."[85] Jefferson was satisfied that he had achieved his ambition in creating a university whose chaste architecture and classical taste would be thought splendid even in Europe and which "leaves every thing in America far behind it."[86] Harvard professor George Ticknor thought the university more attractive than anything in New England. Indeed, during his tour of America in 1824–25, Edward Stanley, later 14th Earl of Derby and prime minister of Britain, said of Harvard that it consisted "of several high plain red brick buildings, without any pretensions to Architecture."[87] After visiting the Grounds in 1828, Margaret Bayard Smith wrote tellingly that the university was "one of the finest specimens of art & the most magnificent Institution I have ever seen—It has a most imposing effect. . . . Were I a young man & a student there—methinks the place, alone, would purify & elevate my mind."[88]

To Joseph Cabell, Jefferson justified the expense of the buildings, reminding him that "the great object of our aim from the beginning has been to make the establishment the most eminent in the United States, in order to draw to it the youth of every state." They had therefore sought to recruit professors of the first order of science in Europe, "as well as our own country; and, not only by salaries and the comforts of their situation, but by the distinguished scale of its structure and preparation, and the promise of future eminence which these would hold up, to induce them to commit their reputations to its future fortunes." He asked Cabell, "Had we built a barn for a College, and log-huts for accommodations, should we ever have had the assurance to propose to an European Professor of that character to come to it?"[89]

6

Useful Knowledge

IN JANUARY 1825, George Long, professor of ancient languages, was the first member of the faculty to arrive on Grounds, which, "being almost without inhabitants," looked "like a deserted city," with no other faculty or students and all the buildings complete, except for the dome of the Rotunda.[1] Among eight faculty members, Long was one of five professors who had been recruited in Britain. He felt lonely in the absence of his colleagues and worried that their delayed sailing might harm the prospects of the new university, causing the postponement of the first day of classes. Embarking on an American ship from Liverpool to New York, he arrived two months ahead of his other colleagues coming from Britain. They had sailed at the same time from London to Norfolk, Virginia, in an English vessel named the *Competitor*, which was "something like an old hay stack: it could just float and go before the wind," with "an unpolished selfish person" as a skipper" who had "no great liking . . . for 'philosophers.'"[2] During a bitterly cold winter, Long lived in solitude without any furniture in the newly constructed Pavilion V.

Long had been apprehensive about accepting a position at the new University of Virginia. A Craven Scholar at Cambridge University, he was a fellow of Trinity College, still one of the wealthiest and arguably most attractive colleges, where he had been appointed instead of the later-famous historian Thomas Babington Macaulay. Long was concerned at the prospect of relocating abroad, especially as he was the guardian of his younger brother and two sisters. He wanted to know whether the location of the university would enable his siblings to continue to live in a respectable manner and whether they would be able to acquire "a little property to advantage." The salary offer from the university seemed "adequate," but he worried about the comparative cost of living. He suspected that food might be cheaper but feared that other articles, such as clothing and furniture, might be dearer "than they are here" in England. He questioned whether the university had sufficient support to survive or whether it was just an experiment with the risk of failure. He asked, "Is there in the county of Albemarle, or town of Charlottesville, tolerably agreeable society, such as would in some degree compensate for almost the only comfort an Englishman would leave behind him?" He wanted to know whether the teaching demands and vacations would "leave sufficient time for literary pursuits, and the studies connected with the profession." He was concerned about job security and on what grounds a professor could be removed. He concluded, "I have no attachment to England as a country; it is a delightful place for a man of rank and property to live in, but I was not born in that enviable station, to which most men here are led to aspire and often in vain. If comfortably settled therefore in America I should never wish to leave it."[3] Nevertheless, he admitted that he was conflicted at the thought of leaving his native country and some valuable friends.[4]

A few days after his arrival in Charlottesville, Long "walked up to Monticello to see Mr. Jefferson." He recollected that he arrived at the Entrance Hall and made himself known to Jefferson's "servant," almost certainly the enslaved valet Burwell Colbert, who was a nephew of Sally Hemings. After "a few minutes a tall dignified old man entered" and after looking at him for a moment said, "Are you the new professor of ancient languages?" When the twenty-four-year-old professor answered in the affirmative, Jefferson said, "You are very young," to which Long answered, "I shall grow older." His host smiled and replied that "that was true." Born the same year that Jefferson first mooted the idea of a University of Virginia to Joseph Priestley, Long recognized that the eighty-two-year-old Jefferson "was evidently somewhat startled at my youthful and boyish appearance: and I could plainly see that he was disappointed." They started to talk, and he then stayed to dine with Jefferson at Monticello. Long initially thought his host "was grave and rather cold in his manner, but he was very polite," simply dressed, and "free from all affectation." Fifty years later from England, Long wrote that he remembered "this interview as well as if it took place yesterday."[5] He won the respect of Jefferson, who came to think of him as "a most amiable man, of fine understanding, well qualified for his department, and acquiring esteem as fast as he becomes known."[6]

During his two months of solitary residence on the Lawn, Long made several subsequent visits and occasionally passed the night at Monticello. He was relieved that the founder of the university "became better satisfied with the boy professor" as they talked together "on all subjects." When he revealed his interest in the geography of his adopted country and "the story of the revolution," Jefferson "told me much about it, but in a very modest way as to himself" and showed him the original draft of the Declaration of Independence.[7] On subsequent visits to the university, Jefferson generally called on Long, and the two of them met frequently over the course of the next year. On one occasion Jefferson spoke about the character of George Washington. Later, reading a similar account of Washington written by Jefferson, Long observed that as "a mere writer" he "might have excelled most men of his day." Long would also meet James Madison and James Monroe. Of Madison, Long wrote, "I think he was one of the most sensible men that I ever spoke to." He thought Monroe "rather a dull companion" after sitting next to the former president at dinner. During the dinner, Monroe said nothing, other than asking Long, "How is your father?" Long replied, "I have no father," leaving Monroe silent. As to his former student Edgar Allan Poe, Long wrote, "I have a faint recollection of the name, but no real remembrance of what he was or what he did at the University."[8]

GEORGE LONG TYPIFIED the outstanding early faculty at the University of Virginia. He would come to be regarded as a pioneer and authority in etymology and comparative languages. Like Thomas Cooper, he became an early and leading expert in Roman law. Burwell Clark, an alumnus of the first year of the university, recalled Long as a "very popular, enthusiastic and efficient teacher," who "was quite a handsome man, a very agreeable and social companion." He used to eat at the hotels with the students. They were "very much attached to him," because he always partook in their conversation and "made us feel at ease."[9] For the rest of his life, Long continued to correspond with fellow classicist and former student Henry Tutwiler, of Alabama. Known by the students as the "Colonel" because he had the temperament of an army officer, Long married a Virginian, Harriet Selden, a relative of the provost, Arthur Brockenbrough, who had helped supervise the building of the "Academical Village." As the first romance on the Lawn, their courtship was the subject of comedy among students, who made vulgar play of lines from Oliver Goldsmith's *The Hermit* (1765): "Harriet wants but little here below / But wants that little Long."[10] During these first months, Long was looked after by his future wife and father-in-law. His first son was born in Pavilion V and later became a lawyer in London.

While teaching at the University of Virginia, Long wrote *Two Dissertations on the Roman Law* (1827). An indication of the early intellectual and research life of the university, he also coauthored two books with colleagues, which included an *Introduction to the Study of Grecian and Roman Geography* (1829), with Robley Dunglison, the professor of medicine. Long later said that he wanted to save the classics from "dusty pedantry." At the invitation of the British statesman Lord Brougham in 1828, Long returned to England to become the first professor of Greek at University College in London, which had been established two years earlier, based on the radical ideas of Jeremy Bentham and sharing the secular vision of Jefferson. As the first new university in England in centuries after Oxford and Cambridge, it became one of the two founding colleges of London University.[11]

After resigning his professorship at University College in protest over the dismissal of a colleague in 1831, Long became an editor of the *Quarterly Journal of Education*, published by the Society for the Diffusion of Useful Knowledge. For the same organization he edited twenty-nine volumes of the *Penny Cyclopaedia* and *Knight's Political Dictionary*. He was one of its most active members and used the journal to champion the reform of secondary education. Long resumed his position at University College London, only to resign again when he became a reader in jurisprudence and civil law at the Middle Temple, one of the Inns of Court in London. As editor of the *Bibliotheca Classica*, he produced the first series of scholarly classical translations with English notes, to which he contributed his own edition of *Cicero's Orations* (1851–62). As late as the first half of the twentieth century, these were still standard texts in universities, with the *Encyclopedia Britannica* crediting Long with having exercised "a wide influence on the teaching of Greek and Latin languages in England."[12] As a founder, honorary secretary, and twenty-year member of the Royal Geographical Society, he published *The Geography of America and the West Indies* (1841) and an *Atlas of Classical Geography* (1854). He wrote a five-volume history of the *Decline of the Roman Empire* (1864–74). Matthew Arnold, the poet and cultural critic, wrote that Long's "reputation as a scholar is a sufficient guarantee of general fidelity and accuracy of his translation," but that his real gift was engaging his readers and giving life to his subject matter. Long continued to contemplate a return to America and was disappointed to be unable to accept an invitation to the fiftieth anniversary of the first class of the University of Virginia, writing, "I should be delighted to see the old country again."[13] His scholarship received national recognition when Prime Minister William Gladstone, the British leader most comparable in intellect to Thomas Jefferson, whom he greatly admired, awarded Long a pension on the Civil List in 1873.

The other four professors from England were delayed another month before they joined Long. In the meantime, he was "amused with the curiosity my new friends showed to hear some news about England." As if he knew everyone in Britain, one man asked him about the welfare of the Scottish poet Thomas Campbell. The four newly arrived professors from England were Robley Dunglison, professor of medicine and anatomy; Charles G. Bonnycastle, professor of natural philosophy; George Blaettermann, professor of modern languages; and Thomas Hewitt Key, professor of mathematics. Stuck in the British Channel, they had a "long and tedious passage" of over three and a half months as opposed to the usual thirty-seven-day voyage from England. They were feted on arrival and treated like celebrities in America.[14] Awaiting their delayed arrival from Britain, people in Charlottesville had "nothing better to do [than] amuse themselves with inventing stories on this unfortunate subject."[15] In Richmond, a Mrs. Camp, who was "a kind of Mrs Malaprop," spread the word that "the Universal confessors" had reached Norfolk. There was a ball given in their honor in Richmond that was so well attended "the grave seemed to have given up the dead," according to Maria Randolph, "for there came ladies whom I never heard of being out before for years to see the English people." At the same ball, she observed a portrait painter dance on the top of a piano, "the most elegant hornpipe and jig I ever saw."[16]

One of the four late arrivals, Dr. Robley Dunglison and his wife, Harriette, had an arduous journey from Richmond to Charlottesville, traveling seventy miles along notoriously bad roads, during which their carriage was involved in an accident when trying to ford Moore's Creek. "Such was the unpropitious introduction to the University," Dunglison wrote, "a Roman would have regarded it as a bad omen, and been disheartened. We are not Romans, however, and the affair only excited amusement." In Charlottesville, the group was welcomed by Jefferson, who sympathized with them "on the discomforts of our long voyage, and on the disagreeable journey" along the roads of Virginia. He spoke of his "great distress ... lest we had been lost at sea" and admitted that "he had almost given us up." Dunglison recalled how the ex-president "welcomed us with dignity and kindness for which he is celebrated," and that "he was then aged eighty-two years old, with his intellectual powers, unshaken by age; and the physical man so active, that he rode to and from Monticello and took exercise on foot with all the activity of one 20 or 30 years younger."[17]

The first full-time professor of medicine and anatomy in the United States, the twenty-eight-year-old Dunglison had trained at the University of Edinburgh, as well as the École de Médecine in Paris, the Royal College of Surgeons, and the Society of Apothecaries in London, acquiring his M.D. at the University of Erlangen in Germany. Living with his wife in Pavilion X, he was pleasantly surprised to find it "much better furnished than we had expected." Known as the "Father of American Physiology" for his book *Human Physiology* (1832), he wrote this, his most acclaimed work, at the University of Virginia and dedicated it to James Madison "Rector ... a zealous promoter of Science and Literature" and "the friend of Mankind." Dated "University of Virginia, October 1832," he published the *New Dictionary of Medical Science and Literature* in early 1833, which he dedicated to his fellow faculty member Robert M. Patterson, the professor of natural philosophy. By 1852, the latter work had gone through eight editions and sold 17,250 copies. Dunglison spent much of the latter part of his career teaching at Jefferson Medical College in Philadelphia during which time one of his sons, Richard James, became the first editor of *Gray's Anatomy* (1859). Later in life, Dunglison became vice president of the American Philosophical Society.[18]

While local society celebrated the arrival of the professors, the recruitment of Europeans also caused a backlash. Dunglison said that his own selection as professor of medicine "excited the most feeling amongst my professional brethren." The announcement of his appointment in the *London Medical Repository* occasioned "a long and excited article," some five pages in length, under the title of "American Medicine" in the *Philadelphia Journal of Medical and Physical* Sciences, then "the most prominent medical journal in America." It warned that the American medical societies "will protest against this act of injustice." As late as 1842, the editor of the journal wrote of the gall of Dunglison, who without ever having "felt an American pulse" or made "a visit to an American sick room," thought that he had "a complete knowledge of American diseases and was perfectly competent in their treatment and care, and also to become an instructor in them to others." Dunglison retorted in his memoirs that excellence, not nationality, should be the criteria for the selection of a scholar, which he extolled as the practice at the University of Virginia.[19]

In his quest to recruit some of the most outstanding faculty in the country, Jefferson set a new standard in the United States that followed the practice of such German institutions as the University of Göttingen and the University of Berlin.[20] From the beginning, Jefferson considered "the high qualification of our professors as the only means by which we could give to our institution splendor and preeminence over its sister seminaries."[21] He thought that favoritism and nepotism had led to the relative decline of the University of Pennsylvania and the University of Edinburgh.[22] Jefferson stressed the importance of breadth. Professors ought to be familiar with the sciences in general and not just their own discipline, to be able to converse with colleagues, and to participate in discussions, without which a professor "will incur their contempt, and bring disreputation on the institution."[23] He hoped that his successors would always consider the good—"the sublimation"—of the university in appointing professors. After Jefferson's death, Madison continued this tradition of excellence, asking regarding the selection of Gessner Harrison to replace George Long "if he was a man of genius." Madison smiled when Dunglison replied that he scarcely knew "what that was, but he was certainly an excellent scholar, and possessed those mental qualities which would enable him to be eminently useful as a professor of ancient languages, while his moral character was entirely without reproach."[24]

In the United States at the time, it was difficult to find and recruit faculty because there was no career structure in academia. The word "career" was not even introduced until the mid-nineteenth century. As late as the 1870s, William Graham Sumner, the first professor of sociology in the country, wrote that "there is no such thing yet at Yale as an academic career. There is no course marked out for a man who feels called to this work, and desires to pursue it." Until the emergence of professional associations in the 1890s, the formal concepts of tenure, promotion, academic freedom, and salary incentives had not been developed. As the social reformer Henry Ward Beecher asked rhetorically, "Who ever heard of a college professor that is not poor?"[25]

Although an embryonic academic culture was emerging, it remained true from colonial times that professors were typically men in their early twenties who regarded teaching as a pit stop on the way to a more lucrative and promising career in the church or one of the professions.[26] High turnover of faculty was consequently common. Although the proportion of clergymen was declining, they represented at least a third of all college faculty. At Harvard, the majority of the professors were recent college graduates, and most stayed less than three years. The same was true of Columbia College (Columbia University).[27] At the University of Virginia, the majority of the original faculty had not pursued teaching as their first choice of profession. The death of his uncle had prevented Robley Dunglison from joining his practice as a plantation doctor in the British Caribbean. Similarly, but for the death of his father, George Long had intended to purchase a commission in the British Army. Despite all of his academic achievements, Long later contemplated returning from Britain to farm in America and ended his career teaching at an English secondary school called Brighton College. For much of the nineteenth century, it was common for professors to leave universities to teach in secondary schools or become headmasters. In his inaugural address at Harvard in 1869, Charles William Eliot still spoke of the difficulty of finding competent professors and complained that few of his countrymen "of eminent ability are attracted to this profession."[28]

THE UNIVERSITY OF VIRGINIA enticed new faculty by offering rent-free accommodations in one of the pavilions and by paying the highest salaries in the country, rivaled only by Harvard.[29] As Adam Smith had advocated in *The Wealth of Nations* (1776), the faculty received additional income beyond their salary from fees paid directly to them by students, which gave them an incentive to teach larger classes. This led to wide discrepancies between professors, with salaries varying from $1,600 per annum to $3,500. As professor of ethics, George Tucker was the lowest paid professor, owing to the unpopularity of his subject. Older than the rest of the faculty and one of the only professors educated in America, Tucker resented it. Jefferson was insistent that the faculty should be full-time professionals who did not "moonlight" or make money in other professional work. The teaching load involved lecturing three times per week for two hours each session, but expectations could vary between schools.[30]

Jefferson did actually first try to recruit within the United States and insisted that both the professors of law and of politics be Americans. He attempted to appoint Samuel Bowditch from Salem, Massachusetts, to teach mathematics, but Bowditch accepted double the salary to work for the Essex Fire and Marine Insurance Company. Jefferson's offer to George Ticknor from Boston to teach languages also failed, with Ticknor instead becoming one of the most prominent faculty members at Harvard. As noted earlier, although the recipient denied receiving the invitation, Jefferson claimed that he made a rejected offer to the Reverend Samuel Knox, who in 1796 had co-won the prize for the best essay on public education from the American Philosophical Society.

Yet as early as 1794, Jefferson had thought in terms of obtaining the best talent in Europe. As we have seen, he wanted to move the entire University of Geneva to Virginia. He made clear his wish to appoint Europeans in his first letters to Joseph Priestley outlining his interest in the creation of a University of Virginia in 1800.[31] When attempting to win support for the creation of Central College, he claimed that three of the most eminent Europeans had already indicated their willingness to join the faculty, including the great French political economist Jean-Baptiste Say. Jefferson also tried to lure the natural scientist George Pictet from Geneva, the natural philosopher Dugald Stewart from Scotland, and the philosopher Antoine Destutt de Tracy from France. Jefferson confided to architect Benjamin Henry Latrobe that, since "all Europe seems to be breaking up," the time was ripe to snap up geniuses.[32]

In 1819, Jefferson wrote to John Adams that "our wish is to procure natives where they can be found . . . of the first order of acquirement in their respective lines; but, preferring foreigners of the 1st order to natives of the 2d we shall certainly have to go, for several of our Professors, to countries more advanced in science than we are."[33] Adams was unconvinced, writing that "I do not approve of your sending to Europe for Tutors, and Professors. I do believe there are sufficient scholars in America to fill your Professorships and Tutorships with more active ingenuity, and independent minds, than you can bring from Europe. The Europeans are all deeply tainted with prejudices both Ecclesiastical, and Temporal which they can never get rid of; they are all infected with Episcopal and Presbyterian Creeds, and confessions of faith."[34] Distrustful of Europeans' religious and political principles, the Reverend Joseph Caldwell, the president of the University of North Carolina, similarly opposed recruiting professors from Europe, adding that they could not enforce discipline because they did not understand "the disposition of American youth . . . especially the southern variety."[35] At Yale, President Timothy Dwight was so opposed to hiring Europeans that he appointed Benjamin Silliman to be professor of chemistry, despite his having no qualifications in the subject, which necessitated Silliman's leaving the university to study chemistry at Edinburgh University. Fortuitously, he became one of the leading scientists in the United States.[36]

Jefferson was undeterred. After failing to persuade Joseph Cabell to go on a recruiting trip to Europe, he assigned the task to the thirty-three-year-old attorney Francis Walker Gilmer of Pen Park, near Charlottesville. Offering him the professorship of law, Jefferson regarded Gilmer as one of the brightest young men in Virginia. As Jefferson explained to Richard Rush, "We determined to receive no one who is not of the first order of science in his line; and as such, in every branch, cannot be obtained with us, we proposed to seek some of them at least in countries ahead of us in science and preferably in Great Britain, the land of our own language, habits and manners."[37] Jefferson provided introductions for Gilmer to some of the most progressive thinkers and advocates of educational reform in both England

and Scotland, including Major John Cartwright, a radical pamphleteer and proponent of universal male suffrage; Reverend Samuel Parr, an influential writer and bibliophile; James A. Murray, the associate editor of the highly prestigious *Edinburgh Review*; Lord Brougham, a statesman and founder of University College London; and Dr. George Birkbeck, a distinguished physician and later namesake of one of the colleges at London University. Gilmer experienced some comic mishaps, such as when he arrived at Oxford and Cambridge when both universities were on their summer vacation and the majority of their fellows were on holiday, scattered in different parts of Britain. He considered going to the University of Göttingen in Germany but decided to wait until after his trip to Edinburgh.

Although committed to the building of the university, Gilmer did not share Jefferson's interest in educating the broader population or in reforming Virginia. A protégé who owed some of his education and reading interests to Jefferson, Gilmer was capable of being sarcastic in his private correspondence about his former mentor, whom he variously dubbed "Citizen Thomas," "Red breeches," and the "worthy St. Thomas of Cantingbury" (a pun on St. Thomas of Canterbury), echoing Jefferson's bitter political opponent John Randolph of Roanoke.[38] Nevertheless, throughout his short life Gilmer corresponded with Jefferson. While successful in fulfilling Jefferson's wishes to recruit new faculty, Gilmer's return voyage proved tragic for him personally. Despite becoming ill on the passage back to New York, he managed to appoint a sixth faculty member to teach chemistry: John Patten Emmet, a resident of the city and émigré from Ireland. Gilmer lived long enough to greet first George Long and then Robley Dunglison in Norfolk but died the same month and never assumed the law professorship.

After meeting Gilmer in the rooms of the poet Winthrop Mackworth Praed at Trinity College, Cambridge University, the twenty-five-year-old Thomas Hewitt Key accepted the professorship of mathematics. Switching fields to Latin, he would later become one of the founding professors at University College London (1828), where his former colleague George Long joined him as professor of Greek and later succeeded him as professor of Latin (1842). A few years older than the others at the age of thirty, Charles G. Bonnycastle, who became professor of natural philosophy, was a graduate of the Royal Artillery School in Woolwich, where his late father had been professor of mathematics. Bonnycastle distinguished himself by issuing an expanded thirteenth edition of his father's textbook, *An Introduction to Algebra* (1824). As professor of modern languages, a German, and the oldest member of the group at the age of forty-two, George Blaettermann was the only professor to apply for the job and the only recruit from Continental Europe, although living in Britain. The three remaining faculty of the original eight were Americans, but as Dunglison observed, two of the three were actually immigrants: the professor of ethics, George Tucker, was from Bermuda, and the professor of chemistry, John P. Emmet, was not only from Ireland but the nephew of the revolutionary Irish hero Robert Emmet, who was executed for treason by the British in 1803. Unlike Tucker, who came to America as an adult, Emmet arrived at the age of eight, when his father moved to New York after being imprisoned for patriot activities in Ireland. John Tayloe Lomax, the professor of law, was the sole native-born U.S. citizen.

The first faculty engaged in a vigorous intellectual life. Robley Dunglison and George Tucker were both elected to the American Philosophical Society. They each presented papers there and published in its journal. Tucker conducted an important study of Siamese twins, Chang and Eng, who had toured Virginia. Unable to persuade them to make a detour to Charlottesville, he interviewed them in New York. He published his findings first as a book, *The Siamese Twins* (1830), and later as an article in the *Proceedings of the American Philosophical Society* (1841), arguing that the twins offered an unparalleled opportunity to understand the relative roles of nature and nurture in social development. Between June 1829 and June 1830, Dunglison and Tucker combined to edit a weekly faculty journal called the *Virginia Literary Museum and Journal of Belles Lettres, Arts, Sciences, &c.*, which aimed to publish "original and interesting contributions," scientific discoveries, and a "taste for polite literature" to general readers. It excluded discussion of party politics and theology. It ran for fifty weeks, totaling eight hundred pages in the course of a year.[39] Tucker had wanted to include fictional stories but Dunglison opposed him. While they both wrote the majority of the articles, "all the professors, or nearly all, wrote papers for it." The journal stopped because the circulation was too limited to make a profit. During his twenty years at the university, Tucker also contributed articles, including biographical accounts of Jefferson and Madison, to the *Penny Cyclopedia*, edited in England by his former faculty colleague George Long. He later took a yearlong leave to visit England and met with Long at University College. In his memoirs, Tucker recalled that "my colleagues were all agreeable and well informed men and had all travelled in foreign countries. We were very sociable often dining and passing the evening together, and that life which we then led, tho' seemingly monotonous and devoid of interest, had no doubt appeared to all, on retrospect, one of the happiest portions of our lives."[40]

POSSIBLY INFLUENCED BY Chevalier Quesnay's 1787 plan for a projected academy in Richmond or Pierre Samuel du Pont de Nemours's *National Education in the United States of America* (1812), Jefferson separated the teaching into different schools and departments.[41] The traditional medieval university was composed of four faculties, reflecting the prevailing conception of the main realms of human knowledge: theology, law, medicine, and arts (philosophy and sciences). Although Jefferson originally intended to have ten departments, the university opened with eight, with one professor in each. It was comparatively smaller than the twenty-member faculty at Harvard University, thirty-six professors at the University of Berlin, and forty at the University of Göttingen. It was, though, larger than most colleges in America: Columbia College, the wealthiest college in the nation, had only four professors in the early 1800s and six by 1854.[42] The president of many smaller colleges did all or most of the teaching. Jefferson's arrangement, in which a single professor taught a group of disciplines, represented a growing movement toward greater academic specialization. As Jefferson wrote to Dr. Thomas Cooper, parodying the course offerings of other colleges, "Caesar and Virgil, & a few books of Euclid do not really contain the sum of all human knolege, nor give to a man figure in the ranks of science."[43]

Aware of the rather arbitrary division of academic disciplines elsewhere, Jefferson was striving to offer every branch of human knowledge at the highest level. Beginning in 1825, the university was one of the first to teach economics, then called political economy, in the United States. Yet Jefferson's desire to create specialized departments was compromised by the small size of the faculty and the aim to offer a comprehensive curriculum. Each professor was responsible for a wide range of subjects, which in practice were often artificially grouped together. In addition to Latin and Greek, George Long was expected to teach rhetoric, *belles lettres* (poetry, rhetoric, history, and moral philosophy), ancient history, geography, and Hebrew. Some of the first faculty were overwhelmed by the demands on them. Long thought himself unqualified to teach Hebrew.

In his anonymous article in the *North American Review*, Edward Everett was especially critical of the number and range of subjects expected of the faculty, writing that "one professor of Latin, Greek and Hebrew is too little" and claiming that the most ill-provided grammar school was better staffed. He thought it too much for one person to be expected to be "perfectly skilled" in so many modern languages, feeling it necessary to remind readers that it was necessary "not only for a professor's reputation, but for the actual success of teaching, that he know a great deal more, than that he is obliged to teach." Everett spoke against the lack of specialization regarding the professorship of ethics as particularly "overcharged" with moral philosophy, the science of ideas ("ideology"), general grammar, rhetoric, *belles lettres*, fine arts, and natural theology, which were "surely branches too numerous and too dissimilar for any man, however unwearied his industry, or versatile his talents." The teaching requirements for one professor represented at least four subject areas "usually held to be great departments of themselves."[44] This proved a major limitation, forcing the dropping of some areas like agriculture and the merging of other fields like politics and law. Admitting to feeling unqualified to teach all the subjects required of them, the faculty swapped subjects among themselves, as when George Tucker persuaded the law professor to let him teach moral philosophy and George Long to give up rhetoric and *belles lettres*.

Overall, the curriculum aimed to liberate the living generation from the past. While Jefferson wished it to be as comprehensive as possible, the main emphasis was on "useful knowledge," with a particular orientation toward science, relevance, and vocational training. Accepting Enlightenment ideas of a hierarchy of knowledge, with a premium on the sciences, Jefferson recognized that "what was useful two centuries ago is now become useless" and regarded science as progressive. In his eyes, the Universities of Oxford, Cambridge, and the Sorbonne "were from a century and a half to two centuries out of date," since they were still essentially teaching the humanist curriculum of the Renaissance.[45] Some newer colleges also promoted science, including Amherst (1821), Hobart (founded as Geneva College in 1822), Trinity (founded as Washington College in 1823), and especially Union (1795). Elsewhere, science was grudgingly admitted if at all. At Yale, the scientists were segregated in chapel services and were siphoned off into the separate Sheffield School.[46] The Yale Report of 1828 even reasserted the centrality of the classics in the curriculum at the expense of modern science. As the university that produced the most college presidents and boasted the most alumni, Yale's national influence was particularly great.

Jefferson regarded medicine as the most important of the sciences because it was "useful" and afforded "the greatest opportunity and the widest scope for the exercise of humanity." He abhorred the contemporary practice of medicine with its "fanciful and ephemeral theories under which prac-

titioners are so wantonly sporting with human life."[47] Condemning the
"pious fraud of the adventurous physician" who "substitutes presumption
for knowledge," he believed in the capacity of the body for self-healing and
opposed any form of surgery not based on good empirical evidence, clini-
cal observations, and long experience. He thought nature "preferable to an
unskillful" doctor.[48] In a scarcely veiled reference to Dr. Benjamin Rush,
who had popularized the practice of bleeding patients, Jefferson vented that
"our country is overrun with young lads from the Philadelphia school, who
with their mercury and lancet in hand are vying with the sword of [Napo-
leon] Bonaparte [to see] which shall have shed the most human blood."[49]
From the time of Hippocrates, following "a succession of hypothetical systems each having its day in vogue," physicians "have ever had a false knowledge, worse than ignorance."[50] Influenced by Dr. Thomas Cooper, Jefferson
enjoyed reading exposés of sham medical theories and the failures of past
treatments. He was also critical of contemporary hospitals. He believed
in a holistic philosophy of health and advocated a lifestyle of moderation,
strict habits, physical exercise, a low-meat/high-vegetable diet, and regular
sleeping hours.[51] He was receptive to good medical science but opposed un-
supported experimentation that threatened the patient. Familiar with the
research of Edward Jenner and John Lettsom, Jefferson became one of the
first in the United States to promote the cowpox vaccine against smallpox,
personally seeing to the vaccination of members of his family and some two
hundred enslaved laborers. He worked with Dr. Benjamin Waterhouse at
Harvard to spread awareness of the vaccine in the United States, which won
him a letter of recognition from the Royal Jennerian Society in London.

Recommended to be the first professor of medicine at the University
of Virginia by Dr. George Birkbeck in London, Robley Dunglison proved
to be a sympathetic ally who shared a compatible vision with Jefferson's.
Only once accepting a fee, he became Jefferson's personal physician, visiting two or three times a week at Monticello. He was amused rather than
affronted by Jefferson's gentle jibes at the charlatanry of the medical profession, including an occasion when the ex-president greeted him and a couple
of other doctors by saying that "whenever I see three physicians together,
I look up to the sky to discover whether there's a turkey buzzard [i.e., vul-
ture] in the neighborhood."[52] Dunglison similarly befriended James Madison and James Monroe. He later observed that although Jefferson "had
more imagination, Mr. Madison excelled him perhaps in judgment," while
Mr. Monroe "made a much less favorable impression in regard to his intellectual powers than Mr. Jefferson or Mr. Madison."[53]

Hindered by the absence of a hospital, one of the drawbacks of the location in Charlottesville, Dunglison succeeded in persuading Jefferson to design and add an anatomical theater that was completed in 1826 and demolished to make way for the Alderman Library in 1939, the only one of the original Jefferson-designed buildings that has been lost. He expanded the medical book collection in the library and introduced rigorous examination requirements, an important innovation in a period when formal testing was not required to obtain a medical qualification and most medical schools were designed to maximize income for their faculties. At the few colleges offering the subject—including Pennsylvania, Harvard, and Yale—medical schools ran as separate entities, not integrated into the university. Columbia University actually abolished its Faculty of Medicine, terminating five faculty members in 1813, and did not revive medical training until 1891.[54]

Influenced by Jefferson, Dunglison offered a preclinical training through the medical school in which students were exposed to the fundamental branches of medical science. They were offered lectures in anatomy, human physiology in health and disease, pathology, and pharmacology. Virginia was the first school in the nation to offer lectures in the history of medicine within the medical curriculum.[55] Three days a week, Dunglison offered a free outpatient clinic and pharmacy to the poor and charged fifty cents per visit to other members of the local community. After Jefferson's death, Dunglison combined with John P. Emmet, the professor of natural history (chemistry, botany, zoology, mineralogy, comparative anatomy, and geology) to offer M.D. degrees. Emmet assumed responsibility for pharmacology and *materia medica*. Dr. Thomas Johnson was added as an instructor in anatomy. The university, well in advance of the teaching of medicine at other colleges, anticipated in many respects what remains the gold standard of medical training outlined in the 1910 Flexner Report.[56] About a fifth of students who studied at the university during the antebellum period became doctors.

This more scientifically oriented curriculum was not synonymous with an exclusive focus on what we would now describe as science, technology, engineering, and mathematics (STEM). For much of the eighteenth century, the term "science" was interchangeable with knowledge and inquiry. In a conversation with the British actor John Bernard, Jefferson said that he considered "scientific knowledge to be that food which alone can enable the mental functions to acquire vigor and activity; but elegant literature as the wine that should invariably follow, because without it the mind would never rise to the full measure of its enjoyment." His favorite poets were William Shakespeare and Alexander Pope, who jointly represented "the perfection of imagination and judgement, both displaying more knowledge of the human heart—the true province of poetry—than he could elsewhere find." His favorite prose writers were Jonathan Swift and Lord Bolingbroke. As Jefferson told Bernard, his background in law "gave me a view of the dark side of humanity. Then I read poetry to qualify it with a gaze upon its bright side; and between the two extremes I have contrived through life to draw the due medium."[57]

Jefferson thought that students studying for the professions must also have a grounding in other fields, including the liberal arts. In the tradition of his own mentor George Wythe, he advised students to spend at least three years reading broadly before embarking on professional studies like law and medicine, which anticipated the idea of professional degrees taught at the graduate level.[58] He saw modern languages, which were not then offered at most universities, as an "instrument of attainment in the sciences" by enabling scholars to read leading scientific works published in Continental Europe, which were ahead of England and Scotland.[59] At the University of Virginia, modern languages received equal treatment with ancient languages. The school offered French, German, Spanish, Italian, and Anglo-Saxon. Having an intercontinental view of the Americas, Jefferson appreciated the importance of Spanish. In acknowledging the gift by Professor George Ticknor at Harvard of a copy of his Spanish-literature syllabus, regarded as a milestone in the history of language teaching, Jefferson observed that "nobody, in this country, within my acquaintances, has so much knowledge of this particular subject as you have."[60]

Indeed, Jefferson thought most subjects *useful* in some capacity. He was the first advocate in America for the teaching of Anglo-Saxon. Although later invoked in support of racist theories, he thought the subject important for understanding law, the origins of representative government, and the development of the English language.[61] Unlike Benjamin Franklin, Benjamin Rush, and Pierre Samuel du Pont de Nemours, who favored the removal of "dead languages" in colleges, Jefferson wanted to include Latin and Greek at the university, without according to them the priority and privileged position in the curriculum advocated at Yale. Jefferson thought that classical literature offered some of the best and most beautiful examples of good writing. He acknowledged that he was grateful for his own classical education, for the sheer pleasure that it had given him, and for relieving the boredom of an enfeebled old age during which one of his favorite pastimes was reading the original texts of classics.[62] In a wonderful testimony of the joy and reward of learning for its own sake, he wrote to Joseph Priestley, "I thank on my knees those who directed my early education for having put into my possession this rich source of delight. . . . I would not exchange it for anything which I could then have acquired and have since acquired."[63] He credited Peter Jefferson for enabling him to read the classics, thinking himself "more indebted for this to my father than for all the other luxuries his cares and affection have placed within my reach."[64]

Jefferson did not dismiss the idea of study for its own sake and was well aware that a proportion of the wealthy students would not need to qualify for a profession. Even for those who sought professional careers, it was not necessary at the time to have a degree or formal qualification to become a lawyer or doctor. His inclusion of vocational training was consistent with the role of the earliest medieval universities, which first and foremost provided professional training for lawyers, clergymen, government officials, and doctors.[65]

However, Jefferson had no patience for metaphysics or abstract philosophical speculation, particularly disliking theological arguments because they could not be verified by empirical evidence. He excluded the fine arts from the curriculum because he thought that art and art history were too expensive to teach without sculptures and old-master paintings to provide visual reference, writing that "it would be useless therefore and preposterous for us to endeavor to make ourselves connoisseurs in those arts. These are worth seeing, but not studying."[66] It was to be many years before the formal teaching of the fine arts was introduced into any American college. Still, along with the Board of Visitors, he gave the faculty discretion to hire lecturers and proposed at their first meeting to find someone to teach music and art while still emphasizing practical knowledge. It is more remarkable that Jefferson wanted to provide access to the arts in the form of a museum, galleries, books, and musical concerts in the Rotunda. The university was an expensive essay in architecture for the students, which was in itself a powerful statement of Jefferson's own appreciation of the arts and his belief in their importance.

BECAUSE OF HIS WISH to create an egalitarian intellectual community, combined with the traditional republican fear about the dangers of concentrating power, Jefferson instituted a flat administrative structure that departed from the hierarchical tradition of other colleges in America. Until the appointment of Dr. Edwin A. Alderman in 1905, the university had no president, a dominant position at most other universities whose prestige helped

attract prospective students.⁶⁷ Jefferson instead introduced a rotational system of faculty governance with professors serving as chairman of the faculty
for one-year terms, a system that proved impractical according to George
Tucker because "persons may be well qualified to teach, but too devoid of
personal dignity or moral propriety to be head of the Institution."⁶⁸ The
university was very different from the German model in Berlin, where Wilhelm von Humboldt thought it "no more advisable for teachers to govern
themselves than it is for a troupe of actors to direct their own affairs."⁶⁹ Although faculty governance continued until 1905, the system was soon modified to enable faculty to elect their chairman and to provide some financial
incentive for professors to serve in that position.

The Board of Visitors oversaw the operations and management of the
university. The board elected its chairman, known as the rector, beginning
first with Thomas Jefferson in the role and then with James Madison. The
rector was merely first among equals, presiding over the deliberations of the
board but lacking a casting vote or any delegated authority. Jefferson envisaged a board composed of individuals whose academic abilities matched
those of the faculty. Since there were few such people in the state, he originally suggested limiting the board to five members, but the number was
expanded to seven, and these men retained their membership when Central College became the University of Virginia. The board members were
chosen by the governor and council of the state of Virginia. In placing the
university under public control, Jefferson was influenced by his experiences
with the College of William and Mary, where the governing body was also
called the Board of Visitors and where the faculty enjoyed a greater degree of self-government in common with the colleges of Oxford and Cambridge. When Jefferson attended the college, its unelected board had been
in disastrous conflict with the General Assembly in Williamsburg.⁷⁰ Public
oversight accorded with Jefferson's belief in accountability to the electorate,
which in turn would contribute to the survival and funding of the university. Still, state control was (and remains) much less intrusive than at universities in Europe, where central governments oversaw a national system
of universities, often integrating professors into the civil service, making appointments, and determining the curriculum.

Professor Robley Dunglison likened the governance of the university to
a separation of powers between the executive branch (the faculty) and the
legislative branch (the Board of Visitors). After six years of experience at
the university, he suggested that a professor be allowed to sit as a faculty
delegate on the Board of Visitors, "who even if he had no vote might be

expected to take a part in those deliberations which regarded the rules and regulations of the university." The faculty member "would have the advantage of the voice of experience," while the rest of the faculty, by choosing a delegate, "could always be represented, should discussions arise between them and their presiding officer."[71] Unlike the governing board of the University of Pennsylvania, which was one of the few other universities without a president, the Board of Visitors did not micromanage, but it was involved in decisions that are now left entirely to the discretion of departments and administrators, such as the selection of faculty.[72]

WRITING TO THE British historian and abolitionist William Roscoe in December 1820, Jefferson penned his great vision of academic freedom when he wrote that "this institution will be based on the illimitable freedom of the human mind. for here we are not afraid to follow truth wherever it may lead, not to tolerate any error as long as reason is free to combat it."[73] Historian Richard Hofstadter argued that "in one important respect Jefferson's philosophy of academic liberty was deficient and inconsistent: for all the fine and deeply felt rhetoric about the illimitable freedom of the human mind he could not transcend the tendency, almost universal at the time, to subordinate intellectual freedom in some considerable measure to considerations of partisan politics." It demonstrated to Hofstadter that "even Jefferson, the most enlightened lay educator of his time, had not thoroughly thought out the intensely perplexing problems of freedom in education."[74] This oft-repeated criticism alluded to Jefferson's efforts to have the teaching of law and politics be consistent with Republican Party principles.

Like many old revolutionaries, Jefferson was concerned with ideological purity, which for him meant preserving the "spirit of 1776." This was particularly true in his plans for the law school, which he regarded as especially important to ensure the survival of the republican system. He hoped that within twenty years, "a majority of our own legislatures, will be from our school, & many disciples will have carried its doctrines home with them to their several states."[75] Likening lawyers to priests, he was suspicious of their ability to "throw dust in the eyes of the people" and their "endless quibbles, chicaneries, perversions, vexations and delays" when serving in legislatures.[76] Of his particular *bête noire*, the Federalist Supreme Court chief justice John Marshall, he wrote that Marshall treated the law as "nothing more than an ambiguous text to be explained by his sophistry into any meaning which may subserve his personal malices."[77]

In law and politics, Jefferson thought it his and Madison's duty "to lay down the principles which are to be taught."[78] He wanted to end what he saw as the corruption of American law occasioned by the continued influence of a Tory version of British law spread by William Blackstone's *Commentaries on the English Law* and the opinions of William Murray, the Earl of Mansfield, the lord chief justice of the King's Bench, who had served in the cabinet of Lord North under George III.[79] The word "Tory" was used to describe loyalists during the American Revolution and had previously applied to those said to espouse ideas of divine-right monarchy and passive obedience under the Stuart monarchy in seventeenth-century England. Jefferson saw their influence in the interpretations by the Federalist government of the First Amendment in upholding the Sedition Acts (1798) and in the judgments of Chief Justice Marshall.

Jefferson believed that the "honied [honeyed] Mansfieldism" of Blackstone's *Commentaries* gave an indolent student the dangerous illusion that he was "master of the whole body of the law." It threatened to lead students astray, especially when supplemented by David Hume's Tory *History of England*.[80] According to Jefferson, in one of many instances of his hyperbole, Blackstone and Hume "made tories of all England and are making tories of those young Americans" and had done "more towards the suppression of the liberties of man, than all the millions of men in arms of Bonaparte."[81] In other words, he associated this legal tradition with support for authoritarian government and the royal prerogative and believed that the remedy was to have students read the English jurist Sir Edward Coke, especially his *Institutes of the Lawes of England* (1628–44), a work that invoked the common-law tradition against the newly assumed powers of Charles I.

As with Jefferson's views on the education of physicians, he was critical of the system of training lawyers through apprenticeships, in which he thought they received little guidance in return for their work. "As other branches of science, especially history, are necessary to form a lawyer," he believed that students needed two to three years of broad reading. To one aspiring law student, he recommended a background in French, mathematics, Latin, natural philosophy (physics, chemistry, and astronomy), ethics, religion, natural law, *belles lettres*, criticism, rhetoric, and oratory.[82] He wanted to train republican lawyers as an antidote to Federalists, whose jurisprudence he regarded as a hybrid combining Old Testament law with "a little dash of Common law, & great mass of original notions of their own." Jefferson also dismissed what he called "Richmond lawyers" who were protégés of Marshall.[83]

Jefferson and Madison devoted more time recruiting a law professor than any other faculty position at the university. Their difficulty was partly due to the university requirement that the professor not practice law. Francis Walker Gilmer turned down the post three times and died soon after finally accepting it. Jefferson and Madison were so ambitious to obtain an outstanding candidate that they offered it to William Wirt, the U.S. attorney general. With Jefferson's reluctant agreement, they were even willing to create the office of president to increase the salary and to entice Wirt. After Wirt rejected the offer in April 1826, at his recommendation they appointed John Tayloe Lomax, a graduate of St. John's College and a lawyer in Fredericksburg, who agreed to begin teaching on July 1. Lomax was an influential jurist and author whose *Digest of the Laws Respecting Real Property* was adopted throughout the United States.[84] He and his successor expounded a radical interpretation of states' rights.[85]

Jefferson was in reality less prescriptive than critics like Richard Hofstadter allege, since he was capable of appointing faculty with opposing views to his own. A fifty-year-old former three-term U.S. congressman, George Tucker was the most senior member of the original faculty and its first chairman, despite the fact that his political views conflicted with those of Jefferson. A contemporary of Joseph C. Cabell and John Hartwell Cocke as undergraduates at the College of William and Mary, Tucker attributed his appointment to his *Essays on Various Subjects of Taste, Morals, and National Policy* (1822), "of which I had learnt both Mr. Jefferson and Mr. Madison had spoken highly." He was ambivalent about accepting the professorship since he felt himself unqualified, which he "frankly stated to Mr. Jefferson," who "made light of my objection, which he regarded as merely temporary." After meeting at Monticello with Jefferson, "whose address and powers of pleasing were very great" and who "so favorably represented the life I should lead," Tucker hesitated no longer.[86] His appointment was remarkable because the volume that so impressed both Jefferson and Madison repudiated some of the former's most cherished beliefs. An essay on national debt argued that government debt redistributed wealth, gave employment to unproductive parts of the country, and represented no threat as long as government was able to borrow. Another essay, on banks, dismissed Jefferson's notion that they created bogus capital. He defended dueling and once nearly engaged in a duel himself.

Elsewhere, Tucker wrote in favor of manufacturing and industry. He privately admitted that he thought the tariff issue "greatly overrated."[87] He distrusted France. As a whole, these were classic Hamiltonian positions, the acceptance of which had led Jefferson to resign from the cabinet at the end of 1793. Tucker also defended the classical curriculum against an emphasis on utilitarian subjects. In the *Richmond Enquirer*, he wrote an article about luxury and its positive effects. He even admitted to being fond of Chief Justice Marshall. With a scar in one eye impairing his vision, Tucker was also a well-known gambler who lost $1,000 in one game against another congressman, "a notorious swindler," whom Tucker claimed wore glasses to read the marks and scratches on the backs of some of the cards.[88]

A prolific writer, Tucker claimed to have published over ten thousand pages by the end of his career.[89] As author of *The Laws of Wages, Profits and Rent, Investigated* (1837) and *The Progress of the United States in Population and Wealth* (1843), he was not only a leading economist in the South but, according to scholar Eugene D. Genovese, "arguably the ablest political economist in the United States."[90] He contributed to periodicals and journals like the *British Spy, North American Review, American Quarterly, Southern Literary Messenger*, and *Democratic Review*. He wrote two novels, published by the same New York press that printed James Fenimore Cooper, beginning with *The Valley of Shenandoah; or, Memoirs of the Grayson* (1824), a two-volume work reprinted in England and translated into German that attempted to emulate Sir Walter Scott. Tucker also published one of the first science-fiction novels in America, *Voyage to the Moon* (1827), a satire that he claimed James Fenimore Cooper imitated in *The Monikins* (1835). Tucker published his last set of essays at the age of eighty-five.

Tucker wrote one of the first and most substantial biographies of Thomas Jefferson (1837), which he dedicated to James Madison. It won the admiration of Lord Brougham, who "said that he had previously entertained a strong prejudice against Jefferson."[91] Tucker had first met Jefferson while the latter was vice president of the United States in 1797. Tucker "was struck by his easy politeness and familiar conversations" and by "his library, his philosophical instruments, and his workshop." These objects of curiosity had "augmented the interest which his character and his position as head of the republican party excited." In his two-volume biography of Jefferson, Tucker claimed to draw a veil "over his faults and defects to which I was not blind"; although critical of some of his policies, it was generally very favorable. He was more ambivalent in his private memoirs, where he described Jefferson as having the "most winning manners when he chose to exert them, but he was occasionally somewhat dictatorial and impatient of contradiction, which Madison never appeared to be."[92]

James Madison was less concerned about political orthodoxy than Jefferson and tellingly did not want the syllabus for law to include his own

Virginia Resolves (1799), which represented a classic statement of states' rights against the Federalist Alien and Sedition Acts. He thought that the document was controversial, even among fellow party supporters, and that it might alienate potential students, including those who were applying to study subjects other than law. Madison argued for avoiding extremes "by referring to selected standards without requiring an unqualified conformity to them."[93] It is one of the few occasions over forty years on which he and Jefferson disagreed.

Whereas the trustees specified textbooks in many universities, Jefferson deferred to the faculty in most subject areas, believing that he and other members of the board lacked the knowledge to impose their choices and that it was "better left to the professors."[94] Even so, Jefferson did assign a list of readings "on the principles of government" to accompany the study of law. His preferences were described by the late Curry School professor Jennings Wagoner as "prescriptive not proscriptive."[95] Many works of which Jefferson disapproved were available in the library, and indeed the students checked out copies of Blackstone more frequently than any other law book. By the 1830s, the law tutor was even assigning Blackstone's *Commentaries*. The students ultimately decided for themselves. As Jefferson was the first to acknowledge, the earth belonged to the living, and the living generation sometimes subverted his wishes. Tucker assigned Hume's *History of England*, believing that students could read his work "without any danger of being contaminated by his principles of government" and turned into British Tories.[96]

In the end, Jefferson did not try to institutionalize republicanism—unlike Dickinson College, which tried to indoctrinate students in republican ideas through a special lecture series in 1798.[97] At the University of North Carolina, the trustees tried at one stage to ban all political debate, decreeing that "no speech by a student shall have any allusion to party politics."[98] Jefferson's vision of the curriculum was also very different from the example of Napoleon, who wanted a state monopoly of Europe's universities and teaching corporations. The French emperor simply abolished courses on political science and ethics, and he destroyed the economic independence of the colleges by confiscating their endowments.[99]

At the University of Virginia, the faculty furthermore enjoyed reasonable guarantees of tenure. George Long asked about job security while he was still in England. He was told that professors could only be removed by a majority of five votes among the seven members of the Board of Visitors. When the board tried to reduce faculty salaries in 1848, a dismayed George

Tucker recalled "an assurance from Mr. Jefferson that he considered the tenure of office to be equivalent to a life estate, the professor removable only by 5 votes out of 7, which could not be expected to take place except in cases of delinquency."[100] Jefferson gave similar pledges to John Tayloe Lomax and John Patten Emmet. While academic freedom and tenure were hardly discussed in nineteenth-century America, Jefferson was aware of their importance. He had heard from George Ticknor that the vitality, productivity, motivation, and quality of the faculty at the University of Göttingen "now leaves England at least twenty years behind" in the classics, a situation Ticknor attributed to the lack of political interference owing to the university's location in the tolerant British kingdom of Hanover.[101]

In terms of the freedom of ideas, the library's failure to purchase any antislavery texts was far more troubling. Jefferson went to great lengths to draw up lists for the library to purchase and consulted with many others, including Madison and John Adams. The absence of abolitionist literature was a stunning omission and an indication of Jefferson's willingness to appease the proslavery interest in his late retirement to garner their support for the university. However, the most obvious area in which he was doctrinaire was his insistence that there be no department of religion and no chapel. He was only willing to permit the study of religion in the context of classes on history, politics, philosophy, ethics, or literature. This was the most controversial feature of his vision among contemporaries, who asked, with some justification, why religion should be treated differently from any other subject.

7

A Wall of Separation

T HE YEAR OF the creation of the University of Virginia in 1819, Thomas Jefferson resumed an editing project that he had started while in the White House (then called "the President's House"). Using the King James edition of the Bible, the process involved cutting and pasting passages from the four Gospels of the New Testament. He performed the task with a sharp razor knife, deleting some verses and arranging the rest in chronological order, from four editions of the Gospels (English, French, Latin, and Greek). With the different languages side by side, he pasted the extracts in four columns onto blank pages with the aim of extracting the "diamonds" from what he called the "dunghill" of accretions and falsifications of the life of Jesus.[1]

Seeking to create a rational, demystified version of the Gospels and excluding the rest of the New Testament, Jefferson edited the parallel texts to remove passages, including all the stories of miracles performed by Jesus, the immaculate conception, the virgin birth, the resurrection, and the visible ascension. He rejected the Trinity, which he regarded as a return to the polytheistic religions of the ancient world, and the concepts of original sin, predestination, transubstantiation, atonement, and the deification of Jesus. Jefferson aimed to restore the Gospels to their original form, which he argued had been corrupted by generations of religious leaders, in alliance with government, intent on controlling, duping, and keeping ordinary people under subjection. He retained only those passages that contained moral and ethical teachings, including many parables such as that of the Good Samaritan.

Jefferson's actions would have been regarded as sacrilegious in an increasingly evangelical age, and he was at pains to keep the project secret, but it demonstrated moral courage in his willingness to question an entrenched system of beliefs, even in private. It also reflected the originality of his intellect in an early application of hermeneutics that treated the Gospels as any other literary text, ignoring claims for their divine inspiration. Indeed, it was in some ways similar to the project of the current Jesus Seminar (1985–). Much influenced by the writings of Joseph Priestley's *A History of the Corruptions of Christianity in England* (1782), Jefferson's undertaking was all the more remarkable for having been begun by a sitting president of the United States.

Jefferson started editing the Gospels in 1803, when he informed Benjamin Rush that he was working on a "Syllabus" or "Outline," which he eventually titled "The Syllabus of an Estimate of the Merit of the Doctrines of Jesus, Compared with Those of Others."[2] It was inspired by a contemporary pamphlet by Priestley on *Socrates and Jesus Compared* (1803), which argued that many passages in the Bible were false additions that had accrued over the centuries. He called for a return to the pure teachings of Jesus. Jefferson was concerned at the time by political attacks during the election of 1800 accusing him of being an atheist. He was trying to clarify his beliefs for his own benefit as well as that of Rush, who spent many years trying to convert him to practicing Christianity and who, failing in that, did succeed in reconciling Jefferson and John Adams. Jefferson sent the "Syllabus" to Rush to fulfill a promise that he had made during their debates on religion in the late 1790s. Consisting of three parts, the work compared the moral thought of "the most esteemed" philosophers of the classical worlds of Greece and Rome, the Jews of the Old Testament, and the teachings of Jesus of Nazareth. Jefferson sent a copy to Priestley as well, adding that he had ordered from Philadelphia two copies of a Greek edition and two copies of an English edition of the New Testament, "with a design to cut out morsels of morality, and paste them on the leaves of a book."[3] Jefferson had wanted Priestley to write a volume that summarized the beliefs and moral codes of the major religions of the world, thinking that the common elements would offer a universal system of social ethics more accurately reflecting the will of God.

Aimed at removing what he regarded as corruptions of the text, Jefferson compiled a forty-six-page manuscript edition of the Gospels that he called "The Philosophy of Jesus of Nazareth Extracted from the Account of His Life and Doctrines as Given by Matthew, Mark, Luke, and John." According to his own account, "it was the work of 2. or 3. nights only at Washington, after getting thro' the evening task of reading the letters and papers of the day."[4] Completed by March 10, 1804, he said that it was for "the use of the Indians who were unembarrassed with matters of fact or faith beyond the level of their comprehensions." The reasons for his claiming to have written for Indians are disputed. By "Indians" he may well have been referring in a veiled way to the Federalists, whom he regarded as superstitious and unreflecting. Intended only for himself and a few intimate friends, his pretense about the intended audience may alternatively have been a ruse to disguise the work's purpose if it ever became public knowledge. Jefferson was unable to spend sufficient time as president to complete the task to his own standard. As late as October 1813, he told John Adams that he would never be capable of completing the task, which he regarded as too broad a canvas for a man in his seventies.[5]

Acknowledging in retirement that his first efforts to edit the Gospels had been "attempted too hastily," Jefferson wrote that, "with one foot in the grave," it would become one of his "idle projects," aiming to "beguile the wearisomeness of declining life."[6] In the year of the bill establishing Central College (1816), he credited his rekindling of interest to his correspondence with John Adams, who was concerned with the continuing influence of state-supported church establishments by Congregationalists in Massachusetts and Connecticut. Jefferson sent Adams a copy of his "Syllabus" and another copy to a correspondent who was writing a history of the life of Jesus. He urged the latter to use "caution, lest it should get out in connection with my name," since he was "unwilling to draw on myself a swarm of insects, whose buz is more disquieting than their bite." Nevertheless, he encouraged the biography of Jesus in order that "the world will see, after the fogs shall be dispelled, in which for 14. centuries he has been inveloped by Jugglers to make money of him, when the genuine character shall be exhibited, which they have dressed up in the rags of an Imposter, the world, I say, will at length see the immortal merit of this first of human Sages."[7]

In retirement, Jefferson returned to his project, using additional copies of the Gospels that he had purchased as president. He was more secretive than ever, working alone in his study and sharing the text with no one, not even his daughter Martha Randolph. His return to the project was indicative of its importance for his own spiritual quest. When it was complete in 1820, he had it bound in red leather in Richmond with the title on the spine reading, "The Life and Morals of Jesus of Nazareth Extracted Textually from the Gospels in Greek, Latin, French & English." The small volume, 8½ inches in height and 5 inches wide, contained a total of eighty-one pages.

On behalf of the Smithsonian Institution in 1895, librarian Cyrus Adler purchased the original of what affectionately became known as the "Jefferson Bible" from Jefferson's great-granddaughter Carolina Ramsay Randolph. Adler had earlier discovered and privately purchased two copies of the New Testament that could be traced to the posthumous sale of Jefferson's possessions at Monticello. With entire passages cut out by Jefferson's razor to paste into the final version, Adler's family donated these volumes to the Smithsonian in 1920. First published by order of Congress in 1902, at the behest of Congressmen John F. Lacey, nine thousand copies of *The Jefferson Bible* were distributed to members of both chambers, and thereafter every new senator received a copy until the supply ran out in the 1950s. The decision to publish a volume that by omission denied the divinity of Christ was protested at the time by the Presbyterian Ministers' Association. A practicing Christian, Lacey responded that "no one that examines this little volume, whether he be saint or sinner, will rise from his perusal without having a loftier idea of the teachings of our Savior."[8]

JEFFERSON WAS MORE dogmatic about the teaching of religion than any other subject at the University of Virginia. His treatment of it was the most distinctive and controversial feature of the entire enterprise. As with so much else in the creation of the university, in order to understand his approach, we need to consider the evolution of his private beliefs and why he was so fearful of the influence of organized religion.

In 1819, as he returned to his project of editing the Gospels, Jefferson declared, "I am of a sect by myself, as far as I know."[9] Certain that his opponents wished "it to be believed that he can have no religion who advocates its freedom," he insisted that religion was a private and voluntary matter.[10] Like every other subject, it should be based on factual evidence and rigorous examination, not inherited tradition or authority. He characteristically advised Peter Carr, his nephew, that he should "lay aside all prejudice . . . and neither believe nor reject any thing because any other person, or descriptions of persons have rejected or believe it." Jefferson reminded Carr that "your own reason is the only oracle given you by heaven" and suggested that he read the Bible with the same critical facilities "as you would read Livy or Tacitus."[11] The former president was very much an empiricist who accepted only factual evidence and provable propositions. With respect to the apocalypse, he commented that "what has no meaning admits no explanation."[12]

Jefferson saw religion as providing a moral system whose practice would promote happiness. He grounded the validity of a particular faith on its promotion of benevolence, charity, and kindness, rather than the niceties of theological doctrines. He maintained that action and good deeds were more important than words and beliefs. Influenced by the ideas of the Scottish Enlightenment, he thought that God had given everyone an innate moral sense, a natural benevolence, and a predisposition to do good, but that these characteristics could be developed more fully through education. The truth of a religious proposition could best be gauged by what all could approve. Where there were disagreements and sectarian feuds, the dictum was "most probably wrong."[13] He was raised an Anglican and continued to be an Episcopalian. Until the Episcopalians built Christ Church in 1825, the Methodists, Baptists, Presbyterians, and Episcopalians rotated their religious services at the courthouse in Charlottesville. Jefferson sporadically attended and donated money to all the churches in Charlottesville. Reuben Maury, an Episcopalian parishioner, later recalled how Jefferson "sat very far back" on a collapsible three-legged cane stool, which he carried into the church service under his arm.[14] In retirement, Jefferson's correspondence referred to daily prayers, while he spent the last hour in the evening reading texts that inspired moral thought.[15] He rejected the central idea associated with deists that God was a clockmaker who stood aside after creating the universe, leaving humanity to live without divine intervention.[16]

While he never used the title, "The Jefferson Bible" essentially consisted of moral sayings that reflected his creed and beliefs. The project was not an arid intellectual exercise, for it helped to fulfill his own spiritual quest, which followed a long period of doubt. He thereafter regarded himself as a "Christian in the only sense in which [Jesus] wished anyone to be," which Jefferson defined as being "sincerely attached to his doctrines, in preference to all others" while insisting that Jesus made no claims to divine powers or to being the son of God.[17] This view was shared by John Adams. After reading Jefferson's "Syllabus," Adams asserted that the character and doctrines of Jesus had suffered through the shortcomings of his followers, who had embellished and "disfigured" the truth to such an extent that it caused many to "throw off the whole System in disgust" and see Christ as an "Impostor," a tragic misrepresentation of "the most innocent, the most benevolent, the most eloquent and sublime Character, that ever has been exhibited to Man."[18] Jefferson similarly blamed those purporting to promote their faith as "the greatest enemies to the doctrines of Jesus," people who had "perverted them for the structure of a system of fancy absolutely incomprehensible, and without any foundation in his genuine words."[19] "Of this band of dupes and imposters," he regarded Saint Paul as "the great Coryphaeus [the leader of the chorus in Athenian plays], and first corrupter of the doctrines of Jesus."[20] He felt that as a religion, Christianity in its unadulterated form offered "the most sublime and benevolent code of morals which has ever been offered to man."[21]

Jefferson denied being an atheist, but he was doubtful of his own beliefs and skeptical about organized religion from at least his time as a college student. He was especially influenced by the writings of the English author Henry St. John, Viscount Bolingbroke. In Jefferson's Literary Commonplace Book, he copied more passages from Bolingbroke than any other author and later claimed to have read him five times. Bolingbroke wondered why the God of the universe would reveal himself to a single nation in the eastern Mediterranean. He condemned the bigotry and persecution done in the name of religion, noting that in England, "men have been burned under one reign, for the very same doctrines they were obliged to profess in another."[22] Jefferson was also acquainted with the work of the English deists John Toland and Matthew Tindall. Jefferson's belief that Christianity had been corrupted found contemporary confirmation by such writers as Edward Gibbon, who recounted in *The History of the Decline and Fall of the Roman Empire* (1776–89) the politics behind the selection of approved sacred texts over the course of several centuries. The historical arguments of how religion had led to war in the Comte de Volney's work *Les Ruines; ou, Méditations sour les révolutions des empires* (The Ruins; or, Meditations of the Revolutions of Empires, 1791) so impressed Jefferson that he wanted it translated. Drawing on passages from the *Essays on the Principles of Morality and Natural Religion* (1751) by the Scottish Enlightenment thinker Lord Kames, Jefferson believed in what he called a natural religion based on principles shared between different faiths.

Jefferson found his own religion in the demythologized Christianity of Priestley, supplemented by the moral teachings of earlier classical authors, particularly Epictetus and Epicurus. After reading Priestley, Jefferson no longer accepted Bolingbroke's claim that the ancient philosophers offered a more complete and coherent system of morals than Jesus. The main object of his ire was not religion per se but organized religion, in which sects and denominations claim an exclusive monopoly of the truth in their doctrines and biblical interpretations. He denounced what he called "priestcraft," originally an anti-Catholic term used in the Protestant Reformation that deists adopted to critique clergy who they believed had adulterated the teachings of Christianity. Jefferson was especially critical when political leaders used religion to strengthen their support.[23]

JEFFERSON REGARDED THE Virginia Statute for Religious Freedom (drafted in 1779 and enacted in 1786) as one of his three greatest achievements, to be included on his tombstone along with the drafting of the Declaration of Independence and the founding of the University of Virginia. Until Chief Justice William Rehnquist moved the Supreme Court in a different direction in the late twentieth century, the statute was the main source used to interpret the freedom-of-religion clause in the First Amendment.[24] It also informed his friendship with James Madison. Although Jefferson drafted the bill for religious freedom in Virginia, Madison was especially passionate on the subject and responsible for handling the successful passage of the statute while Jefferson was away in Paris. The statute grew out of their view that simply tolerating religious diversity was inadequate; only the legal free exercise of any or no religion would suffice. It famously declared that "no man shall be compelled to frequent or support any religious worship, place, or ministry whatsoever, nor shall be enforced, restrained, molested or burthened in his body or goods, nor shall otherwise suffer, on account of his religious opinions or belief." In his incomplete autobiography of 1821, not published during his lifetime, Jefferson took pleasure in the fact that legislative attempts to insert the words "Jesus Christ" into the preamble, and thereby limit religious freedom to Christians, was defeated. Preferring the free exercise of religion to the more passive concept of religious toleration, he insisted that it was "meant to comprehend, within the mantle of its protection, the Jew and the Gentile, the Christian and Mahometan [Muslim], the Hindoo and the infidel of every denomination."[25] This position was more comprehensive than the limited religious toleration advocated by John Locke.

Like so many of his ideas, Jefferson's views on religion have become so commonplace as to be taken for granted, while we forget the extent of religious bigotry and persecution at the time, such as the whippings of Baptists in Virginia before the American Revolution. In North Carolina, Catholics did not enjoy full legal equality until 1835 and Jews until 1868.[26] The Virginia Statute for Religious Freedom attracted the support of some religious groups, including the Baptists, whose petitions even mentioned religious freedom for Muslims and other non-Christians. The statute inspired similar legislation in other states, which all began a process of religious disestablishment after the American Revolution, with the exception of the

Federalist strongholds of Connecticut and Massachusetts, where Congregationalism continued to be the state-supported religion until 1818 and 1833, respectively.

In a letter to the Danbury, Connecticut, Baptists in 1802, Jefferson famously wrote that the First Amendment created "a wall of separation between church & state," a concept illustrated in his treatment of religion at the University of Virginia.[27] With a few noted parallels such as in France, Australia, and Turkey, it remains one of the more exceptional features of the United States. Most other countries have avoided clarifying the relationship, while some 40 percent of countries still have a state religion. Unlike separationists in France and Turkey, Jefferson and Madison were not simply concerned with the corruption of the state by religion but also the corruption of religion by government, which could, unchecked, interfere in religious activities.

As president, Jefferson attended religious services in the House of Representatives. The distinction was that these were private meetings, in which no one was subject to proselytizing against their will. However, he refused to follow the example of George Washington and John Adams, who proclaimed national fast days, which he thought contrary to the Constitution. Jefferson regarded organized religion as having been instrumental in the rise of Old World tyrannies through an alliance of kings, nobles, and priests. He disliked theology and any kind of metaphysical speculation in which people fought over abstractions that they did not understand. He had no time for dogmas, particularly the Protestant Puritan doctrines of John Calvin, so influential among New England Presbyterians and Congregationalists, and the Catholic religious exercises formulated by Ignatius Loyola, who founded the Jesuit Order. Because he was not interested in theology, he often had an almost caricatured view of these other dogmas while failing to be aware of the dogmatism and inconsistencies in his own religious thinking.

JEFFERSON'S PLAN FOR the university is such a powerful example of his ideas of religious separation that it has been the subject of heated debate in interpreting the First Amendment.[28] Jefferson prevented the teaching of theology and the physical presence of a chapel at the University of Virginia. He justified the exclusion of religion from the university both because it was a public institution and because the different denominations would constantly feud for control. As Madison explained to Edward Everett, if religion were allowed at the university, it would either become a sectarian monopoly or, with "professorships of rival sects, it would be an arena of theological gladiators."[29] Based on his knowledge of history, Jefferson's belief that the effort to impose doctrinal uniformity had led to "millions of innocent men, women and children" being "burnt, tortured, fined, [and] imprisoned," making "one half the world fools, and the other half hypocrites."[30] To him traditional religions were a form of tyranny whose dogmatism often bolstered political tyrannies in which their leaders returned the favor by giving special privileges to state churches.

Jefferson regarded the clergy as analogous to lawyers, both equally dangerous because of their claims to a monopoly of truth and to special powers. He saw each as an obstacle to progress for thinking that "institutions established for the use of the nation, cannot be touched nor modified." Each believed that "the earth belongs to the dead, & not the living."[31] Organized religion was one of the ultimate threats to freedom of the mind and freedom of inquiry, which is why Jefferson thought it so important to exclude it from the university. It was in the context of religion that he wrote his much-quoted phrase, inscribed on the walls of the Jefferson Memorial in Washington, D.C., "I have sworn upon the altar of god eternal hostility against every form of tyranny over the mind of man."[32] In matters of religion, he inverted the revolutionary slogan to read, "Divided we stand, united we fall," meaning that it was healthier to have many competing religions instead of one dominant religion.[33] He despised the demands for conformity in "vestments, ceremonies, physical opinions, & metaphysical speculations, totally unconnected with morality & unimportant to the legitimate objects of society."[34] This only led to factions, separations, and bloodshed.

Jefferson doubted that contemporary revolutions in South America would succeed, partly because illiteracy was so widespread in the region but also because the inhabitants were not prepared for religious freedom, being too bigoted to accept it for themselves, "much less to trust others with it."[35] Like Priestley, he believed that unfettered religious and intellectual freedom would enable science to demystify religion. He predicted that "the day will come" when the story of the virgin birth of Jesus "will be classed with the fable of the generation of Minerva in the brain of Jupiter."[36] His own interest in geology and fossils made him an early exponent of a secular explanation for the origins and development of the earth.[37] He anticipated that religious freedom would engender a competitive marketplace in religious ideas through which the public would gradually gravitate to a rational faith, writing that "I confidently expect that the present generation will see Unitarianism become the general religion of the United States."[38]

Yet as he did with his views on the abolition of slavery, Jefferson became more guarded and less public about his religious opinions over time, not least because they became less politically acceptable as Americans in the early nineteenth century became more evangelical. He was similarly more reticent about his abolitionist views as they became increasingly taboo in the South with the reinvigoration of slavery owing to the rise in the production of cotton. He did not reveal his views on religion to anyone, except for a few very trusted, sympathetic friends; he insisted they keep his correspondence private. He declared that "not for the world" would he see his letters on the subject published, saying that he would sooner "undertake to bring the crazy skulls of Bedlam [the mental asylum in London] to sound understanding."[39]

Jefferson's revolutionary idea of a secular university was at odds with the prevailing opinion of his time, replete with popular religious revivals and the Second Great Awakening. The period of the founding of the university also coincided with the birth of such evangelical religious organizations as the American Tract Society (1814), American Bible Society (1816), American Education Society (1816), American Sunday School Union (1824), American Home Missionary Society (1826), and American Temperance Society (1826). Throughout the antebellum period, seminaries and church-sponsored colleges proliferated, such as the Furman Institution (1826) for Baptists, the Columbia Theological Seminary (1828) for Presbyterians, Randolph Macon College (1830) and Wesleyan College (1831) for Methodists, and the University of the South at Sewanee (1857) for Episcopalians.

As with ending slavery, Jefferson thought that his generation would have to leave "to others, younger & more learned than we are," the task of restoring "the primitive simplicity" of early Christianity.[40] Like the early 1640s in England and the late 1960s in the United States, the period of revolution had been conducive to radical and utopian ideas. By 1822, Jefferson was warning "that the atmosphere of our country is unquestionably charged with a threatening cloud of fanaticism, lighter in some parts, denser in others, but too heavy in all."[41] Jefferson's Virginia Statute for Religious Freedom most likely would not have passed twenty years later. Again, in common with his views on slavery, he made few public statements on religion after the publication of his *Notes on the State of Virginia* (1787). There he made the case for treating religion as a private matter between individuals and their creator, famously declaring that "it does me no injury for my neighbor to say there are twenty gods, or no God. It neither picks my pocket nor breaks my leg."[42]

Jefferson was ahead of his time. As late as 1873, Cardinal John Henry

Newman was still contending that religion and theology ought to be at the center of a university. In his classic statement on liberal arts education, *The Idea of a University Defined and Illustrated*, Newman regarded theology as the capstone science giving coherence and meaning to knowledge. Writing the original lectures for his book over thirty years after the founding of the University of Virginia, Newman specifically characterized a college that excluded such a "special and important" subject as religion as a "seat of learning [that] calls itself what [it] is not" and "an intellectual absurdity." In his view, "religious doctrine is knowledge and therefore should be included in the curriculum." Newman warned that knowledge would become over-specialized and fragmented "if you begin the mutilation with the divine," since religious truth was not simply a field of study but "a condition of general knowledge."[43] He was consequently critical of what he regarded as an exclusive emphasis on empirical evidence and reason. This view that religion should be at the heart of a university was shared by many of Jefferson's colleagues in the struggle for independence. Benjamin Rush similarly insisted that "the only foundation for a useful education in a republic is to be laid in RELIGION. Without this, there can be no virtue, and without virtue there can be no liberty, and liberty is the object and life of all republican governments. . . . The religion I mean to recommend in this place is the religion of JESUS CHRIST."[44]

Despite this major divide, Newman's and Jefferson's visions had much in common. Both thought that universities should be committed to the pursuit of knowledge, the teaching of science, and a philosophical approach to knowledge. Both decried overspecialization and men with only one idea. Both regarded a true university as one that offered the most comprehensive coverage of the span of subject areas. Both believed that the university should be a nurturing family "knowing her children one by one," in Newman's words, "not a foundry, or a mint or a treadmill."[45] While Jefferson's idea of a secular university has become the standard model, the approach of Newman and Rush prevailed in the short term, and the tension persists.

ALTHOUGH HISTORIANS OFTEN highlight the conflict between organized religion and the rise of science, it is equally true that religion played a critical role in fostering the development of education at all levels. European universities owed their original existence to the Catholic church. Institutions like Oxford University can point to no exact founding date but rather to a gradual emergence that began with clerical scholars gathering together to share ideas and supplement their income by teaching. Despite their informal early development, the medieval universities became the incubators of such later teaching methods as recitations and lectures. Until the French Revolution, universities continued to be religious institutions with faculties composed predominantly, and often exclusively, of clergymen. Indeed, the nomenclature of modern universities still harkens back to their religious origins with words like "fellowship," "rector," "chancellor," "provost," and "dean," and with title of degrees and degree ceremonies that include the laying on of hands. The idea of a residential community engaged in reflection, scholarship, and a life of contemplation featured both in the monasteries and in early medieval universities. Despite the English Reformation against the Catholic church, teaching fellows at Oxford and Cambridge, with a few exceptions, were expected to be celibate and to resign if they married, which only ended with the intervention of Parliament in the passage of the Oxford and Cambridge Universities' Act in 1877. Similarly, Oxford students had to subscribe to the Thirty-Nine Articles of the Anglican church, which, apart from some exemptions permitted in 1854, continued until 1871. The requirement continued at Cambridge University for undergraduates until 1856 and for professors until 1871. It was often a condition of accepting a fellowship that faculty take holy orders. They were first and foremost clergymen rather than university teachers who made up only 9 percent of the faculty. As late as 1912, the clergy still held a fifth of the fellowships at Oxford.[46]

While the Protestant Reformation stimulated an emphasis on education in northern Europe, the Jesuits (the Society of Jesus), growing out of the Counter-Reformation, became the Catholic order most active in establishing schools and colleges. Meanwhile, Scotland, Massachusetts, and Connecticut had the highest literacy rates in the transatlantic world, thanks to the role of Presbyterians and Congregationalists. Even without public schools, literacy rates in the antebellum South rose to 80 percent of the white population, owing largely to Sunday schools and the desire of parents to teach their children to read the Bible.[47] The South may have lagged behind the North, but in its literacy rates among whites and late introduction of public education, the region's rates were comparable to England, even though the latter was the first industrial nation in the world, governing an empire overseeing a fifth of the global population.

Whereas universities in Continental Europe became increasingly secularized in areas conquered by Napoleon, this was not the case in the early nineteenth-century United States. At the time of the founding of the University of Virginia, fully 104 of the 119 colleges had religious origins. In the 1820s and 1830s, more theological schools and seminaries than colleges were created.[48] The colleges often functioned like theological seminaries: Williams (1795), Middlebury (1802), Bowdoin (1806), and Amherst (1822) aimed "especially to meet the needs of poor New England boys who wished to better themselves by entering the ministry."[49] Colleges all required students to attend chapel, often twice daily, which was the expectation at the College of William and Mary when Jefferson attended.[50] Yale did not drop mandatory Morning Prayer at 7:45 a.m. until 1926. Founded in 1785, the University of Georgia's charter required that all governors and faculty shall be "of the Christian religion." Although the proportion of graduates entering the ministry declined, they still accounted for roughly 18 percent of students at Yale. The ratio was even higher elsewhere, with a third of graduates becoming clergymen at Williams, 43 percent at Middlebury, 46 percent at Amherst, and 50 percent at Hampden-Sydney. Harvard was the lowest with 11 percent, a figure still much higher than the 3.8 percent at the University of Virginia. During the first two decades of the nineteenth century, between 20 and 30 percent of all university graduates were entering the ministry in North America.[51] Even in France, the Bourbon Restoration (1815–30) reversed the secularization of higher education under Emperor Napoleon.

Yale University had the nation's largest enrollment and alumni with the widest geographical dispersal. Its graduates founded Congregational "daughter colleges," adopting the same curriculum throughout the Northwest, at schools like Western Reserve University (1826) and Oberlin College (1833) in Ohio, Illinois College (1829), Beloit College (1846) in Wisconsin, and Grinnell College (1846) in Iowa. Princeton graduates created a similar Presbyterian empire in the South at Hampden-Sydney and Washington Colleges (later Washington and Lee University) in Virginia. Yale and Princeton collectively produced the majority of college presidents and had the greatest influence on curricula nationally.[52] Religious imperatives and theology played less of a role at the University of Pennsylvania (formerly the College of Philadelphia) and Columbia University (King's College). In 1754, a promotional advertisement for King's College declared, "It is to be understood that, as to Religion, there is no Intention to impose on the Schollars the peculiar Tenets of any particular Sect of Christians; but to inculcate upon their tender Minds the great Principles of Christianity and Morality in which true Christians of each Denomination are generally agreed." Still, appointing only Episcopalians to its presidency between 1828 and 1948, Columbia University became so sectarian that it was one of the least religiously diverse antebellum colleges.[53] During the colonial period, both Columbia and the University of Pennsylvania nearly failed, owing to sectarian struggles for control between Presbyterians and Anglicans. Jefferson specifically wanted to avoid their example and the likely outcome of one denomination dominating the university.

Nevertheless, despite their religious affiliations, colleges were relatively tolerant and seldom excluded students from other Protestant denominations. This was due in part to their need for tuition funds, owing to a lack of endowments and insufficient funding from their respective churches, and also because boards composed of laymen often governed the colleges. Episcopalians like James Madison from the South were able to attend Presbyterian Princeton because its charter affirmed that "every religious denomination may have a free and equal liberty and advantage of education."[54] After the American Revolution, colleges did not require religious tests or oaths, theoretically making it possible for anyone to attend. Their tolerance, though, was largely confined to fellow Protestants since there remained considerable anti-Catholicism and anti-Semitism. As late as the 1930s and 1940s, anti-Semitism at Yale "restricted the development and health of scientific and humanistic study."[55] Even religious liberals could fall afoul of the prevailing orthodoxy, as did Andrew Dickson White, the founder and first president of Cornell University, whose religious liberalism was too much for the Yale Corporation. In the 1850s, it blocked his appointment as the first history professor at Yale.[56]

While some precedents existed nationally for the idea of a secular university, they were all short-lived. At its beginning in 1789, the University of North Carolina was a nondenominational college, albeit one that required students to attend daily prayer. The curriculum designed by William R. Davie was similar to that later adopted at the University of Virginia. During the presidency of Joseph Caldwell (1804–12, 1816–35), North Carolina became more conventionally religious and predominantly Presbyterian. Described by a historian of the university as "a member of the church militant," Caldwell appointed class monitors to report the use of profanities and check on attendance at twice-daily prayer and Sunday chapel services.[57] The faculty was increasingly composed of Presbyterian preachers appointed by Caldwell.

Founded in Kentucky in 1780, Transylvania University represented the most impressive attempt to create a secular university before the University of Virginia. With the aim of becoming a public university, it forbade religious tests from being administered to the faculty, officers, or trustees. When the university appointed a Presbyterian to be its first professor, the

Kentucky Gazette published letters protesting what was seen as the failure to keep religion from encroaching in a state university, written by pseudonymous authors like "Paddy Money-Man," "A Transylvanian," and "A Sectarian." In 1794, Presbyterians were temporarily defeated with the appointment to the presidency of an English Unitarian and Republican, Harry Toulmin, who was a friend of Jefferson and a protégé of Joseph Priestley. His tenure, however, lasted only two years. In 1804, the university reverted with the appointment to the presidency of James Blythe, who regarded the separation of church and state as a product of the atheism of the French Revolution and Jeffersonian Republicans. In 1818, officials tried again to create a secular university with the appointment of Horace Holley, another Unitarian, who on his way to Kentucky met to discuss his plans with Jefferson at Monticello. Following continued conflict with Presbyterians, however, he resigned in 1826.[58]

Harvard was an exception to the increasing Protestant Christian sectarianism of universities in the United States. It became a Unitarian stronghold in the early nineteenth century and in 1810 appointed John Thornton Kirkland, a Unitarian minister, as its president. It became more tolerant than most colleges, with as many as three Catholic instructors and administrators in 1831. In 1815, the Corporation of Harvard announced its desire that students inquire for themselves about the doctrine of revelation. Nevertheless, it still required students to go to chapel twice a day. As late as 1885, students petitioned the governing board against compulsory chapel attendance as "a remnant of ancient encroachments on civil liberty."[59] The Harvard Divinity School disclaimed sectarian bias but appointed only Unitarians until 1870. It also remained politically conservative in the short term, supporting Federalists.

As with so many of the influences on Jefferson, the idea of secular education originated in Europe and was tried in many universities following the French Revolution. In the seventeenth century, the Jewish philosopher Benedict de Spinoza had argued that ecclesiastical control of education restricted intellectual freedom and that theology discouraged skepticism. In an *Account of Denmark as It Was in 1692* (1692), Robert Molesworth argued that philosophers would make better teachers than priests, since they would cater more to vocational training outside of the ministry and devote less time to classical languages. Scottish universities in fact did not require students to take religious tests and were lax regarding the orthodoxy of the faculty. Joseph Priestley was so fearful of religious indoctrination that he actually opposed public education, seeing it as a vehicle for the state to impose religious orthodoxy. It is extraordinary that Jefferson preceded European models by attempting to make the College of William and Mary a secular institution as early as 1779.

JEFFERSON WAS ADAMANT about the separation of church and state at a public university. In the Rockfish Gap Commission (1818), he was explicit in his uncompromising stance against the teaching of religion, which he justified as conforming "with the principles of our constitution" and reflecting the "sentiments of the legislature in favor of freedom of religion." The report declared, "We have proposed no professor of Divinity," while it assigned questions about religion and the existence of God to the professor of ethics.[60] In the wake of the fallout from the appointment of Thomas Cooper, the Board of Visitors in 1822 approved a plan for allowing the establishment of independent schools of theology around the perimeter of the university.[61] Despite the provision in the original commission report for a room for worship in the Rotunda, Jefferson denied a request from Arthur Brockenbrough, the proctor, to allow religious services to be conducted in a lecture room and insisted that the university buildings should not be used other than for "University purposes." When someone applied to preach a sermon in one of the pavilions, Jefferson observed that the university buildings belonged to the state and declined the request.[62] He argued that there were already conveniently located churches in Charlottesville and that a room on the Grounds would be too small, given the competition between different denominations for its use. While he was alive, no religious services were held anywhere on the Grounds. The University of Virginia was the only college in the country not to require compulsory chapel and not to provide a space for worship.

While historians have been critical of what some describe as Jefferson's doctrinaire views about the teaching of politics and law, they rarely make the same observation about his views on the teaching of religion, about which he was much more inflexible. In his instructions to Francis Walker Gilmer, who was tasked with appointing professors in Britain, Jefferson specifically asked him to avoid recruiting clergymen to the faculty. In the field of ethics and moral philosophy, his desire that a layman be appointed was a novelty. He consulted with James Madison, Madison's cousin Bishop James Madison, and John Adams about appropriate books on theology for the library. He classified book titles on religion under subject headings like "ethics" and "jurisprudence." President James Madison found it difficult to exclude "moral and metaphysical" books and regarded the effort as "extremely tedious."[63] Historian Robert M. Healey is one of the few authors to question Jefferson's dogmatic view that sectarians were wrong and that he was right, arguing that his rigidity led him to do "exactly what he condemned as sinful and tyrannical; he tried to compel others to furnish contributions of money for the propagation of opinions which they disbelieved and abhorred." Healey thought Jefferson's refusal to accept that religious believers were amenable "may have made him more literally sectarian than they," with Jefferson revealing "an unconscious but powerful drive to put his own religious beliefs in a position of unusual strength so as to receive a hearing from the students."[64]

UNLIKE ALEXIS DE TOCQUEVILLE, whose *Democracy in America* (1835) appeared exactly one decade after the opening of the university, Jefferson was not concerned about the impact of the possible decline of traditional religious beliefs and regular church attendance. De Tocqueville feared that the absence of formal religion would weaken the bonds and morality of society. Influenced by the moral-sense philosophy of the Scottish Enlightenment, Jefferson believed that people were naturally ethical and able to distinguish right from wrong, but that their innate moral sense could be improved and developed by encouragement and continual exercise until it became habitual.[65] He was very much of the view that bad habits acquired while growing up would be difficult to shake off later and therefore believed it important to teach good moral habits to children by encouraging them in regular study and reading.

Like many of the founding elite, Jefferson thought that students, as future leaders of the country, should cultivate and improve their moral sense. He gave priority to developing the qualities of benevolence, compassion, empathy, humanity, and charity, all of which he believed could be perfected by following the unadulterated teachings of Jesus, whose "system of morality was the most benevolent and sublime probably that has been ever taught." These ideas he thought best summarized in two of the commandments: "to love our neighbors as ourselves, and to do good to all men."[66] This was the path to human happiness. For this reason, he respected the Quakers, liking the absence of theology in their religion but disliking what he suspected was their partiality toward Britain and their lukewarm support for the War of 1812. Sharing their belief in an innate good and inner light in everyone, he

FIGURE 1. *Thomas Jefferson*, by Thomas Sully, finished 1830. One of the last portraits of Thomas Jefferson, completed when he was seventy-eight years old, it captures the intelligence and expressiveness of his face. (Courtesy of the American Philosophical Society)

FIGURE 2. Aerial photograph of Monticello. Jefferson lived at Monticello throughout the period of his creating the University of Virginia. Known affectionately as "The Sage of Monticello," once a phrase of derision by his political opponents, Jefferson was already the object of pilgrimages in which "his mountain" was "made a sort of Mecca." (Courtesy of the Thomas Jefferson Foundation at Monticello)

Figure 3. Entrance Hall at Monticello. Jefferson was a natural teacher and enjoyed sharing and displaying his knowledge at Monticello. Like modern visitors, the students and faculty entered the house through the East Portico into the Entrance Hall. This was the most public room in the house and acted as a museum aimed at instructing visitors. (Courtesy of the Thomas Jefferson Foundation at Monticello)

Figure 4. Cabinet, Monticello. Within Monticello, Jefferson had a private suite of rooms, like an apartment, with his "Cabinet" (study), library, greenhouse, and "Chamber" (bedroom). Margaret Bayard Smith described this secluded place as Jefferson's *Sanctum Sanctorum*, where he did the majority of his writing and reading. (Courtesy of the Thomas Jefferson Foundation at Monticello)

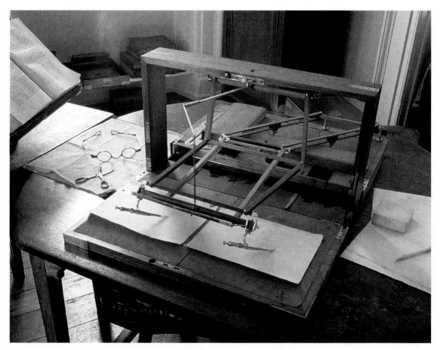

FIGURE 5. Polygraph Machine. Marked "Hawkins & Peale's Patent Polygraph No. 57," this machine was used by Jefferson from 1806 until his death. The writer's hand moves one pen whose action is duplicated by the second one, producing a copy strikingly like the original. (Courtesy of the Thomas Jefferson Foundation at Monticello)

FIGURES 6 (a) *Francis Bacon*, studio of Paulus van Somer I, ca. 1617–1620; (b) *Sir Isaac Newton*, by John Vanderbank, 1726; (c) *John Locke*, copy by Stewart (or "Stuart") after Sir Godfrey Kneller, 1789. Through the double doors from the Entrance Hall, the parlor at Monticello contained portraits of the three men whom Jefferson called "my trinity of the three greatest men the world has ever produced." (Courtesy of the Thomas Jefferson Foundation at Monticello)

FIGURE 7. Photograph of William and Mary College, Wren Building and Courtyard. The College of William and Mary was the only college in the South before 1775 and the second oldest college in British America. In his vision for the University of Virginia, Jefferson tried to recreate the learning environment that he experienced at William and Mary. (Credit: Stephen Salpukas/William and Mary)

FIGURE 8. *William Small*, by Tilly Kettle, ca. 1765. Dr. William Small was the only lay professor among the six faculty members at the College of William and Mary. Jefferson later wrote that their relationship was one of his greatest fortunes and "what probably fixed the destinies of my life." (Courtesy of the Muscarelle Museum of Art at William and Mary)

FIGURE 9. *Martha Jefferson Randolph*, by James Westhall Ford, 1823. In his retirement, Jefferson persuaded his daughter Martha Jefferson Randolph (1772–1836) to move with her husband and family to live with him at Monticello. An alumnus of the first year of students at the university, Henry Tutwiler suggested that the university should commemorate Martha's role in supporting her father. (Courtesy of the Thomas Jefferson Foundation at Monticello)

FIGURE 10. Photograph of Poplar Forest, Historic American Buildings Survey, 1933. During his retirement, Jefferson regularly visited his other octagonal plantation home at Poplar Forest in Bedford County, near Lynchburg, Virginia, which he began designing in 1806. He kept a library there and wrote many letters from this location in regard to the construction of the university. (Courtesy of the Library of Congress)

FIGURE 11. *View of the West Front of Monticello and Garden*, by Jane Braddick Penticolas (1825). Monticello during Jefferson's retirement and the construction of the University. Featuring three of his white grandchildren by his daughter Martha Randolph, this image illustrates how Jefferson enjoyed, in his own words, living "like a patriarch of old," a life made possible through the labors of some 140 enslaved workers on his surrounding plantation. (Courtesy of the Thomas Jefferson Foundation at Monticello)

FIGURE 12. *John Adams*, by Gilbert Stuart, 1826. Throughout the time that he was overseeing the creation of the University of Virginia, Jefferson was engaged in a remarkable correspondence with his former political opponent and predecessor as president, John Adams. Over a period of fourteen years, their correspondence traversed an expansive array of intellectual, personal, and mutual interests. This was the last portrait done of Adams. (Courtesy of the Smithsonian American Art Museum)

FIGURE 13. *The Declaration of Independence, July 4, 1776*, by John Trumbull, 1817–1818. Like Benjamin Franklin, one of the founders of the University of Pennsylvania, Jefferson might well have pursued educational reform and founded a university even if America had remained British, but the American Revolution provided the impetus that led him to propose a public school system and craft a distinctly republican conception of a university, whose foundations lay in the "spirit of 1776." (Courtesy of the Yale University Art Gallery)

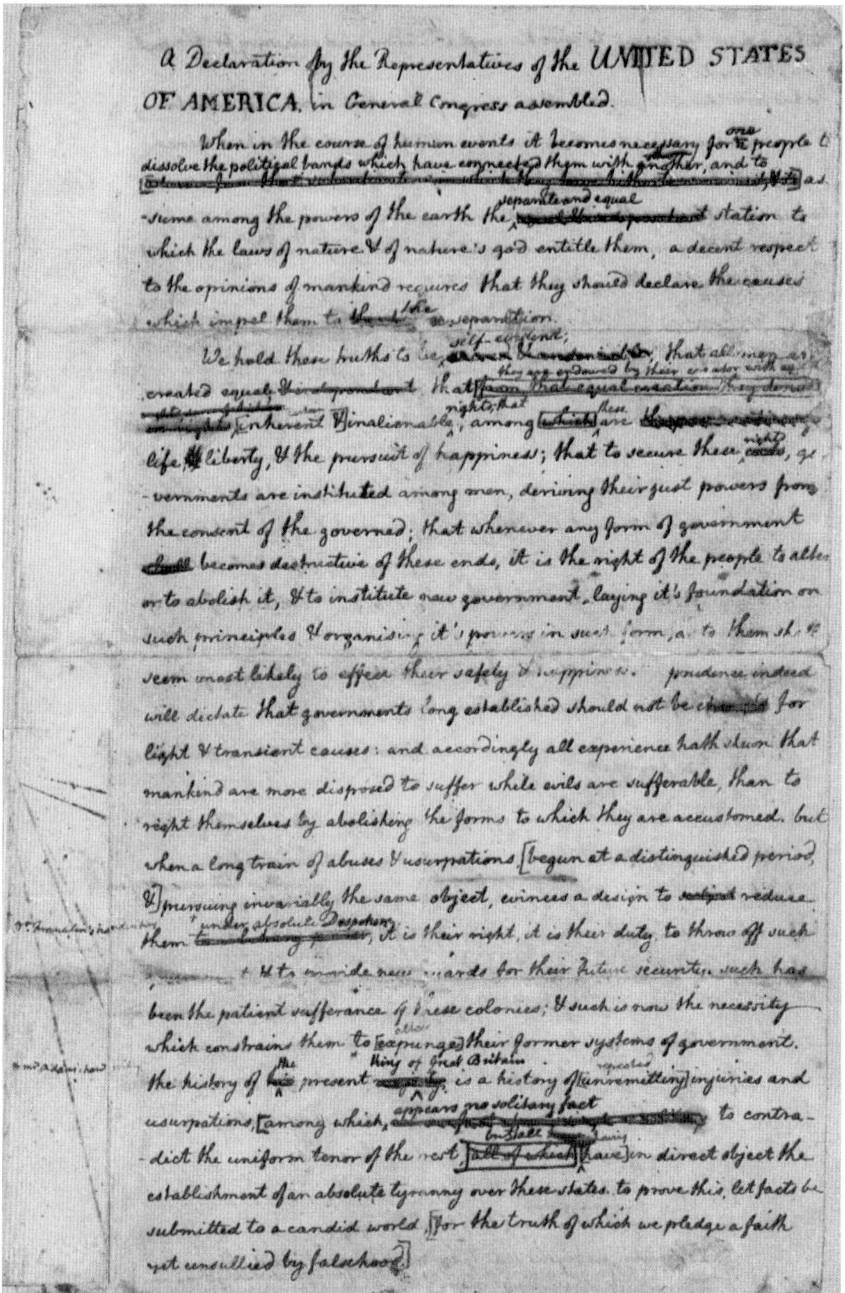

A Declaration by the Representatives of the UNITED STATES OF AMERICA, in General Congress assembled.

When in the course of human events it becomes necessary for one people to dissolve the political bands which have connected them with another, and to assume among the powers of the earth the separate and equal station to which the laws of nature & of nature's god entitle them, a decent respect to the opinions of mankind requires that they should declare the causes which impel them to the separation.

We hold these truths to be self-evident; that all men are created equal; that they are endowed by their creator with equal rights, [inherent & inalienable] rights; that among these are life, liberty, & the pursuit of happiness; that to secure these rights, governments are instituted among men, deriving their just powers from the consent of the governed; that whenever any form of government becomes destructive of these ends, it is the right of the people to alter or to abolish it, & to institute new government, laying it's foundation on such principles & organising it's powers in such form, as to them shall seem most likely to effect their safety & happiness. prudence indeed will dictate that governments long established should not be changed for light & transient causes: and accordingly all experience hath shewn that mankind are more disposed to suffer while evils are sufferable, than to right themselves by abolishing the forms to which they are accustomed. but when a long train of abuses & usurpations [begun at a distinguished period, &] pursuing invariably the same object, evinces a design to reduce them under absolute Despotism, it is their right, it is their duty, to throw off such government & to provide new guards for their future security. such has been the patient sufferance of these colonies; & such is now the necessity which constrains them to [alter] their former systems of government. the history of the present King of Great Britain is a history of [unremitting] repeated injuries and usurpations, [among which, appears no solitary fact to contradict the uniform tenor of the rest, but all have] in direct object the establishment of an absolute tyranny over these states. to prove this, let facts be submitted to a candid world, [for the truth of which we pledge a faith yet unsullied by falsehood]

FIGURE 14. Jefferson's original draft of the Declaration of Independence. For faculty and student visitors at Monticello, Jefferson liked to relate anecdotes about the pantheon of heroes of the American Revolution and to show his guests his copy of the original draft of the Declaration of Independence. He thought the original much superior to the version revised by Congress. (Courtesy of the Library of Congress)

FIGURE 15. *Joseph Priestley*, by Ellen Sharples, ca. 1797. Jefferson wrote his first letter proposing the University of Virginia in 1800 to Joseph Priestley (1733–1804), the émigré British theologian and scientist. (Courtesy of the National Portrait Gallery, London)

FIGURE 16. *Thomas Jefferson*, by Thomas Sully, 1821–1822. As president in 1802, Jefferson drafted and signed into law a bill to create the U.S. Military Academy at West Point. He saw it as an opportunity to create a Republican officer corps in an army dominated by Federalists. This portrait was one of the last of Jefferson before his death in 1826. (Courtesy of the West Point Museum Collection, United States Military Academy)

FIGURE 17. *The Providential Detection*, ca. 1797–1800. Jefferson was depicted by his Federalist opponents as an atheist and French Jacobin. In 1800, the Reverend Timothy Dwight, the president of Yale, helped lead the Federalist attack on Jefferson's supposed atheism and asked students the following year to take an oath never to vote for Jefferson. Because the majority of colleges were Federalist, Jefferson was determined to create a southern Republican university. (Courtesy of the Library Company of Philadelphia)

ROCKFISH GAP AND THE MOUNTAIN HOUSE.

FIGURE 18. *Rockfish Gap and the Mountain House Central R.R. Augusta Co. Va.*, by Edward Beyer, lithograph, 1858. Located twenty miles west of Charlottesville, a dramatic opening at the top of Rockfish Gap enables travelers to contemplate sweeping vistas of the Shenandoah Valley. In August 1818, a group of twenty-one commissioners met at the Mountain Top Inn to create the blueprint for the future University of Virginia, in what became known as the Rockfish Gap Commission. (Courtesy of the Albert and Shirley Small Special Collections Library, University of Virginia Library)

FIGURES 19 (a) *Joseph C. Cabell*, by Louis Mathieu Didier Guillaume, 1856; (b) Insert of a cane given by Joseph Cabell to Jefferson. Joseph Carrington Cabell (1778–1856) became Jefferson's front man in the Virginia State Senate. Thirty-five years his junior, Cabell presented Jefferson with a whalebone and ivory walking stick upon his retirement from the presidency, which was engraved "TJ. Joseph Cabell to his friend Christmas 1809." (Courtesy of the Fralin Museum of Art at the University of Virginia and the Thomas Jefferson Foundation at Monticello)

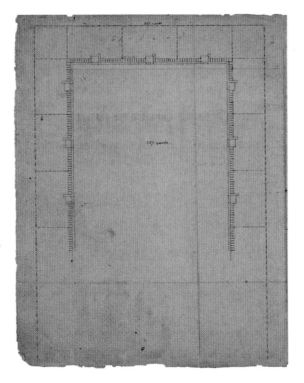

FIGURE 20. Plan for Albemarle Academy, by Thomas Jefferson, 1814. In 1814, Jefferson's plan for building the Albemarle Academy contained many of the key principles that would later be enshrined in the layout of the Lawn. He proposed nine pavilions flanked by ten dormitories on each side, with covered walkways surrounding a square with one side open, which symbolically distinguished the design from the enclosed quadrangles of religious institutions and medieval colleges. (Courtesy of the Albert and Shirley Small Special Collection Library, University of Virginia)

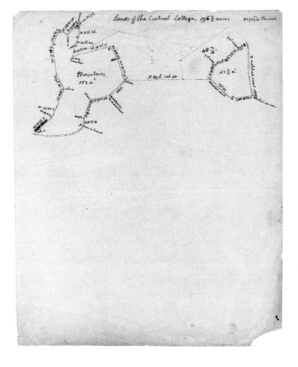

FIGURE 21. Plans showing "Lands of the Central College," by Thomas Jefferson, ca. 1819. On July 18, 1817, Jefferson personally surveyed the site for Central College. Using a little ruler that he always carried with him in his pocket, he "measured off the ground and laid off the foundation" before assigning the enslaved work crew to begin leveling the surface. (Courtesy of the Albert and Shirley Small Special Collection Library, University of Virginia)

FIGURE 22. *Thomas Cooper*, by Charles Willson Peale, 1819. Jefferson invited Thomas Cooper (1759–1839) to become the first faculty member of Central College of Virginia and again to be the first professor at the University of Virginia. Regarded by Jefferson as "one of the ablest men in America," Cooper was a polymath and prolific writer on subjects ranging from economics and law to chemistry, geology, and medicine. (Courtesy of the College of Physicians of Philadelphia; photograph by Evi Numen)

FIGURE 23. *Abbé José Corrêia da Serra*, by Rembrandt Peale, ca. 1812–1813. Jefferson was able to discuss his ideas on education and to keep informed about educational institutions through his transatlantic network of fellow intellectuals, which included José Corrêia da Serra, the Portuguese philosopher, politician, diplomat, and scientist who cofounded the Academy of Science in Lisbon and who had a room named after him at Monticello. (Courtesy of the Thomas Jefferson Foundation at Monticello)

FIGURE 24. *James Madison*, by Joseph Wood, 1816. Madison was an important ally of Jefferson in founding and building the University of Virginia. He was one of the most regular attendees of the meetings of the Board of Visitors and later succeeded Jefferson as rector, in which capacity he served until 1834. (Courtesy of the Virginia Museum of History and Culture, 1967.13)

FIGURE 25. *James Monroe*, by John Vanderlyn, 1816. As governor of Virginia in 1801, James Monroe also championed public education, and while president of the United States, Monroe attended the foundation stone–laying ceremony for Central College. (Courtesy of the National Portrait Gallery, Smithsonian Institution)

FIGURE 26. Silver Jefferson cup. Jefferson loaned the Freemasons three of his famous silver cups for use during the foundation stone–laying ceremony of Central College, the future University of Virginia. The presence of Freemasons was a longstanding tradition at such occasions, whether for public, private, or religious buildings. (Courtesy of the Thomas Jefferson Foundation at Monticello)

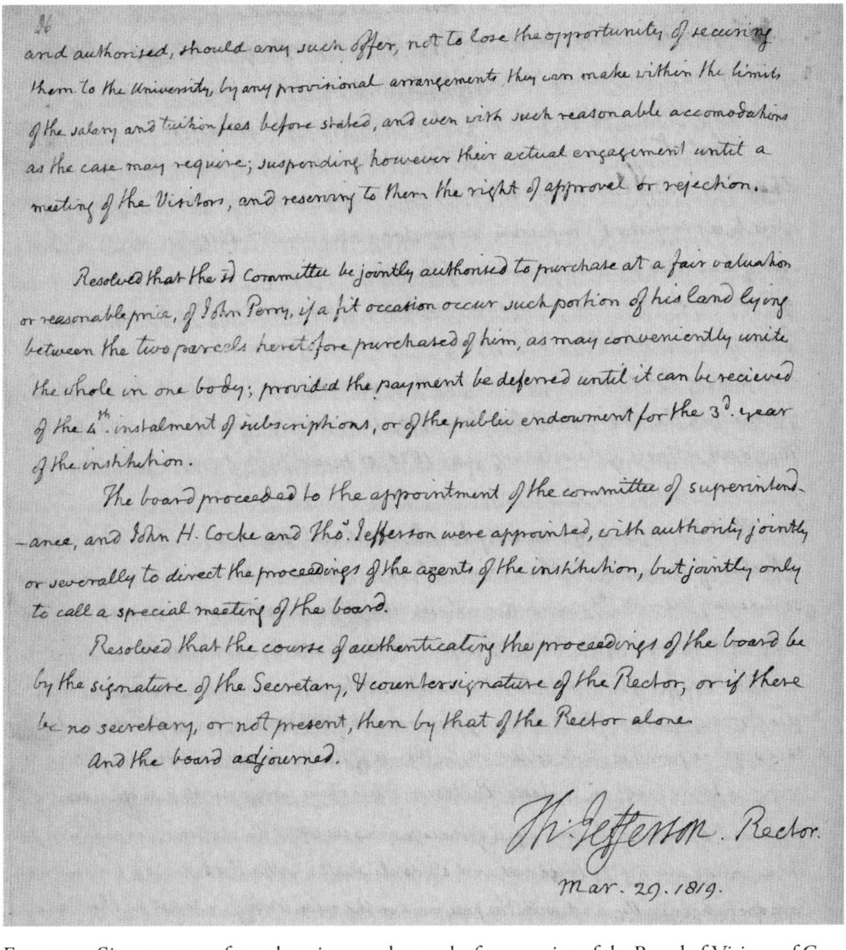

and authorised, should any such offer, not to lose the opportunity of securing
them to the University, by any provisional arrangements they can make within the limits
of the salary and tuition fees before stated, and even with such reasonable accomodations
as the case may require; suspending however their actual engagement until a
meeting of the Visitors, and reserving to them the right of approval or rejection.

    Resolved that the sd committee be jointly authorised to purchase at a fair valuation
or reasonable price, of John Perry, if a fit occasion occur such portion of his land lying
between the two parcels heretofore purchased of him, as may conveniently unite
the whole in one body; provided the payment be deferred until it can be recieved
of the 4th. instalment of subscriptions, or of the public endowment for the 3d. year
of the institution.
    The board proceeded to the appointment of the committee of superintend-
-ance, and John H. Cocke and Tho. Jefferson were appointed, with authority jointly
or severally to direct the proceedings of the agents of the institution, but jointly only
to call a special meeting of the board.
    Resolved that the course of authenticating the proceedings of the board be
by the signature of the Secretary, & countersignature of the Rector, or if there
be no secretary, or not present, then by that of the Rector alone.
    And the board adjourned.

Th: Jefferson. Rector.
Mar. 29. 1819.

Figure 27. Signature page from the minutes taken at the first meeting of the Board of Visitors of Central College, ca. February 26, 1819. Jefferson spent the last decade of his life preoccupied with the quest to establish the University of Virginia. He undertook the seemingly dull task of writing the minutes of the Board of Visitors, which ensured that his version became the final record of their meetings. (Courtesy of the Albert and Shirley Small Special Collection Library, University of Virginia)

MARIA COSWAY

as the Act directs 1 Jan? 1785 by G.Bartolozzi to be had at M. Torres Hay Market 23

FIGURE 28. *Maria Cosway,* by Francesco Bartolozzi, engraving, 1785. Jefferson described his first encounter with Maria Cosway (1760–1838) in Paris "as long as a Lapland summer day." That same day he also first saw a Delorme-constructed dome at the Halle aux Blé, which he would adapt at Monticello and the Rotunda. In retirement at Monticello, Jefferson would later write to Cosway about his architectural plans for an Academical Village. (Courtesy of the Thomas Jefferson Foundation at Monticello)

FIGURE 29. Photograph of Pavilion VII. Pavilion VII was the site of the original groundbreaking ceremony and the first building to be completed on the Lawn. The cellar was insufficient for a kitchen, lacking enough space to keep food, while the living spaces for enslaved servants in all of the pavilions were inadequate, confined, and windowless. (Courtesy of Dan Addison/UVA University Communications)

FIGURE 30. *University of Virginia*, engraved by Benjamin Tanner, 1826, from an 1824 drawing. As early as June 1820, Jefferson wrote to his son-in-law that "our University is now so far advanced as to be worth seeing." Jefferson was satisfied that he had achieved his ambition in creating a university whose chaste architecture and classical taste would be thought splendid even in Europe. (Courtesy of Special Collections; University of Virginia)

FIGURE 31. *View from Monticello Looking toward Charlottesville,* by Jane Braddick Peticolas, 1825. A rare contemporary view from Monticello during Jefferson's lifetime, with Charlottesville in the background and a clearing in the trees through which he watched the construction of the University of Virginia. (Courtesy of the Thomas Jefferson Foundation at Monticello)

FIGURE 32. Cartoon of Jefferson's plans for a planetarium, "The Celestial Dome." Jefferson considered astronomy to be the most sublime of the sciences and a high point of an enlightened education. He envisaged using the ceiling of the library as a planetarium in which an astronomy professor mounted on a saddle with stirrups could be elevated thirty feet to the concave ceiling by a mechanical boom, guided by a student operator. (Courtesy of Charles Peale)

FIGURE 33. Photograph of the Rotunda. Receiving drawings from Benjamin Henry Latrobe, Jefferson adopted his idea of a principal building at the top of the Lawn, which would become the Rotunda. On his final visit to the university, Jefferson watched as workmen lifted the first Carrara marble Corinthian capital to the southwest corner of the south portico of the Rotunda. (Courtesy of Dan Addison/UVA University Communications)

FIGURE 34. Nineteenth-century photograph of the interior of the Rotunda. Jefferson demonstrated his Enlightenment vision of the university by placing the library, rather than a chapel, at the head of the Lawn in the Rotunda. In 1824, Jefferson achieved a publicity coup by dining with the Marquis de Lafayette in the unfinished Rotunda. (Courtesy of the Library of Congress)

Books to be procured for the Anglo-Saxon course in the school of Modern Languages.

£ ster.

1 - 16 - 0   Institutiones Grammaticae Anglo-Saxonicae et Moeso-Gothicae Hickesii. Oxon. 1689. 4to

0 - 7 - 6   Grammatica A-Saxonica ex Hickesiano Thesauro excerpta. 8vo
            Elstob's Saxon Grammar: p. 4to

3 - 3 - 0   Junius's Etymologicon

6 - 16 - 6   Lye's Dictionarium Saxonico- et Gothico-Latinum ab Owen Manning. 2. to. in 1. fol.

1 - 8 - 0   Benson's Saxon Vocabulary. 8vo

8 . 0 . 0   Somneri Dictionarium Saxonico-Latino-Anglicum . Oxon .1659. fol.

1.1.0.0   Orosius Saxon by Alfred and English by Barrington . 8vo
            Chronologia A-Saxonica. à Wheeloc. fol.

2 - 2 - 0   Chronicon Saxonicum. Gibson. A-Saxon et Latine. Oxon 1692. 4to

0 - 15 - 0   Gurney's transln of the Saxon Chronicle. Lond.1819. 9. et A. arch

3 - 13 - 6   Ingram's Saxon Chronicle, with an Eng translin, notes &c 4to

1 - 7 - 0   Alfredi magni vita, à Spelmanno, appendicibus Oxon 1678. fol.

0 - 18 - 0   Spelman's life of Alfred. Eng. 8vo

2 - 2 - 0   Bedae Historia Ecclesiastica. Lat et A. Saxon et chronologia Saxonica Cant.1643 4to

1 - 1 - 0   Bede's Ecclesiastical history. Eng. 8vo. Lond.1723.

4 - 4 - 0 { Asser Menevensis de rebus gestis Alfredi. Lat. in A-Saxon characters.}
           { Chronica et ypodigmata Neustria Thomae Walsingham.   } Lond.1574 4to

0 . 10 . 6   Annales rerum gestarum Aelfridi Asseri Menevensis à Wise, et Chronologia vitae
             Alfridi, Spelmanni. Oxon. 1722 8vo
             Lambardi Archaionomia. Saxon. et Lat. folio.

1 . 1 . 0   the same Lond.1658. 4to

0 - 5 - 0   Lambard's antient laws by Day. 4to 1658. [see Clarke's Bibliotheca&c p a .108.1819]
            Spelmanni Concilia. fol. Lond.1639.

1 . 1 . 0   Wilkins's leges A-Saxonicae. fol. Lond.1721.

2 - 4 - p   Wheeloc leges A-Saxonicae. fol. Cantabr. 1644.

1 - 7 - 0   Heptateuchus, Job, et Evangelium Nicodemi, A-Saxonice, à Thwaites. Oxon 1698. 8vo

0 - 5 - 6   the apocryphal Newtestament, with the gospel of Nicodemus. Lond.1821 8vo
            Caedmonis Paraphrasis Genesios. Junii 4to Amstel.1655.

1 - 7 - 0   Psalterium Davidis Lat-Saxonicum vetus. Spelmanni. 4to Lond.1640.

1 . 16 . 6   Evangeliorum versiones Gothica et A-Saxonica à Junio et Mareschallo, et
             Gothicum Glossarium Junii 2. v. in 1. 4to Dordrechti .1665.

——————
36 . 10 . 6

FIGURE 35. Thomas Jefferson's list of "Books to be procured for the Anglo-Saxon course," ca. April 1824. In 1824, Jefferson prepared a handwritten desiderata list of 6,860 books for the library. Within five years the library contained some eight thousand volumes, more than any other college in the United States except Harvard and Yale. (Courtesy of the Albert and Shirley Small Special Collection Library, University of Virginia)

FIGURE 36. Photograph of covered walkways. Jefferson envisaged a cluster of buildings, similar to a village, which allowed for "varieties of the finest samples of architecture" and made the university "a model of beauty, original and unique." Although the view is now obscured by Cabell Hall, the university looked out southward toward the mountains, the frontier, and the future. (Courtesy of Dan Addison/ UVA University Communications)

FIGURE 37. Aerial view of the university. Using the term "academical village," Jefferson envisaged a community dispersed among small buildings in which professors lived among and even dined with the students, an enlightened model of intergenerational relations and mentorship. (Courtesy of Dan Addison/UVA University Communications)

FIGURE 38. Photograph of Professor George Long, by Louise Savage, 1871. George Long (1800–1870), professor of ancient languages, was one of the "imported professors" from Britain. He typified the outstanding quality of the early faculty. (Courtesy of the Albert and Shirley Small Special Collections Library, University of Virginia Library)

FIGURE 39. *Francis Walker Gilmer,* ca. 1820–1826. After failing to persuade Joseph Cabell to go on a faculty recruiting trip to Britain, Jefferson assigned the task to young attorney Francis Walker Gilmer (1790–1826). Offering him the professorship of law, Jefferson regarded Gilmer as one of the brightest young men in Virginia. (Courtesy of the Fralin Museum of Art at the University of Virginia)

FIGURE 40. *Robley Dunglison, M.D.,* engraved print, ca. 1846. Robley Dunglison (1798–1869) was the first full-time professor of medicine and anatomy in the United States. He became known as the "Father of American Physiology" for his book *Human Physiology* (1832), which he wrote at the University of Virginia. (Courtesy of the Library of Congress)

FIGURE 41. *Thomas Jefferson*, statue by Moses Ezekiel, 1910. Dedicated in 1910, this statue outside the Rotunda commemorates Jefferson's ideas of religious freedom by listing, in different faiths and languages, the various names for God, which are carved on a tablet held in the hands of the spirit of Brotherhood and titled "Religious Freedom, 1786." (Courtesy of James Bowen)

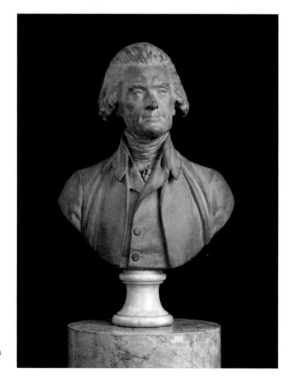

FIGURE 42. *Thomas Jefferson*, bust by Jean Antoine Houdon, 1789. (Courtesy of the Thomas Jefferson Foundation at Monticello)

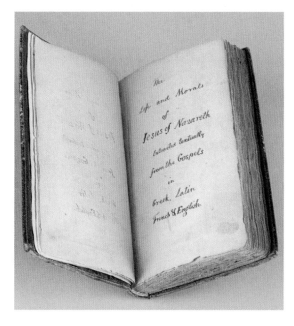

FIGURE 43. "The Life and Morals of Jesus of Nazareth Extracted Textually from the Gospels in Greek, Latin, French & English." In 1819, the year of the creation of the University of Virginia, Jefferson resumed an editing project that he had started while president. He pasted extracts from the King James version of the Bible in four columns to blank pages with the aim of extracting the "diamonds" from what he called the "dunghill" of accretions and falsifications of the life of Jesus. (Courtesy of the Division of Political and Military History, National Museum of American History, Smithsonian Institution)

FIGURE 44. Photograph of a (a) Chinese gong and (b) clock at Monticello. On each hour and half-hour, the chimes of the Great Clock in the Entrance Hall were struck by a Chinese gong on the roof, which could be heard by enslaved laborers across Jefferson's plantation, reputedly as far as three miles away. Plantations were like factories in a field, anticipating the synchronization of work in an era that increasingly equated time with money. (Courtesy of the Thomas Jefferson Foundation at Monticello)

FIGURE 45. Photograph of Sally Cottrell Cole, by William Roads, ca. 1867–1873. The enslaved laborers at the university included slaves from Monticello such as Sally Cottrell Cole (d. 1875). Cole was sold for four hundred dollars to Thomas Hewitt Key, the professor of mathematics, who planned to free her. Her legal status as a free person, however, was still being questioned as late as 1850. (Courtesy of the Albert and Shirley Small Special Collection Library, University of Virginia)

FIGURE 46. Photograph of Isaac Granger Jefferson. Isaac Granger Jefferson (1775–1846), an enslaved tinsmith and blacksmith, dictated a memoir in the 1840s that recollected life at Monticello. In 1796, he had a supervisory role in the nailery, which employed about a dozen enslaved teenage boys. Working anywhere from ten to fourteen hours a day, they hammered out between five and ten thousand nails per day in seven different sizes. (Courtesy of the Thomas Jefferson Foundation at Monticello)

Figure 47a and b. Photographs of Edgar Allan Poe's room. Poe lived on the West Range along what was called Rowdy Row in room number 13, which has been furnished and maintained by the student Raven Society since 1904. (Courtesy of Dan Addison/UVA University Communications)

FIGURE 48. *Edgar Allan Poe*, 1836–1839. Poe, the most famous alumnus of the first year, enrolled at the university on February 15, 1826. He was a member and acted as secretary pro tempore of the Jefferson Literary and Debating Society. (Courtesy of the Edgar Allan Poe Museum, Richmond, Virginia)

FIGURE 49. Photograph of students on the Lawn. Jefferson envisaged the University of Virginia as the last best hope for transmitting the untainted legacy of the American Revolution. He wanted the university to be what he called "a bulwark of liberty." In his view, the living generation was responsible for educating the succeeding generation to chart a new path for the happiness and prosperity of the people. (Courtesy of Dan Addison/UVA University Communications)

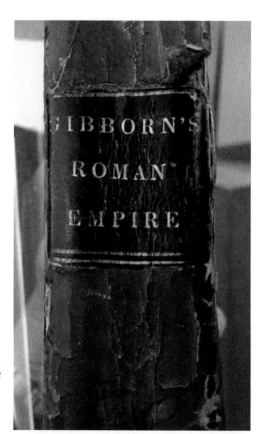

FIGURE 50. Misspelled book spine of Edward Gibbon's *Decline and Fall of the Roman Empire*. On his last visit to the university, Jefferson inspected the boxes of books in Pavilion VII intended for the library in the Rotunda. He instructed the librarian to return this copy of Gibbon's book because the binder had misspelled Gibbon's name on the spine to read "Gibborn." (Courtesy of Endrina Tay, 2018)

FIGURE 51. *Thomas Jefferson Randolph*, by Charles Willson Peale, ca. 1808. Thomas Jefferson Randolph (1792–1875) was Jefferson's favorite grandson; he managed his grandfather's plantations and was an executor of Jefferson's will. He served as a member of the Board of Visitors (1829–57) and as rector of the University of Virginia (1857–64). (Courtesy of the Thomas Jefferson Foundation at Monticello)

FIGURE 52. *Ellen Wayles Randolph Coolidge*, by Francis Alexander, ca. 1830–1845. Ellen Wayles Randolph Coolidge (1796–1876) was Jefferson's favorite granddaughter. She described the conversation during dinner parties at Monticello as "completely the feast of reason," and wrote that she often thought "that the life of a student must be the most happy and innocent in the world." (Courtesy of the Thomas Jefferson Foundation at Monticello)

FIGURE 53. Jefferson's tombstone at Monticello. Along with his authorship of the Declaration of Independence and the Virginia Statute for Religious Freedom, Jefferson regarded the founding of the university as one of the three greatest achievements in life he wanted acknowledged on this tombstone. (Courtesy of the Thomas Jefferson Foundation at Monticello)

FIGURE 54. Photograph of "Walking the Lawn," a graduation tradition that dates from the early twentieth century. Thomas Jefferson looked to the graduates of what he described to the Marquis de Lafayette as "this Athanaeum of our country" to secure his legacy. Jefferson felt the University of Virginia represented the culminating achievement of a career dedicated to promoting the ongoing progress of Enlightenment and republican self-government in America. (Courtesy of Dan Addison/UVA University Communications)

was also attracted to their emphasis on charity and good works, which he thought should be the ultimate objective of any religion.

AFTER JEFFERSON'S DEATH in 1826, the University of Virginia continued to be controversial, facing mounting pressure to change its stance on religion.[67] The perception of infidelity reduced its appeal to students and their parents, especially from the more evangelical western states, with the result that until the 1850s, student enrollments were much lower than Jefferson had anticipated. Henry Tutwiler, one of the first students to attend the university, recollected a clergyman saying to someone who was about to send his son to the university, "'Much as I love your son,' who had been a favorite pupil, 'I would this day, rather follow him to the grave than see him enter the University.'"[68] Robert Lewis Dabney, a student between 1839 and 1842, similarly recalled that the university opened "under infidel auspices, without prayers, chaplain, Bible classes, Sabbath school—yea we may say, without Sabbath: so that almost all godly parents kept their sons away from it."[69] In Fredericksburg, Virginia, a teacher wrote to his brother that he regarded the university "as a School of infidelity—a nursery of bad principles."[70] Following a typhoid epidemic among the students in 1828 and 1829, the Reverend William Meade, an assistant bishop in the Episcopal Diocese of Virginia, in a sermon to the university, attributed the outbreak to divine judgment against the absence of religion at the University of Virginia. In 1840, the Reverend S. H. Tyng, a newspaper editor and leader of the evangelical wing of the Episcopal church in Philadelphia, wrote that "this university was set up in direct and designed hostility to Christianity." He claimed that "it was considered, and was undoubtedly intended to be, an infidel institution, and a school in which the principles of infidelity, negatively at least, should be taught. I believe this character was maintained during the life of its founder."[71] In 1845, a report of the General Assembly attributed the low enrollments of the university primarily to the lingering impression of irreligious sympathies.[72]

Jefferson's approach to religion diminished his own posthumous popularity, not least in the more evangelical climate in Charlottesville after 1829. Other than the issue of slavery, it remains the most controversial area of his life. Reverend Tyng claimed that he had "never heard [Jefferson's] name spoken with so little respect, and so much aversion, as in this very neighborhood in which he lived and died. I never conceived of his character so bad as I have found it here." Tyng was elated that the community had "awakened against the spirit and tendency of Mr. Jefferson's example. All his greatness has perished and is forgotten because he was an infidel."[73] The anonymous author of an 1837 review of George Tucker's biography of Jefferson in the *New-York Review and Quarterly Journal* criticized Jefferson for "having designed to make this institution a place where the minds of young and unsuspecting youth were to be poisoned with the venom of atheism—where they were to be taught that the Sabbath was to be abolished—that God Almighty was not the Lord of the universe—and where a deliberate attempt was made to overthrow the whole fabric of the Christian religion."[74] As late as the 1850s, the student-edited *Monument Magazine* complained that there was a prejudice against the memory of Jefferson, which contributed to the defeat of a student campaign to build a monument in his honor.[75]

After 1826, the University of Virginia began to relax the rigid wall of separation that its founder had established. The changes resulted from mounting pressure from faculty, students, and members of the Board of Visitors. Within the board, Chapman Johnson and John Hartwell Cocke had combined to pressure Jefferson to rescind the appointment of the Unitarian Thomas Cooper. Following Jefferson's death, Johnson wrote that the "old sachem was gone and that they should appoint an educated clergyman from Oxford or Cambridge." He wrote to Cocke that he should "tell Cabell it is time to give up his old prejudice on the subject, the offspring of the French Revolution, long since a bastard by a divorce of the unnatural alliance between liberty and atheism."[76] When James Madison demurred at the appointment of a clergyman to the faculty in 1828, Johnson, after consulting with Cocke, explained that the candidate in question was not a church minister. Still, he protested that they did not think it was a valid objection and that the addition of a clergyman would protect the university "from the injurious imputation of being a school for infidelity, and a nursery of irreligion."[77] A member of the board from 1819 to 1845, Johnson became rector of the university from 1836 to 1845.

Under the leadership of their chairman, George Tucker, the faculty supported the allocation of a room for religious observance in the eastern basement wing of the Rotunda. From 1828 to 1829, the Reverend Frederick W. Hatch, the Episcopalian rector at Christ Church in Charlottesville, and the Reverend Francis Bowman, a Presbyterian minister, alternately preached in the Rotunda. In 1830, Edward Dunlap Smith, a Presbyterian minister from Philadelphia and a graduate of Princeton, acted as an unofficial and unsalaried chaplain to the university and lived in one of the faculty pavilions. Beginning in 1833, the faculty appointed a rotating chaplain annually who was subsequently housed in Pavilion VII on the Lawn. From 1835, the students and faculty began remunerating the chaplain with voluntary subscriptions, simultaneously setting up a Sunday school and founding a Bible society. The same year, George Tucker wrote on behalf of the faculty to every member of the Board of Visitors that the faculty wanted to set up a subscription for a chapel in front of the Rotunda, for which they had already selected an architect. According to one visitor critical of what he regarded as a university that had been created "in direct and designed hostility to Christianity," the majority of the students were practicing Christians.[78] On her American tour in 1837, Harriet Martineau, a British writer, thought that the University of Virginia's students heard a wider variety of sermons from different denominations and that church attendance among them was more popular because it was voluntary.[79]

The proponents of religious worship justified the changes as consistent with the original vision to create a nonsectarian university, arguing that they were not advantaging a specific religious denomination and that it was all funded by private subscription. As historian Harry Y. Gamble astutely observes, their innovations "marked an extremely important shift" from Jefferson's vision for the university. While the evangelical movement initially made slow progress in the South, it was increasingly embraced by the majority of white and Black southerners to the extent that it became an irresistible force at the University of Virginia. Jefferson intended that the university not favor any religion, including Christianity, whereas the faculty and board interpreted their mandate as "not favoring any particular denomination of Christianity."[80] In reality, the chairman of the faculty issued the invitations and chose only preachers from four Protestant denominations: Episcopalians, Methodists, Presbyterians, and Baptists. In 1845, William Holmes McGuffey, professor of moral philosophy, became the first clergyman to be appointed to the faculty. He was an important force for change, leading the movement to build a chapel and parsonage. He is remembered as the author of the nationally bestselling school textbooks known as the *McGuffey Readers*, which notably lauded Alexander Hamilton and never even mentioned Jefferson.[81]

Within twenty years of the school's opening, a student could attend Morning Prayer daily, Bible lectures given by faculty members, Sunday school, and numerous organizations, such as a temperance association, the Bible Society, and the Society for Missionary Inquiry.[82] The university had become so evangelical that the majority of the faculty abstained from alcohol and joined the temperance society, despite the indignant refusal of

George Tucker, who had led the movement for a place of worship, along with his fellow faculty member and first cousin once removed Henry St. George Tucker.[83] In 1858, the university permitted the first college Young Man's Christian Association (YMCA) in the United States. Between 1883 and 1885, after a successful private subscription campaign, the present gothic-style chapel was constructed.

RESPONDING TO AN evangelical's claim that the original "experiment" of a secular university was failing in 1838, George Tucker wrote anonymously that "religion has no further connection with the University at this moment, than it had upon the day" that it opened.[84] Despite all attempts to the contrary, a distinguishing feature of the university was that it lacked either a department of religion or compulsory chapel. The Board of Visitors was resistant to such changes, while even the proponents of religion wanted to avoid the appearance of deviating from Jefferson's founding vision. The initial secularity of the university enabled it to attract outstanding faculty and students who either held unorthodox views on religion or belonged to religious minorities. Condemned as a "materialist and an infidel" by the *American Medical Recorder,* John P. Emmet had been unable to find an academic position for three years after he attributed the formation of organic matter to chemical factors. This pioneering thesis was not proven until 1844. Nevertheless, he held the chair of chemistry and medicine at the University of Virginia from 1825 until 1842.

In 1841, the twenty-seven-year-old James Joseph Sylvester became the first Jewish professor in America when he was appointed from England to the faculty of the University of Virginia. He was chosen over forty other candidates.[85] Recommended by Thomas Hewitt Key, a former University of Virginia faculty member, Sylvester had been a colleague of Key's at University College, London University, and a fellow of the Royal Society in London. Prevented from subscribing to the Thirty-Nine Articles of the Church of England by his Jewish faith, he was unable either to graduate from Cambridge University or apply for a fellowship or its Smith Prize, despite having ranked second in Cambridge's famous mathematical tripos exams.

James Joseph Sylvester was not simply of Jewish ethnicity but an observant Jew. He later became an immensely distinguished mathematician, awarded the Copley Medal by the Royal Society in London. At the University of Virginia, he taught mathematics, chemistry, moral philosophy, ancient languages, and law. As a scholar, he made foundational contributions to matrix theory, variant theory, number theory, partition theory, and combinatorics. He introduced many well-known terms into the language of science, including the word "graph," and he pioneered the mathematical use of letters from the Hebrew alphabet. A lover of poetry, he translated works from Italian, French, Greek, German, and Latin. In 1928, the British political scientist Harold J. Laski recalled hearing a judge saying, "The greatest man he had ever met was J. J. Sylvester."[86] Sylvester was revered by Charles Babbage, who invented the calculating machine that was the basis for computers, and he was the inspiration for the great astronomer and logician Sir John Herschel.

In 1840, the University of Virginia also appointed a Hungarian Roman Catholic, Charles Kraitsir (also Kratzer). He was selected out of an applicant pool of forty-six candidates. Although a professor of mathematics, he also offered to teach French, Spanish, Italian, German, Provençal, Portuguese, Danish, Swedish, Icelandish, Dutch, Bohemian, Polish, Russian, and Magyar.[87] Kraitsir and Sylvester were both condemned in the *Watchman of the South*, a Richmond publication of the Presbyterian church, as showing that infidelity was "unashamed of its colors" in seeking "to form alliances with Papism, Unitarianism, Judaism, and other errors subversive of Christianity." It asked, "Could there be a more flagrant demonstration of contempt for Protestantism than the Board had exhibited" in appointing a Catholic and a Jew?[88] William Barton Rogers, a faculty colleague who later became the first president of the Massachusetts Institute of Technology, denounced this illiberality "on the subject of religion . . . as displayed in the bigoted publications . . . respecting the appointments of Sylvester and Kraitzir."[89]

The subsequent brief careers of both men reveal the limits of religious toleration. Their resignations were aggravated by the prejudices against them. In 1843, the university dismissed Kraitsir, whose class enrollments were low, after he was ejected from his house several times in the night and even whipped once by his wife. Subject to anti-Semitic barbs by students, Sylvester fled the university within four months of his arrival, after defending himself with a cane and sword from physical assault by a student who resented his antislavery views. Sylvester justifiably feared for his life, since only the previous year the law professor, John A. G. Davis, had been shot dead by a student. In a hearing before the faculty, the student who assaulted Sylvester complained that the professor had said the student was no gentleman and had spoken to him "in an authoritative manner—as an overseer speaks to a negro slave."[90]

The consequences were tragic in the short term for Sylvester. Although supported by the faculty, he failed to obtain testimonials from the Board of Visitors in Virginia, which included many of Jefferson's old associates, like Cabell and Thomas Jefferson Randolph. Sylvester then tried unsuccessfully to obtain a position at Columbia University and thereafter lost ten years of academic life working as an actuary for an insurance company in England. Nevertheless, he remained undaunted. He developed actuarial models for the insurance company and became its de facto director. He later joined the faculty of the Woolwich Academy. In 1876, Sylvester crossed the Atlantic again to become professor at the new Johns Hopkins University, now regarded as the first university in America to be modeled on the German research tradition of colleges like Berlin University. While at Hopkins, Sylvester founded the *American Journal of Mathematics* and intervened to enable Christine Ladd to be admitted as the first woman graduate student in the country. At the time of his death in 1897, he was the Savilian Professor of Geometry at Oxford University, and the Royal Society honored him by creating the Sylvester Medal. After his departure from the University of Virginia, no other Jewish professor was appointed to the faculty until 1920. Similarly, following Kraitsir's dismissal, throughout the rest of the nineteenth century there would be no Roman Catholic members of the faculty. Despite Jefferson's best efforts, the university was a product of its environment.

NOTWITHSTANDING ALL EFFORTS to the contrary, Jefferson's original vision of religious tolerance and separation continued to inspire later generations. The university never required attendance at chapel, and it admitted Catholics and Jews. Entering in October 1862, Gratz Cohen, a Jewish student from Savannah, Georgia, was unanimously elected president of the prestigious Jefferson Literary and Debating Society. The university became so attractive to Jewish students, especially from New York, that they represented 8.5 percent of the total student body by 1926–27.[91] Like many universities in the Northeast, their numbers were thereafter restricted by a quota system. Jefferson's home of Monticello was preserved owing to its purchase by Uriah Phillips Levy, who was the first Jewish commodore in the U.S. Navy. Purchasing the house in 1834, he had earlier paid for the sculpting of a statue of Jefferson, the only privately funded monument in the U.S. Capitol. Levy ascribed his admiration in part to the fact that Jefferson did "much to mold our Republic in a form in which a man's *religion* does not make him ineligible for political or governmental life."[92] On April 13, 1923, the 150th anniversary of Jefferson's birth, the property was purchased from the Levy family by the Thomas Jefferson Foundation, which maintains it to this day.

When he became the first Muslim ever elected to Congress, Keith Ellison of Minnesota took the oath of office using the copy of the Qur'an that Jefferson had included in his sale to the Library of Congress in 1815. Purchased by Jefferson while he was still studying law in Williamsburg in 1765, this English translation was edited by George Sale and titled *The Koran; Commonly Called the Alcoran of Mohammed* (1734). Published in London in 1764, Jefferson's copy of a second edition, in two octavo volumes, included a "Preliminary Discourse" by the translator, who avoided the general tendency to try to demonstrate the superiority of Christianity. This Qur'an is identifiable as part of Jefferson's library by the characteristic addition of his initials T and I (J in the Latin alphabet), before and after a printed signature T.

In the *North American Review*, Edward Everett—later president of Harvard—wrote that the absence of religion "is probably the first instance, in the world, of a university without any such provision." He described it as a "hazardous experiment."[93] Jefferson's desire to exclude organized religion was fundamental to his educational vision. It was a leading factor in his preference for a public system because it would help to maintain a wall of separation between the university and sectarian control. It was one of the reasons he wanted schools funded at the equivalent of the town or village level, what he called ward republics, rather than the state, and why he opposed Charles Fenton Mercer's public-school bill, which was backed by Presbyterians in 1817. One major reason for his opposition to southern youth attending northern colleges was their domination by Presbyterians and Congregationalists, in addition to their alliance with his opponents in the Federalist Party. He was more extreme than most of the revolutionary generation in wanting to prohibit clergy from teaching at either school or university level. He went so far on this issue that he risked the support of the legislature and had to be forced by the rest of the Board of Visitors to renege on the appointment of Thomas Cooper to the faculty. Although racial discrimination has become an issue of much greater concern, it is easy to forget that differences in religion historically have led to ethnic cleansing, persecution, and prejudice, which in Europe reached its apogee with the Nazi murder of 6 million Jews.

Dedicated in 1910, a statue of Jefferson outside the University of Virginia's Rotunda depicts him holding the Declaration of Independence and commemorates his ideas of religious freedom by listing, in different faiths and languages, the various names for God: Jehovah, Allah, Brahma, Ra, Atma, Zeus, and God. Cast from an earlier mold used for the same statue with a larger base in Jefferson County, Kentucky, it also features Jewish symbols on the scrolls and the Hindu "aum" sign. This piece was sculpted by Ezekiel Moses, a native of Richmond, who was the first Jewish cadet at the Virginia Military Institute (VMI) and who particularly admired Jefferson. At VMI, he had been a roommate of Jefferson's great-nephew Thomas G. Jefferson. His statue includes an inscription from the book of Leviticus—"Proclaim Liberty Throughout All the Land Unto the Inhabitants Thereof"—along with allegorical figures of four spirits representing Freedom, Equality, Justice, and Religious Freedom (Brotherhood). Described at the dedication by President Edwin Alderman as a "sermon in stone," the names of God are carved on a tablet held in the hands of the spirit of Brotherhood and titled "Religious Freedom, 1786," to commemorate the Virginia Statute for Religious Freedom. It aims to show that each religion believes in a God and that all have "equal right to protection of our just laws as Americans."[94]

8

This Deplorable Entanglement

O N AUGUST 19, 1791, the year of the adoption of the Bill of Rights, Benjamin Banneker, whose father had been enslaved, wrote to Secretary of State Thomas Jefferson. Banneker acknowledged that he was taking a liberty that "seemed to me scarcely allowable" when he considered the "distinguished, and dignified station in which you Stand" and "the almost general prejudice and prepossession which is so prevalent in the world against those of my complexion." A Black astronomer and mathematician, Banneker had been a member of a team that surveyed the District of Columbia for the future national capital. In a tone as bold as that used by Jefferson in addressing George III in *A Summary View of the Rights of British America* (1774), Banneker continued, "We are a race of Beings who have long laboured under the abuse and censure of the world, that we have been long looked upon with an eye of contempt, and that we have long been considered rather as brutish than human, and Scarcely capable of mental endowments." Appealing to Jefferson's belief in the moral equality between the races and the innate moral sense of all mankind, Banneker hoped that Jefferson would "eradicate that train of absurd and false ideas and oppinions which so generally prevails with respect to us," since regardless of differences in religion and color, "we are all of the Same Family, and Stand in the Same relation" to the "one universal Father."[1]

Just as Jefferson had reminded George III of his obligations to his imperial subjects, the fifty-nine-year-old Banneker told Jefferson that it was the "indispensible duty" of those professing a belief in natural rights and Christianity "to extend their power and influence to the relief of every part of the human race, from whatever burthen or oppression they may unjustly labour under." If Jefferson were sincere in his proclaimed beliefs, he would be active in ensuring that every individual "of whatsoever rank or distinction, might with you equally enjoy the blessings" of the rights of man, neither should he rest satisfied until he had exerted himself to the fullest to remove the oppressed from a state of "degradation, to which the unjustifiable cruelty and barbarism of men may have reduced them." Identifying himself "freely and Chearfully" as "of the African race" and Black "of the deepest dye," Banneker reminded Jefferson of the time when the British tried "to reduce you to a State of Servitude" and when "you clearly saw into the injustice of a State of Slavery." Confronting Jefferson with his own words from the Declaration of Independence, Banneker asserted that Jefferson's abhorrence of slavery "was so excited, that you publickly held forth this true and invaluable doctrine, which is worthy to be recorded and remember'd in all Succeeding ages. 'We hold these truths to be Self evident, that all men are created equal, and that they are endowed by their creator with certain unalienable rights, that among these are life, liberty, and the pursuit of happyness.'"[2]

With the accusatory tone of the list of grievances against George III in the Declaration of Independence, Banneker charged Jefferson with having betrayed his own revolutionary beliefs, when he had held "proper ideas of the great valuation of liberty" and the free possession of natural rights:

> How pitiable it is to reflect, that altho you were so fully convinced of the benevolence of the Father of mankind, and of his equal and impartial distribution of those rights and privileges which he had conferred upon them, that you should at the Same time counteract his mercies, in detaining by fraud and violence so numerous a part of my brethren under groaning captivity and cruel oppression, that you should at the Same time be found guilty of that most criminal act, which you professedly detested

when committed by the British. He recommended "to you and all others to wean yourselves from these narrow prejudices which you have imbibed" and instead follow the biblical exhortation in the book of Job to "put your Souls in their Souls stead." Through this empathy for the enslaved, "thus shall your hearts be enlarged with kindness and benevolence."[3]

Banneker concluded that his main purpose in writing was to send Jefferson a copy of an almanac that he had handwritten and calculated. Aided by the loan of books and equipment from two Quaker brothers named Ellicott, Banneker had commenced the study of astronomy at an "advanced Stage of life" and succeeded in publishing a series of almanacs beginning with the one he was sending to Jefferson. As Banneker explained in his accompanying letter, he had succeeded against all adversity, "difficulties and disadvantages," motivated by a determination to gratify his curiosity and his "unbounded desires to become acquainted with the Secrets of nature."[4] His almanacs included material aimed at improving the condition of African Americans and looked forward to a "time, [which] it is hoped *is not very remote*, when those ill-fated people, dwelling in this land of freedom, shall commence a participation with the white inhabitants, in the blessings of liberty, and experience the kindly protection of government, for the essential rights of human nature."[5] The Philadelphia astronomer David Rittenhouse pronounced the book "a very extraordinary performance, considering the Colour of the Author," adding that the "calculations are sufficiently accurate for the purposes of a common Almanac." Well aware of the condescension of Rittenhouse's assessment, Banneker was "annoyed to find that the subject of my race is so much stressed" when his "calculations were perfect."[6]

Ignoring the accusation of having connived in a system of fraud and violence to subjugate African Americans, Jefferson wrote a brief reply that ostensibly commended Banneker's efforts. Thanking him for his letter and the copy of the almanac, Jefferson wrote that "no body wishes more than I do to see such proofs as you exhibit, that nature has given to our black brethren, talents equal to those of the other colours of men, and that the appearance of a want of them is owing merely to the degraded condition of their existence both in Africa and America." He claimed that he ardently wished to see "a good system commenced for raising the condition both of their body and mind to what it ought to be, as fast as the imbecillity of their present existence and other circumstances which cannot be neglected, will admit," and that he regarded the almanac as a "document to which your whole color had a right for their justification against the doubts which have been entertained of them."[7] Jefferson added that he had sent a copy of the almanac to the Marquis de Condorcet, a noted mathematician and abolitionist who was the secretary of the Academy of Sciences in Paris and a member of the French Society of Friends of the Blacks (Société des Amis des Noirs). Condorcet called Black people his brothers in his radical antislavery manifesto *Réflexions sur l'esclavage des Nègres* (1781). In his cover letter to Condorcet, Jefferson wrote, "I am happy to be able to inform you that we have now in the United States a negro, the son of a black man born in Africa, and of a black woman born in the United States, who is a very respectable Mathematician," and that he had "seen very elegant solutions of Geometrical problems by him." Describing Banneker as "a very worthy and respectable member of society," Jefferson claimed that he would "be delighted to see these instances of moral eminence so multiplied as to prove that the want of talents observed in them is merely the effect of their degraded condition, and not proceeding from any difference in the structure of the parts on which intellect depends."[8] Three years after Banneker's death in 1806, however, Jefferson disparaged his abilities to Joel Barlow, concluding that "he had spherical trigonometry enough to make almanacs, but not without the suspicion of aid from Ellicot, who was his neighbor & friend, & never missed an opportunity of puffing him." It described his long letter from Banneker as showing "a mind of very common stature indeed."[9]

IN THE WAKE OF the civil rights movement and Black Lives Matter, Jefferson's demeaning racial views and his failure to free his enslaved workers has rightly been condemned. In our era of greater sensitivity to racial justice, the issues of race and slavery have diminished his reputation as an "Apostle of Liberty." Jefferson condemned slavery throughout his life and acknowledged that it was an urgent issue; if not addressed, he feared that a slave uprising would lead to a race war similar to the Haitian Revolution. However, his self-imposed limits on a piecemeal or national plan of emancipation, other than through the impractical method of removal abroad, ultimately left him intellectually bankrupt as to a solution and implicated him in the survival of the system. He could not imagine an interracial society, which is all the more surprising given his fathering of the children of Sally Hemings. He was elusive about both race and slavery, especially since his views changed and evolved, partly in response to less propitious circumstances. He was often addressing and trying to appeal to two diametrically different audiences: the antislavery sentiments of Enlightened thinkers and his political base in the South. Consequently, beginning from the time of his death, there was debate about his actual views on the subject, with the result that he was invoked by both champions of the defense and abolition of slavery.[10] His flawed response was of course not limited to him individually but reflected a national problem and a prevalent belief in white supremacy. African American historian Roger Wilkins describes Jefferson "as America writ small."[11] Slavery contaminated not only life at Monticello but also the University of Virginia. Benjamin Banneker articulated a question that remains a riddle: how Jefferson justified his belief that all men are created equal and yet remained implicated in this moral evil.

Jefferson's racial attitudes were rooted in the system of slavery, the prevalent form of labor at both his plantations and the University of Virginia. Often regarded as the first female sociologist, Harriet Martineau, a British writer and intellectual, visited the University of Virginia in 1835 and commented that "the evil influences of slavery have entered in to taint the work of the great champion of liberty," adding in prophetic anticipation of the Civil War that "the eyes of the world will be fixed on Jefferson's University during the impending conflict between slaveholders and freemen."[12] The Board of Visitors included large planters, such as Joseph Cabell, Thomas Jefferson, James Madison, John Hartwell Cocke, and James Monroe, who each enslaved more than a hundred people but who all favored abolition through colonization, the idea of sending Black Americans back to Africa. Like all colleges in the South, the domestic staff consisted largely of enslaved laborers employed by the faculty, hotelkeepers, or the university on contract from their owners. The only aspect that distinguished the university from other southern colleges were the regulations that prohibited students from bringing enslaved servants onto the Grounds.

There were many interconnections between slavery at Monticello and the University of Virginia. The domestics employed by the faculty and the enslaved laborers at the university included slaves from Monticello such as Sally Cottrell Cole. She had been the enslaved maid of Jefferson's granddaughter Ellen Randolph, who upon marrying Joseph Coolidge in May 1825, wrote a power of attorney "to dispose of Sally and to protect her" in which she emphasized that "her own wishes . . . must direct the disposition that is made of her for I would not for the world that after living with me for fifteen years any kind of violence should be done to her feelings." Randolph requested that Cottrell be allowed to choose her own master, whether sold or hired out, and that "she should not be sent any where she is unwilling to go."[13] She was sold for four hundred dollars to Thomas Hewitt Key, the professor of mathematics, who planned to free her after she nursed his infant daughter by his wife, Sarah. After Key returned to England, Cottrell served as a seamstress and nurse in the household of another professor, John Patten Emmet. In 1846, she married Reuben Cole. Her legal status as a free person was still being questioned as late as 1850.

After Jefferson's death, 130 of his enslaved laborers were sold off to pay his debts, tragically causing the separation of families. Harriett Dunglison, the wife of the medical professor, wrote to the executor of the estate concerning Fanny Hern. In as much "as she has once lived with me," she expressed her "fear she may be sent to a distance." Professor Dunglison accordingly authorized his wife "to try to obtain her at the sale as well as her youngest child, should they go at a reasonable price." The Dunglisons did succeed in purchasing Hern and her youngest child, Bonnycastle, named

188   THE ILLIMITABLE FREEDOM OF THE HUMAN MIND

after another professor, Charles Bonnycastle, who also owned a former Monticello slave named Patsy.[14] Two years later, the Dunglisons additionally bought "Waggoner David," Hern's husband. Lucy Cottrell; her mother, Dorothea Cottrell; and their extended family were purchased from Jefferson's estate by George Blaettermann, the professor of modern languages, for whom she worked as a cook, living with her relatives in the cramped cellar of Pavilion IV.[15]

Born at Monticello in the year of Jefferson's death in 1826, Henry Martin was purchased by the Carr family. He later recalled that he first began working as a server in the dining room and hauling wood at a boardinghouse for students run by Mrs. Dabney Carr at Carr's Hill in 1850. During the Civil War, he was rented out to a plantation in Richmond, but he ran away and returned to Charlottesville dressed as a Confederate soldier. As a free man after the war in 1868, he worked at the university as a janitor and bell ringer until his retirement in 1910. In a letter to the university magazine in 1890 briefly describing his life and work, he said that over the course of forty years he had known students who would occupy places of honor and distinction in the government. Martin continuously rang the bell on the day he learned of the surrender of the Confederacy at Appomattox Court House and on the day of the great fire of the Rotunda on October 17, 1895. When he died at the age of eighty-nine in 1915, the Charlottesville newspaper, the *Daily Progress*, noted that Martin had made sure that all of his twenty-four children could read and write. The paper also described his funeral as attracting "the largest and most distinguished crowd of white people that ever attended a colored man's funeral in Charlottesville."[16]

In 1820, Virginia was the largest slave state, accounting for some 425,153 slaves of a total of 1.5 million in the United States. They composed almost a third of the total enslaved population in the South, even after the exodus of some fifty thousand enslaved persons sold or transferred to the new cotton-belt states in Mississippi and Alabama between 1810 and 1820.[17] In Albemarle County, the location of Charlottesville and one of the four wealthiest counties in Virginia, the proportion of slaves relative to the total population was even higher at over 50 percent. At the University of Virginia, there were typically between 125 and 200 enslaved domestics and workers who were owned by faculty members and hotelkeepers or hired from owners by the university. Unlike South Carolina College (University of South Carolina), the university itself did not own slaves, with the single exception of the bell ringer Lewis Commodore, who was purchased first by the faculty and then the university after his owner threatened to sell him. The en-slaved domestics were assigned menial tasks like washing, cleaning out the privies, changing bedding, and cooking. Most belonged to the hotelkeepers. The 1830 census reveals that some 31 percent of the enslaved community at the university were children employed in delivering food, waiting on tables, and cleaning rooms.[18] The university also employed free Black workers like William Spinner, the first janitor at the university, while others profited from the school's presence, such as Jack Kennedy, who sold alcohol in the precincts of the university.[19] Jesse Scott, whose mother was a Pamunkey Indian and who was married to Sally Jefferson Bell, the daughter of Mary Hemings Bell, performed with his sons—Robert, James, and Thomas—at university dances as part of the "famous fiddling Scots."[20]

THE RACIAL TENSIONS inherent in slave societies were replicated within the university, sometimes leading to outbreaks of violence that were only occasionally recorded for posterity. The absence of any legal protection exposed enslaved people to arbitrary and demeaning treatment in a situ-ation that subjected them to the conflicting authority of students, profes-sors, and hotelkeepers. Early in the history of the university in 1828, the potential for arbitrary treatment was well illustrated when a student named Thomas Boyd assaulted an enslaved waiter in the dining hall of the hotel kept by Warner W. Minor.[21] According to Minor, Boyd complained that his waiter had served him rancid butter. The waiter did not respond until the student had left the room, when he commented sarcastically to a fellow servant that he was surprised that the student "having read so many books should not know the difference between water & butter." Upon hearing the comment secondhand, Boyd returned to the dining room the next day to insist that the waiter leave. When the latter refused, Boyd and a fellow stu-dent beat him and tried to force him out of the room until prevented by the hotelkeeper and his wife. Finding the student armed with a broken stick and the Black waiter covered in blood, they reported the incident to the faculty. During the resulting hearing, Boyd "expressed astonishment and in-dignation at being called before the faculty for so trifling an affair as that of chastising a servant for his insolence." Boyd subsequently challenged the hotelkeeper to a duel and threatened to shoot him in front of a crowd, with a student shouting, "Whip him Boyd, whip him." As historian Ervin L. Jor-dan reminds us, the enslaved waiter was never named in the proceedings, and the incident was only recorded because a white hotelkeeper brought a case against a white student.[22] Boyd went unpunished until a second incident with the hotelkeeper, after which he was moved to another dormitory.

On a Sunday afternoon on February 24, 1839, Charles Bonnycastle, the mathematics professor, scuffled with a group of students who were assaulting one of Bonnycastle's enslaved servants called Fielding. The incident began near the entrance of the university on the road leading to the center of Charlottesville. Two Black men were fighting, surrounded by others who cheered them on. Upon the intervention of two students, Franklin English and Benjamin Johnson, Fielding shouted and waved his stick saying, "These men are free, and they shall fight as much as they choose." English and Johnson turned on Fielding and began to beat him with their canes, but he managed to wrestle himself free and then threatened them with a stone before being pursued. A third student joined the fight, striking the enslaved boy with his fist and forcing him to the ground as he begged for mercy. Although they allowed him to get up, Fielding promptly picked up another stone, "motioned to strike with it, and was again insolent." A fourth student helped to tie Fielding and carry him but the enslaved boy grabbed a fence and said he would go no further since they might kill him.[23]

Professor Bonnycastle arrived on the scene and seized the collar of one of the students, who shouted verbal abuse and profanities, saying "that any man who would protect a negro . . . is no better than a negro himself." English grabbed Bonnycastle from behind while another student continued to beat Fielding. The students screamed profanities at the professor, shook him violently, struck him, and threatened him. Having freed Fielding, Bonnycastle encouraged him to run, but the enslaved, now exhausted boy was overtaken and knocked to the ground by a fifth student who drew a small dagger and threatened to stab him. One witness observed that Fielding was on his knees but unwilling to be subdued. Fielding managed to break the watch of one of the students before finally giving up the struggle. While they later admitted that they had been disrespectful toward the professor, the students argued that Bonnycastle had "thrown off the garb of a Professor and (as they supposed) assumed that of a man recklessly interposing to screen his servant from merited chastisement and to protect him in a course of extravagant impudence and abuse." At their hearing, the faculty left their punishment to the courts, which took no action.[24] One of the only times in which an effort was made to apprehend students who attacked a slave occurred in 1850, after an especially heinous crime when three students — George H. Hardy, Armistead C. Eliason, and James E. Montandon — raped a "small negro girl, a slave about 12 years old" near the University Cemetery. After the offenders were reported by other students, the culprits were merely expelled from the university.[25]

IN HIS PAMPHLET *Taxation No Tyranny* (1775), Samuel Johnson famously asked, "How is it that we hear the loudest yelps for *liberty* among the *drivers* of negroes?"[26] In Virginia, the first enslaved persons were imported in 1619, the same year that the first elected assembly in colonial America met in Jamestown. The contradiction between slavery and republican ideals of freedom and equality is quaintly described by some as a paradox and by others as rank hypocrisy, in what has been called the original sin of America. This is not just a retrospective judgment by historians.[27] Since the time of the American Revolution, Johnson and others have satirized the hypocrisy of slavery in a republican society. Ironically, it can be argued that southern whites' experiences of slavery and tyrannical authority were the prime reasons they were so vigilant of their freedom and more willing to embrace ideas of equality among themselves. In his 1775 speech on "Conciliation with the American Colonies," Edmund Burke attributed the "more high and haughty" spirit of liberty in the southern colonies to the multitude of slaves in the region. Wherever slavery existed in the world, "those who are free, are by far the most proud and jealous of their freedom. Freedom is to them not only an enjoyment, but a kind of rank and privilege."[28] In Virginia, Edmund Randolph similarly observed that "the existence of slavery, however, baneful to virtue, begat a pride which nourished a quick and acute sense of the rights of a freeman" and engendered "disdain" for any "abridgement of personal independence."[29] Historian Edmund S. Morgan has argued it was slavery that "enabled Virginia to nourish representative government in a plantation society, slavery that transformed the Virginia of Governor Berkeley to the Virginia of Jefferson, slavery that made the Virginians dare to speak a political language that magnified the rights of freemen, and slavery, therefore, that brought Virginians into the same commonwealth political tradition with New Englanders."[30] Although such arguments help explain why planters were so jealous of their own freedom as to play a major role in establishing the nucleus of representative government, Jefferson understood well the contradiction between slavery and the expressed ideals of liberty, regarding it as a blot on the republican system.

In spite of his enslavement of other human beings, Jefferson was one of the earliest and most eloquent critics of slavery in the new republic. Unlike contemporary planters in the British Caribbean, he recognized the immorality of slavery and acknowledged the contradiction it posed to professed beliefs in liberty, writing, "What a stupendous, what an incomprehensible machine is man! Who can endure toil, famine, stripes, imprisonment & death itself in vindication of his own liberty, and the next moment be deaf to all the motives whose power supported him thro' his trial, and inflict on his fellow men a bondage, one hour of which is fraught with more misery than ages of that which he rose in rebellion to oppose."[31] In his correspondence, he described slavery as a "hideous blot," an "abomination," and a "moral and political depravity."[32] In a letter to Edward Coles in 1814, he wrote that "the love of justice & the love of country plead equally the cause of these people, and it is a mortal reproach to us that they should have pleaded it so long in vain."[33]

As a young lawyer in Williamsburg in the 1760s, Jefferson defended several freedom suits on behalf of African Americans. As in the case of Samuel Holwell in *Holwell v. Netherland* (1770), he seems not to have charged his nonwhite clients a fee for his services.[34] Upon entering the House of Burgesses in 1769, Jefferson supported a bill to allow the private manumission of slaves. In *A Summary View of the Rights of British America* (1774), which he gave to his enslaved servant Jupiter to carry to the House of Burgesses in Williamsburg, Jefferson wrote, "The abolition of domestic slavery is the great object of desire in those colonies where it was unhappily introduced in their infant state."[35] In his original draft of the Declaration of Independence, he blamed George III for the slave trade, calling it a crime against the liberties of one people and a "cruel war against human nature itself." The paragraph was deleted at the behest of the members from South Carolina.

In Paris in 1786, Jefferson wrote of slavery, "I tremble for my country when I reflect that God is just: that his justice cannot sleep forever." In the event of a great slave rebellion or war between the races, "the Almighty has no attribute which can take side with us in such a contest."[36] In his so-called autobiography (1821), he claimed that he had proposed a manumission bill in the House of Burgesses as early as 1769. During the revision of the state statute on slavery in the 1770s, he wanted to include a plan for general emancipation but found that "the public mind would not yet bear the proposition," adding in his autobiography that public opinion "will not bear it even at this day."[37] He included such a plan in his *Notes on the State of Virginia*.[38] In his *Report of a Plan of Government for the Western Territories* to the Confederation Congress on March 1, 1784, Jefferson proposed resolutions banning slavery after 1800 in all the new western territories, both North and South, to be ceded to the national government. Such a ban would have included Alabama, Mississippi, and Tennessee. Gaining support from only one southern state, it fell by a single vote in Congress. In retrospect, the failure of this initiative was particularly significant given that the initial crisis that led to the Civil War concerned the expansion of slavery to new states, such as Missouri, Kansas, and Texas. Jefferson lamented that "the fate of millions unborn was hanging on the tongue of one man, and heaven was silent in that awful moment."[39] His draft ordinance did influence the 1787 Northwest Ordinance, which prohibited slavery in the future states of Ohio, Illinois, Wisconsin, and Michigan. In 1846, David Wilmot, a congressman from Pennsylvania, invoked the precedent set by Jefferson when he proposed the famous Wilmot Proviso (1846), which aimed to prevent the spread of slavery in areas conquered in the Mexican War. During the debate on the Compromise of 1850, Salmon P. Chase, the antislavery leader from Ohio, called Wilmot's Proviso "a revival after the lapse of sixty-two years, of the territorial policy of Jefferson." The Free Soil Party (1848), and later the Republican Party, celebrated what they dubbed "The Jefferson Proviso."[40]

After the Revolutionary War, Jefferson wrote to the British radical Richard Price that Virginia was the next place "to which we may turn our eyes for the interesting spectacle of justice in conflict with avarice & oppression: a conflict wherein the sacred side is gaining daily recruits of young men," suckled in the "principles of liberty," to whom he looked "with anxiety to turn the fate" of slavery.[41] Indeed, the College of William and Mary professor St. George Tucker pointed out that Virginia had more free Blacks living in the state than in all of New England, with some 30,750 by 1810.[42] In 1791, Jefferson contributed money to Richard Allen's building of the first Black church in Philadelphia, which became the African Methodist Episcopal church. As president of the United States in December 1806, Jefferson urged in his annual message to Congress that the earliest opportunity be taken to interpose its constitutional authority to prohibit the international slave trade, thus ending "those violations of human rights which have been so long continued on the unoffending inhabitants of Africa."[43] On March 2, 1807, he signed into law the act abolishing the slave trade, to commence on January 1, 1808, the earliest possible date allowed by the Constitution. While some modern critics dismiss this measure as a cynical ploy that actually increased the value of his own slaves, the radical journalist and politician John Binns praised Jefferson in the Philadelphia Democratic press for advocating legislation to end the slave trade, declaring that "the ax is therefore at length, effectually laid to the root of slavery."[44] Jefferson's role in closing the transatlantic slave trade and his ordinance to prevent slavery in the Midwest represented significant victories for freedom and contributed to weakening the institution of slavery.[45]

Short of emancipation, Jefferson and his fellow planters responded to the challenge of abolitionists with what they called a system of amelioration that sought to improve the lives of the enslaved and, not coincidentally, their productivity. This combined a more humane and enlightened approach to the work and care of the enslaved with the planters' own economic self-interest. Beginning in the 1790s, while rebuilding Monticello, Jefferson sought to improve the efficiency of his plantations by adopting a more scientific approach to agricultural production and applying humanitarian principles to the enslaved workforce. He ceased to grow tobacco and instead cultivated diverse crops, such as wheat, while also raising livestock. Because tobacco was more labor intensive, the change required breaking up the larger field gangs and giving more individual responsibility to slaves. On Mulberry Row, the principal street and hub of the plantation at Monticello, smaller single-family dwellings replaced large multifamily tenements. Jefferson offered financial incentives and other inducements, allowing some of his enslaved laborers to cultivate small plots of land for their own benefit, which enabled them to engage in the consumer economy and even occasionally to lend cash to Jefferson. His ideals and the reality of slavery were often in conflict. Frances Wright, the English feminist and author who saw the slave quarters at Monticello, acknowledged the efforts of the planters to ameliorate the conditions of their slaves but regarded it as "gilding" rather than breaking the chains of slavery.[46]

Just as he became more reticent about the subject of religion, Jefferson was more guarded in his statements about emancipation later in life, but his options for a national solution were limited. It was not merely a matter of his being unwilling to risk his political capital; it would have been politically unfeasible for him to have been more active in promoting abolitionism while pursuing an active political career. Where there had seemed a very real chance of progress in the era of the American Revolution, with abolitionist sympathies on the rise in Virginia, times had changed and attitudes had shifted. The embryonic antislavery sentiment in the state was stifled by the expansion of the cotton economy, which led to an increase in the value of each enslaved person; the burgeoning free Black population; and alarms over racial violence with the success of the Haitian Revolution (1791–1804) and notably Gabriel's slave rebellion in Virginia in 1800. The revolutionary spirit that made it possible to contemplate radical ideas of beginning the world anew was subsiding.

By 1800, Jefferson's taking a strong stance for emancipation would have cost him the presidency, since he needed the support of the southern states whose votes dominated the first decades of national politics, thanks not least to the Constitution's three-fifths clause counting the enslaved population for apportionment purposes. If Jefferson did nothing in office against slavery other than help abolish the slave trade, even that was more than his Federalist opponent John Adams had achieved. Even though most Federalists were northerners who stood to lose less financially than southerners if slavery were abolished, they were divided on the subject of slavery and generally only expressed antislavery views when they were in opposition to the Republicans. Proslavery Federalists in South Carolina even used Jefferson's correspondence with Benjamin Banneker against Jefferson. In the presidential election of 1796, South Carolina Federalist William L. Smith claimed that Jefferson was friendly to free Blacks and hostile to slavery, and the same tactic was used against him in the election of 1800.[47] Jefferson was especially vulnerable because of having fathered children by Sally Hemings. If he had acknowledged the fact, it would have made him unelectable in 1800.[48]

OTHER THAN HIS children by Hemings and some of the extended Hemings family, Jefferson freed none of his slaves and advised against others doing so. He opposed incremental plans for freeing individuals and small groups, fearing that they would deflect from the urgency of collective action and a general plan of emancipation, without which a race war would ensue and lead to "convulsions which will probably never end but in the extermination of the one or the other race."[49] Referring to the Black population as a separate nation, he could only envisage a general plan of emancipation that entailed removal elsewhere to avoid a race war. The belief might be dismissed as self-serving but it had the merit of candidly acknowledging the oppressive and immoral nature of slavery, and the just resentment of the oppressed, in contrast to the view soon to prevail among southern whites that slaves were happy with their status. Credited with writing the boldest antislavery pamphlet in the South in 1796, St. George Tucker shared Jefferson's belief that a general emancipation within the nation would lead to civil war, thereby threatening the lives of the planters and their natural rights to self-preservation. Like Jefferson, he argued that Black people would never be able to survive economically in the United States.[50] Consequently, Jefferson's and Tucker's arguments about the dangers of emancipation actually lent support to the institution's continuance.

Indeed, St. George Tucker was one of several prominent Virginians who spoke against slavery but similarly failed to free their own slaves and thereby helped perpetuate the system. Others included Patrick Henry, one of the leading patriots of the revolution and a governor of Virginia; George Mason, the author of the Virginia bill of rights; David Rice, the Presbyterian evangelical who helped found Hampden-Sydney College and Transylvania University; John Hartwell Cocke, a member of the Board of Visitors at the University of Virginia; and James Madison, often called the father of the Constitution. Against the advice of Jefferson, who opposed piecemeal emancipation, Edward Coles freed his slaves, but he was forty years younger than Jefferson and, in order to carry out his intentions, had to leave Virginia for Illinois. Credited with having said "give me liberty, or give me death," Patrick Henry admitted his dilemma and recognition of his own moral failing when he said, "Would any one believe that I am the Master of Slaves of my own purchase! I am drawn along by ye general inconvenience of living without them; I will not, cannot justify it!"[51] The Virginia legislature actively discouraged emancipation by enacting a law in 1806 that required freed slaves to leave the state within a year.

Jefferson never wavered from the view that the system of slavery was morally repugnant and that it should be ended. Less than a year before his death, when his own granddaughter Ellen Coolidge compared the South unfavorably to the North, likening slavery to a canker that "eats into their hearts, & diseases the whole body by this ulcer at the core," he replied that with "one single circumstance [slavery] changed," the South would be superior but that this "one fatal strain deforms what nature had bestowed on us of her fairest gifts."[52] Furthermore, while thinking it both inexpedient and beyond his powers in old age to take up the challenge of slavery, likening it to asking "Old Priam to buckle the armour of Hector," Jefferson continued to warn his correspondents of the urgency of the issue and the likelihood that, if not addressed, it would lead to a bloody war like the revolution in Haiti.[53] As he had written to St. George Tucker in 1797, "if something is not done, and done soon, we shall be the murderers of our own children."[54]

Jefferson admitted that he saw "not how we are to disengage ourselves from that deplorable entanglement" of slavery, lamenting that "we have the wolf by the ears and feel the danger of either holding or letting him loose."[55] Using the same analogy of holding "the wolf by the ears" to slavery, he wrote to another correspondent, "We can neither hold him, nor safely let him go. justice is in one scale, and self-preservation in the other."[56] He consoled himself late in life with the illusory hope that the diffusion of slavery across the nation would lead to its gradual demise by diluting its impact and relevance.[57] He additionally hoped that a better-educated generation of leaders would solve the problem of slavery, writing, "I shall not live to see it but those who come after us will be wiser than we are, for light is spreading and man improving. to that advancement I look, and to the dispensations of an all-wise and all-powerful providence to devise the means of effecting what is right."[58]

Despite his hopes for a better future, Jefferson was well aware—and fearful—of the consequences of emancipating his own slaves, as was clearly illustrated by the fate of one of his contemporaries, Robert "Councillor" Carter III. The latter was one of the leading political figures in Williamsburg on the eve of the American Revolution. He was the most conspicuous emancipator of the era, a Virginian freeing nearly five hundred slaves and providing them with land and houses. Carter was ostracized for his efforts and moved to Baltimore. George Washington freed 123 slaves but only to occur after his wife Martha's death. He enjoyed the benefits of their labor throughout his life and died wealthy in contrast to the bankrupt Jefferson. Furthermore, the majority of the enslaved at Mount Vernon remained in bondage after his death because 195 slaves belonged to Martha outright. In any event, Washington never spoke out publicly against slavery, an act that could have had real impact coming from a president who was a legend in his own lifetime and regarded by contemporaries as the father of his country. During his presidency, Washington avoided Pennsylvania laws that would have freed his enslaved servants by shuttling them back and forth to Mount Vernon.[59] He relentlessly pursued one enslaved person, Ona Judge, after her escape to New Hampshire, incensed by her demand that she would return only if she received a pledge that she would be freed when Washington and his wife died. By the time Jefferson founded the University of Virginia, hostility to abolitionists was so extreme that Francis Walker Gilmer, the favorite choice to hold the law professorship, believed that Federalist Charles Fenton Mercer should be imprisoned for his antislavery views.[60]

Like most people then and now, Jefferson had multiple and conflicting objectives. Given that politics is the art of the possible, he made tradeoffs as to what was most important to him and what could be achieved. His overriding goal was to ensure the survival of the republican system and the union of the states. The Missouri Crisis exposed the very real possibility that debates over slavery might lead to disunion. Jefferson gave priority to establishing the university in the belief that it would train a generation of political leaders who would not only perpetuate the republic but solve those problems left by his own generation, telling Edward Coles, "I had always hoped that the younger generation," having benefited themselves from the blessings of liberty, "would have sympathised with oppression wherever found, and proved their love of liberty beyond their own share of it."[61] Explaining his decision not to subscribe to an antislavery tract in 1805, Jefferson said that he would avoid saying or doing anything in regard to the subject until the right moment arose for him to interpose himself "with decisive effect," since "it would only be disarming myself of influence to be talking small means."[62] He had similarly argued once before, in regard to possible action in the state legislature, that "an unsuccessful effort, as too often happens, would only rivet still closer the chains of bondage, and retard the moment of delivery to this oppressed description of men."[63] Later he complained more generally, "How difficult it is to move or inflect the great machine of society, how impossible to advance the notions of a whole people suddenly to ideal right."[64]

Jefferson's antislavery views influenced some of his family members and protégés who, after his death, were almost alone in advocating emancipation in Virginia and throughout the South. As a girl of fifteen, his daughter Martha wrote to him, "I wish with all my soul that the poor negroes were all freed. It grieves my heart when I think that these our fellow creatures should be treated so terribly as they are by many of our fellow country men." Possibly influenced by Martha, her husband, Thomas Mann Randolph, later governor of Virginia, wanted to farm on a smaller scale "without employing slaves in the cultivation of the lands," a plan he told his father-in-law was approved by Martha. Jefferson deplored what he called "the new morality which tolerates the perpetuity of slavery," which he would later detect in the debates over Missouri statehood in 1820. Thomas Jefferson Randolph, Jefferson's eldest grandson, became a self-described "unflinching advocate of abolition" who presented a plan of gradual emancipation to the Virginia legislature, similar to that of his grandfather, as late as 1832. He lost his seat in the legislature when he supported Andrew Jackson in the Nullification Crisis, a stance his mother, Martha, supported.[65] Ellen Randolph Coolidge wrote that "slavery is a hateful thing" and that "though born & brought up in a Slave State. I was early taught to abhor an odious system." Nevertheless, Martha and Ellen shared Jefferson's distrust of radical abolitionists, who they suspected of trying to incite insurrection.[66] Ellen, who wrote so eloquently against slavery to her grandfather, was disgusted by what she regarded as the extremism and radicalism of the abolitionists that she met in London in 1838–39, such as Charles Sumner and Harriet Martineau, of whom she wrote that "the lady's animosity against slave-holders had become a monomania."[67] Antislavery southerners took the view that the decision to end slavery should ultimately be made by the southern states and not by northerners, a position consistently held in the South from the beginnings of the republic. Their argument had more validity in the 1780s, when there seemed a real chance of change, than the 1820s and 1830s.

AT THE UNIVERSITY OF VIRGINIA, a small faction among the faculty and students opposed slavery. They included St. George Tucker's older cousin Professor George Tucker and the former's son Professor Henry St. George Tucker. There were also students who opposed slavery, such as Gessner Harrison and Henry Tutwiler. Having been taught to read as a child by a boy of mixed race in Bermuda, George Tucker professed "doubts about the inferiority of the coloured race." In his *Letters from Virginia* (1816), he attributed the cause of racial differences solely to "time and circumstance." In his later biography of Jefferson, he wrote that the latter had blundered in asserting the "natural inferiority" of Blacks in the *Notes on the State of Virginia*.[68] With a career spanning twenty years at the University of Virginia between 1825 and 1845, Tucker wrote extensively on the subject of slavery. In his first book, *Letter on the Conspiracy of the Slaves* (1801), he advanced a practical rather than a moral argument against the institution, warning that as the enslaved became more educated, they were more likely to rebel, just as they had done in Gabriel's Rebellion (1800). He wrote that slavery was impeding southern economic progress. Along with fellow professors Charles Bonnycastle and Robley Dunglison, Tucker joined the American Colonization Society. Like Jefferson, he later concluded that colonization was impractical and that the problem would only be solved by the diffusion of African Americans throughout the United States. He predicted that the system of slavery would become uneconomic and uncompetitive compared to cheap white labor, leading to its implosion in sixty to eighty years. He based this claim on analysis of population growth and the impact of technology, which he thought would lead to massive discrepancies in wealth among whites. After moving to Philadelphia, he freed his own slaves in 1845.[69]

As rector of the University of Virginia, James Madison believed in the intellectual potential of Blacks and favored a gradual plan of emancipation with compensation to the masters.[70] Arguing that the people, not the states, were the parties to the original compact, Madison denied the claims of John C. Calhoun and William Branch Giles that nullification and secession were permissible under the Constitution. During the South Carolina Nullification Crisis (1832–33), Madison wrote three essays in which he not only denied the constitutionality of the actions of South Carolina but refuted any parallel to his and Jefferson's Virginia and Kentucky Resolutions.[71] Often dubbed the father of the Constitution and the author of the Virginia Resolves, Madison's words carried weight against extreme assertions of states' rights and reinforced the arguments of northern unionists, such as Senator Daniel Webster of Massachusetts.

Henry Tutwiler, the former student who described dining at Monticello, called slavery the source of "almost all moral and political evil in the state." While he was teaching ancient languages at the University of Alabama, Tutwiler was recruited by the abolitionist James Birney to help him set up a chapter of the American Colonization Society in Tuscaloosa. In 1830, a group of women connected with the University of Virginia sponsored a fair "for the benefit of the Colonization Society," which was attended by Gessner Harrison, an alumnus of the first-year student intake who replaced George Long as professor of ancient languages.[72] Harrison and Professor John B. Minor conducted Sunday schools for slaves, while some students taught at other such schools and made weekly visits for the same purpose to the enslaved community in the Ragged Mountains.[73] In 1832, when the Jefferson Society chose Merritt Robertson to speak at a public event, he denounced the immorality of slavery and championed the cause of emancipation.[74]

Only in the decade before the Civil War did it become virtually impossible to debate the subject of slavery at the university. Writing from Philadelphia in 1855, George Tucker asked his daughter Elizabeth in Charlottesville about the veracity of an article alleging that the sister of Harriet Beecher Stowe, author of *Uncle Tom's Cabin* (1852), was given a mock serenade while the novelist was burnt in effigy at the university.[75] In 1857, Charles B. Shaw, a former adjunct professor of engineering, challenged his colleague Albert Taylor Bledsoe in a book titled *Is Slavery a Blessing?* Writing from the safe distance of Massachusetts, Shaw lamented the gradual decline of open discussion and dissent on the subject of slavery, with southern abolitionists having to resort to whispering to confidants.[76] Although Bledsoe became a leading intellectual exponent of proslavery ideology, he did not join the faculty until 1853. He had been a friend of Abraham Lincoln. James Philemon Holcombe, another leading faculty exponent of secession, later elected to the Confederate Congress, similarly did not become a professor at the university until 1852. As late as 1858, the Jefferson Society was still debating slavery when the faculty intervened to rescind their invitation, along with two other clubs, to the abolitionist and alumnus Henry Winter Davis to give one of the annual addresses on the Grounds.[77]

SOME HISTORIANS DOUBT the sincerity of Jefferson's antislavery convictions in light of his pseudoscientific race theories. He posited that Black people were mentally inferior to whites and that they constituted a separate nation. His influential racial views rightly elicited sharp criticism by contemporary defenders of racial equality.[78] In *Notes on the State of Virginia*, Jefferson offered his "opinion" and his "suspicion" that Blacks were "inferior" to whites "in the faculties of reason and imagination." While he conceded that their moral sense was equal to whites, he claimed that "in imagination they are dull, tasteless, and anomalous." Jefferson made negative physical comparisons in which he stated that Blacks secreted a "very strong and disagreeable odour." He hypothesized that they were only capable of sexual, not romantic, feelings, while orangutans preferred Black women to their own species, although he twice later revealingly compared himself to an orangutan.[79] He disparaged the talents of those Blacks who had been heralded for their abilities, such as the Massachusetts poet Phillis Wheatley, of whom he wrote, "The compositions published under her name are below the dignity of criticism." While he admitted that such opinions "must be hazarded with great diffidence," Jefferson still asserted that enslavement had not caused what he considered to be their lesser intelligence, which he attributed to nature having "been less bountiful to them in endowments of the head."[80] His original draft of the manuscript, in which he wrote of "permanent inferiority," was even more damning, but he introduced qualifiers like "opinion" and "suspicion" in response to the criticism of his friend Charles Thomson, who encouraged him to remove the section altogether, arguing that it would undermine his case for emancipation.[81] Yet, in all subsequent revisions of the *Notes*, Jefferson never amended his discussion of race.

Jefferson's views on race did not go unchallenged. Even in his own lifetime authors questioned the validity of a comparison between slaves and freemen, recognizing the absurdity of comparisons that ignored the inequality of conditions, the absence of opportunities, and cultural deprivation, as if they inhabited a level playing field with whites. The strongest repost to Jefferson's racial views came from the Reverend Samuel Stanhope Smith, a Presbyterian clergyman and the founding president of Hampden-Sydney College, in an *Essay on the Causes of Variety of Complexion and Figure in the Human Species* (1810). Although expressing concern about slavery corrupting whites, he conceded that Black people were the real victims of the system. Smith argued for the unity of mankind and explained physical differences in terms of climate and adverse conditions. Refuting the claim that Blacks were emotionally inferior, he said that he had personally seen many instances of the highest manifestations of love among them.[82] David Walker's *Appeal* (1829), one of the first antislavery tracts written by an African American, denounced Jefferson's racial views. The son of an enslaved man, Walker found it surprising that "a man of such great learning, combined with such excellent natural parts, should speak so of a set of men in chains." He accused Jefferson of having fueled racism by his "remarks respecting us," which "have sunk deep into the hearts of millions of whites" and "never will be removed this side of eternity."[83]

Jefferson's views on race represent what some writers like Jamelle Bouie call "the dark side of the Enlightenment." The eighteenth-century Prussian philosopher Immanuel Kant, who coined the term "Enlightenment," reminded contemporaries that they lived in an age of enlightenment, not an enlightened age.[84] Even Kant was himself guilty of the same racial disparagement as Jefferson. In his *Observations on Feeling of the Beautiful and the Sublime* (1764), the most popular of his works among contemporaries, Kant repeated the claim of the Scottish philosopher David Hume that there was not a "single example in which a Negro has shown talents." Although modifying his views in the late 1790s, Kant originally concluded that the difference between the two races was fundamental, arguing that "it appears to be as great in regard to mental capacities as in color."[85] David Hume supported abolition, but in his essay "Of National Characters" (1748), in words very similar to those later used by Jefferson, he suspected "negroes to be naturally inferior to the white. There never was a civilized nation of any other complexion than white, nor even any individual eminent either in action or speculation. No ingenious manufactures amongst them, no arts, no sciences." Arguing that even the most barbaric Europeans exhibited some ingenuity, Hume maintained that "such a uniform and constant difference could not happen, in so many countries and ages, if nature had not made an original distinction between these breeds of man."[86] These racial views were shared by other leading intellectuals of the period, including Voltaire and Volney.

Jefferson's writings on race are particularly shocking in their resort to unscientific language. He speaks of his opinion and suspicion while making invalid and incorrect comparisons between classical and southern plantation slavery. He seemed impervious to contrary evidence. In 1809, Abbé Henri Jean-Baptiste Grégoire, a French abolitionist and champion of equality, sent Jefferson a copy of his book *De la littérature des nègres* (1808), with a dedication to him, in which the author meticulously presented evidence of Black accomplishments. Jefferson responded by assuring Grégoire that "no person living wishes more sincerely than I do to see a complete refutation of the doubts I have myself entertained and expressed." He admitted that they resulted from "personal observation on the limited sphere of my own State, where the opportunities for the developement of their genius were not favorable, and those of exercising it still less so. I expressed them therefore with great hesitation."[87] As in the case of the letter from Benjamin Banneker, Jefferson's response was insincere for he wrote to Joel Barlow that *Grégoire*'s book was a collection of fantastic tales and that he had given the author a "very soft answer."[88] Indeed, Jefferson declined the request that he find a translator for the book, which eventually appeared in a corrupted version in English that omitted its dedication to Jefferson. The translation manipulated the evidence in ways that undercut its argument, deleted criticism of American slavery, and omitted the only complete chapter on one individual, Angelo Soliman (1721–96).[89]

Jefferson has justifiably been described as confused in his views on race since he was not consistent and did on occasion write favorably of the physical attributes of people of mixed ancestry.[90] About the time of the publication of the notorious passage on race in his *Notes*, he wrote that "though the black man, in his present state might not be equal in body and mind to the white," this could change if "equally cultivated for a few generations."[91] Furthermore, he insisted that "whatever be the degree of talent, it is no measure of their rights."[92] In the last years of his life, he appointed Patrick Henry, a free Black man, to be caretaker and supervisor of his property at Natural Bridge.[93]

If Jefferson was sometime conflicted, the majority of the white population, in both the North and the South, believed in the racial inferiority of African Americans. Visiting from England between 1824 and 1825, twenty-five-year-old Edward Stanley formed opinions about slavery that would eventually be significant in his own political career and his involvement in abolition of slavery in the British Empire in 1833. Stanley had originally hoped to meet Jefferson and visit him at Monticello, but his trip was cut short before he could do so. His travels outside of Virginia, however, gave him ample opportunity to observe that "free Blacks are held . . . equally low" as slaves, and that "the prejudice respecting them" was "equally strong in the Northern & Eastern States," further noting that such racist feelings were more strongly held in Philadelphia than those opposing slavery.[94] Although generally laudatory of America, his impressions motivated him to go into politics where, in addition to being the longest-serving head of a political party, he became prime minister of Britain three times, as the 14th Earl of Derby. With the perspective of an outsider, he denounced the deep-rooted and universal prejudice that made it dangerous to be seen walking with a Black person and which prompted passengers to avoid sitting in the same carriage. In Pennsylvania, Stanley was refused a discount for his servant at a toll bridge because the man was white, not Black.

Stanley opined that it was "extremely convenient to be able to justify an antipathy, by a sweeping assertion of the natural inferiority of the whole negro race; a position which is accordingly assumed and certainly acted upon throughout the United States." He questioned these assumptions, believing that the character of slaves was "fostered and strengthened by their treatment," and that their moral degradation was "the effect, and not the cause, of their political and social abasement." The heir of one of the oldest noble families in England, which helped put the Tudor dynasty on the throne during the Battle of Bosworth (1485), he believed that everyone in the United States was terrified of becoming a "mongrel" race, "perhaps more than half black," and "even in time perhaps have a black President!!"[95] His observations align with the evidence of the legal and social exclusion of African Americans, who were prohibited from voting in Pennsylvania or Connecticut, limited in their voting by property requirements in New York, or prevented from engaging in interracial marriage in Massachusetts. Frederick Douglass said of the northern states, "If they are not actual slave-holders. . . . they stand around the slavery system and support it."[96]

PARTLY AS A CONSEQUENCE of his view that the races could not inter-mix, Jefferson's preferred method of emancipation was colonization, which aimed to banish Black Americans to Africa. He viewed them as a captive nation that could not coexist with white America. In his *Notes on the State of Virginia*, Jefferson's emancipation scheme involved colonization.[97] He re-stricted his colonization plans to those yet unborn or to infants, with the cruel implication of breaking up families and turning children into orphans. As late as 1824, he put forward yet another plan that envisaged the state purchasing infant slave children, some sixty thousand a year, and shipping them to Haiti. According to Joseph Cabell, Jefferson was unwilling to vio-late private property rights by emancipating slaves already alive, calculating that "at an average of two hundred dollars each, young and old," their total value amounted "to six hundred million dollars, which must be paid or lost by some body."⁹⁸ While his plans respected the property rights of planters, he showed a lack of empathy for the enslaved parents and children, which he defended on the grounds that any father would rather see a child free than "entail his own miserable condition on endless generations proceeding from him."⁹⁹

Although ridiculed for its costs and impracticality, not to mention its unpopularity among its supposed beneficiaries, colonization was the only emancipation scheme that enjoyed national support. Formed as late as December 1816, the members of the American Colonization Society included James Madison, James Monroe, John Marshall, John Hartwell Cocke, James Birney, John Randolph of Roanoke, William Short, and later Edward Coles, but not Jefferson. Other supporters of colonization included Daniel Webster, Andrew Jackson, Stephen A. Douglas, Henry Clay, and Bushrod Washington, a nephew of George Washington. Some were skeptical as to whether a biracial society could succeed while many were simply averse to racial integration in America. The popularity of colonization as a solution to slavery continued almost up until the Civil War. In 1848, the society succeeded in founding Monrovia, named after James Monroe, in imitation of British Sierra Leone. Up until the time of his Emancipation Proclamation (1862), Abraham Lincoln continued to advocate colonization, saying that he had "expressly disclaimed all intention to bring about social and political equality between the white and black races." In his annual message to Congress in 1862, Lincoln said, "I cannot make it better known than it already is, that I strongly favor colonization," and called for a constitutional amendment to fund a colonization scheme.¹⁰⁰

In his *Notes*, Jefferson envisaged the education of Black children in "tillage, arts or sciences, according to their geniuses," as part of his plan of colonization.¹⁰¹ Historian Terry L. Meyers argues that "until 1814, Jefferson was an advocate for more education for the enslaved, and, indeed, for free black children than has generally been recognized."¹⁰² In 1796, in response to a plan for the education of Black children by Robert Pleasants, a Quaker philanthropist in Virginia, Jefferson replied that he considered "the Instruction of black Children to be a duty we owe to that much degraded part of our fellow Creatures, and probably would tend to the spiritual and temporal advantage of that unhappy race, as well as the Community at large." He thought it would prepare them for freedom, "which at this enlightened day is generally acknowledged to be their right," adding that he "much desired to see some su[i]table steps taken to promote such work."¹⁰³ Rather than create separate schools for Black children, he encouraged Pleasants to revive the "Bill for the General Diffusion of Knowledge" and amend it to specifically include the education of free Black children, which "more desireable as they would in the course of it be mixed with those of freed condition." In regard to schooling enslaved children, Jefferson thought it questionable at a practical level, since "ignorance and despotism seem made for each other."[104] When the legislature passed a truncated version of his education bill in 1796, Jefferson regretted that "although those of Colour are not exempted from the benifit of such schools, yet I can't help fearing that the prevailing prejudices against that unfortunate race of people, will be an obstruction to an equal participation in the proposed benifit."[105]

Jefferson thereafter took little interest in the education of African Americans. Israel Gillette Jefferson, an enslaved person, recalled overhearing Jefferson tell the Marquis de Lafayette that slaves should be taught to read but not write, as it would "enable them to forge papers, when they could no longer be kept in subjugation." In contrast to many slaveholders, Jefferson did not prohibit his slaves from learning to read, but he did little to encourage their education at Monticello even among his own children by Sally Hemings. A member of the free Black community in Charlottesville, Robert Scott, a fiddle-player and grandson of Mary Hemings Bell, claimed that Jefferson had encouraged his father to educate his children. Likewise, Peter Fossett recalled that Jefferson "allowed his grandson to teach any of his slaves who desired to learn."[106] Fossett was taught by Meriwether Lewis Randolph. Jefferson's son Madison Hemings, however, described having to induce his white cousins to teach him to read and write.[107] Indeed, in 1819 one of Jefferson's white granddaughters asked to teach a young slave girl who had lost her mother.[108] Still, Jefferson did ensure that his sons were trained as craftsmen to enable them to make a living independently.

Despite Jefferson's seeming lack of interest in teaching his enslaved workers to write, several were fully literate. He corresponded with his enslaved carpenter John Hemmings about construction work at Poplar Forest.[109] Hemmings was able to read the Bible to his wife. His half-brother, James Hemmings, who was Jefferson's cook, wrote an inventory of the kitchen at Monticello.[110] There are surviving blacksmith accounts written by Peter Fosset's father. When Jefferson was too ill to go to Poplar Forest in November 1818, an enslaved woman named Hannah wrote to him to assure him that all was well at his summer home.[111] Archaeological evidence points to lessons held along Mulberry Row, where a triangular fragment of slate was discovered with letters that appear to be part of a verse. Israel Gillette

Jefferson recollected in 1873 that often his "duties as a laborer would not permit me to acquire much of an education," but upon reaching Ohio in the 1840s, he learned to read and write, regarding "what education I have a fruit of freedom."[112]

The literacy rates among the free Black population were higher than those of whites in Albemarle County. In the census of 1840, only 3 of a total of 297 free Black males were illiterate.[113] Despite the requirement that manumitted slaves leave the state, many remained without even obtaining formal papers, and some even fought successful lawsuits.[114] Other than Benjamin Franklin, the Presbyterian David Rice was one of the few members of the founding generation who argued for the education of African Americans.[115] A small number of Black students graduated from northern colleges, usually as part of the colonization movement, such as Andrew Twilight from Middlebury College in 1832, Edward Jones from Amherst College in 1826, John Russwurm from Bowdoin College in 1826, and Edward Mitchell from Dartmouth College in 1828. Similarly, in the 1830s, radical abolitionists attempted to establish three Black colleges in the North, but they were short-lived. By 1860, only twenty-eight African Americans had earned degrees in America.[116]

The University of Virginia was one of the last among its peer institutions to admit Black students, a process it only began in earnest in the 1960s. The "deplorable entanglement" of the university and its founder with slavery should be a subject for humility and reflection about the limitations of higher education, not merely an opportunity for the present to reproach the past. As Andrew Delbanco reminds us in *College: What It Was, Is, and Should Be* (2012), "Colleges are no more independent of the larger culture than any other institution."[117] The truth of this statement was demonstrated by the first generation of faculty, who were mostly young radicals and all of whom had been born outside the United States, with the single exception of the law professor, John Tayloe Lomax. Thomas Cooper, the first professor appointed at the University of Virginia and regarded as one of the most brilliant men in America by Jefferson, had previously participated in the earliest campaign against the slave trade, writing articles in a local newspaper that he eventually published as a pamphlet in England in 1787. After resigning from the faculty, owing to opposition against his unconventional religious views, he became president of the College of South Carolina, where his youthful radicalism dissipated. He began owning enslaved people, "went out of his way to express his conviction of the essential inferiority" of Blacks, championed states' rights, and became known as "the high priest of nullification," saying publicly in 1827 that it was time for the state "to calculate the value of the Union."[118]

George Long, the first professor to arrive on Grounds in early 1825, remained only two years before returning to London to teach at University College. An early proponent of education for women and supporter of public education, he wrote that he would die thinking about the southern states and was so enamored of the Confederacy that he dedicated one of his books to General Robert E. Lee.[119] When John Neale, a free Black man, asked the proctor if he could rent one of the vacant hotels at the university, the faculty ordered his removal and added their general disapproval of "free negroes permitted to reside within the University."[120] Harriet Martineau was especially critical of the views of the faculty wives, who she claimed speak "lightly on the great subject, asking me if I did not think the slaves were happy," while their husbands "use a very different tone, observing with gloom, that it was a dark subject every way."[121] George Tucker, a member of the American Philosophical Society, regretted emancipating his slaves and ceased writing publicly on the subject of slavery after 1824. His biographer maintains that he became an apologist for the system, arguing that enslaved laborers in the South were better off than factory workers in the North. John P. Holcombe had been raised by parents who freed their slaves, and in order to raise their children in a free state, moved from Lynchburg to Indiana, but Holcombe himself became a leading champion of secession at the university.[122]

The various reactions of the faculty members to slavery are a reminder that all too often education can simply help rationalize existing prejudices. The early champions of antislavery were religious evangelicals who also played a pioneering role in expanding educational opportunities to Blacks and women, but whom Richard Hofstadter denounced as the source of anti-intellectualism in nineteenth-century America. Nevertheless, he acknowledged that "the academic culture of the Northern states did not make a striking contribution to a rational discussion and sober exchange of views on the possible solutions of the slavery question."[123] Writing of his student days at Princeton in the antebellum period, Edward W. Smith of Alabama recalled that the politics of the university was "entirely conservative, and friendly to the South."[124] In 1838, Josiah Quincy, Harvard's president, instructed the dean of the divinity school to prevent a planned public debate on slavery. In 1850, Ralph Waldo Emerson was hissed at by students when he spoke against Daniel Webster's defense of the Fugitive Slave Act. As late as the early 1860s, the president of Harvard condemned the tone of articles on antislavery and freedom of religion by Oliver Wendell Holmes Jr., the editor of the *Harvard Magazine*. Harvard faculty member George Ticknor, who offended Ellen Coolidge in London by decrying her grandfather and fashionably associating himself with antislavery advocate Charles Sumner, later condemned abolitionism as "a virus that was a disease fatal to the republic, and must be quarantined." In his article "The Diversity of Origin of the Human Races" (1850), Harvard professor Louis Agassiz promoted pseudoscientific theories of racial differences and the inferiority of Black people.[125]

WHILE JEFFERSON'S OWN VISION of liberty and equality was limited in some ways and pitiful in regard to his attitudes on race, a key part of his achievement was crafting a capacious language that could be broadened to be more inclusive and provide hope for future generations of different races, genders, and nationality. Although regarded as the historian most critical of Jefferson for his views on race and slavery, Paul Finkelman writes that "we honor him for the words of the Declaration of Independence, even as we remember his lifelong failure to implement liberty at the most personal level." Finkelman concedes that it is possible to admire Jefferson for many things, "such as his advocacy of religious freedom, his brilliant articulation of the patriot position during the revolution, and his lifetime support of public education—while at the same time recognizing his failure to come to terms with slavery and race."[126] Annette Gordon-Reed states it succinctly and elegantly: "Jefferson's vision of equality was not all-inclusive but it was transformative."[127]

Respect for Jefferson's transformative legacy is shared by John Charles Thomas, who matriculated at the University of Virginia in 1968 when only a handful of African American students were enrolled. He received his undergraduate degree in 1972 and went on to complete a law degree at the university's law school in 1975. He became the first African American law partner at the formerly all-white southern firm of Hunton & Williams in 1982. When Governor Charles Robb appointed him to the Supreme Court of Virginia at the age of thirty-two in April 1983, Thomas became the first Black and the youngest justice on the court in history. Since 1990, he has read the preamble to the Declaration of Independence each year during the festivities on Independence Day in front of a bunting-covered Monticello. A raconteur and a poet, he is one of the longest serving trustees in the history of the Thomas Jefferson Foundation. In 2007, observing that its founder's name was otherwise absent, he helped persuade the U.S. Military Academy to name its new library after Jefferson. In a speech to a gathering of some of the descendants of the enslaved people at Monticello in 1997, Judge Thomas said that "even the ideas of a flawed man can spark the creation of a more perfect union" by giving expression to the idea that "all men are created equal."[128]

In front of the Lincoln Memorial in 1963, Martin Luther King Jr. called Jefferson's words a promissory note for the future in his "I Have a Dream" speech. The descendants of the enslaved community at Monticello have also appealed to the words of the Declaration. They included Coralie Franklin Cook, a graduate of the University of Wisconsin and a founder of the National Association of Colored Women, who applauded the "uncompromising opposition" of a few members of Congress "who have not forgotten the Declaration of Independence" in their efforts to uphold the Fourteenth and Fifteenth Amendments. A graduate of Harvard, where he was the first African American in its Phi Beta Kappa chapter, William Monroe Trotter was one of the most prominent descendants of the slaves at Monticello. He called on President Calvin Coolidge to end segregation in government on the anniversary of the "Republic's first document which enunciated equality and freedom."[129] Beginning with the African American writer David Walker and continuing through the Declaration of Rights and Sentiments by the women at Seneca Falls in 1848, Jefferson's words, amplified by his evolving university, have been invoked by many different marginalized groups seeking their own freedom and justice in the United States.[130]

9

Idle Ramblers Incapable
of Application

Standing in a packed room in the unfinished Rotunda on October 3, 1825, Thomas Jefferson burst into tears before the entire student body and faculty of the University of Virginia. Aged eighty-two, he had summoned a disciplinary hearing into a student riot two days prior. "Declaring that it was one of the most painful events of his life," while flanked behind a long table by fellow members of the Board of Visitors, Jefferson became speechless and fell back into his chair. Unable to continue, he turned toward James Madison and Chapman Johnson, uttering "that he must commit to young hands the task of saying that which he felt unable to say." Johnson called on the guilty students to identify themselves to spare the innocent, "but as one of the young men told me it was not his words, but Mr. Jefferson's tears that melted their stubborn purpose."[1]

Jefferson's and Madison's call for the culprits to identify themselves "could not be resisted" by the students, who venerated the two former presidents for their age, "their services and their authority." The fourteen responsible stepped forward to admit that on the first night of the month of October, "they had masked & disguised themselves and gone out on the lawn where they had made some noise." They denied, however, that they had insulted the professors. The leading offenders included Jefferson's own grandnephew Wilson Miles Cary, who had resisted the authority of a professor, "used violence against him, and excited others to follow his example." He was expelled "for abusive epithets."[2] Shocked by the discovery that "the last ten years of his life had been foiled by one of his own family," Jefferson ceased to cry and became angry, unable to "forebear using, for the first time, the language of indignation and reproach."[3]

The day preceding the riot, a student had thrown a bottle of urine and a pack of cards through the open window of George Long, the professor of ancient languages, who was sitting with some students and guests inside

Pavilion V. While throwing the bottle, the student cursed "European pro-fessors" and challenged them to come out so "that they might be taken to the pump & & &."[4] The following evening an inebriated party of fourteen students, disguised by masks, "marched about the lawn, as they had often done before." Jefferson later downplayed the incident to friends, saying that the young men acted "with no intention, it is believed, but of childish noise and uproar," but George Tucker, the chairman of the faculty and a former U.S. congressman, thought that the students were deliberately "inviting and defying the notice of the Faculty."[5]

Tucker and John Patten Emmet, the professor of chemistry and *materia medica*, were together in Pavilion IX when they heard the din of raucous students and ran out to restore order, only to be met by insults and ob-jects hurled at them too. Tucker and Emmet each seized a student and de-manded their names. The offenders refused to reveal their identities and responded with verbal abuse. Tucker ripped the collar of his captive as he ran away, but Emmet "got into a boxing match" with the nineteen-year-old Wilson Miles Cary. Other students hurled stones and sticks at the two fac-ulty members. In the course of the scuffle, the students allegedly searched the pockets of Tucker's enslaved man. When Tucker tried to reason with them, he was told "to go to my logic" and threatened with personal violence, as some of them picked up pieces of wood. "Gentlemen," Tucker pleaded, "you seem as if you meant to use violence against me. What can I do against you all?" He then folded his arms and said, "If *you are mean enough* to do so, you are welcome."[6] The students threw down their weapons and fled.

The following day, "in consequence of the serious riot and disturbances," the faculty held a special meeting in which they voted to suspend lectures until the perpetrators were discovered. They requested the assistance of the students in obtaining names. The "brutal design" and "unmanly attack on the dwellings" of the professors was aggravated by the "presence of terrified females," their wives. In a letter addressed to the board, the faculty resolved to resign en masse "unless an efficient Police were immediately established in the University." This attempt to quell the situation failed. The riot leaders won the support of their fellow students, who sent a remonstrance to the faculty with sixty-five signatures giving notice of "their determination not to act the part of Informers and of their indignation at the aspersion thrown upon them by the Faculty in expressing a belief that they were capable of such baseness." They not only denied having assaulted any of the professors but claimed that the two professors "had attacked *one* student and that he was justified in making resistance."[7] With his faculty on the verge of quitting, Jefferson made his emotional appeal to the students.

On October 5, the fourteen instigators of the riot appeared individually before the faculty, led by Wilson Miles Cary who claimed that he had not been intoxicated and that he had not made a noise but that he had been grabbed first by Tucker and then by Emmet. He admitted that he aimed a blow at Emmet, shouting "the damn'd rascal has torn my shirt," and then picked up a brick in self-defense as he retreated, but he denied throwing it. Cary had already been expelled successively from the College of William and Mary and Hampden-Sydney College before matriculating at the University of Virginia.[8] According to his aunt Martha Jefferson Randolph, "it was a place of too great temptation for him ... good tempered, *plausible*, (they say *clever*), vain, self conceited, with ungovernable *appetites*," his "situation was fraught with danger to him self, and mischief to others over whom he had great influence." Nevertheless, in spite of the personal embarrassment, she and her father had "asked him to come over to stay with us till his mother sent for him." She seemed surprised that ten days later, he "has not come yet" to Monticello.[9] The other student revelers acknowledged they had worn masks but denied throwing sticks, bottles, or bricks. They claimed that they had been under the impression that the professors had attacked the students. According to one of them, they did cry "Damn the European Professors," but they "did it 'for fun' without any evil design."[10] Even after the board expelled three of the students, committing another for judgment by the civil courts, and formally admonished the remaining ten, Thomas Hewitt Key, the professor of mathematics, and George Long proffered their resignations, claiming that "it is not consistent with either our feelings of self-respect, or our notions of happiness, to remain any longer in our present situations."[11] They planned to go to Princeton where Long had been offered a job. The pair reconsidered when they were reminded that breaking their contract would incur a $5,000 penalty. While all of the faculty returned to their classes, Jefferson wrote to Madison that Key and Long, "the two Cantabs" (graduates of Cambridge University), were "somewhat in the pouts as yet."[12]

Jefferson fell ill in the immediate aftermath of the crisis, leaving him feverish, weak, and in pain. He had spent the previous five months "confined to the house by a painful complaint, which, permitting me neither to walk nor to sit, obliges me to be constantly reclined, and to write in that posture, when I write at all."[13] His health had been improving sufficiently to enable him to ride two to three miles a day in a carriage, "but going backwards and forwards on the rough roads to the University for five days successively" had caused him "a great degree of sufferance."[14] Martha wrote to her daughter Ellen that "the fatigue of the last week has thrown him back a good deal and obliged me to increase his nightly dose of laudanum to 100 drops."[15] Later the same month, Jefferson nearly died when he sat for a life mask by John Henri Isaac Browere. The artist had sculpted other prominent revolutionaries, including Alexander Hamilton and the Marquis de Lafayette, with a view to creating a gallery of busts and statues in Washington, D.C. Promised that the procedure would take about twenty minutes and be "less unpleasant than Houdon's method," Jefferson recalled that it was a risky experiment for an octogenarian "worn down by sickness as well as age." The artist applied successive coats of "thin grout" plastered over Jefferson's face, head, and throat, which one of the granddaughters likened to being buried alive. Jefferson began to suffocate when the plaster was allowed to dry too long, without sufficient oil to prevent it from sticking to the skin. Browere had to use a mallet and chisel to remove the plaster, which was so slow and painful as he broke off and removed only a small piece at a time that Jefferson was reduced to "groans & even hysteric sobs."[16]

OWING TO A postponement of the intended opening date in early February 1825, due to the late arrival of the professors from Britain, the university began operation without ceremony on March 7. Forty students arrived in dribs and drabs, but the number had reached 116 by the last day in September. Still, disciplinary problems were immediately noticeable. At a meeting in June, the faculty heard that "some cows belonging to persons attached to the University have been shamefully mutilated" and that "Ben, a black man, was in the habit of selling spirituous Liquor in the cellar of one of the Pavilions." Then on September 19, there was the earlier incident with drunken students in which one had insulted and used indecent language to Professor Emmet. As with the later riot in October, a group of sixty-four students signed a petition to the faculty requesting that they revoke the punishment of the revelers because the guilty parties had been of "irreproachable character" heretofore. The faculty began issuing new stipulations to the Enactments (university regulations), including one requiring hotelkeepers to stop serving student breakfasts after 7:30 a.m. They required hotelkeepers to report students who were away for more than three days and to keep regular report cards on student attendance at lectures, to be sent to their parents. They moved to prohibit students who were under the age of nineteen from living in the rooms on the Lawn situated between the faculty pavilions.[17]

The student disturbances threatened to damage the public reputation of the new university and its financial support from the legislature. William Short heard that in Washington, D.C., stories were circulating in October that "the students were in a state of absolute insurrection—that they had pulled down a house or houses in Charlottesville," and "that the whole institution had come to an end, or something like it."[18] Jefferson engaged in damage control, writing letters downplaying the affair and again enlisting the reliable support of Thomas Ritchie's *Richmond Enquirer*, which dismissed the events as "boyish pranks."[19] Jefferson was well aware that student unrest represented one of the greatest threats to the survival of the university, writing before it opened that "the article of discipline is the most difficult in American education." He gloomily foretold student unrest "as a breaker ahead which I am far from being confident we shall be able to weather."[20] In correspondence with George Ticknor at Harvard in 1823, he confided that "the rock which I most dread is the discipline of the inst[itutio]n and it is that on which most of our public schools labor." Jefferson feared that "premature ideas of independance, too little repressed by parents, beget a spirit of insubordination, which is the great obstacle to science with us, and a principal cause of its decay since the revolution."[21]

Other universities had suffered from declining enrollments in the wake of student disturbances. Following a riot at the University of North Carolina in 1799, the state legislature withdrew funding and only desisted after losing a court case brought by the university. Thereafter, the university moved away from the secular republican tradition of its founder, William R. Davie, whose vision paralleled Jefferson's. The decline of the College of William and Mary was accelerated by its student rebellion of 1802, described by St. George Tucker, the most distinguished member of its faculty, as a "blow, from which it will never recover." Following the introduction of draconian regulations, he resigned his professorship, thinking it demeaning to have to supervise the student living quarters and "perform the duties of a beadle [i.e., policeman]."[22] Although the University of Virginia staved off faculty resignations in the aftermath of the riot of 1825, Key resigned the following year to teach at University College in London. With political sentiments that "were decidedly liberal, if not radical," he had earlier declared "he would wish to live and die" in the United States, but within two years, he "emphatically stated, that 'he would rather live in England on six pence a day.'"[23] George Long followed him to University College in 1827.

Jefferson had envisaged students in his own mold, men who would render themselves "valuable members of society, and fit successors of their fathers in the government of their country."[24] He described himself as a "hard student" with a "canine appetite for reading."[25] John Page, his student contemporary and future state governor, later recalled how Jefferson "could tear away from his dearest friends to his studies."[26] Jefferson urged those whom he personally mentored to acquire industrious habits since "every day you lose, will retard a day your entrance on that public stage whereon you may begin to be useful to yourself." In making decisions, "ask yourself how you would act were all the world looking at you, and act accordingly."[27] To a grandson embarking on college life in Philadelphia, he advised, "Be very select in the society you attach yourself to, avoid taverns, drinkers, smokers & idlers & dissipated persons generally; for it is with such that broils & contentions arise, and you will find your path more easy and tranquil."[28] Chapman Johnson, a member of the Board of Visitors, complained that Jefferson's standards were too high, making impossible demands of the students and unrealistically expecting them to be better than their professors.[29]

The disorderly conduct of the students continued to tarnish the image of the university throughout its first two decades of existence. On two nights in November 1836, the student military corps rioted, frequently firing their muskets, attacking the homes of faculty members, lighting a bonfire on the Lawn, going on a destructive rampage through Charlottesville, and occupying the Rotunda. The rebellion was suppressed only by the intervention of the militia. The problem climaxed in 1840 with the murder of the law professor, John A. G. Davis, who was the husband of Jefferson's grandniece and a friend of James Madison. On this occasion, the students helped identify the perpetrator, who still managed to escape and supposedly committed suicide. The incident occurred the same year that a drunken student at Yale stabbed his tutor, who later died from complications.[30]

IN HIS *Notes on the State of Virginia,* Jefferson wrote one of the most penetrating and critical accounts of the sense of entitlement and "unremitting despotism" displayed by the sons of his fellow planters, faults he attributed to their observing the behavior of their fathers toward their enslaved workers. Believing that "man is an imitative animal," he described how "the child looks on, catches the lineaments of wrath, puts on the same airs in the circle of smaller slaves," and encourages by example "his worst passions, and thus nursed, educated, and daily exercised in tyranny, cannot but be stamped by it with odious peculiarities."[31] Even at Princeton, where southerners made up a third of the student population, they seemed to be disproportionately delinquent in their behavior.[32] They were more likely than northern students to engage in dueling, gambling, drinking, smoking, and horse racing. They were distinguishable in the North for their foppish clothing and extravagant tastes. Their more intense sense of honor manifested itself in their refusal to testify against one another, acute sensitivity to slights, concern with the opinion of their peers, and defiance of authority. By wearing masks in some disturbances, the students acknowledged that they were not behaving honorably and therefore needed to disguise their identities. The objective was to be seen to uphold a high standard in which appearances were everything.

In his classic study of southern character, Bertram Wyatt-Brown argued that honor substituted for a moral code in the South: "Honor, not conscience, shame, nor guilt were the psychological and social underpinnings of Southern culture."[33] Associated with their desire to be considered gentlemen, the honor code among students worked against student discipline and the pursuit of the life of the mind. It encouraged conformity and intensified peer-group pressure, which acted as catalysts, allowing for trivial encounters to turn violent. The lack of precise definitions of honor led to random incidents. Its openness to individual perception and interpretation created a herd mentality in dealing with the faculty and sharp divisions among individual students as they defended their honor against each other. In the southern mindset, honor was the badge of liberty in a system in which slaves theoretically could have no honor, even though the enslaved themselves constantly resisted such disparagement.

While the honor system—comparable at the elite level with the aristocracies of Europe—was more culturally pervasive and more broadly disseminated within all ranks of society in the South, it was not exclusive to the region even in United States. The problem of student riots was not limited to the South but was also widespread in both the North and Europe. European students even went so far as to engage in political assassinations and the creation of paramilitary groups aimed at the overthrow of government. In the most famous example, Prussian students followed rigid social codes as members of fraternities collectively known as the *Burchenschaften* participated in the March Revolution of 1848. Although more overtly political, aristocratic students in elite fraternities throughout Germany engaged in dueling and binge drinking much like students in the American South.[34]

Although the presence of slavery and the honor code were contributory factors, they are not a sufficient explanation of the indiscipline of the students in the South when student riots were just as rife in the North. At the University of Virginia in the decade after 1850, there were no riots despite enrollments reaching their highest levels. An authority on college life in New England, David F. Allmendinger Jr. argues that from 1760 to 1860, American colleges generally experienced "a rising curve of collective student disorder."[35] There were student rebellions at Harvard in 1766, 1769, 1805, 1807, 1808, 1817, 1818, 1823, and 1834. The issues sparking the riots were often petty, such as the quality of the food and the behavior of a faculty member.[36] In 1818, Harvard students threw bread through the oriels of the windows of the main hall and smashed nearly all the crockery. That year Harvard expelled all eighty members of the sophomore class. Ralph Waldo Emerson declared the decision tyrannical and resigned from Harvard, whereas John Adams, incensed by the student shenanigans, called for the return to flogging. The "Great Rebellion of 1823" began as a dispute between students, when "the high fellows" sought retribution against a student informant whom they dubbed a "black" player while blaming him for the expulsion of another student. They swore an oath at the Liberty Tree, vowing to leave the college if the informant was not expelled and their hero reinstated. The faculty expelled forty-three students from a class of seventy, including the son of President John Quincy Adams and the future antislavery leader Ellis G. Loring.[37]

The Yard at Harvard excelled the Lawn at the University of Virginia in student excesses. Unlike Princeton, with its large proportion of southerners, Harvard had an overwhelming majority of students from New England, mostly from Boston. The students commemorated the uprising of 1818 with a poem called "The Rebelliad":

> When Nathan threw a piece of bread
> And hit Abijah on the head,
> The wrathful freshman, in a thrice,
> Sent back another bigger slice,
> Which being buttered pretty well,
> Made greasy work wher'er it fell
> And thus arose a fearful battle,
> The coffee-cups and saucers rattle,
> The bread-bowls fly at woeful rate,
> And break full many a learned pate.[38]

While sounding relatively harmless, one of the bread crusts hit the eye of Professor Charles Prescott, a historian of late Renaissance Spain and the Spanish Empire in the Americas. Prescott's sight thereafter began to deteriorate. In 1836, the college erupted into a rebellion that took three months to quell during which students set fire to a recitation room, assaulted two night watchmen, exploded a bomb in the chapel, and hung the president in an effigy filled with gunpowder at the celebrated Rebellion Tree. Harvard expelled the entire sophomore class and brought criminal charges against three students.[39]

Andrew Peabody wrote of his time at Harvard that "crimes that were worthy of the penitentiary were of frequent occurrence."[40] Edward Everett complained that he was little more than the "submaster of an ill-disciplined school," despite being president of Harvard, the "most famous institution of learning in America." After admonishing some students for beckoning a "loose woman," he lamented, "Is this all I am fit for?" Harvard faculty member George Ticknor vented his frustration that "we neither have an University—which we call ourselves—or a respectable high school . . . the morals of great numbers of the young men who come to us are corrupted."[41]

At Yale, Andrew Dickson White recalled the bacchanalian lifestyles, rowdiness, profane language, and defiance of regulations that were characteristic of students. He described "the fatal wounding of Tutor Dwight" and the killing of two town rioters by students at Yale.[42] President Timothy Dwight of Yale thought that America did not have any real universities or colleges but something more akin to British prep schools or what he called "collegiate schools, such as Eton [College]." The English custom of "fagging," in which young students acted as servants to upperclassmen, continued at Harvard until 1798 and Yale until 1804.[43]

In his study of college rebellions between 1798 and 1815, Steven J. Novak makes no distinction between the North and South but rather suggests a common cause of student rebellion: the "decline of the colleges, confusion about their purpose, falling academic standards, and deteriorating student-faculty relations all resulting directly or indirectly from the Revolution."[44] Although they paled in comparison to student violence in France and Germany, Novak argues that student disturbances in America became a tradition, partly because subsequent generations found it difficult to define their roles in relation to the heroes of the revolution. The problem was exacerbated by the youth of the students; many were adolescents who today would be in high school. Furthermore, the students at the major colleges were an elite, representing less than 1 percent of the population. The major universities were therefore aristocratic enclaves where those in attendance looked at faculty as little more than servants. While the term "aristocratic" seems to fit Europeans better than Americans, Edward Stanley, the heir to one of the oldest earldoms in the House of Lords in England, used it to describe Boston in 1824, saying, "established here [is] a complete Aristocracy of Society." Like John Adams, Stanley thought that, regardless of the system of government, wealth and luxury made aristocracy inevitable in any country.[45]

THE STUDENTS AT the University of Virginia were conscious of belonging to a privileged caste, with many of them descended from the first families of Virginia. Related to one another through intermarriage, these families regarded their lineages much as horse breeders thought about pedigrees and thoroughbreds. They aimed to cultivate what Edmund Burke called "an uncontending ease and unbought grace of life" as the true hallmark of a gentleman. They associated their origins with the Cavaliers, the royalist supporters of Charles I during the English Civil War (1642–51).[46] Virginia was the last colony in America to relinquish its allegiance to Charles I and the first to proclaim Charles II in the Restoration of 1660. Personified by the Frans Hals portrait of *The Laughing Cavalier* (1624), they were aristocratic courtiers who wore their hair long; dressed in gaudy, colorful clothes; engaged in decadent behavior; gambled; enjoyed the theater at court; and belonged to the established Church of England.[47]

While much about Virginia's Cavalier connections is mythical, it was certainly true that many Cavaliers had fled republican England during the authoritarian rule of Oliver Cromwell, (1651–58), such as the ancestors of George Washington, who came from Northamptonshire. After Charles II rewarded their loyalty to the royalist cause with a grant of much of the land on the Northern Neck in Virginia, Lord Fairfax and his descendants became the only members of the British House of Lords to live in colonial America.[48] The opponents of the Cavaliers were the Roundheads or Parliamentarians, supported by Congregationalists and Presbyterians who had emigrated in large numbers to New England during "the great migration" of the 1620s. They were known as "Roundheads" for their short hair, while they dressed plainly, shunned the theater, and prided themselves on sobriety, frugality, temperance, and chastity. The term "Cavalier" became a popular self-designation more generally among southerners in the lead up to the

Civil War. Only in 1923, with the composition of "The Cavalier Song," was the term formally adopted at the University of Virginia.

IDENTIFYING WITH the English Parliamentarians rather than the Cavaliers, Jefferson tried to break with the tradition of a hierarchical structure and encourage student self-government consistent with his republican political philosophy. Instead of what he called the "degrading motive of *fear*," he wished to appeal to "pride of character, laudable ambition, & moral dispositions" as "innate correctives of the indiscretions of that lively age." He believed that all humanity, including enslaved people, had an innate moral sense. While the first code of laws governing Harvard College sanctioned corporal punishment, Jefferson believed that "hardening [students] to disgrace, to corporal punishments, and servile humiliations, cannot be the best process for producing erect character." Using the metaphor of family and seeing the college community as an extended patriarchy, he wanted to emulate "the affectionate deportment between father & son" that, he thought, "offers in truth the best example for that of tutor & pupil."[49] In contrast to the raised desks for masters and ushers common in school and college classrooms on both sides of the Atlantic, he envisaged less formal and hierarchical exchanges. The university discouraged the use of titles like "professor" or "doctor," which accorded with both republican ideals and aristocratic traditions, since it was similarly the practice at Oxford University, a bastion of high Tory politics. In the European tradition, Jefferson was particularly keen to give the university autonomy from civil authorities and allow a proctor to exercise all judicial power within the university community. In his words, he aimed "to sheild the young and unguarded student from the disgrace of the common prison, except where the case was an aggravated one," and to allow students "a compleat police of their own, tempered by the paternal attentions of their tutors."[50]

Little was done to implement Jefferson's liberal ideas of student self-government. He had wanted to create a faculty-appointed student court, called "a board of censors," whose six members would hear minor cases among fellow students. However, he did not receive the necessary legal authority for the court. It was unlikely to have succeeded in any event since it required students to report one another to the faculty. Used to more hierarchical and authoritarian societies in Europe, the faculty for its part resisted what it regarded as Jefferson's overindulgent treatment of students. Robley Dunglison described Jefferson as being "under the erroneous impression" that "the 'patriotism and honor' of the students were more effective than 'positive punishment.'" Dunglison dismissed as fanciful the belief that students could participate in their own oversight.[51]

While the students lacked discipline, the professors themselves exacerbated the problem by their inexperience and pettiness. George Long revealingly recalled that the Board of Visitors "thought that we were sometimes too severe." He said he had "not the least reason to regret anything that I did," admitting that he "always had the temper of a soldier, and it was only the accident of my father's loss at sea that caused me to be sent to the University of Cambridge to seek my fortune instead of wearing a red coat."[52] Jefferson described George Blaettermann, the German professor of modern languages and a veteran of Napoleon's army, as unrefined, coarse looking, and speaking rough English, "although having an excellent mind and qualifications." Blaettermann was unpopular with the librarian for keeping books beyond their return date and writing in their margins. At a faculty meeting, he once kicked Professor Key under the table, causing the latter to cry out, "You kick like an ass." He accused George Tucker of giving nonsensical lectures.[53] Blaettermann was the only member of the original faculty to be dismissed after he publicly beat his wife. Although Dunglison thought Thomas Hewitt Key a competent and faithful teacher, he remembered Key, the professor of mathematics, as unfriendly, "fond of controversies," often rude, and getting "in to personal altercations . . . indeed one of the most impracticable men with whom I have ever been thrown in contact."[54] Cornelia J. Randolph, Jefferson's granddaughter, described Key "as one of those Englishmen who have succeeded in making their nation hated in every part of the known world!"[55] George Tucker later acknowledged that only Blaettermann "had ever been a teacher—and our want of skill in the management of young men was manifest."[56]

Indeed, the problem of student discipline only improved when something akin to Jefferson's original scheme was introduced. At the recommendation of Professor Henry St. George Tucker, the spirit of Jefferson's vision was revived with the introduction of the honor system on July 4, 1842. Remaining in force till this day, it was the first student-run honor system in America. Along with the influence of evangelical religion and the temperance movement, it is often credited with the decline in student disturbances and riots that occurred, despite higher enrollments, after 1850.

THE SIZE OF the student body, with little more than a hundred students that first year, was comparable to the College of South Carolina but fell

TABLE I. Age distribution of students (March 1825)

	Numbers	Percent (%)
Aged 21	6	10
Aged 20	9	15
Aged 19	23	38
Aged 18	10	16
Aged 17	10	16
Aged 16	3	5

Source: Philip Alexander Bruce, *History of the University of Virginia, 1819–1919: The Lengthened Shadow of One Man*, 5 vols. (New York: Macmillan, 1920), vol. 2, p. 262.

short of the much higher predictions given by Jefferson, who had planned dormitories for 218 students.[57] He blamed the low attendance partly on the late start to the law school, which immediately attracted thirty students on the appointment of a law professor. Although Jefferson had hoped to attract students from the North and West, two-thirds of the students were Virginians. In another feature that set it apart from many other colleges but which reduced potential enrollments, the university did not admit students under the age of sixteen. Jefferson was pleased that nearly two-thirds of the students were nineteen years of age or older, with only a fifth aged between sixteen and seventeen (table 1). Harvard permitted students as young as twelve, while the median age of students was fifteen and a half and did not surpass seventeen until 1845. At the University of Pennsylvania, the minimum age of admission was meant to be fourteen but a class of thirty-six students included eight freshmen who were even younger.[58]

Despite inauspicious early enrollments, the university became the third largest in the country during the antebellum period and the largest in the South. By 1840, the only other American colleges with more than 150 undergraduates were Yale, Dartmouth, Princeton, Harvard, Union, Brown, Amherst, Bowdoin, and South Carolina.[59] Until the Civil War, except for the competitive rates paid by medical students, tuition fees at Virginia were the highest in the country.[60] Between 1825 and 1860, the students paid $75 for three courses, plus $25 for each additional course, compared to $71 at Harvard (which rose to $75 in 1845 and $106 in 1860), $40 at Princeton, $50 at North Carolina, $50 at South Carolina, $30 at Williams, and $18 at Oberlin. The rates elsewhere varied between $20 and $40.[61] The high cost of a university education partly motivated the founding of less expensive colleges like Bowdoin, Amherst, Middlebury, Colby, and Williams. Until

1850, the students at the University of Virginia paid each professor an additional fee of $50, which along with $100 for board and lodging, the purchase of books, and other expenses, amounted to a minimum of $218, compared to $245 at Harvard ($300 by the 1850s), $245 at Princeton, $195 at Yale, and $110 at Amherst and Williams.[62] Some of the wealthier students were spending over $400 at a time when $100 was a typical annual salary for some plantation managers and overseers. Like plantation overseers, the faculty received free housing and were among the highest paid in America with an annual salary of $1,500. Gessner Harrison, a student in the opening year of the university and later a distinguished faculty member, initially thought that he was not getting value, writing that "if the money had not been paid in advance I should have been home by this time."[63]

Not until 1846 did scholarships become available, finally beginning to realize Jefferson's vision of state scholarships to the very brightest. The scholarships were limited to thirty-two students, one from each senatorial district, and they still required that successful applicants pay part of their lodging costs. The higher cost of attending the university resulted from buildings maintenance, limited occupancy to two students per room, low enrollments in the early years, the absence of economies of scale in providing food through private hotels, and the much longer length of the sessions (semesters) than elsewhere. By 1856, salaries had fallen so far behind that the faculty complained collectively to the Board of Visitors. The annual state $15,000 subsidy did not cover the costs of running the university, which amounted to $28,628 in 1832–33. Before the Civil War, the state never used direct taxes to fund the university, raising the money through fines, escheats, and forfeitures. Furthermore, throughout the antebellum period, it did not increase its annuity to the university.[64] The failure of the state to provide more money undermined Jefferson's meritocratic intentions.

During the antebellum period, enrollment at the University of Virginia peaked at 645 students in 1856–57.[65] Thanks in part to the profitability of cotton, the students coming from outside Virginia were almost exclusively from the South. While only 8 percent of the students of South Carolina College came from outside the state in the antebellum period, 41 percent at the University of Virginia were not from Virginia.[66] During the first fifty years of the university, the highest proportion of students from outside the state were from Alabama (6.2%) followed by South Carolina (5.6%), Maryland and the District of Columbia (4.2%), North Carolina (4%), Mississippi (3.9%), Georgia (3.4%), Louisiana (2.9%), Tennessee (2.5%), Kentucky (2.2%), Texas (1.4%), Missouri (1.2%), Florida (0.7%), Arkansas (0.5%), and outside of the South entirely (1.7%).[67] Although limited in terms of its national appeal, the school still attracted more out-of-state students than Harvard, where early in the century 82 percent of students were from Massachusetts, primarily from Boston, rising to 86 percent in 1830 and then falling slightly to 77 percent in the 1840s.[68] Yale was more successful in attracting students from the Midwest, and Princeton with students from the South. Between 1809 and 1825, 25 percent of Princeton's students were from outside New England and 10 percent from the South.[69]

Jefferson instituted the shortest vacation period of any university in America with one six-week break from December 15 to the end of January, which became a major cause of student unrest. Referring to what he called the "common abuse" of two and three months of time lost "under the name of Vacations," he justified the brevity on the grounds that with too lengthy a break, the "thread of their studies is broken," requiring yet more time to recover, and that this "loss, at their ages from 16 and upwards, is irreparable to them. Time will not suspend its flow during these intermissions of study."[70] There was no remission from lectures even on Saturdays. The shortness of the vacations occasioned a student petition to the faculty in late June 1825. Signed by seventy-eight students, it requested a ten-day or longer vacation over the July 4 commemoration. They argued on the grounds of the "unusual length of the session" and "the immoderate heat" during the summer weather.[71] The dearth of vacations may indeed have been the underlying cause of the first student riot. The short holidays were also an obstacle to recruiting faculty in England, when Oxford and Cambridge universities each scheduled three vacations a year.[72] While Virginia did eventually introduce longer holidays, it still exceeded "the number of working days in any collegiate institution in the world" as late as 1888.[73]

Also engendering student resentment were the Enactments, the strict and sometimes petty rules of the university that governed student life. The students were required to bank their money with the proctor, who gave them a weekly allowance. They were prohibited from smoking, drinking, and gambling. They had to go to bed at 9 p.m. The students were not permitted to carry guns, noteworthy given that the rules were made by a Board of Visitors that included James Madison, the author of the Second Amendment. This restriction on gun ownership is one of a number of early examples of regional gun control both by institutions and local government. After the death of Jefferson, the rules became even more draconian. Between late April and July, students now had to attend their first lecture at 5:30 a.m., as opposed to the original time of 7:30 a.m. Beginning in December 1826, students were required to wear a uniform, which was very unpopular and caused a riot in 1831. The uniform consisted of a black hat, a single-breasted waistcoat, a braided standing collar, flat buttons, and pantaloons. Students were required to put gaiters over their shoes in winter and wear stockings in the summer. Rather than flamboyant silk fabrics preferred by the students, the clothing was to be made from an inexpensive cloth in a dull grayish color. Boots were prohibited because they concealed "the introduction of forbidden liquors."[74] The dress code aimed to improve discipline and prevent the wearing of extravagant clothes. It was not repealed until 1845.

THE ELECTIVE SYSTEM was one of the distinguishing features of the University of Virginia. It had first appeared in Europe. During the Convention of the First French Republic in December 1792, the Marquis de Condorcet, a correspondent of Jefferson, put forward ideas for turning colleges into institutes. This ultimately led to the famous lycées, which gave greater emphasis to mathematics and natural sciences, together with complete freedom for students to select preferred courses.[75] With the conquests of Napoleon, the elective system spread elsewhere in Continental Europe. His subordinates closed some of the oldest universities, such as Louvain and Wittenberg, while reforming others along the principles of metropolitan France.[76] First pioneered at the College of William and Mary in the United States, the elective system became one of the defining characteristics of American higher education. In the belief that students should not "waste" their time on subjects they "think will not be useful," Jefferson told one of his grandsons that it would be "the fundamental law of our University to leave everyone free to attend whatever branches of instruction he wants, and to decline what he does not want."[77] Noah Webster had thought it one of the great errors in higher education that "the students are all restricted to the same course of study and, by being classed, limited to the same progress."[78]

At the University of Virginia, the elective system gave students greater freedom than elsewhere in selecting their courses. They were not required to pass through any specific course or term of study, or to attend specified classes, known as "tickets," but rather selected their own courses of studies. However, there were restrictions. Once chosen, they could withdraw from a department only with the written permission of their parents or guardian and of the faculty. They were required to register for three courses unless they obtained an exemption through their parents and the faculty. Otherwise, they enjoyed more flexibility than modern students in that they could specialize and focus on a few subjects without having any mandatory foun-

TABLE 2. Student choices of subject (March–October 1825)

	Numbers	Percent (%)
Mathematics	68	24
Modern languages	64	23
Ancient languages	55	19
Natural philosophy	33	12
Natural history	30	10
Anatomy and medicine	20	7
Moral philosophy	14	5
Total	284	100

Source: Annual Report of the University of Virginia Board of Visitors to the President and Directors of the Literary Fund, Minutes of the Board of Visitors, 6 Oct. 1825; Philip Alexander Bruce, *History of the University of Virginia, 1819–1919: The Lengthened Shadow of One Man*, 5 vols. (New York: Macmillan, 1920), vol. 2, pp. 81.

dation courses in other areas. Thus, students went through the university not as a class but at their own individual pace. In contrast, Harvard required students to take twelve classes, three per year, and a total of thirty-three subjects in which students were given little choice. This allowed for no concentration in a particular subject area and provided little sequential development in the arrangement of the courses over a period of study. Based on his experience at the University of Göttingen and knowledge of the University of Virginia, George Ticknor tried to persuade Harvard University to adopt an elective system, but he largely failed outside of his own teaching of Spanish.

The elective system had its critics. As early as 1802, the president of Bowdoin derided the idea of an elective curriculum, saying a student would benefit more from intensive study of a subject that might have no professional benefit than devote their time to what he called "light reading which requires no thinking."[79] After reading the Rockfish Gap Commission's report, Edward Everett criticized its failure to allow students sufficient time to learn a language, as if "a few weeks of attention would be sufficient for [studying] Anglo-Saxon."[80] Although the majority of students entered the professions, more of them chose to take liberal arts courses than vocational disciplines like law and medicine. The latter was more popular among older students, who likely already had a background within the liberal arts. Within twelve years of the opening of the university, the number of medical students rose from 25 to 130. Contrary to the caricatures of a dissolute and frivolous student body, the most popular courses were mathematics and languages, which alone required preliminary exams (table 2).

Jefferson also concerned himself with the learning environment and quality of teaching. He wanted professors to be not only scholars but good teachers. Owning books on education by John Locke and the Swiss educator Johann Heinrich Pestalozzi, Jefferson favored a student-centered approach to teaching aimed at developing the innate faculties of the individual. He opposed recitation from memory, one of the most popular teaching methods of the day, which he thought appropriate only for young children. He hoped to reestablish the intimate circles of discourse and intellectual exchange that he had known in Williamsburg with his tutors William Small and George Wythe. This was one reason he wanted the university to be residential for faculty as well as students. Sharing the vision of German philosopher Johann Gottlieb Fichte for the University of Berlin, Jefferson envisioned a community of students and professors who would interact, meet informally, and engage in dialogue.[81]

The faculty were required to set written exercises daily, which, along with the length of time spent on each assignment and the number of lectures delivered, they were required to list in a weekly report for the Board of Visitors.[82] During the first year, some professors even began to publish their syllabi and lecture outlines.[83] George Tucker initially wrote all his lectures but then began to speak extemporaneously, finding this more effective in engaging students. By comparison, Harvard continued to use a teaching system based on recitations and fixed tasks. While it did offer lectures, they were unrelated to the courses.[84] In 1824, the Eton- and Oxford-educated Edward Stanley likened Harvard to the prep schools in his native England and thought it "suited only for boys, and from which a young *man* can derive but little benefit."[85] At the University of Virginia, the lectures were open to the public. According to George Tucker, John Patten Emmet's lectures on chemistry and natural history "were well attended by the public," and that "a large part of the auditory often consisted of ladies."[86]

A rigorous examination system was another distinguishing feature of Jefferson's vision for the university. In 1831, Robley Dunglison claimed that it was the only university in America to have introduced "the English system" of written exams, with a numerical marking scale, dating from the opening of the university.[87] While president of Yale (1778–95), Ezra Stiles had devised the first grading system in the United States, but it was not widely adopted.[88] The use of written, rather than oral, exams was beginning to be introduced in the 1820s, first at Harvard in 1825. They did not become the norm in most colleges until after 1870. At Virginia, George Tucker attributed the introduction of exams to the influence of Key and Long, "according to the model of the Cambridge [University] system."[89]

The baccalaureate degree at most colleges was little more than a certification of attendance. Students at the University of Virginia were initially eligible only for diplomas, which were certificates "attested" by one of the professors and declaring the recipient "eminent."[90] A student was "permitted to become a candidate for graduation" whenever he felt "sufficiently informed on the subject, taught in any one of his schools."[91] The rules originally required a proficiency in Latin in order to graduate with a diploma, but the faculty successfully petitioned for it to be replaced in favor of an "ability to write the *English language* correctly." There were two general examinations every year, written in a lecture room, excepting only the school of languages, whose exams were "partly oral."[92] The university began awarding additional degrees with the Doctor of Medicine in 1828, the Master of Arts in 1831, the Bachelor of Law in 1841, and the Bachelor of Arts in 1848. The university had awarded only ninety-eight masters' degrees by 1856 and forty baccalaureate degrees by 1861.[93] The University of Virginia did not and still does not give honorary degrees, awarding instead Jefferson Medals in law, architecture, global innovation, and citizen leadership, all sponsored by the independent Thomas Jefferson Foundation.

Most students stayed at the university for less than a year. College education was regarded as desirable but not essential to advancing a career. In relation to the population, only 1 percent attended college in the early nineteenth century, while the proportion rose only marginally for the rest of the antebellum period.[94] Formal qualifications were not needed, even for professional vocations like law and medicine, where clerkships and apprenticeships sufficed. As Robley Dunglison observed, degrees were "little esteemed," especially when the standard varied so radically between colleges.[95] It did not help that the benefits of degrees were dismissed by some of their most influential graduates, such as the historian-politician George Bancroft, the poet Ralph Waldo Emerson, and the essayist Henry David Thoreau, all of whom attended Harvard. As New Yorker George Templeton Strong complained in his famous diary in 1858, "We have to create a demand for higher education as well as the supply," and thought the people "not yet ripe for higher education."[96] The gradual increase in demand for credentials to enter the professions would play an important role in the rise of universities. During the first fifty years of the University of Virginia, only 13.7 percent of students took degrees, with 3.5 percent staying for four years,

11 percent staying for three years, and 28.5 percent for two.[97] While possibly lower in proportion to some other colleges, it was typical for students not to take their degrees. At the University of Pennsylvania between 1809 and 1825, fewer than a quarter of students ultimately graduated.[98]

In 1831, a committee consisting of two of the original faculty members created an alumni association, which arranged for an oration at the university every July 4. Over half the students who attended the university became lawyers and doctors with only about 12.5 percent becoming planters and farmers (table 3). During the first half-century, many alumni became political leaders. The university produced 2 presidential cabinet members, sixty-two members and 2 Speakers of the U.S. House of Representatives, 348 representatives in state legislatures, 167 judges, 30 brigadier generals, 8 state attorneys general, and 5 secretaries of state. During the first year of operation, the students included William Preston of Abingdon, who became secretary of the navy during the presidency of Zachary Taylor, and Robert T. Hunter, who later became Speaker of the U.S. House of Representatives. Just as the alumni dominated the legal and medical professions in the South, they also accounted for a significant proportion of the leadership of the Confederacy, with thirty-one congressional representatives and five cabinet members serving under Jefferson Davis.[99]

VALUED FOR DEVELOPING public-speaking skills and originating in the mid-eighteenth century, literary and debating societies proved to be among the most popular student activities in all the major colleges in the United States. During the first few months of the session of 1825, the majority of students joined the Patrick Henry Literary Society. The choice of this particular founder was curious in that Jefferson himself disliked Henry, who had supported an attempt to investigate Jefferson for his behavior as governor during the British invasion of 1781. Indeed, Jefferson did much to besmirch the character of Henry in the information he gave his first biographer, William Wirt. The society was short-lived. On July 4, 1825, a group of sixteen former members met in Dormitory no. 7 on the West Lawn and founded the Jefferson Literary and Debating Society, known more commonly as the Jefferson Society. Their first announcement captured the spirit of the founding vision of the university and drew for inspiration on the Declaration of Independence and the Virginia Statute for Religious Freedom: "Holding it to be true, that opinions, springing out of solitary observation and reflection, are seldom, in the first instance, correct; that the faculties of the mind are excited by collision; that friendships are cemented, errors cor-

TABLE 3. Career choices of students (1825–1875)

Career	Number	Percent (%)
Medicine	1907	26.6
Lawyer	1411	19.7
Farmer/Planter	1139	16
Died in war	441	6.1
Merchant	379	5.3
Government and law	311	4.3
Church	275	3.8
Higher education	272	3.8
Teacher	236	3.3
Government	157	2.2
Engineering	118	1.6
Secondary education	110	1.5
Lawyer and farmer	100	1.4
Military	89	1.2
Journalism	68	0.9
Teacher and farmer	40	0.6
Banker	34	0.5
Hospitality	33	0.5
Insurance agent	31	0.4
Land agent	12	0.2
Law enforcement	6	0.1
Dentist	2	0.0
Total	7,171	100.0

Source: [Maximilian Schele De Vere], Students of the University of Virginia: A Semi-Centennial Catalogue with Brief Biographical Sketches (Baltimore: C. Harvey, 1878); Herbert Baxter Adams, Thomas Jefferson and the University of Virginia: With Authorized Sketches of Hampden-Sidney, Randolph-Macon, Emory-Henry, Roanoke, and Richmond Colleges, Washington and Lee University, and Virginia Military Institute (Washington, D.C.: Government Printing Office, 1888), pp. 167–68.

Notes: (1) Maximilian Schele De Vere, professor of modern languages, compiled this list based on questionnaires sent to former students or their survivors. A student at the university from 1853 to 1855, Captain John Van Holt Nash spent three years completing the list and undertook its publication.

(2) The table does not include 2,001 individuals whose career choices were unknown.

rected and sound principles established by society and intercourse; and, especially in a country where all are free to profess and by argument maintain their opinions that the powers of debate should be sedulously cultivated."[100] As with such societies elsewhere, the Jefferson Society assumed some of the role of the university. It maintained its own library. Its early meetings included the reading and discussing of each other's essays.[101] The society had its own insignia, mottoes, colors, and Greek letters. Indeed, students often regarded such clubs as the best part of their education. Recalling a similar organization during his undergraduate days at Yale, F. A. P. Barnard, the president of Columbia University, thought that no part of his training was more beneficial than that "which I derived from the practice of writing and speaking in the literary society to which I belonged."[102]

In August 1825, the Jefferson Society offered honorary membership to Thomas Jefferson to demonstrate the "sincere respect which we entertain for your character as a man, and the profound gratitude with which we are impressed for your eminent services as a patron of science, a politician and a philanthropist."[103] He declined the offer, on the grounds the he could not show partiality to any group within the university, but added that the highest reward for him and the Board of Visitors was "the anticipated hope and belief that they are rearing up in science and in virtue those on who the hopes of their country rest for its future govmt and prosperity."[104] The society was more successful in extending membership to James Madison and James Monroe. Moving to Hotel C in 1837, the Jefferson Society remains located there in the renamed Jefferson Hall. After 1831, it had a strong contender in the Washington Literary Society and Debating Union. The two societies debated one another, supported literary events, and hosted celebrations. They counted most of the university's students among their membership in the days before fraternities, which did not appear until the 1850s. The Jefferson Society has survived as the oldest continuous student organization at the University of Virginia.

Other opportunities for curricular activities emerged. Like the faculty, the students ran their own magazines and publications, which included the *Jefferson Monument*, the *Collegian*, the *University Literary Magazine*, and the long-running *Virginia University Magazine*. Encouraged by John Hartwell Cocke, a leading figure in the national movement, the students established a Sons of Temperance organization (1849), which was so popular that it was able to build its own hall (1856).[105] It was related to the rise in evangelical fervor, which gripped the university as students engaged in regular worship. While there were no organized sports, Jefferson always stressed the value of

exercise to supplement study and arranged for a gymnasium in the colonnades under the terraces of the Rotunda. The games included running, ice
skating, and pitching quoits. To the disappointment of Madison, Jefferson
required students to participate in military drills.

The most popular celebration for the students was Independence Day.
The highlight of the calendar during the first year of students was the return of the Marquis de Lafayette for a last visit to Jefferson, Madison, and
Monroe. In another publicity coup for the university, he dined again at the
Rotunda. While walking on the Lawn, Lafayette was intercepted by John
Lee, a student, who invited him to become an honorary member of the Jefferson Society. In accepting, Lafayette thanked Lee for the student recognition of the soldiers of independence and freedom and their "attachment
to the republican principles for which we have had the honor to fight and
bleed." Jefferson was too ill to attend the dinner during which Lafayette
toasted "The University of Virginia: May it more and more diffuse through
every part of mankind, the principles, the feelings, and the benefits of true
knowledge, general philanthropy and unalloyed republicanism."[106] Lafayette found Jefferson weaker than during his visit the previous year, describing him as in "enfeebled health and a state of painful inaction."[107] Jefferson
still managed to entertain his fellow patriot and invite at least one student,
Thomas W. Gilmer, to the dinner party at Monticello, sending Gilmer one
of his handwritten invitation cards, in which Jefferson always drew an oval
around the name of the recipient and the date of the dinner, possibly representing the oval tables on which they dined.[108]

Edgar Allan Poe, the most famous alumnus of the first year, enrolled
at the university on February 15, 1826. He lived on the West Range along
what was called Rowdy Row in room number 13, which has been furnished
and maintained by the student Raven Society since 1904. Born in Boston,
the seventeen-year-old Poe "often fascinated" his fellow students in private
reading groups "with his weird creations," which in addition to his writings
included charcoal drawings on the wall of his room. He used to go on long
walks around the hills, which "furnished him with both mood and material."[109] Echoes of his life at the university appeared in short stories like
A Tale of the Ragged Mountains (1844) and possibly his long poem "Tamer-
lane" (1827). Poe was a member and acted as secretary pro-tempore of the
Jefferson Society. His library records indicate eclectic reading interests.

Having a flair for languages and sufficient funds for only two courses,
Poe studied ancient languages with George Long and modern languages
with George Blaettermann. Both of them gave him their highest commen-

dations for his exam performance in French and Latin. He endeared himself to Blaettermann as the only student in his class to complete an optional recitation from the Renaissance Italian poet Torquato Tasso. In a letter to his stepfather on September 21, 1826, in which he mentioned that the Rotunda was almost complete, Poe complained of his impending exams and long hours of study. His fellow students remembered him as "tolerably regular" for classes. Participating in sports on the Lawn, he excelled at the broad jump. Unable to procure adequate financial support from his stepfather, he turned disastrously to drinking and gambling, which left him $2,000 in debt. He was so poor that he broke up the furniture in his room to use as firewood. On his final evening at the university, he expressed his deep regret to the librarian William Wertenbaker, who later described Poe as "a sober, quiet, and orderly young man" who may have occasionally "entered into a frolic" but who was never seen "in the slightest degree under the influence of intoxicating liquors."[110]

BASED ON THE VIEWS of the faculty, Jefferson classified one-third of students as working "very hard," "another third reasonably diligent and employing themselves to good account," and "the remaining third idle ramblers incapable of application." He thought these proportions were "as satisfactory as one could expect."[111] In a letter to the university bookseller, he claimed that "we have a very fine collection of youths, much disposed to order & study, but much obstructed by about a dozen of vicious & worthless scapegraces [i.e., mischievous or wayward young people]".[112] As with any university at any time, the students ranged across a spectrum of abilities. An exceptionally gifted one was Henry Tutwiler, who gave the address to fellow alumni in Charlottesville in 1882 in which he described dining with Jefferson at Monticello. Tutwiler was the favorite student of George Long with whom he corresponded until his former professor wrote from Brighton in 1879, "I am dying slowly and painfully. My last letter is this in which I assure you of my remembrance, as long as the poor body shall endure."[113] A self-effacing and modest man from Harrisonburg, no student of his generation graduated in so many different subject areas, including ancient languages, mathematics, moral philosophy, political economy, and law.

When Tutwiler applied for a faculty position at the newly opened University of Alabama, he received glowing references from many of his former professors, not only George Long but also Robley Dunglison, John P. Emmet, Gessner Harrison, and George Tucker. Emmet wrote that "his [Tutwiler's] general acquirements are more profound, his judgement riper, and his mind altogether freer from conceit and prejudice than is the case with any other young man of my acquaintance." Tutwiler became the acting president of the University of Alabama in his first year there and twice later rejected formal offers of the presidency. His students included the novelist and U.S. senator Jeremiah Clemen, the poet and historian Alexander Meek, the governor of Texas Oran M. Roberts; the author and U.S. congressman William Russell Smith; the U.S. senator Clement Claiborne Clay, and "scores of others who were foremost among the torch-bearers of literature and learning in the first half century of Alabama's statehood."[114] In 1853, President Franklin Pierce appointed Tutwiler to the Board of Visitors of the U.S. Military Academy at West Point, an institution founded by Jefferson during his presidency in 1802.

Tutwiler's career reflected the influence of the University of Virginia. In teaching ancient languages, he applied lessons from George Long on the necessity of understanding literature in the context of history and geography. According to his former student William Russell Smith, who established the state of Alabama's first literary magazine and served as a U.S. congressman, "he was a whole faculty within himself" and "as much at home in the chemical laboratory as he was in his own room with the classics. He was as familiar with all the sciences, and always at work."[115] Tutwiler's hobby was astronomy, and every night he looked at the skies through his telescope, discovering a previously unknown star in 1866, *T Coronae Borealis*. In 1847, he founded the Greene Springs School, known as the "Rugby of Alabama."

Tutwiler devoted thirty-seven years to running the school he founded, with great financial success. Like Jefferson, he chose to locate the school in the countryside near Havana, Alabama, at an isolated and healthy site, renowned for its spa waters. Like Jefferson, he emphasized science, especially those "sciences which have revolutionized the whole domain of industry, and diffused the comforts and luxuries of life among the great mass of mankind." He therefore equipped the school with the necessary apparatus. He emphasized utility and practical benefits, not just teaching mathematical theory but also "the practical applications of trigonometry to heights and distances, filed surveys, levelling, navigation, etc."[116] As with Jefferson, he emphasized modern languages. A committed Methodist, he broke from Jefferson's model by teaching religion, but he allowed his students to recite poems with moral messages rather than limiting themselves to the Bible. In his speech to his fellow alumni in 1882, he remembered how Jefferson's treatment of religion nearly prevented the university from ever being realized.

To write a history of the university that exclusively focuses on the "idle ramblers" is unjust to the institution, the equivalent of writing the history of Yale University through the lens of the Skull and Bones Society. After having taught at University College, George Long wrote of his time at the University of Virginia "that I never had more youths of good abilities under me, nor youths more capable of being made good and useful men."[117] Robley Dunglison had worried that the large proportion of foreign professors "would be unfavorable to discipline; and might lead the disorderly to rebel against the authority of the University." Nine years later, he recalled that he had been wrong and that "no single act came to my knowledge of insubordination from that cause; whilst ample evidence afforded of their respect of those who had left their homes, and were zealously engaged in instructing them."[118] His recollection was inaccurate but suggests that initial student hostility to foreign professors did not leave a strong impression. A member of the first session of the university in 1825, Burwell Stark recalled that his "time at the school was very profitably and pleasantly spent." He remembered the faculty as "competent and gentlemanly, while the students were clever and sociable." He conceded that many of his peers "indulged in prank and mischief, but not to very serious excess."[119] According to the record of library loans during the first session of the university, all but 10 of the 123 students borrowed books, despite the limited hours and the need to ask the written permission of a professor for each loan.[120]

Jefferson was enough of an elitist to believe that a few individuals could make a significant difference in society. Henry Tutwiler represented such a former student, greatly influencing a generation of future writers and leaders in Alabama and throughout the Southwest. His school was unusual in that he early on began to admit women. One of his daughters, Julia Strudwick Tutwiler, became a writer and advocate of education and prison reform. She served as co-principal of the Livingston Female Academy and was the first female president of Livingston Normal College. Tutwiler himself never forgot dining at Monticello and hearing Jefferson describe slavery as a moral and political evil in Virginia. Speaking of slavery as the source of "almost all the moral and political evil" in Virginia, Tutwiler was admirable for his moral courage in the Deep South in holding to his antislavery views and for his work with James Birney in setting up a branch of the American Colonization Society in Tuscaloosa.[121] He represented the founding ideal of the university that the students would use reason as their oracle and follow truth wherever it might lead.

Jefferson never intended his own views to be prescriptions for the future, quite the opposite. He did not want the living generation to be held back by tradition and the dead hand of the past but to chart a new path and improve upon his example, bringing about progress for the general happiness and prosperity of the people. He hoped also that even students who were not diamonds, but were reasonably committed, might become useful members of society. Possibly even those "incapable of application" might benefit from their time at the university. Despite being one of the worst of the "idle ramblers" who caused his great uncle's tears to turn into anger by leading the first major outbreak of student rebellion at the university, even Wilson Miles Cary overcame a long struggle with alcoholism to become a productive member of the community as a newspaper editor and lawyer in Charlottesville.[122]

10

This Athenaeum

"THOMAS JEFFERSON" were likely the last full words uttered by John Adams before he died on July 4, 1826, on the same day as the fiftieth anniversary of the Declaration of Independence.[1] Bostonian Edward Everett, who was once likened to the "Pericles of Athens," embellished his final indistinct muttering in a eulogy, claiming that Adams's last words were "Thomas Jefferson survives."[2] Spoken in the late afternoon, Adams would in any case have been wrong. Jefferson had died a few hours earlier and been delirious for a couple of days during which family members said that he had a tendency to revert to the scene of the Revolution. He had previously spoken freely of approaching death, updating his will and discussing arrangements with his grandson Thomas Jefferson Randolph. Before falling into unconsciousness, he "expressed anxiety for the future of the University" but confidence in the "exertions in its behalf of Mr. Madison and the other visitors."[3] Jefferson was treated during the final week of his life by Dr. Robley Dunglison, the professor of medicine, who stayed at Monticello for the duration of Jefferson's illness, which saw him eating less and suffering from dysentery.

On July 2, Jefferson had begun to drift in and out of consciousness, a state that became "almost permanent" until the next day when he suddenly awoke at about 7 p.m. Seeing Dunglison by his bedside, he exclaimed in a husky and indistinct voice, "Ah! Doctor are you still here?" and then asked, "Is it the 4th?" to which Dunglison replied, "It soon will be." Two hours later, Dunglison woke him to relieve him with a dose of laudanum (a tincture of opium with associated alkaloids, including morphine and codeine), which his patient refused by saying, "No, doctor, nothing more." According to Dunglison, Jefferson then fell back into a comatose state, "wholly unconscious of all that was passing around him." His circulation was gradually "becoming more languid; and for some hours prior to dissolution, the pulse

238

at the wrist was imperceptible." Attended by his daughter and his grandson, along with enslaved domestics, he spoke his last words during the night, calling to one of his enslaved servants with a strong, clear voice.[4] Just as Jefferson's first memory was of an enslaved woman adjusting his pillow as a baby, Burwell Colbert, his enslaved butler and valet, fluffed his pillow for the last time. Jefferson died at about 1 p.m. on July 4, 1826. An hour later, while canons were still booming in celebration of Independence Day, the sudden slow toll of the courthouse bell alerted the population of Charlottesville to the death of the author of the Declaration of Independence.

Jefferson's greatest concern at the time of his death was the way history would treat his term as governor of Virginia during the American Revolution. He had been accused of failing to prepare the defenses of Virginia against Lord Cornwallis and was later subjected to an inquiry by the legislature. He was not mollified by the unanimous vote of approval for his conduct that followed, calling the investigation a wound that would only be "cured by the all-healing grave." The criticism resurfaced in the popular published memoirs of Major General Henry ("Light-Horse Harry") Lee, the father of Robert E. Lee. After hearing that a son of the elder Lee was intending to republish the memoir, Jefferson invited him to Monticello in the hope of persuading the son to remove the offending passages about his governorship of Virginia. On July 1, 1826, Henry Lee Jr., a controversial figure sometimes referred to as "Black Horse Harry," arrived at Monticello. Lee later described how Jefferson treated his impending death "as an event rather unpleasant than terrible—like a traveler expressing apprehension of being caught in the rain." Lee observed Jefferson's daughter Martha beside his bed "with grief at her heart."[5]

Americans regarded as providential the deaths of the two self-styled Argonauts of the revolutionary age on the same day as the much-celebrated jubilee of the Declaration of Independence. Horace Greeley, the founder and editor of the *New-York Tribune*, recounted how the public first learned the news when the messengers bearing the sad tidings, on their respective rides from Charlottesville, Virginia, and Quincy, Massachusetts, coincidentally met one another under the shadow of Independence Hall in Philadelphia. To Greeley, "it seemed that a Divine attestation had solemnly hallowed and sanctified the great anniversary by the impressive ministration of Death."[6] Speaking at Faneuil Hall in Boston on August 2, 1826, the Massachusetts statesman and orator Daniel Webster gave a rousing eulogy: "No two men now live, fellow citizens, perhaps it may be doubted whether any two men have ever lived, in one age, who, more than those we now commemorate, have impressed their sentiments in regard to politics and government, on mankind, infused their own opinions more deeply into the opinions of others, or given a more lasting direction to the current of thought. Their work doth not perish with them."[7] Jefferson and Adams had continued their correspondence until the very end. In their final years, they increasingly reflected on their lives, commiserated with each other about their respective health problems, reflected on their experiences of grief, and discussed their thoughts on death and the question of an afterlife. In these playful and sometimes humorous exchanges, they asked one another whether they would like to live their lives over again, to which Jefferson replied, "Yea. I think with you that it is a good world on the whole," with "more pleasure than pain dealt out to us."[8]

Adams acknowledged that he too had known greater pleasure than pain in life, but he gave a conditional response as to whether he would relive it. He replied in the affirmative but admitted that he would also shrink at the prospect. To his own question "what is human Life," Adams reflected that it is "a Vapour, a Fog, A Dew, a Cloud, A Blossom a flower, A Rose a blade of Grass, a glass Bubble, a Tale told by an Idiot, a Boule de Savon, Vanity of Vanities, an eternal succession of which would terrify me, almost as much as Annihilation."[9] Jefferson then refined his own answer to say that he would not want to return any younger than twenty-five, nor any older than sixty, "for, at the latter period, with most of us, the powers of life are sensibly on the wane, sight becomes dim, hearing dull, memory constantly enlarging its frightful blank and parting with all we have ever seen or known, spirits evaporate, bodily debility creeps on palsying every limb, and so faculty after faculty quits us, and where then is life?" While he found the prospect of bodily decay gloomy, Jefferson thought that "of all human contemplations the most abhorrent is body without mind."[10] He reflected that "when all our faculties have left, or are leaving us, one by one, sight, hearing, memory, every avenue of pleasing sensation is closed," leaving only debility and malaise "when the friends of our youth are all gone, and a generation is risen around us whom we know not, is death an evil?" He admitted that he "dreaded a doting old age" when his health had "been generally so good."[11]

Both having lost their wives and some children, they reflected on their feelings of grief and loss. As to bereavements, Jefferson wrote to Adams that "these afflictions cloud too great a portion of life" and that even setting aside the time of mourning, "all the latter years of aged men are overshadowed with its gloom."[12] Following the death of Abigail Adams in 1818, Jefferson wrote to John Adams that "the same trials have taught me that, for ills so immeasurable, time and silence are the only medecines."[13] In the last six months of his life, Adams reconsidered his wish to live his life over again and said that he would "rather go forward and meet my destiny," lamenting the loss of his parents, his wife, some of his children, and some of his friends.[14] Jefferson did not reconsider, having "enjoyed a greater share of health than falls to the lot of most men; my spirits have never failed me except under those paroxysms of grief which you, as well as myself, have experienced in every form: and with good health and good spirits the pleasures surely outweigh the pains of life." However, he admitted that he would have preferred "to cut off from the train" before his health was "destroyed" by his 1819 visit to Warm Springs. With a humorous flourish, Adams wrote to Jefferson, "We shall meet again, so wishes and so believes your friend, but if we are disappointed we shall never know it."[15]

IF JEFFERSON WAS SERIOUS in wishing to have died in 1819, it was hardly due to his health, which remained relatively robust until almost the end. Furthermore, it would surely have derailed his plans for the university. The claim is more explicable in the context of his deteriorating financial situation and imminent bankruptcy. His fortunes plunged with the great financial crisis of 1819. Jefferson died with debts amounting to over $107,000, the equivalent of $2.5 million today. What he termed the final *coup de grâce* was his becoming liable for $20,000, part of the debt of his friend and political ally the former state governor Wilson Cary Nicholas. Having agreed to guarantee some of his friend's obligations, he thereafter found himself paying $1,200 per annum just on the interest.[16] This liability coincided with a drop in crop sales and a steep decline in the value of land by as much as a quarter. Defending him from the charge of extravagance, his family later blamed his period in government service, which prevented him from managing his plantations during an absence of seventeen years and increased his expenses beyond his salary.[17] Furthermore, he did not receive either a federal or a state pension during a retirement in which strangers seeking hospitality inundated him. While agricultural yields improved under his grandson Thomas Jefferson Randolph, from 1816 on his estates were never particularly profitable. By the time he died, he owed Randolph $60,000.[18]

Because of his mounting debts, in January 1826 Jefferson was reduced to asking the state legislature for permission to hold a lottery on his behalf, which would otherwise have been illegal. Explaining to Joseph Cabell, his old ally in the cause of the university and now his intermediary in the cause of the lottery, he wanted to "pay my debts and leave a living for myself in my old age, and leave something for my family."[19] Randolph also tried to raise support among the legislators in Richmond. He found initial enthusiasm, but the timing was unfortunate because of public resentment at a letter published in the newspaper claiming that Jefferson had boasted and chuckled about deceiving the state as to the real cost of the university. In the ensuing backlash, the legislature refused a new request to fund the university and postponed a decision on the lottery. His friends initially lost a vote on the lottery in the House of Delegates, with opposition voiced even among his neighbors in Albemarle. During this tense time, he told his mother, Martha, "for godsake keep up your spirits . . . without you all events will be like a blank to me."[20] The measure authorizing a lottery to raise up to $60,000 eventually passed on February 20 by margins of 125 to 62 in the House and 13 to 4 in the Senate. The final bill limited the proceeds of the lottery to the fair market value of the property. The family had hoped just to offer the mill and some land to make the total. When Randolph advised his grandfather that Monticello must be included, he turned white but capitulated, realizing there was no other option.[21]

In the meantime, subscriptions on behalf of Jefferson were begun in New York, where the mayor raised $8,500; in Philadelphia, which raised $5,000; Baltimore with $3,000; and smaller sums elsewhere for a total of $17,000–18,000. Still, after his death, people were less willing to help his family than they might have been to help him. The prizes in overvalued land made the tickets for the lottery unappealing. After his death, the legislatures of South Carolina and Louisiana, concerned that his daughter would be left indigent, each contributed $10,000. They paid in stock worth $24,000 when redeemed.[22] Thomas Jefferson Randolph managed Jefferson's remaining affairs with his creditors, paying interest up until the time of his own death in 1875. The family never received any aid from the state of Virginia, which did nothing to commemorate Jefferson.

JEFFERSON HAD REQUESTED that only family members attend his funeral, which he wanted to occur soon after his death. Held at 5 p.m. the next day, the burial was marred by a public quarrel between Thomas Mann Randolph and his eldest son, Thomas Jefferson Randolph. The former had stayed away the last few days during the period of Jefferson's decline, but he appeared at the funeral, where his son accused him of being "more ferocious than the wolf & more fell than the hyena, hating [Jefferson] in life, neglecting him in death, and insulting his remains when dead."[23] Bad blood already existed between the two. Jefferson had put his grandson, rather than his son-in-law, in charge of his affairs. Thomas Jefferson Randolph bought his father's heavily mortgaged property at auction, including the family plantation at Edgehill, leaving Thomas Mann Randolph landless. They quarreled publicly at the funeral about who should instruct the Reverend Frederick Hatch to commence the funeral and disagreed about whether to await the arrival of a procession of the townspeople and members of the university who had gathered in expectation at the courthouse in Charlottesville. In the meantime, the grave was dug by one of Jefferson's most trusted enslaved workers, Wormley Hughes, who was the head gardener at Monticello.

While a bell pealed and the militia fired a gun salute, the townspeople, wearing black crepe on their arms, assembled at the courthouse, ready to process to Monticello. There followed a town-gown dispute as to whether the students and faculty of the university should precede or follow the local citizens. In the pouring rain, some students were so anxious not to miss the event that they mounted their horses and galloped ahead. Because of the short notice and the family squabble, only some thirty to forty people witnessed Jefferson's interment. The small group of students who arrived in time for the burial included Edgar Allan Poe. After the grave was covered up, the mourners began their descent down the mountainside, where they met the procession of 1,500 people arriving from Charlottesville, who were "sorely disappointed, and in some cases, angered" when they discovered that they would not be able to pay their respects and attend the funeral service.[24]

Two days before his death, Jefferson had told his daughter that "she would find something intended for her" in a drawer with an old pocketbook. There, she later found a poem that he had composed:

> *A death-bed Adieu. Th:J to MR.*
> Life's visions are vanished, its dreams are no more.
> Dear friends of my bosom, why bathed in tears?
> I go to my fathers; I welcome the shore,
> which crowns all my hopes, or which buries my cares.
> Then farewell my dear, my lov'd daughter, Adieu!
> The last pang of life is in parting from you!
> Two Seraphs await me, long shrouded in death:
> I will bear them your love on my last parting breath.

Among his belongings, she found some little packages containing locks of the hair of his deceased wife, his daughter Maria, "and even the infant children that he had lost." He had labeled one of them, in which there were a few strands of soft, silky hair evidently taken from the head of an infant, "A lock of our first Lucy's hair, with some of my dear, dear wife's writing." Another package, marked simply "Lucy," contained "a beautiful golden curl."[25]

The family also found a note written on the torn back of a letter with directions for his monument with some verse in Greek (here translated):

Could the dead feel any interest in Monuments or other remembrances of them, when, as Anacreon says:

> My soul to festive feelings true;
> One pang of envy never knew;
> And little has it learn'd to dread
> The gall that Envy's tongue can shed.
> the following would be to my Manes the most gratifying.

Regarding the grave, he wrote,

a plain die or cube of 3.f without any mouldings, surmounted by an Obelisk of 6.f height, each of a single stone: on the faces of the Obelisk the following inscription, & not a word more

> "Here was buried
> Thomas Jefferson
> Author of the Declaration of American Independance
> of the Statute of Virginia for religious freedom
> & Father of the University of Virginia."

because by these, as testimonials that I have lived, I wish most to be remembered. to be of the coarse stone of which my columns are made, that no one might be tempted hereafter to destroy it for the value of the materials. my bust by Ceracchi, with the pedestal and truncated column on which it stands, might be given to the University if they would place it in the dome room of the Rotunda.

on the Die of the Obelisk might be engraved

> "Born Apr. 2. 1743. O.S.
> Died _____ "[26]

As early as 1771, Jefferson had written a note to himself about his "burying place," which he wanted to be on his mountaintop on a site that was devoid of sound and lacked any evidence of human habitation. He designed an obelisk for his tomb, which reached toward the sky from the mountaintop. In the words of historian Andrew Burstein, it has "an upward movement, future-directed, and decidedly hopeful." He was buried in a family circle, between his wife and his daughter Maria "Polly" Eppes (d. 1804), near his sister Martha Carr (d. 1811) and her husband, and his childhood friend Dabney Carr (d. 1773).

Ellen Coolidge was on her way to visit her grandfather when she learned of his death. She continued on to the place that she had called home for most of her first thirty years and where she had experienced the dinner parties that she dubbed "feasts of reason." She later recalled that upon arrival, she found "he was gone. His place was empty. I visited his grave, but the whole house at Monticello, with its large apartments and lofty ceilings, appeared to me one vast monument. yet I could not always feel that I should see him no more. I wandered about the vacant rooms as if I were looking for him. Had I not seen him there all the best years of my life?" She was now a mother but felt saddened that she could never show her child to her grandfather and never see him smile in response. She spent many hours in his bedchamber, which was just as he had left it, with the chair where she always found him sitting and even his clothes still in their place: "In the cabinet adjoining were his books, the beloved companions of his leisure — his writing table from which I gathered some small relics, memoranda and scraps of written paper which I still preserve. All seemed as if he had just quitted the rooms and there were moments when I felt as if I expected his return." For days she thought she might hear "the sound of his step or his voice, and caught myself listening for both." The dining room still had the low armchair by the fireside where he would sit. The sofa where she sat by his side remained in the tearoom. In the parlor, with its parquet floor, she saw the Campeachy chair "where, in the shady Twilight, I was used to see him resting." In the Entrance Hall, she was reminded of him by the large glass doors "where, in bad weather, he liked to walk." She remembered "how much I liked to walk with him! — Every thing told of him. An invisible presence seemed every where to preside!" Such was the void left by his death that she departed, never to return to a place to which she could no longer feel attached.[27]

Apart from leaving some minor bequests to the university and his estate at Poplar Forest to his grandson Francis Eppes, Jefferson directed in his will that all his property be first subject to the payment of his debts, with the residue to be held in trust for his daughter Martha Randolph. He appointed as executors his grandson Thomas Jefferson Randolph; Nicholas P. Trist, who was the husband of granddaughter Virginia Jefferson Randolph; and Alexander Garrett, the treasurer of the university. The will specifically excluded as an executor, in consideration of "the insolvent state" of his affairs, "my friend & son in law Thomas Mann Randolph." Jefferson explained in a codicil that this provision was intended to protect the estate from the creditors of his son-in-law. Also, he asked that his "gold-mounted walking staff of animal horn" be given to James Madison, "as a token of the cordial and affectionate friendship which for nearly now an half century, has united us in the same principles and pursuit of what we have deemed for the greatest good of our country." He left a gold watch to each white grandchild to be given to the boys when they turned twenty-one and the girls at sixteen, with the exception of the adult grandchildren who had already received their watches. To his grandson Thomas Jefferson Randolph, he left all his papers and a silver rather than a gold watch, "because of its superior excellence." Excepting books they already owned, he bequeathed his library to the University of Virginia.[28]

MADE LESS THAN four months before his death, the codicil of Jefferson's will was notable for promising freedom to his remaining children by Sally Hemings. Beverly and Harriet had already left Monticello by the 1820s. After they served as apprentices until the age of twenty-one, Madison and Eston Hemings were to be freed. They both later acknowledged that they were sons of Thomas Jefferson. In order that they might remain "where their families and connections are," Jefferson further requested that the state legislature waive the law which required emancipated slaves to leave Virginia, "as an additional instance of the favor, of which I have received so many other manifestations, in the course of my life, and for which I now give them my last, solemn, and dutiful thanks." He also freed three other relatives of Sally Hemings, including Burwell Colbert, whom Jefferson called his "good, affectionate, and faithful servant," with a gift of three hundred dollars "to buy necessaries to commence his trade of painter and glazier, or to use otherwise as he pleases."[29]

John Hemmings, Sally's brother and an extraordinarily able carpenter, and Joe Fossett, Sally's nephew, were granted their freedom a year after Jefferson's death. Jefferson bequeathed them "all the tools of their respective shops or callings." For Burwell Colbert, John Hemmings, and Joe Fossett, he insisted that "a comfortable log-house be built for each," for use during their lifetimes, with a life-interest in an acre of land in the environs of Charlottesville and the university, "where they will be mostly employed." Jefferson did not officially grant freedom to Sally Hemings, but she was listed as a free white woman in a Charlottesville census of 1830. In the wake of the Nat Turner Rebellion (1830), a special census in 1833 was taken in which Hemings described herself as a free mulatto woman who had lived in Charlottesville since the year of Jefferson's death in 1826. Until Heming's death in 1835, Martha Jefferson gave her "her time," which meant her freedom in all practical respects, while still technically leaving her a slave. As argued by Annette Gordon-Reed and Peter S. Onuf, Jefferson would never have freed her in a public document, which might either have risked his legacy or "would publicly hurt and humiliate the most important person in his life, Martha Randolph."[30]

Owing to the failure of the lottery to raise funds, Jefferson's family was forced to sell almost everything in his estate, including Monticello, to pay off his debt. The local community was shocked by the size of it. On November 3, 1826, an advertisement in the Charlottesville *Central Gazette* announced the auction of "the whole of the residue of the personal property of Thomas Jefferson." The resulting public sale in January 1827 included Jefferson's furnishings from the public rooms, clocks, and some of his paintings. It most tragically also included "130 valuable negroes," which an advertisement claimed were the most valuable for their number ever offered at one time in Virginia. During a harsh winter, the sale was conducted over five days and attracted a large number of bidders, with prices for the enslaved servants greatly exceeding their appraised value. At a subsequent auction in 1829, thirty people formerly enslaved by Jefferson were sold.[31]

The slave auctions represented the heart-breaking rupture of a long-established community, dispersing husbands, wives, children, and friends. People of all ages and both sexes stood on the block as local citizens made their bids at Monticello. Many of the families had served Jefferson and his kin for generations. After the first auction in 1827, Martha wrote to Ellen Coolidge that her daughter was fortunate to have moved to Boston to be spared the trouble and distress of the auctions, "for nothing can prosper under such a system of injustice." Reacting to the sale of a favorite maid of her daughter Virginia Randolph Trist, Martha admitted that "the discomfort of slavery I have borne all my life, but its sorrows in all their bitterness I had never before conceived."[32] Before the first auction, she personally intervened to prevent the sale of three domestics and eight young girls.

Although Thomas Jefferson Randolph tried to ensure that families remained together and prevent their removal to cotton plantations, the auctions separated families and children as young as eight or nine, who were still sold in individual lots. The stories of the families' persistent and determined struggles to reunite are heartrending. Put on the auction block and sold to strangers at the age of eleven, Peter Fossett recalled that "then began our troubles. We were scattered all over the country, never to meet each other again until we meet in another world." He later described how Jefferson's death left the entire Black community of Monticello in anguish at the implications for its future. He recollected that he had thought of himself as a free person until the auction, telling one newspaper that he "knew nothing of the horrors of slavery till our good master died." While his father, Joseph Fossett, was freed in Jefferson's will, his mother and three siblings were sold to different bidders for a total of $1,350. Peter remained in slavery for almost three more decades and twice tried to run away. He secretly taught himself to write and successfully forged manumission papers for his sister Isabella, who used them to go to freedom in Boston.[33]

Remarkably, by 1837, Peter Fossett's father had succeeded in purchasing freedom for his wife, five children (two born after the auction), and four grandchildren. Despite his father's efforts on his behalf, Peter was not among them, because his owner failed to keep a promise that he would sell him to his father when the latter raised sufficient capital. Finally, his family and friends banded together and enabled him to join the rest of his family in Cincinnati. Peter served that city's Black Brigade during the Civil War, and he and his wife worked with Levi Coffin in the Underground Railroad. In 1870, he became a church minister and founded the First Baptist Church in Cumminsville, Ohio. In 1900, his congregation raised the money to fund his ambition of returning to his childhood abode. Aged eighty-five, Peter made the trip that May, ascending the famous mountaintop in a carriage driven by the son of one of the slaves that he had taught to read and write. He was welcomed at the front door at Monticello "with most gracious hospitality" by the owner, Jefferson Monroe Levy.[34] Fossett's story and that of his family is heroic; sadly, others were less successful. The collected stories of the descendants of all of the slave families are the subject of a project of the Thomas Jefferson Foundation titled *Getting Word*, begun in 1993 by Lucia Stanton and Dianne Swann-Wright, in association with Beverly Gray. It represents a unique study of one plantation, the dispersal of its inhabitants, and the lives of their descendants through documentary sources and oral histories.

THE SALE OF Monticello took longer. Five years after Jefferson's death, an eccentric Charlottesville druggist, Dr. James Turner Barclay, finally purchased it for $7,500. He was interested only in the land, not the house, and he detested Jefferson's political principles. Despite the fact that construction had continued almost until Jefferson's death, with the addition of the pillars of the east portico and slate paving on both porticoes, the house looked neglected even in his lifetime. By September 1827, one visitor described it as "dark & much dilapidated with age & neglect."[35] Commenting on its decline since her previous visit eighteen years earlier, the author and political commentator Margaret Bayard Smith wrote a haunting description of it in 1828: "No kind friend with gracious countenance stood in the Portico to welcome us, no train of domestics hastened with smiling alacrity to show us forward. . . . Ruin has already commenced its ravages."[36] In the Entrance Hall, where public visitors were once welcomed, she found a "defaced floor" with walls stripped of their pictures and emptiness, removed of its "busts, and statues and natural curiosities." For a decade beginning in 1827, it was customary for university students to enter the premises secretly and initial the underside of the roof shingles on the dome. Of some sixty extant examples, the first known student to inscribe his name, along with an unidentified companion, was William Augustine Washington Spottswood, who wrote, "WAWS Student of the University of Virginia January 13, 1827." Others included their department, such as "James A. Leitch Student of Medicine and Chemistry 1830."[37] The house very nearly did not survive its additional neglect during the brief ownership of Barclay. It was saved by Commodore Uriah Philips Levy, who admired Jefferson for his views on religious freedom and whose family maintained the house until it was sold to the Thomas Jefferson Foundation in 1923.

At Monticello, Burwell Colbert, who had a cabin on the estate, tried to assist in maintaining the property, thereby earning the gratitude of Jefferson's granddaughter Virginia Randolph Trist, who wrote that he "seems to take pleasure in keeping things as they used to be."[38] Although now a freeman, he had no authority over whites and consequently fought a losing battle against vandals and trophy seekers. In a letter to her oldest sister in March 1827, Virginia wrote, "It will grieve you both very much to hear of the depredations that have been made at Monticello by the numerous parties who go to see the place. Mama's choicest flower roots have been carried off, one of her yellow jasmines, fig bushes." [39]

Martha Randolph was left destitute after her father's death with seven children, aged seven to twenty-eight, living with her. After the Richmond banks denied her a loan through her son in 1828, she even had to resort to borrowing through her son $19,777 from the University of Virginia.[40]

Still hoping to save Monticello, Martha and her daughters tried to raise money by publishing a selection of Jefferson's letters. Spending five to eight hours a day reading and copying the letters, they used a magnifying glass to help them decipher some of the more scrawled or faded correspondence. According to one of the daughters, "We worked very hard with the manuscript which leaves us little time to do anything else," but only their brother Thomas Jefferson Randolph was credited as editor on the title page.[41] After publication in 1829, the letters proved highly controversial, blemishing Jefferson's reputation within Virginia because of the hostility they expressed toward Presbyterians. Acknowledging that recourse to make a living was to profit from her own education, given "in happier days and for a different purpose," Martha decided to set up a school with her three oldest daughters in Charlottesville. Regarding the prospect "a bitter heartache," she became physically ill when hearing of the sale of Monticello.[42] In 1836, she died and was buried next to her husband in the Monticello cemetery, which was all that remained in the family's possessions there. Despite the university being all-male when he addressed it in 1882, Henry Tutwiler suggested that it should commemorate Martha's role in supporting her father, while he oversaw the creation of the university and during his final days: "Do not the labors and sacrifices of this noble woman in the interests of the University demand something more than they have yet received?"[43]

JEFFERSON REMAINED INVOLVED with the operation of the university up until a couple of weeks before his death. As late as February 1826, when he wrote a long letter on the problems of fundraising, he was corresponding almost weekly with Madison.[44] He even continued his daily rides to look at the university. On days that he remained at home, "his pet scheme towards the end of his life" was to look at the university through his telescope from the North Terrace near his dining room at Monticello.[45] He continued to invite four or five students to dinner every Sunday and to write the minutes for the Board of Visitors. In conjunction with Professor John Emmet, he was planning a botanical garden for the university. In May, he wrote to John Hartwell Cocke to say that he had located a site for the garden. Aware that his days were numbered, he sent all his correspondence with Emmet to Madison. During a trip that led to a North American travel account, the distinguished European soldier Bernhard, Duke of Saxe-Weimar-Eisenach, toured the university and dined at Monticello with Thomas Hewitt Key, the professor of mathematics, and his wife, Sarah, along with Martha Randolph and Jefferson. The duke observed that the university was his host's favorite subject and that he was optimistic about its future, believing that it and "Harvard University near Boston, would in a short time be the only institutions, where the youth of the United States would receive truly classical and solid education."[46]

A few weeks before his death, Jefferson made his final visit to the university to open boxes of books for the library. Unable to rise from the stirrup to mount his aging horse, Eagle, he had to get into the saddle from the terrace above. Refusing any escort, he rode unaccompanied over the familiar terrain, but two friends secretly followed him. Although his previous visits were so familiar as to be virtually unnoticed, "those who saw him on this occasion never after forgot the beaming eye, the kindly smile, and the still erect, noble form which they then beheld for the last time."[47] Arriving at Pavilion VII, where the first shipments of books awaited the completion of the Rotunda, the student librarian William Wertenbaker described how Jefferson "manifested interest in getting everything rightly placed at an early date," and that with "feeble hands he helped to unpack the books and place them on the shelves, in the order and the way that he had chalked out in his mind."[48] After inspecting the boxes, Jefferson called the librarian to him and pointed to a copy of Edward Gibbon's *Decline and Fall of the Roman Empire*, saying, "You ought not to have received that book. It should be returned." "Why," replied Wertenbaker, "it is a very handsome edition." "That may be so," answered Jefferson, "but look at the back." On the spine, the binder had misspelled it to read "Gibborn's Roman Empire."[49] From the balcony of Pavilion VII, now the Colonnade Club, Jefferson sat down on a chair provided by the student librarian and watched for an hour as workmen lifted the first Carrara marble Corinthian capital to the southwest corner of the south portico of the Rotunda. The arrival of the capitals had been delayed by low water and the winter in Richmond. After watching the positioning of the last capital, Jefferson rose, descended the stairs, mounted his horse, and rode away for the final time. The balustrades and bookcases were yet to be installed.

AFTER JEFFERSON'S DEATH, George Tucker recalled that Jefferson's "agreeable society and hospitality were greatly missed by the professors and the University lost its greatest attraction."[50] As a memorial tribute to Jefferson, the university faculty voted to wear crepe on the left arm for two months. On July 11, they published a tribute to their founder in the *Richmond Enquirer*, feeling themselves "impelled to record this testimony of their exalted respect for his talents, admiration for his virtues, and grateful sense of kindness and attention to themselves." They regarded the university as especially indebted to him because "he was substantially their founder: for his genius suggested the plan, his patience and unwearied assiduity combatted every prejudice, and his efforts, after having overcome all opposition, were extended to its course of instruction—the laws for its government—and the minutest detail of its regulation and policy." Jefferson's public stature and devotion to its interests had greatly augmented the status of the institution. Despite his advanced age, Jefferson labored with "a diligence and zeal that would have signalized the most fervid course of youthful ambition." The faculty wrote that the loss of their patron was also irredeemable on a personal level, having "experienced his accommodating spirit—his liberal hospitality—his kind offices on every occasion." They all felt themselves instructed "by the rare and versatile powers" of his "intellect which time had enriched with facts, without distracting from its lustre." They had been charmed by his "inimitable manners which, dictated by delicacy and benevolence, mere rules can never teach."[51]

In his will, Jefferson bequeathed to the university his personal library at Monticello of 1,600 books. He also wanted it to have his bust by Giuseppe Ceracchi, complete with the pedestal and truncated column. His grandson Thomas Jefferson Randolph wrote to the university afterward of his earnest desire to comply with Jefferson's wishes, "particularly" the bequests to the university, but he found that "the deeply embarrassed state in which his affairs were left renders it extremely doubtful whether his property will be sufficient to meet claims upon it."[52] Randolph requested that the books be kept at the university for safekeeping. In any event, the only books from Jefferson's personal collection that went to the university library at that point were those he gave while alive. Thanks to Ann Lucas and Endrina Tay at Monticello in 2011, some of the books from his retirement library were rediscovered at Washington University in St. Louis, where they were presented to the founder by the grandson-in-law and granddaughter of Ellen Coolidge. The bust and its pedestal were sold by the family to Congress, where they were destroyed in a fire in 1856. Some of his collection from the Entrance Hall, including the fossils, was given to the university and became the nucleus of a Museum of Curiosities, which was probably destroyed in the great fire of the Rotunda and the adjacent humanities building in 1895.[53] Others were kept by different departments and eventually returned to Monticello.

Faculty member George Long recalled that, although Jefferson thought the first few months of the university "were not quite satisfactory," he had "confidently looked forward to the future and the advantages that the state would derive from the young men who were educated in the University of Virginia."[54] His friends continued to oversee the university until long after his death. James Madison succeeded him as rector, bequeathed his own library to the university, and donated $1,500, despite his own impending bankruptcy. In a letter to Madison in February 1826, Jefferson wrote that it was a solace to "leave the institution under your care" and additionally to know that Madison would continue to protect and perpetuate the pure version of republicanism and the blessings of self-government. He thanked Madison for having been his "pillar of support thro' life" and asked him to "take care of me when dead," meaning his reputation and legacy.[55] Madison was followed as rector by James Monroe, Chapman Johnson, and Jefferson's great ally Joseph Cabell, who were all members of the original Board of Visitors in 1819. Cabell survived to hold the office until 1856, and Thomas Jefferson Randolph served as rector almost until the end of the Civil War in 1864.

HISTORIANS OF HIGHER EDUCATION have had difficulty categorizing the University of Virginia in relation to other colleges in America. Roger Geiger describes the university as "sui generis" in the United States. "When the University of Virginia opened in 1825," Geiger writes, "it was both a new model for American higher education and a belated realization of the old dream of republican universities."[56] It anticipated many of the features of the modern university precisely because it looked back to the values and ideas of the Enlightenment and the republicanism of the American Revolution. The separation of religion alone distinguished the university from all others in United States. While other universities had briefly experimented with separating religion, the secular tradition at the University of Virginia explains why it became the first in America to appoint a Jewish professor. Along with the University of South Carolina, it was the first truly public university in that it received annual funds from the state of Virginia.[57] Although it followed the College of William and Mary and the University of North Carolina in offering an elective curriculum, the University of Virginia gave visibility to the idea of letting students choose their own courses, which became a defining feature of higher education in the United States. Jefferson's emphasis on a broad curriculum that would teach both science and vocational subjects was in marked contrast to the continued emphasis elsewhere on a traditional education in the classics.

In the United States, the University of Virginia was the first to have a professional academic chair in medicine and a major innovator in the teaching of medicine. It was one of the earliest to teach chemistry, modern languages, and economics. It was a pioneer in the division of universities into separate schools, each holding some autonomy and different graduation requirements. Ahead of Yale and Harvard, Jefferson's pedagogical preference for lectures over recitation and his emphasis on written examinations also anticipated the modern university. His desire to recruit first-rate faculty from Europe was a half-century ahead of the example of Daniel Coit Gilman, who followed the same strategy in establishing Johns Hopkins University. The physical concept of an "academical village" with the university as a community in which the buildings are dispersed and faculty live among residential students was creative. The egalitarian system of faculty and student governance, with no university president and an emphasis on self-government, was also contrary to the norm of the more typical all-powerful college president.

The originality of Jefferson's vision of a university is not sufficiently appreciated largely because his ideas have either become so commonplace as to attract no attention or because the university itself has dispensed with some of his innovations, including faculty self-governance. With the celebrity of college presidents gaining momentum in the late nineteenth century and the increasing administrative workload shared by the faculty, the University of Virginia finally capitulated to prevailing practices with the appointment of Edwin Alderman in 1904. The same fate doomed the unusually short vacations and long semesters, a system that was not based on the traditional agricultural or Christian calendars. The failure of the state to increase the budget for the university made it one of the most private public universities in America.

Jefferson's pioneering political and religious ideas are also all too often taken for granted because they are so familiar that we forget their genesis. The secular arrangements of the university did not entirely disappear, but over time it became increasingly sectarian and evangelical. Jefferson's achievement was all the more remarkable because he did it in what Richard Hofstadter called "the age of the great retrogression," when the country was retreating from the values and rational emphasis of the Enlightenment, thanks to the rise of evangelicalism and the Romantic movement.[58] While he did not fully articulate the concept of a research university, an ideal that only emerged gradually during the nineteenth century, Jefferson did anticipate some of its associated features by giving priority to empirical evidence to support any claim, recruiting faculty based on reputation, prohibiting them from engaging in professional practice outside the university, recognizing the importance of a good library, supporting subscriptions to academic journals, and purchasing the latest equipment for experiments and research. He was aware that knowledge was constantly changing and that it should be deployed for the benefit of society.

THE UNIVERSITY OF VIRGINIA provided an alternative model for universities in America that were otherwise dominated by the influence of Yale and Princeton. Furthermore, Virginia's vision proved the more durable over time by avoiding the emphasis of other colleges on classics and religion. Jefferson promoted his ideas for the university by publishing many of the key documents in its creation, including the Rockfish Gap Report, which was also reprinted in the *Analectic Magazine* in Philadelphia in 1819.[59] Its purpose as a publicity effort is suggested by his asking the *Richmond Enquirer* editor Thomas Richie to print additional copies for other states. While recruiting faculty, Francis Walker Gilmer distributed copies to key individuals in England. One of the recipients was Lord Brougham, who would later help found University College London, the self-styled "University of London" and now part of London University. The college was primarily modeled after the University of Edinburgh but was also influenced by the University of Virginia.[60] Brougham and the other founders became more active in implementing their plan after receiving the Rockfish Gap Report from Gilmer. Unaffiliated with any religious sect and with a broad curriculum that included the sciences, the college shared many features with the University of Virginia.

Jefferson's celebrity brought his university national attention. The University of Virginia was the subject of a twenty-three-page article in the *North American Review* in January 1820. Its author, Edward Everett, was professor of Greek at Harvard at the time, where he taught Ralph Waldo Emerson. Although critical of some features, he upheld the university as a model of public funding that other states and the federal government should follow. The northern newspapers even printed articles about the "imported professors" as they arrived from England. By the time of the Civil War, Virginia had the largest enrollment of any southern university and was originally known for much of the nineteenth century simply as "the University." According to Herbert Baxter Adams, the prominent late nineteenth-century educator and historian, "scarcely any college in the South . . . has not to a greater or lesser extent modelled its system of teaching after that of the University of Virginia. Furthermore, it "has always furnished these various colleges with a large proportion of their professors."[61] Lawrence A. Cremin, a leading authority on higher education in the United States, states that "the influence of Jefferson's educational thought, during the nineteenth century and into the twentieth century, was powerful and pervasive." Comparing the influence in other states to that of the Virginia Statute for Religious Freedom, Cremin argues that the university "became a model of the American state university from the time of its founding through the passage of the Morrill Act in 1862."[62]

The most influential feature of the university was its elective curriculum, which had been adopted by at least thirty-five southern colleges by 1884.[63] It was also imitated in the North. In 1849, Professor William Barton Rogers was contacted through his brother Henry by Francis Wayland, the president of Brown University (1827–55), who was proposing major reforms to the curriculum and wanted to obtain details of the elective system of courses at the University of Virginia.[64] In the United States, Andrew Delbanco observes that, with a few notable exceptions, colleges now "give students virtually unlimited freedom to study whatever they want."[65] The secular tradition also gained adherents with institutions like Cornell, which was founded as a nonsectarian university in 1868.

Jefferson's vision was spread by faculty, alumni, friends, and even family members. A leading founder of the University of Michigan in 1817, known at the time as Catholepistemiad or the University of Michigania, Augustus B. Woodward had visited Jefferson in Virginia. A chief justice of the supreme court of the Michigan Territory and a lifelong disciple of Jefferson, Woodward embraced a similarly comprehensive vision of a university with libraries, museums, colleges, athenaeums, and botanical gardens, along with feeder institutions.[66] Jefferson's grandson Francis Eppes was involved in the founding of Florida State University, which has a statue of him on campus, although it is now doubted that he was the actual founder.[67]

Jefferson's influence also extended through former faculty members. Professors Thomas Hewitt Key and George Long both resigned to teach at the newly established University College in London, the first university in England to be established since Oxford and Cambridge. Key recommended Joseph Sylvester, a graduate of University College and the first Jewish professor in America, as a faculty member of the University of Virginia. Key and Long each supplied anecdotes for the 1875 jubilee celebration of the first class at the University of Virginia. Finally, the alumni played an important role in educational initiatives, including the founding of the University of Texas (1883).

William Barton Rogers, the founder of the Massachusetts Institute of Technology (MIT, 1865), was a former faculty member at the University of Virginia (1835–53), where he engaged in pioneering geological research on the Appalachian Mountains. According to his widow, Emma, Rogers looked on the University of Virginia as a model when he founded MIT. In an address to the literary societies at the University of Virginia in 1903, Henry Smith Pritchett, the president of MIT from 1900 to 1907, said that "the Massachusetts Institute of Technology was planned in these halls. Its organization as it exists today grew first in the brain of William B. Rogers, whilst he was a professor in this University." When he resigned from the University of Virginia in 1853, Rogers wrote to Joseph Cabell that he valued "more and more the scheme of its organization and method and thoroughness that preside generally in its halls of instruction." He claimed that the university had "been successful in establishing within its borders a higher and more thorough system of scientific and literary training than had previously been successful in the United States." He added that his opinion was shared "by all who are familiar with its course of study."[68] When teaching at the University of Virginia, he defended the policy of not awarding honorary degrees, which he later also instituted at MIT. The tradition continues there to this day.

Demonstrating the direct influence of the university can be difficult because it was typically unacknowledged, and alternative sources for features can be identified, such as the elective curriculum that originated in Europe. There are, however, prominent cases of university reformers and founders who paid direct homage to the influence of the University of Virginia and to Jefferson. The most remarkable example was Harvard, where George Ticknor, supported by Edward Everett, sought to expand the library, end the tradition of learning by recitation, raise admission standards, organize the curriculum by departments, and introduce greater freedom in the student choice of courses. Ticknor was ultimately able to make changes only in his own department of modern languages.[69] While he was predominantly influenced by his education in Germany at the University of Göttingen, Ticknor twice visited Jefferson in retirement and wrote to James Madison that the University of Virginia "is a great & very important experiment; & the Colleges of New England, are, I think, deeply interested in its success." Regarding the backwardness of the teaching at Harvard, he wrote, "I look upon your great experiment in Virginia as very valuable." Ticknor conceded that he could not even have started to make changes "if you had not begun your University of Virginia on principles so truly liberal and wise." He therefore wished Madison "the most serious success . . . as in most such cases the whole must rise or fall together," and "the flourishing condition of your Universities, will be the cause of the same condition in ours."[70]

Upon becoming president of Harvard in 1829, Josiah Quincy traveled as far south as Washington, D.C., with the express purpose of visiting the University of Virginia. As he explained to the rector, James Madison, "My wish . . . is to make myself acquainted with all that relates to the origin, history, constitution, discipline & general regulations of that institution."[71] He was especially interested in the treatment of religious instruction at the university. According to Madison, "Mr. Quincy was so anxious on the subject that he was on his way to the University, when the report of the [typhoid] fever [epidemic at the university] stopped him."[72] Appointed president of Harvard in 1869, Charles William Eliot introduced the elective system and attributed to Thomas Jefferson its origins in America.[73] In 1888, Herbert Baxter Adams published *Thomas Jefferson and the University of Virginia*, a work that recognizes Jefferson as the pioneer of the modern university in America. Adams's reputation as one of the first professors at Johns Hopkins popularized Jefferson's ideas about university education and ensured that they "would play a major role in the establishment and growth of universities in other states beginning in the 1890s."[74] James Bryant Conant, an influential president of Harvard, was a self-described Jeffersonian and wrote a book on *Thomas Jefferson and the Development of American Public Education* (1962). He claimed that "one could almost say that the shape of higher education in the [American] West . . . was largely fashioned in Virginia."[75]

While the University of Virginia was exceptional in the southern states, interesting and pioneering developments took place more generally in higher education in that region. The first explicitly public universities were founded in the South, at a time when the status of northern universities was ambiguous. Transylvania College notably held a charter describing it as a "public school" as early as 1780. The University of North Carolina (1789) is regarded as the first public university by virtue of its charter, but the University of Georgia (1785) actually preceded it as a public foundation. However, the latter merely existed on paper until after the building of the University of North Carolina. Other public universities in the South included the University of Tennessee, which was chartered as Blount College in 1794, and South Carolina College (1801). As president of the latter (now the University of South Carolina), Thomas Cooper wrote that he desired "to leave it on record that a Free College is as necessary as a Free School and that the exaction of Tuition money, for education here can neither be defended on the ground of justice or experience." Regardless of the cost, it would be "a pittance compared to the object in view and not worth a moment's consideration."[76] The University of Virginia and South Carolina College pioneered a new model of public education as the only two universities to receive annual funding from their respective states.

From the time before 1776 when only the College of William and Mary existed in the South, there was a considerable growth in the number of southern colleges. Southerners attended college in greater numbers proportionately than northerners and were similarly more likely to study at the best universities in Europe.[77] In the 1830s, they represented about half of the total number of American medical students in Paris. They also studied at the elite northern universities, where they were a major presence, especially at Princeton and Yale. Like the University of Virginia, many other colleges founded in the South during the two decades after the American Revolution based their curricula on the rational principles of the Enlightenment. The southern colleges were more likely to teach science and medicine, to play down the traditional emphasis on the classics, and to have separate degree programs. They were the first to teach political economy (economics).[78]

Recognition of the quality of southern colleges in the early nineteenth century complements a well-established historical literature that argues for the intellectual vitality of the antebellum South.[79] This vigor was increasingly stifled by the preclusion of the possibility of any discussion of slavery. After resigning from the University of Virginia, Thomas Cooper became president of South Carolina College in 1820. Described by Richard Hofstadter as "one of the most distinguished men in American academic life," he led "one of the best colleges in the United States."[80] Although initially fostering religious and political heterodoxy, South Carolina became the leading intellectual center for proslavery ideology and secession. As with the University of Virginia, the slavery debate ultimately limited the choice of faculty at southern colleges, making them increasingly parochial. In an anonymously published pamphlet entitled "Is Slavery a Blessing?" Charles B. Shaw, a former adjunct professor of engineering at the University of Virginia, claimed that "gradually a funereal pallor has been drawn over any rational discussion of the slavery question and if thereby any now here who hold the [antislavery] sentiment once openly expressed, they are only whispered in confidence." He wrote the pamphlet in reply to fellow faculty member Albert Taylor Bledsoe, regarded as one of the intellectual architects of the Confederacy. Shaw added that "no person can safely reside in the South who is suspected of liberal views on the subject of slavery."[81] The important and pioneering efforts of southern colleges in public education have largely gone unnoticed because they suffered major physical and economic setbacks during the Civil War, when they all ceased operation, with the sole exception of the University of Virginia.[82]

HISTORIAN HAROLD HELLENBRAND writes that the "final project, building a university, reveals Jefferson's core identity . . . a man compelled by psychological and historical circumstances to refine and then reproduce his own education" so that, as Jefferson observed to John Adams, "a 'more instructed race' might complete the revolution that they had only begun."[83] Jefferson believed that future generations must improve existing institutions and not be thwarted by what he called the dead hand of the past. In establishing the university, he provided a way for future generations to think for themselves and foster progress. He wrote dismissively of those who "look at Constitutions with sanctimonious reverence, & deem them like the ark of the covenant too sacred to be touched," and who "ascribe to men of the preceding age a wisdom more than human and suppose they did to be beyond amendment." He insisted that "laws and institutions must go hand in hand with the progress of the human mind." He believed that as society became more developed, more enlightened, as new discoveries are made, new truths disclosed, and manners and opinions change with the change of circumstances, institutions must advance also and keep pace with the times. A man might as well be required "to wear still the suit which fitted him when a boy" as to expect a "civilized society to remain under the regimen of their barborous ancestors."[84]

SHORTLY BEFORE HIS DEATH, Jefferson was asked to celebrate the jubilee of the Declaration of Independence by Robert C. Weightman, the mayor of Washington, D.C., along with John Adams, James Madison, and James Monroe. Jefferson was unable to accept and indeed was hardly able to write. Buckling the armor of Hector, Old Priam roused himself to fire one last brilliantly penned salvo in defense of the cause of liberty and the meaning of the Fourth of July:

> May it be to the world what I believe it will be, (to some parts sooner, to others later, but finally to all,) the Signal of arousing men to burst the chains, under which monkish ignorance and superstition had persuaded them to bind themselves, and to assume the blessings & security of self-

government. that form which we have substituted, restores the free right to the unbounded exercise of reason and freedom of opinion. all eyes are opened, or opening to the rights of man. the general spread of the light of science has already laid open to every view the palpable truth that the mass of mankind has not been born, with saddles on their backs, nor a favored few booted and spurred, ready to ride them legitimately, by the grace of god.

He concluded that these were grounds of hope, for others and ourselves.[85]

In what he once described to the Marquis de Lafayette as "this Athanaeum of our country," Thomas Jefferson looked to the University of Virginia's graduates to secure his legacy. It represented the culminating achievement of a career dedicated to promoting the ongoing progress of Enlightenment and republican self-government in America.[86] Three months before his death, Jefferson wrote, "I am closing the last scenes of my life by fostering and fashioning an establishment for those who are to come after us. I hope its influence on their virtue, freedom, fame and happiness will be salutary and permanent."[87]

NOTES

PTJ   The Papers of Thomas Jefferson, ed. Julian Boyd et al., 44 vols. to date (Princeton, N.J.: Princeton University Press, 1950–).

PJMRS The Papers of James Madison Retirement Series, ed. David B. Mattern et al., 3 vols. to date (Charlottesville: University of Virginia Press, 2009–),

PTJRS The Papers of Thomas Jefferson Retirement Series, ed. J. Jefferson Looney et al., 16 vols. to date (Princeton, N.J.: University of Princeton Press, 2004–).

TJ   Thomas Jefferson

INTRODUCTION

1. TJ to Charles Yancey, 6 Jan. 1816, *PTJRS*, vol. 9, p. 328.
2. Harvard historian Bernard Bailyn wrote of John Thornton Kirkland, one of the most beloved presidents of Harvard University between 1810 and 1828, that Kirkland ultimately failed in his role because he lacked an agenda and the necessary leadership skills. See Bailyn, "Why Kirkland Failed," in *Glimpses of the Harvard Past*, ed. Bernard Bailyn et al. (Cambridge, Mass.: Harvard University Press, 1986), pp. 19–45. Similarly, in discussing Timothy Dwight, the president of Yale between 1795 and 1817, Brooks Mather Kelley argued that his message to students "was at heart anti-intellectual." Kelley further described a sermon that Dwight preached on several occasions denouncing men whose "only object was to be learned." Kelley added that "such anti-intellectualism has not been uncommon among college presidents in America. Not many years later, in fact, the president of Dartmouth said, 'The very cultivation of the mind has frequent led to a tendency to impair the moral sensibilities.'" Kelley, *Yale: A History* (New Haven, Conn.: Yale University Press, 1974), pp. 138, 130.
3. Benjamin Waterhouse to TJ, 22 Oct. 1825, Founders Online, National Archives and Records Administration, Washington, D.C., https://founders.archives.gov /documents/Jefferson/01-35-02-0243.
4. Wilson Cary Nicholas to TJ, 25 Jan. 1819, *PTJRS*, vol. 13, p. 602.
5. James Fieser, ed., *The Life of George Tucker: Excerpted from the Life and Philosophy of George Tucker* (New York: Thoemmes Continuum, 2004), p. 71.
6. James Madison to George Ticknor, 6 Apr. 1825, Founders Online, https://founders .archives.gov/documents/Madison/04-03-02-0513.
7. TJ to Thomas Cooper, 14 Aug. 1820, *PTJRS*, vol. 16, p. 190.
8. Edward Potts Cheyney, *History of the University of Pennsylvania, 1740–1790* (Philadelphia: University of Pennsylvania Press, 1940), p. 27, argues that the term "founder" is inappropriate for Franklin. See also ibid., pp. 76, 173. For Franklin's role, see also

George Boudreau, "'Done by a Tradesman': Franklin's Educational Proposals and the Culture of Eighteenth-Century Pennsylvania," *Pennsylvania History* 69, no. 4 (Autumn 2002): 534, 537; Richard D. Brown, *The Strength of a People: The Idea of an Informed Citizenry in America, 1650–1870* (Chapel Hill: University of North Carolina Press, 2000), p. 37; and Roger L. Geiger, *The History of American Higher Education: Learning and Culture from the Founding to World War II* (Princeton, N.J.: Princeton University Press, 2016), p. 44.

9. Geiger, *History of American Higher Education*, p. 93; Brown, *Strength of a People*, p. 80.

10. George Thomas, *The Founders and the Idea of a National University: Constituting the American Mind* (Cambridge: Cambridge University Press, 2017), p. 93; Lawrence A. Cremin, *American Education, the National Experience, 1783–1876* (New York: Harper and Row, 1988), p. 119; David W. Robson, "College Founding in the New Republic, 1776–1800," *History of Education Quarterly* 23, no. 3 (Autumn 1983): 327.

11. TJ to William Roscoe, 27 Dec. 1820, *PTJRS*, vol. 16, pp. 499–500.

12. Evan Osnos, "Reading the Muller Indictment: A Russian-American Fraud," *New Yorker*, 16 Feb. 2016, https://www.newyorker.com/news/news-desk/reading-the -mueller-indictment-a-russian-american-fraud; Mark Walsh, "Chief Justice Warns That 'Civic Education Has Fallen by the Wayside,'" *Education Week*, 21 Dec. 2019, https://www.edweek.org/education/chief-justice-warns-that-civic-education-has -fallen-by-the-wayside/2019/12.

13. TJ to Lydia Howard Huntley Sigourney, 18 July 1824, Founders Online, https:// founders.archives.gov/documents/Jefferson/98-01-02-4419.

14. Geiger, *History of American Higher Education*, pp. 182, 236.

15. Cameron Addis, *Jefferson's Vision for Education, 1760–1845* (New York: Peter Lang, 2003), p. 155.

16. *President's Commission on Slavery and the University: Report to President Teresa A. Sullivan, 2018* (Charlottesville: The Rector and Visitors of the University of Virginia, 2018); Maurie D. McInnis and Louis P. Nelson, eds., *Educated in Tyranny: Slavery at Thomas Jefferson's University* (Charlottesville: University of Virginia Press, 2019).

17. Cameron Addis is an exception; see *Jefferson's Vision for Education*.

18. [Edward Everett], "Proceedings and Report of the Commissioners for the University of Virginia. Presented 8th of December 1818," *North American Review* 10, no. 26 (Jan. 1820): 130.

19. TJ to Caesar A. Rodney, 23 Oct. 1805, Founders Online, https://founders.archives .gov/documents/Jefferson/99-01-02-2518. My thanks to James Sofka for bringing this letter to my attention.

20. Richard Hofstadter, *Academic Freedom in the Age of the College* (New Brunswick, N.J.: Aldine Transaction, 1996), p. 269.

21. David Waldstreicher. "Founders Chic as Culture War," *Radical History Review* 84 (Fall 2002): 185–94.

22. Daniel J. Galvin, "Thomas Jefferson and Presidential Party Building in the United States," paper presented at the Fifth International Conference of the Lincoln Center for American Studies, Louisiana State University–Shreveport, 2003. My thanks to

Brian Alexander, professor of political science at Washington and Lee University, who ran a current search of the congressional record (1789–2020), finding 23,938 mentions of George Washington; 18,521 of Thomas Jefferson; 9,094 of James Madison; 6,217 of Alexander Hamilton; and 5,984 of John Adams.

23. Abraham Lincoln to Henry L. Pierce et al., 6 Apr. 1859, Speeches and Writings, Abraham Lincoln Online, http://www.abrahamlincolnonline.org/lincoln/speeches /pierce.htm.

24. Scot A. French and Edward L. Ayers, "The Strange Career of Thomas Jefferson: Race and Slavery in American Memory, 1943–1993," in *Jeffersonian Legacies*, ed. Peter S. Onuf (Charlottesville: University Press of Virginia, 1993), p. 419.

25. See "Other Presidents on Jefferson," in *In the Hands of the People: Thomas Jefferson on Equality, Faith, Freedom, Compromise, and the Art of Citizenship*, ed. Jon Meacham (New York: Random House, 2020), pp. 77–89; James L. Golden and Alan L. Golden, *Thomas Jefferson and the Rhetoric of Virtue* (Lanhan, Md.: Rowman and Littlefield, 2002), p. ix.

26. For two excellent discussions of the changing views of Jefferson, see Merrill D. Peterson, *The Jefferson Image in the American Mind* (Charlottesville: University Press of Virginia, 1998), and Frank Cogliano, *Thomas Jefferson: Reputation and Legacy* (Charlottesville: University of Virginia Press, 2006).

27. Annette Gordon-Reed, "Charlottesville: Why Jefferson Matters," *New York Review of Books*, 19 Aug. 2017, https://www.nybooks.com/daily/2017/08/19/charlottesville -why-jefferson-matters/.

28. TJ to Benjamin Waterhouse, 3 Mar. 1816, *PTJRS*, vol. 12, pp. 517–19; TJ to James Madison, 6 Sept. 1789, *PTJ*, vol. 15, p. 392.

29. Meredith Jung-En Woo, *Something New under the Sun: Education at Mr. Jefferson's University* (Charlottesville: University of Virginia College and Graduate School of Arts and Sciences, 2014), p. 8.

1. Feast of Reason

1. Burwell Stark, "Reminiscences," *Alumni Bulletin of the University of Virginia*, May 1894, p. 1.

2. Ellen Coolidge to Martha Jefferson Randolph, 28 Jan. 1818, *Thomas Jefferson's Granddaughter in Queen Victoria's England: The Travel Diary of Ellen Wayles Coolidge, 1838–1839*, ed. Ann Lucas Birle and Lisa A. Francavilla (Charlottesville: University of Virginia Press, 2011), p. xx.

3. [Schele De Vere], "Mr. Jefferson's Pet," *Harper's New Monthly Magazine*, May 1872, p. 824.

4. Henry Tutwiler, *Early History of the University of Virginia: Address of H. Tutwiler, A.M., LL.D., of Alabama, before the Alumni Society of the University of Virginia, Thursday, June 29th, 1882* (Charlottesville, Va.: Charlottesville Chronicle Book and Job Office, 1882), pp. 8–9. Tutwiler gave the number of attendees as three to four students, but Burwell Stark said that each dinner had as many as twelve. Stark, "Reminiscences," p. 1.

5. Tutwiler, *Early History of the University of Virginia*, p. 9.

6. Ibid., p. 3.

7. Ibid., p. 4.

8. Ibid., pp. 4, 5–6.

9. Ibid., p. 6.

10. Ibid., p. 8.

11. Sarah Nicholas Randolph, *The Domestic Life of Thomas Jefferson Compiled from Family Letters and Reminiscences of His Great-Granddaughter* (New York: Harper and Brothers, 1871), p. 238.

12. Margaret Bayard Smith, "Account of a Visit to Monticello," 29 July–2 Aug. 1819, *PTJRS*, vol. 7, p. 387.

13. Lucia Stanton, *"Those Who Labor for My Happiness": Slavery at Thomas Jefferson's Monticello* (Charlottesville: University of Virginia Press, 2012), p. 68.

14. François Jean, Marquis de Chastellux, "A Conversation Always Varied and Interesting" (1782), in *Jefferson in his Own Time: A Biographical Chronicle of His Life Drawn from Recollections, Interviews, and Memoirs by Family, Friends, and Associates*, ed. Kevin Hayes (Iowa City: University of Iowa Press, 2012), p. 2; Randolph, *The Domestic Life of Thomas Jefferson*, p. 239; TJ to Samuel Pierre du Pont de Nemours, 2 Mar. 1809, Founders Online, https://founders.archives.gov/documents/Jefferson /99-01-02-9936.

15. The phrase of Jon Meacham, correspondence with the author, May 2020.

16. TJ to Alexander Donald, 20 May 1795, *PTJ*, vol. 28, p. 366.

17. Auguste Levasseur, *Lafayette in America, in 1824 and 1825; or, Journal of a Voyage to the United States,* trans. Alan R. Hoffman (Manchester, N.H.: Lafayette Press, 2006), p. 236. My thanks to Elizabeth Chew who shared an unpublished article, "Authority and Privilege in Jefferson's Indian Hall."

18. Susan R. Stein, *The Worlds of Thomas Jefferson at Monticello* (New York: Harry N. Abrams, 1993), p. 219.

19. Described in a letter of George Ticknor to his father, reprinted in G. W. Long, *Thomas Jefferson and George Ticknor: A Chapter in American Scholarship* (Williamstown, Mass.: McClelland Press, 1933), p. 7.

20. Stein, *The Worlds of Thomas Jefferson at Monticello*, pp. 404–14.

21. TJ to Benjamin Rush, 16 Jan. 1811, *PTJRS*, vol. 3, p. 305.

22. Margaret C. Jacob, *The Enlightenment: A Brief History with Documents* (New York: Bedford/St. Martin's, 2001), p. vii.

23. Harold Hellenbrand, *The Unfinished Revolution: Education and Politics in the Thought of Thomas Jefferson* (Newark: University of Delaware Press, 1990), p. 66.

24. TJ to Peter Carr, 10 Aug. 1787, *PTJ*, vol. 12, p. 15.

25. TJ to William Johnson, 12 June 1823, Founders Online, https://founders.archives .gov/documents/Jefferson/98-01-02-3562.

26. TJ to James Monroe, 17 June 1785, *PTJ*, vol. 8, p. 227. See also Golden and Golden, *Thomas Jefferson and the Rhetoric of Virtue*, pp. 324–25.

27. Thomas Jefferson, *Notes on the State of Virginia*, ed. Frank Shuffelton (1787; reprint New York: Penguin, 1999), p. 165. There was an earlier unauthorized French edition published in 1785. He completed the actual manuscript in 1782.

28. James Madison, "Notes on Buffon's *Histoire Naturelle*," ca. 1786, Founders Online, https://founders.archives.gov/documents/Madison/01-09-02-0005.
29. Jefferson, *Notes on the State of Virginia*, p. 168.
30. Jack P. Greene, "The Intellectual Reconstruction of Virginia in the Age of Jefferson," in Onuf, ed., *Jeffersonian Legacies*, p. 228.
31. For a study of Jefferson's nationalism and how it related to his views on states' rights, see Brian Douglas Steele, *Thomas Jefferson and American Nationhood* (New York: Cambridge University Press, 2015).
32. Patrick Spero, "The Other Presidency: Thomas Jefferson and the American Philosophical Society," *Proceedings of the American Philosophical Society* 162, no. 4 (Dec. 2018): 321–60.
33. Benjamin Rush, "A Plan for the Establishment of Public Schools and the Diffusion of Knowledge in Pennsylvania," in *Essays on Education in the Early Republic*, ed. Frederick Rudolph (Cambridge, Mass.: Harvard University Press, 1965), p. 15.
34. Spero, "The Other Presidency.," p. 321.
35. Ibid., pp. 330, 338.
36. Chastellux, "A Conversation Always Varied and Interesting," p. 3.
37. Gordon S. Wood, *Friends Divided: John Adams and Thomas Jefferson* (New York: Penguin, 2018), p. 45. Endrina Tay argues that the sale of the library was not motivated so much by financial concerns but a sense of public duty and a desire to influence future decision-makers in Washington, D.C. Jefferson sold the books at much less than market value; see Tay, "'Unquestionably the Choicest Collection of Books in the U.S.': The 1825 Sale of Thomas Jefferson's Library to the Nation," *Commonplace: The Journal of Early American Life* 64, no. 4 (Sept. 2016), http://commonplace.online/article/unquestionably-the-choicest-collection/.
38. TJ to John Adams, 10 June 1815, *PTJRS*, vol. 8, p. 523.
39. *The First Forty Years of Washington Society, Portrayed by the Family Letters of Mrs. Samuel Harrison Smith (Margaret Bayard) from the Collection of Her Grandson, J. Henley Smith*, ed. Gaillard Hunt (New York: Scribner, 1906), p. 71.
40. TJ to John Adams, 10 June 1815, *PTJRS*, vol. 8, p. 523; Kevin J. Hayes, *The Road to Monticello: The Life and Mind of Thomas Jefferson* (New York: Oxford University Press, 2008), p. 566. As per a personal communication on 20 July 2020, Endrina Tay, the associate librarian for technical services at the Jefferson Library (Thomas Jefferson Foundation), writes that the "the actual volume count from Jefferson's library catalogue numbers 1,539 volumes. However, we know that he did not record the actual number of volumes for certain titles or else held more copies of a title than he recorded in his catalogue, it is clear that the actual volume count is greater than 1,539—hence my 'some 1,600 volumes' characterization."
41. TJ to John Wyche, 19 May 1809, *PTJRS*, vol. 1, p. 205.
42. Andrew Burstein, *The Inner Jefferson: Portrait of a Grieving Optimist* (Charlottesville: University Press of Virginia, 1996), p. 3.
43. The original document is missing but a facsimile was published in Henry S. Randall, *The Life of Thomas Jefferson*, 3 vols. (New York: Derby and Jackson, 1858), vol. 1, pp. 44–45. For a different version, see Vegetable Market Report, 1801, Thomas

Jefferson Papers, Library of Congress, Manuscripts Division, https://www.loc.gov/item/mtjbib010905/.

44. Diane Ehrenpreis and Endrina Tay, "Enlightened Networks: Thomas Jefferson's System for Working from Home," *Transactions of the American Philosophical Society* 109 (forthcoming).

45. Thomas E. Buckley, S.J., "Placing Thomas Jefferson and Religion in Context, Then and Now," in *Seeing Jefferson Anew: In His Time and Ours*, ed. John B. Boles and Randal L. Hall (Charlottesville: University of Virginia Press, 2010), pp. 132–33.

46. TJ to John Harvie, 14 Jan. 1760, *PTJ*, vol. 1, p. 3.

47. Terry L. Meyers, "Benjamin Franklin, the College of William and Mary and the Williamsburg Bray School," *Anglican and Episcopal History* 79, no. 4 (Dec. 2010): 368–93.

48. TJ to Thomas Jefferson Randolph, 24 Nov. 1808, Founders Online, https://founders.archives.gov/documents/Jefferson/99-01-02-9151.

49. Hayes, ed., *Jefferson in His Own Time*, p. xii; Randolph, *The Domestic Life of Thomas Jefferson*, p. 31.

50. *Autobiography of Thomas Jefferson*, ed. Dumas Malone (New York: Capricorn Books, 1959), p. 20.

51. Randolph, *The Domestic Life of Thomas Jefferson*, p. 25.

52. TJ to Thomas Jefferson Randolph, 24 Nov. 1808, Founders Online, https://founders.archives.gov/documents/Jefferson/99-01-02-9151; Hayes, *The Road to Monticello*, p. 63.

53. TJ to Louis H. Girardin, 15 Jan. 1815, *PTJRS*, vol. 8, p. 200.

54. TJ to John Hollins, 19 Feb. 1809, Founders Online, https://founders.archives.gov/documents/Jefferson/99-01-02-9834; TJ to George Ticknor, 24 Dec. 1819, *PTJRS*, vol. 15, p. 303.

55. TJ to George Gilmer, 12 Aug. 1787, *PTJ*, vol. 12, p. 26.

56. Richard Rush to Benjamin Rush, 9 Oct. 1816, *PTJRS*, vol. 10, p. 443.

57. Lucinda Stanton, "Perfecting Slavery: Rational Plantation Management at Monticello," in *Jefferson, Lincoln and Wilson: The American Dilemma of Race and Democracy*, ed. John Milton Cooper Jr. and Thomas J. Knock (Charlottesville: University of Virginia Press, 2010), p. 75.

58. Randall, *The Life of Thomas Jefferson*, vol. 3, p. 330.

59. Randolph, *The Domestic Life of Thomas Jefferson*, p. 401.

60. *The Autobiographical Ana of Robley Dunglison, M.D.*, ed. Samuel X. Radbill, *Transactions of the American Philosophical Society* 53, no. 8 (Dec. 1963): 27.

61. Daniel Webster, "Memorandum of Mr. Jefferson's Conversation" (1824), in Hayes, ed., *Jefferson in His Own Time*, p. 92.

62. Randolph, *The Domestic Life of Thomas Jefferson*, pp. 48, 331, 338.

63. Augustus J. Foster, "A Visionary Who Loved to Dream with Eyes Wide Open" (1841), in Hayes, ed., *Jefferson in His Own Time*, p. 130.

64. Randall, *The Life of Thomas Jefferson*, vol. 3, pp. 342–43.

65. TJ to Vine Utley, 21 Mar. 1819, *PTJRS*, vol. 14, p. 157.

66. "Memoirs of a Monticello Slave, as Dictated to Charles Campbell by Isaac," in *Jeffer-*

son at Monticello, ed. James A. Bear Jr. (Charlottesville: University Press of Virginia, 1967), p. 12.

67. James Ogilvie, *Cursory Reflexions on Government Philosophy and Education* (1802); Antoine Destutt de Tracy, *Observations sur le system actuel d'instruction publique* (1800–1801); Joseph Lancaster, *Improvements in Education, as It Respects the Industrious Classes of the Community: Containing a Short Account of Its Present State, Hints Towards Its Improvements, and a Detail of Some Practical Experiments to That End* (1804), and Pierre Samuel du Pont de Nemours, *Sur l'education nationale dans le Etats Unis d'Amerique* (1800). See also Robert F. Haggard, "The Politics of Friendship: Du Pont, Jefferson, Madison, and the Physiocratic Dream for the New World," *Proceedings of the American Philosophical Society* 153, no. 4 (Dec. 2009): 419–40.

68. Daniel Pierce Thompson, "Talking with Jefferson: Two Accounts" (1841 and 1863), in Hayes, ed., *Jefferson in His Own Time*, p. 136.

69. Margaret Bayard Smith, "The Habitation and Philosophy of Virtue" (1809 and 1837), in Hayes, ed., *Jefferson in His Own Time*, p. 45.

70. Thomas Jefferson Randolph, "The Life and Death of Thomas Jefferson" (ca. 1857), in Hayes, ed., *Jefferson in His Own Time*, p. 162.

71. Francis Hall, "Account of a Visit to Monticello," 7–8 Jan. 1817, *PTJRS*, vol. 10, p. 644.

72. George Ticknor, "Account of [a] Visitor to Monticello," 4–7 Feb. 1815, *PTJRS*, vol. 8, p. 241.

73. Thomas Sully actually painted both a so-called bust portrait and a full-length portrait for the U.S. Military Academy. For a discussion of the portrait, see G. S. Wilson, *Jefferson on Display: Attire, Etiquette, and the Art of Presentation* (Charlottesville: University of Virginia Press, 2018), pp. 204–22.

74. Margaret Bayard Smith, "A Visit to Monticello," 29 July–2 Aug. 1809, *PTJRS*, vol. 1, p. 387.

75. Susan R. Stein, "Dining at Monticello: The Feast of Reason," in *Dining at Monticello: In Good Taste and Abundance*, ed. Damon Lee Fowler (Chapel Hill: University of North Carolina Press, 2005), p. 74.

76. Margaret Bayard Smith, "A Visit to Monticello," 29 July–2 Aug. 1809, *PTJRS*, vol. 1, p. 387.

77. George Ticknor, "Account of [a] Visitor to Monticello," 4–7 Feb. 1815, *PTJRS*, vol. 8, p. 241.

78. Webster, "Memorandum of Mr. Jefferson's Conversations," p. 94.

79. Annette Gordon-Reed and Peter S. Onuf, *"Most Blessed of the Patriarchs": Thomas Jefferson and the Empire of the Imagination* (New York: Liveright, 2017), p. 321.

80. TJ to Maria Cosway, 27 Dec. 1820, *PTJRS*, vol. 16, p. 498.

81. Birle and Francavilla, eds., *Thomas Jefferson's Granddaughter in Queen Victoria's England*, p. 180.

82. Cynthia A. Kierner, *Martha Jefferson Randolph, Daughter of Monticello: Her Life and Times* (Chapel Hill: University of North Carolina Press, 2012), pp. 301, 118, 7.

83. Annette Gordon-Reed presents the most compelling case for Jefferson's fathering of the children of Sally Hemings in *Thomas Jefferson and Sally Hemings: An American Controversy* (Charlottesville: University Press of Virginia, 1997). See also Fraser

Neiman, "Coincidence or Causal Connection? The Relationship between Thomas Jefferson's Visits to Monticello and Sally Hemming's Conception," *William and Mary Quarterly*, 3rd ser., 57, no. 1 (Jan. 2000): 198–210.

84. Gordon-Reed and Onuf, *"Most Blessed of the Patriarchs,"* p. 147.

85. JA to Joseph Ward, 8 Jan. 1810, Founders Online, https://founders.archives.gov /documents/Adams/99-02-02-5495. For discussion, see R. B. Bernstein, *The Education of John Adams* (Oxford: Oxford University Press, 2020), pp. 211–12.

86. "The Memoirs of Madison Hemings," reprinted in Gordon-Reed, *Thomas Jefferson and Sally Hemings*, pp. 245–48.

87. For an excellent discussion of Jefferson and debt, see Herbert E. Sloan, *Principle and Interest: Thomas Jefferson and the Problem of Debt* (Charlottesville: University of Virginia Press, 2001).

88. TJ to Martha Jefferson Randolph, 5 Jan. 1808, Founders Online, https://founders .archives.gov/documents/Jefferson/99-01-02-7138.

89. "Jefferson at Monticello: The Private Life of Thomas Jefferson by Rev. Hamilton Wilcox Pierson," in Bear, ed., *Jefferson at Monticello*, p. 51.

90. For a discussion of Jefferson's shifts between optimism and pessimism, see Maurizio Valsania, *The Limits of Optimism: Thomas Jefferson's Dualistic Enlightenment* (Charlottesville: University of Virginia Press, 2011).

91. George Ticknor, "Account of [a] Visitor to Monticello," 4–7 Feb. 1815, *PTJRS*, vol. 8, p. 241.

92. TJ to Thaddeus Kosciusko, 26 Feb. 1810, *PTJRS*, vol. 2, p. 259.

93. TJ to Governor John Tyler, 26 May 1810, *PTJRS*, vol. 2, p. 420.

94. TJ to François Barbé-Marbois, 5 Dec. 1783, *PTJ*, vol. 6, p. 374. I am grateful to Christine Coalwell McDonald for a draft chapter entitled "'His Scholars': Jefferson and the Education of the Randolph Women of Monticello." See also Billy Wayson, "'Considerably Different . . . for Her Sex': A Reading Plan for Martha Jefferson," in *The Libraries, Leadership, and Legacy of John Adams and Thomas Jefferson*, ed. Robert C. Baron and Conrad Edick Wright (Golden, Colo.: Fulcrum, 2010), pp. 133–59.

95. George Green Shackelford, *Thomas Jefferson's Travels in Europe, 1784–1789* (Baltimore: Johns Hopkins University Press, 1995), p. 13.

96. Birle and Francavilla, eds., *Thomas Jefferson's Granddaughter in Queen Victoria's England*, pp. xviii–xix.

97. TJ to Maria Jefferson, 20 Sept. 1785, *PTJ*, vol. 8, pp. 532–33.

98. TJ to John Banister Jr., 15 Oct. 1785, *PTJ*, vol. 8, p. 637.

99. TJ to Marquis de Chastellux, 7 June 1785, *PTJ*, vol. 8, p. 184.

100. TJ to Benjamin Waterhouse, 3 Mar. 1818, *PTJRS*, vol. 12, pp. 518–19.

2. Enlighten the People

1. For a discussion of Benjamin Rush's dreams, see Andrew Burstein, *Lincoln Dreamt He Died: The Midnight Visions of Remarkable Americans from Colonial Times to Freud* (New York: St. Martin's Press, 2013), pp. 6–10.

2. Benjamin Rush to John Adams, 17 Oct. 1809, *Letters of Benjamin Rush*, ed. Lyman

Henry Butterfield, 2 vols (Princeton, NJ: Princeton University Press, 1951), vol. 2, pp. 1021–22.

3. Ibid.

4. Benjamin Rush to John Adams, 17 Feb. 1812, ibid., pp. 1126–27.

5. John Adams to Benjamin Rush, 25 Oct. 1809, Founders Online, https://founders .archives.gov/documents/Adams/99-02-02-5454.

6. Benjamin Rush to TJ, 2 Jan. 1811, *PTJ*, vol. 3, p. 278.

7. Lyman Henry Butterfield, "The Dream of Benjamin Rush: The Reconciliation of John Adams and Thomas Jefferson," *Yale Review* 40, no. 2 (Dec. 1950): 312.

8. Juretta Jordan Heckscher, "'At All Times His Chosen Companions': Some Notes on What Books Meant to Thomas Jefferson," in *The Founding of Thomas Jefferson's University*, ed. John A. Ragosta, Peter S. Onuf, and Andrew J. O'Shaughnessy (Charlottesville: University of Virginia Press, 2019), p. 193.

9. John Adams to TJ, 23 Nov. 1819, *PTJRS*, vol. 15, p. 235.

10. TJ to John Adams, 28 Oct. 1813, *PTJRS*, vol. 6, p. 567.

11. John Adams to Timothy Pickering, 6 Aug. 1822, Founders Online, https://founders .archives.gov/documents/Adams/99-02-02-7674.

12. Pauline Maier, *American Scripture: Making the Declaration of Independence* (New York: Knopf, 1997).

13. John Adams to Benjamin Rush, 21 June 1811, Founders Online, https://founders .archives.gov/documents/Adams/99-02-02-5649.

14. John Adams to Timothy Pickering, 6 Aug. 1822, *Diary and Autobiography of John Adams*, ed. L. H. Butterfield, Leonard C. Faber, and Wendell D. Garrett, 4 vols. (New York: Atheneum, 1964), vol. 3, p. 336.

15. Timothy Pickering, *Observations Introductory to Reading the Declaration of Independence at Salem, July 4, 1823* (Salem, Mass.: Warwick Palfray, 1823); TJ to James Madison, 30 Aug. 1823, *PJMRS*, vol. 3, pp. 114–16; TJ to Henry Lee, 8 May 1825, Founders Online, https://founders.archives.gov/documents/Jefferson/98-01-02-5212.

16. John Adams to TJ, 22 June 1819; TJ to Adams, 9 July 1819, *PTJRS*, vol. 14, pp. 447– 519, 523.

17. John Adams to TJ, 26 May 1817, *PTJRS*, vol. 11, p. 384.

18. Wood, *Friends Divided*, pp. 9, 174, 192, 213, 217, 238, 302–3, 409, 414, 429, 430.

19. For Jefferson's interest in artistic representations of the American Revolution, see Wilson, *Jefferson on Display*, pp. 51–74. For his concern with historical accounts of the American Revolution, see Hannah Spahn, *Thomas Jefferson, Time, and History* (Charlottesville: University of Virginia Press, 2011), and Cogliano, *Thomas Jefferson*.

20. TJ to Maria Jefferson Eppes, 15 Feb. 1801, *PTJ*, vol. 32, p. 593.

21. Jefferson, *Notes on the State of Virginia*, p. 155.

22. TJ to George Wythe, 13 Aug. 1786, *PTJ*, vol. 10, pp. 244–45.

23. TJ to James Madison, 20 Dec. 1787, *PTJ*, vol. 12, p. 442.

24. TJ to Edward Carrington, 16 Jan. 1787, *PTJ*, vol. 11, p. 49.

25. TJ to Pierre Samuel du Pont de Nemours, 24 Apr. 1816, *PTJRS*, vol. 9, p. 702.

26. Benjamin Rush to Richard Price, 25 May 1786, Butterfield, ed., *Letters of Benjamin Rush*, vol. 1, p. 388.

27. Benjamin Rush, "A Plan for the Establishment of Public Schools and the Diffusion

of Knowledge in Pennsylvania," in Rudolph, ed., *Essays on Education in the Early Republic*, p. 9.

28. Noah Webster, *On the Education of Youth in America* (1788), in Rudolph, ed., *Essays on Education in the Early Republic*, p. 66.

29. Simeon Doggett, "A Discourse on Education, Delivered at the Dedication and Opening of Bristol Academy, the 18th Day of July, A.D. 1796," in Rudolph, ed., *Essays on Education in the Early Republic*, p. 156.

30. Brown, *Strength of a People*, p. 101.

31. Robert Coram, "Political Inquiries: To Which Is Added a Plan for the General Establishment of Schools Throughout the United States" (1791), in Rudolph, ed., *Essays on Education in the Early Republic*, p. 145.

32. TJ to George Wythe, 13 Aug. 1786, *PTJ*, vol. 10, p. 244.

33. Frederick Rudolph, *Curriculum: A History of the American Undergraduate Course of Study since 1636* (San Francisco: Jossey-Bass, 1977), p. 25.

34. J. G. A Pocock, "Virtues, Rights and Manners: A Model for Historians of Political Thought," in *Virtue, Commerce and History: Essays in Political Thought and History, Chiefly in the Eighteenth Century* (Cambridge: Cambridge University Press, 1985), pp. 37–51.

35. "Jefferson at Monticello," p. 86.

36. David Hackett Fisher, *Albion's Seed: Four British Folkways in America* (Oxford: Oxford University Press, 1989), p. 347.

37. TJ to George Wythe, 23 Aug. 1786, *PTJ*, vol. 10, p. 244.

38. TJ to John Adams, 28 Oct. 1813, *PTJRS*, vol. 6, p. 566.

39. "A Bill for the More General Diffusion of Knowledge," 18 June 1779, *PTJ*, vol. 2, pp. 526–27.

40. Jefferson, *Notes on the State of Virginia*, pp. 152–55.

41. Cremin, *American Education, the National Experience*, p. 159; Roy John Honeywell, *The Educational Work of Thomas Jefferson* (Cambridge, Mass.: Harvard University Press, 1931), p. 53.

42. TJ to Pierre Samuel du Pont de Nemours, 24 Apr. 1816, *PTJRS*, vol. 9, p. 701; Robert David Anderson, *European Universities from the Enlightenment to 1914* (Oxford: Oxford University Press, 2004), p. 28; Andy Green, *Education and State Formation: The Rise of Education Systems in England, France and the USA* (Basingstoke, U.K.: Palgrave Macmillan, 2002), p. 1.

43. "A Bill for the More General Diffusion of Knowledge," 18 June 1779, *PTJ*, vol. 2, p. 527; author's emphasis.

44. Jefferson, *Notes on the State of Virginia*, p. 154.

45. Pierre Samuel du Pont de Nemours, *National Education in the United States of America*, transl. Bessie Gardner Du Pont (Newark: University of Delaware Press, 1923).

46. John Hammond Moore, *Albemarle: Jefferson's County, 1727–1976* (Charlottesville: University Press of Virginia, 1976), p. 103.

47. Anderson, *European Universities from the Enlightenment to 1914*, pp. 256–57.

48. TJ to Martha Randolph, 17 May 1798, *PTJ*, vol. 30, p. 151.

49. TJ to Nathaniel Burwell, 14 Mar. 1818, *PTJRS*, vol. 12, pp. 533–35.

50. TJ to George Wythe, 13 Aug. 1786, *PTJRS*, vol. 10, pp. 244–45.

51. Alan Taylor, *Thomas Jefferson's Education* (New York: Norton, 2019), p. 3; Michael Zuckerman, "Founding Fathers: Franklin, Jefferson and the Educability of Americans," in *"The Good Education of Youth": Worlds of Learning in the Age of Franklin*, ed. John H. Pollack (New Castle, Del.: Oak Knoll Press, 2009), pp. 37–38; Rhys Isaac, *The Transformation of Virginia, 1740–1790* (New York: Norton, 1982), p. 295.

52. "A Bill for Amending the Constitution of the College of William and Mary, and Substituting More Certain Revenues for Its Support," *PTJ*, vol. 2, pp. 535–38.

53. Ibid., pp. 540–41.

54. Jefferson, *Notes on the State of Virginia*, p. 154.

55. *Autobiography of Thomas Jefferson*, p. 61.

56. "A Bill for Establishing a Public Library," 18 June 1779, *PTJ*, vol. 2, p. 544.

57. Mary Rawlings, ed., *Early Charlottesville: Recollections of James Alexander, 1828–1874* (Charlottesville, Va.: Albemarle County Historical Society, 1942), pp. 22–23; Michel D. Dickens, *Like an Evening Gone: A History of Christ Episcopal Church, Charlottesville, Virginia, upon the Occasion of Its 200th Anniversary* (Charlottesville, Va.: Christ Episcopal Church, 2020), p. 64.

58. Neil McDowell Shawen, "Thomas Jefferson and a 'National' University: The Hidden Agenda for Virginia," *Virginia Magazine of History and Biography* 92, no. 3 (July 1984): 313–15.

59. Thomas, *The Founders and the Idea of a National University*, pp. 70–71, 309–35.

60. TJ to George Washington, 23 Feb. 1795, *PTJ*, vol. 28, p. 276.

61. Thomas, *The Founders and the Idea of a National University*, p. 30; Shawen, "Thomas Jefferson and a 'National' University," pp. 316–25.

62. TJ to François d'Ivernois, 6 Feb. 1795, *PTJ*, vol. 28, p. 263.

63. Du Pont de Nemours, *National Education in the United States of America*.

64. Robert McDonald and Christine McDonald, "'Our Eye Steadily on the Whole System': Jefferson's Evolving Plans for a University for America," paper presented at "Education in the Early Republic and the Founding of the University of Virginia," Robert H. Smith International Center for Jefferson Studies and the American Philosophical Society, Montalto, Charlottesville, Va., 25 May 2018.

65. Thomas Jefferson, Sixth Annual Message to the Senate and House of Representatives of the United States, 2 Dec. 1806, *The Writings of Thomas Jefferson*, ed. Paul Leicester Ford, 10 vols. (New York: Putnam's Sons, 1892), vol. 10, pp. 301–2.

66. Thomas, *The Founders and the Idea of a National University*, pp. 70–71.

67. TJ to John Wayles Eppes, 24 Feb. 1806, *PTJ*, vol. 33, p. 393.

68. TJ to Joseph Priestley, 18 Jan. 1800, *PTJ*, vol. 31, pp. 320–21.

69. Theodore J. Crackel, *West Point: A Bicentennial History* (Lawrence: University of Kansas, 2002), pp. 45, 48, 50, 51.

70. Linda Kerber, *Federalists in Dissent: Imagery and Ideology in Jeffersonian America* (Ithaca, N.Y.: Cornell University Press, 1970), p. 76; Cremin, *American Education, the National Experience*, pp. 250, 81, 91, 92, 74, 75, 134.

71. TJ to Joseph Priestley, 21 Mar. 1801, *PTJ*, vol. 33, p. 393.

72. John Adams to TJ, 10 June 1813, *PTJRS*, vol. 6, p. 180.

73. Robson, "College Founding in the New Republic," pp. 334–35.

74. Samuel Eliot Morison, *Three Centuries of Harvard, 1636–1939* (Cambridge, Mass.: Harvard University Press, 1936), p. 186.

75. Robert A. McCaughey, *Stand Columbia: A History of Columbia University in the City of New York, 1754–2004* (New York: Columbia University Press, 2003), pp. 7, 58, 75.

76. Addis, *Jefferson's Vision for Education*, p. 28. See also John D. Wright, *Transylvania: Tutor to the West* (Lexington: University Press of Kentucky, 2015), p. 55.

77. Helen Duprey Bullock, *My Head and My Heart: A Little History of Thomas Jefferson and Maria Cosway* (New York: G. P. Putnam's Sons, 1945), pp. 149–50.

78. Harry R. Rubenstein and Barbara Clark Smith, "History of the Jefferson Bible," in *Thomas Jefferson, the Jefferson Bible: The Life and Morals of Jesus of Nazareth Extracted Textually from the Gospels in Greek, Latin, French, and English* (Washington, D.C.: Smithsonian Institution, 2011), p. 20.

79. Addis, *Jefferson's Vision for Education*, p. 28; Hellenbrand, *The Unfinished Revolution*, pp. 143–44.

80. TJ to Jeremiah Moore, 14 Aug. 1800, *PTJ*, vol. 32, p. 103.

81. TJ to Joseph Priestley, 21 Mar. 1801, *PTJ*, vol. 33, p. 394.

82. TJ to George Pictet, 5 Feb. 1803, *PTJ*, vol. 39, p. 456.

83. TJ to Littleton Waller Tazewell, 5 Jan. 1805, Founders Online, https://founders.archives.gov/documents/Jefferson/99-01-02-0958.

84. Ibid.

85. *President's Commission on Slavery and the University*, pp. 35, 15; Maurie D. McInnis, "Introduction," in McInnis and Nelson, eds., *Educated in Tyranny*, p. 4. The more polemical claims in both publications were reprinted in the *Atlantic, Washington Post, New York Times*, and *Guardian*.

86. TJ to John Taylor, 4 June 1798, *PTJ*, vol. 30, p. 387.

87. TJ to Littleton Waller Tazewell, 5 Jan. 1805, Founders Online, https://founders.archives.gov/documents/Jefferson/99-01-02-0958.

3. My Single Anxiety in the World

1. Ann Wright, "Afton: Mountain, Myth, Legend," *Virginia Living*, 20 Oct. 2014, http://www.virginialiving.com/culture/afton-mountain-myth-legend/ (no longer available).

2. [De Vere], "Mr. Jefferson's Pet," p. 819; George Tucker, *The Life of Thomas Jefferson, Third President of the United States, with Parts of His Correspondence Never Before Published, and Notices of His Opinions on Questions of Civil Government, National Policy and Constitutional Law*, 2 vols. (London: Charles Knight, 1837), vol. 2, p. 446.

3. My thanks to Ellen Hickman who shared drafts of her paper "Avoiding the 'Appearance of Dictating to the Assembly': Thomas Jefferson and the Establishment of the University of Virginia, 1818–1819," which she delivered at the annual meeting of the American Historical Association in 2016 and the Society of Historians of the Early American Republic in 2018. She has subsequently published the same in Ragosta, Onuf, and O'Shaughnessy, eds., *The Founding of Thomas Jefferson's University*, pp. 102–14.

4. James H. Broussard, *The Southern Federalists, 1800–1816* (Baton Rouge: Louisiana State University Press, 1978), pp. 166–67, 201, 372–73.

5. Archibald Stuart to TJ, 30 May 1818, *PTJRS*, vol. 13, pp. 179–81.

6. Addis, *Jefferson's Vision for Education*, p. 49.

7. "Proceedings of Rockfish Gap Meeting of the University of Virginia Commissioners," 1–4 Aug. 1818, *PTJRS*, vol. 13, pp. 182–84.

8. TJ to Joseph Cabell, 1 Jan. 1819, *PTJRS*, vol. 13, p. 536.

9. "Resolution of the Board of Visitors," 4 Aug. 1818, *PTJRS*, vol. 13, p. 183; Gene Crotty, *Jefferson's Legacy: His Own University* (N.p., 1998), pp. 49–52.

10. Herbert Baxter Adams, *Thomas Jefferson and the University of Virginia: With Authorized Sketches of Hampden-Sidney, Randolph-Macon, Emory-Henry, Roanoke, and Richmond Colleges, Washington and Lee University, and Virginia Military Institute* (Washington, D.C.: Government Printing Office, 1888), p. 89.

11. "The Rockfish Gap Report of the University of Virginia Commissioners," 4 Aug. 1818, *PTJRS*, vol. 13, pp. 211–14.

12. Ibid.

13. TJ to Martha Randolph Jefferson, 7, 14, 21 Aug. 1818, *PTJRS*, vol. 13, pp. 234, 242–43, 250; TJ to Francis Eppes, 11 Sept. 1818, *PTJRS*, vol. 13, p. 278; TJ to John Adams, 7 Oct. 1818, *PTJRS*, vol. 13, p. 309. My thanks to an exchange of emails in regard to the symptoms from members of the medical faculty: Bob Battle, Rebecca Dillingham, and Gerald Donowitz. Given the persistent symptoms, they thought a staph infection most likely but suggested other alternatives, including "hot tub folliculitis" caused by Pseudomonas aeruginosa.

14. TJ to Thomas Cooper, 16 Jan. 1814, *PTJRS*, vol. 7, pp. 454–55.

15. James Axtell, *Wisdom's Workshop: The Rise of the Modern University* (Princeton, N.J.: Princeton University Press, 2016), pp. 151, 156.

16. TJ to John Adams, 5 July 1814, *PTJRS*, vol. 7, pp. 636–42.

17. [De Vere], "Mr. Jefferson's Pet," pp. 815–16. This account claims the trustees were sitting on the lawn outside the Court House rather than at the Stone Tavern. It also collapses the sequence of events by claiming that Jefferson had mooted the idea of a college at his first meeting with the trustees of the Albemarle Academy.

18. Philip Alexander Bruce, *History of the University of Virginia, 1819–1919: The Lengthened Shadow of One-Man*, 5 vols. (New York: Macmillan, 1922), vol. 1, p. 121.

19. Dumas Malone, *The Sage of Monticello* (Charlottesville: University of Virginia Press, 1981), p. 244.

20. TJ to Peter Carr, 7 Sept. 1814, *PTJRS*, vol. 7, pp. 636–40.

21. Ibid.

22. Ibid.; Hellenbrand, *The Unfinished Revolution*, p. 138.

23. "Thomas Jefferson's Estimate and Plans for Albemarle Academy," [ca. 18 Nov. 1814], *PTJRS*, vol. 8, pp. 86–90. Architectural historian Joseph Lasala suggests that this was the "annexed plan" the board minutes mention for the meeting on 19 Aug. 1814.

24. "Thomas Jefferson's Draft Bill to Create Central College and Amend the 1796 Public Schools Act," [ca. Nov. 1814], *PTJRS*, vol. 8, pp. 90–94.

25. "Letters from the College of William and Mary, 1798–1801," *Virginia Magazine of History and Biography* 29, no. 2 (Apr. 1921): 130.

26. TJ to Joseph Cabell, 5 Jan. 1815, *PTJRS*, vol. 8, p. 183; John Shelton Patton, *Jefferson, Cabell and the University of Virginia* (New York: Neale, 1905), p. 26; Bruce, *History of the University of Virginia*, vol. 1, p. 132.

27. Bruce, *History of the University of Virginia*, vol. 1, pp. 147–48; Patton, *Jefferson, Cabell and the University of Virginia*, pp. 24–25; Taylor, *Thomas Jefferson's Education*, p. 171.

28. Joseph Cabell to TJ, 16 Apr. 1824, Founders Online, https://founders.archives.gov /documents/Jefferson/98-01-02-4194.

29. Joseph Cabell to TJ, 3 Dec. 1823, Founders Online, https://founders.archives.gov /documents/Jefferson/98-01-02-3901.

30. Honeywell, *The Educational Work of Thomas Jefferson*, p. 15.

31. Bruce, *History of the University of Virginia*, vol. 1, p. 139.

32. Ibid., vol. 3, pp. 194–95.

33. "Jefferson at Monticello," pp. 32–33. See also Thomas Jefferson, "Notes on the Siting of Central College," 18 July 1817, *PTJRS*, vol. 11, pp. 544–45.

34. *Richmond [Va.] Enquirer*, 17 Feb., 5 Sept. 1817, enclosed in Thomas Richie to TJ, 29 Aug. 1817, *PTJRS*, vol. 11, pp. 664–66.

35. Anonymous (Thomas Jefferson) to the *Richmond Enquirer*, [ca. 29] Aug. 1817, *PTJRS*, vol. 11, p. 664.

36. Addis, *Jefferson's Vision for Education*, p. 42.

37. Robert O. Woodburn, "An Historical Investigation of the Opposition to Jefferson's Educational Proposals in the Commonwealth of Virginia" (Ph.D. diss., American University, 1974), p. 95.

38. Douglas R. Egerton, "To the Tombs of the Capulets: Charles Fenton Mercer and Public Education in Virginia, 1817–1817," *Virginia Magazine of History and Biography* 93, no. 2 (Apr. 1985): 169–70.

39. For an extensive summary of the bill, see Joseph C. Cabell to TJ, 19 Feb. 1817, *PTJRS*, vol. 11, pp. 133–34, and "A Bill 'Providing for the Establishment of Primary Schools, Academies, Colleges and an University';—Passed by the House of Delegates the 18th, and Rejected by the *Senate* the 20th of February, 1817," in Virginia Assembly Literary Fund, *Sundry Documents on the Subject of a System of Public Education, for the State of Virginia* (Richmond, Va.: Ritchie, Trueheart, and Du-Val, 1817), pp. 32–34.

40. "A Bill 'Providing for the Establishment of Primary Schools, Academies, Colleges and an University,'" pp. 32–34; Egerton, "To the Tombs of the Capulets," pp. 155, 160–61.

41. Egerton, "To the Tombs of the Capulets," pp. 165–66.

42. "Bill for Establishing a System of Public Education," 24 Oct. 1817, *PTJRS*, vol. 12, pp. 114–27; TJ to Joseph Cabell, 24 Oct. 1817, *PTJRS*, vol. 12, p. 133.

43. TJ to José Corrêia, 25 Nov. 1817, *PTJRS*, vol. 12, p. 200.

44. "Bill for Establishing a System of Public Education," 24 Oct. 1817, *PTJRS*, vol. 12, p. 126.

45. TJ to José Corrêia da Serra, 25 Nov. 1817, *PTJRS*, vol. 12, pp. 200–202.

46. Zuckerman, "Founding Fathers," p. 39.

47. TJ to Joseph Cabell, 13 Jan. 1823, Founders Online, https://founders.archives.gov /documents/Jefferson/98-01-02-3266.

48. TJ to Joseph Cabell, 24 Oct. 1817, *PTJRS*, vol. 12, pp. 133–34; TJ to Charles Yancey, 6 Jan. 1816, *PTJRS*, vol. 9, pp. 328–31.

49. TJ to Joseph Cabell, 2 Feb. 1816, *PTJRS*, vol. 9, p. 437.

50. TJ to Joseph Cabell, 17 Jan. 1814, *PTJRS*, vol. 7, pp. 134–35.

51. "Proposals to Revise the Virginia Constitution," enclosed in TJ to "Henry Tomkinson" (Samuel Kerchaval), 12 July 1816, *PTJRS*, vol. 10, p. 225.

52. Hellenbrand, *The Unfinished Revolution*, p. 142.

53. TJ to Isaac Tiffany, 26 Aug. 1816, *PTJRS*, vol. 10, p. 349.

54. Suzanne W. Morse, "An International Perspective: The Education of Those Who Govern," in *Thomas Jefferson and the Education of a Citizen*, ed. James Gilreath (Honolulu, Hawaii: University Press of the Pacific, 2002), pp. 265–267.

55. TJ to Joseph Cabell, 2 Feb. 1816, *PTJRS*, vol. 9, p. 436.

56. Addis, *Jefferson's Vision for Education*, pp. 45, 46, 52.

57. Gary Hart, *Restoration of the Republic: The Jefferson Ideal in the 21st-Century* (Oxford: Oxford University Press, 2002).

58. "The Rockfish Gap Report of the University of Virginia Commissioners," 4 Aug. 1818, *PTJRS*, vol. 13, p. 211.

59. TJ to Joseph Cabell, 3 Feb. 1825, Founders Online, https://founders.archives.gov/documents/Jefferson/98-01-02-4932; "The Rockfish Gap Report of the University of Virginia Commissioners," 4 Aug. 1818, *PTJRS*, vol. 13, pp. 209–24.

60. Donald Robert Come, "The Influence of Princeton on Higher Education in the South before 1825," *William and Mary Quarterly*, 3rd ser., 2, no. 4 (Oct. 1945): 369–76.

61. Addis, *Jefferson's Vision for Education*, p. 53.

62. Brown, *Strength of a People*, p. 20.

63. TJ to James Madison, 7 July 1819, *PTJRS*, vol. 14, p. 514.

64. Taylor, *Thomas Jefferson's Education*, pp. 246, 247, 252; Moore, *Albemarle*, p. 106.

65. TJ to John Adams, 19 Jan. 1819, *PTJRS*, vol. 13, p. 589.

66. TJ to Joseph Cabell, 28 Jan. 1819, *PTJRS*, vol. 13, p. 607.

67. Joseph Cabell to TJ, 4 Feb. 1819, *PTJRS*, vol. 14, p. 13.

68. Axtell, *Wisdom's Workshop*, p. 130.

69. Du Pont de Nemours, *National Education in the United States of America*, pp. 121–22.

70. Burton J. Bledstein, *The Culture of Professionalism: The Middle Class and the Development of Higher Education in America* (New York: Norton, 1978), p. 291.

71. Bernard Bailyn, "Foundations," in Bailyn et al., eds., *Glimpses of the Harvard Past*, pp. 10–11.

72. Bledstein, *The Culture of Professionalism*, p. 223.

73. McCaughey, *Stand Columbia*, p. 137. This was a declaration of the then president. Other sources give 1912. Although the Massachusetts Constitutional Convention called Harvard "the University at Cambridge" in 1779–80, Harvard College did not adopt the term until long afterward. See Cheyney, *History of the University of Pennsylvania*, pp. 96, 164.

74. John S. Whitehead, *The Separation of College and State: Columbia, Dartmouth, Harvard, and Yale, 1776–1876* (New Haven, Conn.: Yale University Press, 1973), pp. 138–40.

75. Bailyn, "Why Kirkland Failed," p. 26; Whitehead, *The Separation of College and State*, pp. 3, 151–56, 186.

76. Hofstadter, *Academic Freedom in the Age of the College*, p. 246.

77. Caroline Winterer, *American Enlightenments: Pursuing Happiness in the Age of Reason* (New Haven, Conn.: Yale University Press, 2018), p. 238.

78. James Madison to TJ, 24 Feb. 1826, *PJMRS*, vol. 3, pp. 690–91.

79. TJ to Madison, 17 Feb. 1826, *PJMRS*, vol. 3, p. 688.

80. TJ to Joseph Cabell, 16 Feb. 1818, *PTJRS*, vol. 12, p. 470.

81. TJ to Joseph Cabell, 18 Dec. 1817, *PTJRS*, vol. 12, p. 263.

4. We Shall Have Every Religious Man
in Virginia against Us

1. "Masonic Report on the Central College Cornerstone Laying," 1 Dec. 1817, *PTJRS*, vol. 12, p. 68; TJ to David Knight, 5 Oct. 1817, *PTJRS*, vol. 12, p. 55.

2. "Masonic Report on the Central College Cornerstone Laying," 1 Dec. 1817, *PTJRS*, vol. 12, p. 68; "Jefferson at Monticello," p. 33.

3. "Jefferson at Monticello," p. 33.

4. Bruce, History *of the University of Virginia*, vol. 1, p. 188.

5. TJ to Martha Randolph, 31 Aug. 1817, *PTJRS*, vol. 11, pp. 669–70.

6. "Masonic Report on the Central College Cornerstone Laying," 1 Dec. 1817, *PTJRS*, vol. 12, p. 69.

7. "Alexander Garrett's Order of Ceremonies for the Central College Cornerstone Laying," [before 6 Oct. 1817], *PTJRS*, vol. 12, pp. 61–67; "John H. Cocke's Account of the Central College Cornerstone Laying," 5–6 Oct. 1817, *PTJRS*, vol. 12, pp. 60–61; "Masonic Report on the Central College Cornerstone Laying," 1 Dec. 1817, *PTJRS*, vol. 12, pp. 67–71.

8. John Adams to TJ, 26 May 1817, *PTJRS*, vol. 11, p. 383.

9. Isaac, *The Transformation of Virginia*, pp. 90–91, 295.

10. TJ to William Short, 8 Sept. 1823, Founders Online, https://founders.archives.gov/documents/Jefferson/98-01-02-3750.

11. Anonymous (TJ), *Richmond Enquirer*, ca. 29 Aug. 1817, *PTJRS*, vol. 11, p. 664, enclosed in TJ to Thomas Ritchie, 20 Aug. 1817, *PTJRS*, vol. 11, p. 667.

12. TJ to Joseph Cabell, 10 Sept. 1817, *PTJRS*, vol. 12, pp. 18–19.

13. TJ to Joseph Cabell, 16 Feb. 1818, *PTJRS*, vol. 12, pp. 469–71.

14. TJ to Joseph Cabell, 10 Sept. 1817, *PTJRS*, vol. 12, pp. 18–19.

15. TJ to Joseph Cabell, 9 Sept. 1817, *PTJRS*, vol. 12, pp. 15–16.

16. Birle and Francavilla, eds., *Thomas Jefferson's Granddaughter in Queen Victoria's England*, p. 35.

17. James Madison spelled the name of his home Montpellier.

18. James Madison to William T. Barry, 4 Aug. 1822, *PJMRS*, vol. 2, p. 555.

19. James Madison to William T. Barry, 4 Aug. 1822, *PJMRS*, vol. 2, p. 555.

20. TJ to Joseph Cabell, 26 Feb. 1818, *PTJRS*, vol. 21, p. 511.

21. James Madison to TJ, 24 Feb. 1826, *PJMRS*, vol. 3, p. 691.

22. James Monroe, Address to the Virginia Assembly, 6 Dec. 1801, *The Writings of James*

Monroe: Including a Collection of His Public and Private Papers and Correspondence Now for the First Time Printed, ed. Stanislaus Murray Hamilton, 7 vols. (New York: G. P. Putnam's Sons, 1898–1903), vol. 3, p. 306.

23. TJ to James Monroe, 18 Feb. 1808, Founders Online, https://founders.archives.gov /documents/Jefferson/99-01-02-7452.

24. Frank Edgar Grizzard Jr., "Documentary History of the Construction of the Buildings at the University of Virginia, 1817–1828" (Ph.D. diss., University of Virginia, 1996), p. 15.

25. Dumas Malone, *The Public Life of Thomas Cooper, 1783–1839* (1961; reprint New York: AMS Press, 1979), pp. 8, 259.

26. Adams, *Thomas Jefferson and the University of Virginia*, p. 109; Malone, *The Public Life of Thomas Cooper*, p. 172.

27. Joseph Cabell to TJ, 22 Feb. 1819, *PTJRS*, vol. 14, p. 55; Cabell to James Madison, 10 Mar. 1820, *PJMRS*, vol. 2, p. 273.

28. Patton, *Jefferson, Cabell and the University of Virginia*, pp. 69–71; Addis, *Jefferson's Vision for Education*, p. 74; David E. Swift, "Thomas Jefferson, John Holt Rice and Education in Virginia, 1815–25," *Journal of Presbyterian History* 49, no. 1 (Spring 1971): 32–33, 38.

29. Swift, "Thomas Jefferson, John Holt Rice and Education in Virginia," pp. 42, 43.

30. TJ to Thomas Cooper, 13 Mar. 1820, *PTJRS*, vol. 15, pp. 466–67.

31. Daniel P. Jordan, *Political Leadership in Jefferson's Virginia* (Charlottesville: University Press of Virginia, 1983), pp. 46, 48, 61.

32. TJ to Thomas Cooper, 13 Mar. 1820, *PTJRS*, vol. 15, p. 466.

33. Joseph Cabell to TJ, 29 Dec. 1817, *PTJRS*, vol. 12, p. 285.

34. Samuel Knox, "An Essay on the Best System of Liberal Education, Adapted to the Genius of the Government of the United States," in Rudolph, ed., *Essays on Education in the Early Republic*, p. 307.

35. Cheyney, *History of the University of Pennsylvania*, p. 34; Rush, "A Plan for the Establishment of Public Schools and the Diffusion of Knowledge in Pennsylvania," p. 4.

36. Webster, *On the Education of Youth in America*, p. 52.

37. TJ to William Short, 8 Sept. 1823, Founders Online, https://founders.archives.gov /documents/Jefferson/98-01-02-3750.

38. TJ to Samuel Henley, 14 Oct. 1785, *PTJ*, vol. 8, p. 634.

39. TJ to Elizabeth Trist, 25 Nov. 1816, *PTJRS*, vol. 16, p. 545.

40. Moore, *Albemarle*, pp. 27, 28, 30, 93; Rawlings, ed., *Early Charlottesville*, pp. 30, 63.

41. H. M. White, ed., *Revd. William S. White, D.D., and His Times (1800–1873): An Autobiography* (Richmond, Va.: Presbyterian Committee of Publication, 1891), p. 111.

42. Addis, *Jefferson's Vision for Education*, p. 46.

43. Joseph Cabell to TJ, 3, 28 Dec. 1817, *PTJRS*, vol. 12, pp. 233, 284.

44. Addis, *Jefferson's Vision for Education*, p. 46.

45. Taylor, *Thomas Jefferson's Education*, p. 94.

46. Jordan, *Political Leadership in Jefferson's Virginia*, pp. 42, 46.

47. Joseph Cabell to TJ, 5 Mar. 1815, *PTJRS*, vol. 8, p. 317; Joseph Cabell to TJ, 21 Dec.

1824, Founders Online, https://founders.archives.gov/documents/Jefferson/98-01 -02-4798.

48. TJ to Joseph Cabell, 16 May 1824, Founders Online, https://founders.archives.gov /documents/Jefferson/98-01-02-4271.

49. TJ to Joseph Cabell, 22 Dec. 1824, Founders Online, https://founders.archives.gov /documents/Jefferson/98-01-02-4804.

50. TJ to Joseph Cabell, 16 May 1824, Founders Online, https://founders.archives.gov /documents/Jefferson/98-01-02-4271.

51. For questions as to whether there was really much cohesion among the group, see F. Thornton Miller, "The Richmond Junto: The Secret All-Powerful Club: Or Myth," *Virginia Magazine of History and Biography* 99 (Jan. 1991): 63–80.

52. Scott Taylor Morris, "Southern Enlightenment: Reform and Progress in Jefferson's Virginia" (Ph.D. diss., Washington University, 2014), p. 94.

53. Kevin R. C. Gutzman, *Virginia's American Revolution: From Dominion to Republic, 1776–1840* (Lanham, Md.: Lexington Books, 2007), p. 88.

54. Jordan, *Political Leadership in Jefferson's Virginia*, p. 134.

55. Malone, *The Sage of Monticello*, p. 272; Gutzman, *Virginia's American Revolution*, pp. 154–55.

56. Gutzman, *Virginia's American Revolution*, p. 157.

57. Joseph Cabell to TJ, 21 Jan. 1819, *PTJRS*, vol. 13, p. 592.

58. TJ to Joseph Cabell, 31 Jan. 1821, *PTJRS*, vol. 16, pp. 587–88.

59. Joseph Cabell to John H. Cocke, 31 Mar. 1821, *PTJRS*, vol. 16, p. 588n.

60. William B. O'Neal, "Financing the Construction of the University of Virginia: Notes and Documents," *Magazine of the Albemarle County History* 23 (1964–65): 11.

61. Joseph Cabell to TJ, 6 Mar. 1822, Founders Online, https://founders.archives.gov /documents/Jefferson/98-01-02-2697.

62. Adams, *Thomas Jefferson and the University of Virginia*, p. 104.

63. TJ to Albert Gallatin, 15 Feb. 1818, *PTJRS*, vol. 12, pp. 467–68.

64. Adams, *Thomas Jefferson and the University of Virginia*, p. 103.

65. TJ to Joseph Cabell, 7 Feb. 1826, Founders Online, https://founders.archives.gov /documents/Jefferson/98-01-02-5882.

66. TJ to Joseph Cabell, 28 Dec. 1822, Founders Online, https://founders.archives.gov /documents/Jefferson/98-01-02-3238.

67. TJ to Joseph Cabell, 28 Jan. 1823, Founders Online, https://founders.archives.gov /documents/Jefferson/98-01-02-3290.

68. TJ to John Adams, 8 Jan. 1825, Founders Online, https://founders.archives.gov /documents/Jefferson/98-01-02-4845.

69. "Imported Professors, and Virginia Stump Orators and Presidents," *Central Gazette* (Charlottesville), 25 Dec. 1824, reprinted in *Letters of George Long*, ed. Thomas Fitzhugh (Charlottesville: The Library, University of Virginia, 1917), pp. 29, 30.

70. TJ to Thomas Cooper, 9 Mar. 1822, Founders Online, https://founders.archives.gov /documents/Jefferson/98-01-02-2705.

71. TJ to John Holmes, 22 Apr. 1820, Founders Online, https://founders.archives.gov /documents/Jefferson/98-01-02-1234.

72. TJ to Joseph Cabell, 28 Nov. 1820, *PTJRS*, vol. 16, p. 428.

73. TJ to Joseph Cabell, 22 Jan. 1820, *PTJRS*, vol. 15, pp. 344–45.

74. TJ to Joseph Cabell, 28 Nov. 1820, *PTJRS*, vol. 16, p. 429.

75. Jan Lewis, *The Pursuit of Happiness: Family and Values in Jefferson's Virginia* (Cambridge: Cambridge University Press, 2003), pp. 144–45.

76. Wood, *Friends Divided*, p. 18.

77. Joseph Eaton, *The Anglo-American Paper War: Debates about the New Republic, 1800–1825* (London: Palgrave, Macmillan, 2012), p. 74.

78. TJ to Thomas Ritchie, 21 Jan. 1816, *PTJRS*, vol. 9, pp. 378–80; "Essay on New England Religious Intolerance," as published in the *Richmond Enquirer*, 27 Jan. 1816, *PTJRS*, vol. 9, pp. 381–83.

79. Kemp P. Battle, *History of the University of North Carolina* (Raleigh, N.C.: Edwards and Broughton, 1907; reprint Spartanburg, S.C.: Reprint Company, 1974), p. 156.

80. Bruce, *History of the University of Virginia*, vol. 1, pp. 128–29.

81. TJ to John Holmes, 22 Apr. 1820, *PTJRS*, vol. 15, p. 550.

82. TJ to Hugh Nelson, 7 Feb. 1820, *PTJRS*, vol. 15, p. 382.

83. TJ to James Breckenridge, 15 Feb. 1821, *PTJRS*, vol. 16, p. 611.

84. TJ to John Taylor, 14 Feb. 1820, *PTJRS*, vol. 15, pp. 609–10.

85. Stuart Leibiger, "Thomas Jefferson and the Missouri Crisis: An Alternative Interpretation," *Journal of the Early Republic* 17, no. 1 (Spring 1977): 127.

86. Addis, *Jefferson's Vision for Education*, pp. 92–93.

87. TJ to Albert Gallatin, 26 Dec. 1820, *PTJRS*, vol. 16, p. 490.

88. For the complicity of both northern and southern universities in the system of slavery, see Craig Steven Wilder, *Ebony and Ivy: Race, Slavery, and the Troubled History of America's Universities* (New York: Bloomsbury Press, 2014).

89. Samuel Eliot Morison, *Three Centuries of Harvard*, pp. 254–55; Sven Beckert et al., "Harvard a Short History," in *Slavery and the University: History and Legacies*, ed. Leslie M. Harris, James T. Campbell, and Alfred L. Brophy (Athens: University of Georgia Press, 2019), p. 233.

90. Eaton, *The Anglo-American Paper War*, p. 88.

91. Thomas Jefferson Wertenbaker, *Princeton, 1756–1896* (Princeton, N.J.: Princeton University Press, 1996), pp. 265–66.

92. TJ to John Holmes, 22 Apr. 1820, *PTJRS*, vol. 15, p. 551.

93. TJ to William Branch Giles, 26 Dec. 1825, Founders Online, https://founders.archives.gov/documents/Jefferson/98-01-02-5771.

94. Broussard, *The Southern Federalists*, pp. 167, 168, 176–77, 372.

95. Susan Dunn, *Dominion of Memories: Jefferson, Madison and the Decline of Virginia* (New York: Basic, 2007), p. 141

96. J. Jefferson Looney, "'Merely Personal or Private, with Which We Have Nothing to Do': Thomas Jefferson's Autobiographical Writings," in *Thomas Jefferson's Lives: Biographers and the Battle for History*, ed. Robert M. S. McDonald (Charlottesville: University of Virginia Press, 2019), pp. 25–46.

97. Christine Leigh Heyrman, *Southern Cross: The Beginnings of the Bible Belt* (New York: Knopf, 1997), pp. 5, 9, 265.

98. William J. Cooper Jr., *Liberty and Slavery: Southern Politics to 1860* (New York: Knopf, 1983), p. 145.

99. TJ to William Cabell Rives, 28 Nov. 1819, *PTJRS*, vol. 15, p. 249.

100. Clyde A. Haulman, *Virginia and the Panic of 1819* (London: Pickering and Chatto, 2008), pp. 18, 58, 62, 64–65, 94, 150.

101. TJ to Spencer Roane, 9 Mar. 1821, Founders Online, https://founders.archives.gov /documents/Jefferson/98-01-02-1900.

102. TJ to Joseph Cabell, 7 Feb. 1826, Founders Online, https://founders.archives.gov /documents/Jefferson/98-01-02-5882.

103. Thomas Jefferson, "Thoughts on Lotteries," ca. 20 Jan. 1826, Founders Online, https://founders.archives.gov/documents/Jefferson/98-01-02-5845.

104. TJ to Joseph Cabell, 28 Dec. 1822, Founders Online, https://founders.archives.gov /documents/Jefferson/98-01-02-3238

105. Joseph Cabell to TJ, 25 May 1825, Founders Online, https://founders.archives.gov /documents/Jefferson/98-01-02-5255.

106. TJ to Spencer Roane, 9 Mar. 1821, Founders Online, https://founders.archives.gov /documents/Jefferson/98-01-02-1900.

5. The Academical Village

1. TJ to Maria Cosway, 13 Oct. 1786, *PTJ*, vol. 10, p. 459.

2. Jefferson spelled the name of the building four different ways: Halle au Bleds, Halle au Blé, Halle aux Blés, and Halle au Bled.

3. TJ to Maria Cosway, 12 Oct. 1786, *PTJ*, vol. 10, p. 445.

4. For the following discussion of the Delorme dome method, the author is indebted to the work of Douglas J. Harnsberger, "Elevating Jefferson's High Flying Visions for His Last Delorme Dome Project at the University of Virginia's Rotunda," in Ragosta, Onuf, and O'Shaughnessy, eds., *The Founding of Thomas Jefferson's University*, pp. 115–26.

5. Arthur Young, *Travels in France and Italy during the Years 1787, 1788 and 1789* (London, 1792), quoted in Howard C. Rice Jr., *Thomas Jefferson's Paris* (Princeton, N.J.: Princeton University Press, 1976), p. 18.

6. TJ to Benjamin Latrobe, 8 Sept. 1805, Founders Online, https://founders.archives .gov/documents/Jefferson/99-01-02-2353.

7. Maria Cosway to TJ, 7 Apr. 1819, *PTJRS*, vol. 14, p. 208.

8. TJ to Maria Cosway, 24 Oct. 1822, Founders Online, https://founders.archives.gov /documents/Jefferson/98-01-02-3111.

9. Maria Cosway to TJ, 18 June 1823, Founders Online, https://founders.archives.gov /documents/Jefferson/98-01-02-3580.

10. Margaret Bayard Smith, *A Winter in Washington; or, Memoirs of the Seymour Family*, 2 vols. (New York: Bliss and White, 1824), vol. 2, p. 261.

11. William Short to John H. Cocke, 8 July 1828, John Hartwell Cocke Papers, 1725–1949, Albert and Shirley Small Special Collections Library, University of Virginia, Charlottesville.

12. François Alexandre Frédéric, Duc de Rochefoucauld-Liancourt, [A Stock of Infor-

mation Not Inferior to That of Any Man] (1799), in Hayes, ed., *Jefferson in His Own Time*, p. 12.

13. TJ to David Harding, 20 Apr. 1824, Founders Online, https://founders.archives.gov /documents/Jefferson/98-01-02-4206.

14. TJ to Comtesse de Tessé, 20 Mar. 1787, *PTJ*, vol. 11, pp. 227–28.

15. TJ to Maria Cosway, 1 July 1787, *PTJ*, vol. 11, p. 519.

16. TJ to James Madison, 20 Sept. 1785, with Account Enclosed, *PTJ*, vol. 8, p. 535.

17. Jefferson, *Notes on the State of Virginia*, pp. 158–59.

18. TJ to John Page, 4 May 1786, *PTJ*, vol.9, pp. 444–46.

19. My thanks to Monticello Associate Curator Diane Ehrenpreis for informing me that this was not an architectural table that he commissioned or designed for writing and drafting. It is referred to today as an architect's table but that is a simplification. Ehrenpreis, personal communication, 9 June 2020.

20. TJ to David Rittenhouse, 19 Mar. 1791, *PTJ*, vol. 19, p. 584.

21. TJ to John Wayles Eppes, 18 Sept. 1812, *PTJRS*, vol. 5, pp. 348–49.

22. TJ to Benjamin Latrobe, 10 Oct. 1809, *PTJRS*, vol. 1, p. 595.

23. Jack McLaughlin, *Jefferson and Monticello: The Biography of a Builder* (New York: Henry Holt, 1988), p. 8.

24. Mark Wenger, "Thomas Jefferson, the College of William and Mary, and the University of Virginia," *Virginia Magazine of History and Biography* 103 (July 1995): 359; Patricia Sherwood and Joseph Michael Lasala, "Education and Architecture: The Evolution of the University of Virginia's Academical Village," in *Thomas Jefferson's Academical Village: The Creation of an Architectural Masterpiece*, ed. Richard Guy Wilson (Charlottesville: University Press of Virginia, 1993), p. 9.

25. TJ to Littleton Waller Tazewell, 5 Jan. 1805, Founders Online, https://founders .archives.gov/documents/Jefferson/99-01-02-0958.

26. TJ to Hugh White et al., 6 May 1810, *PTJRS*, vol. 2, pp. 365–66.

27. Benjamin Latrobe to TJ, 17 June 1817, *PTJRS*, vol. 11, p. 453.

28. Bruce Boucher, "Palladio in a Cold Climate: Jefferson, Latrobe, and the Lawn of the University of Virginia," *Annal di archtecturra* 24 (2012): 177.

29. Adams, *Thomas Jefferson and the University of Virginia*, pp. 18, 69; Bryan Little, "Cambridge and the Campus: An English Antecedent for the Lawn at the University of Virginia," *Virginia Magazine of History and Biography* 79 (1971): 190–201. My thanks to Eric Proebsting for information regarding the Oxford and Cambridge College plate series at Poplar Forest. For more information, see Jack Gary, "Ceramics and Jefferson's Aesthetic Philosophy," in *Jefferson's Poplar Forest: Unearthing a Virginia Plantation*, ed. Barbara Heath and Jack Gary (Gainesville: University of Florida Press, 2012), pp. 95–96, 99–100, and Gary, "Acquiring Transfer-Printed Ceramics for the Jefferson Household at Poplar Forest," in *Material Worlds: Archaeology, Consumption, and the Road to Modernity*, ed. Barbara J. Heath, Eleanor Breen, and Lori Lee (London: Routledge, 2017), pp. 109–15.

30. TJ to William Cabell Rives and Littleton Waller Tazewell, 25 Nov. 1825, Founders Online, https://founders.archives.gov/documents/Jefferson/98-01-02-5684.

31. TJ to William Thornton, 9 May 1817, *PTJRS*, vol. 11, p. 343; Ann Lucas, "Thomas Jefferson, Freart de Chambray, and the University of Virginia," *Annali di aritettura*

10, no. 31 (2019): 153. In addition to Leoni's edition of the architecture of Palladio, Jefferson consulted and annotated Charles Errard and Roland Fréart de Cham-bray's *Parallèle de l'architecture antique avec la moderne* (1766). These supplementary sources contained more accurate representations of classical buildings.

32. Richard Guy Wilson, "Inspirational Learning. The Architecture of the University of Virginia," *Journal of Thomas Jefferson's Life and Times* 1, no. 2 (Fall 2017): 20.

33. My thanks to architectural historian Joseph Michael Lasala, who suggested that the arrangement may have been purely by chance, owing to the books that Jeffer-son had available. This chapter owes much to his vetting. Lasala also notes that, in Jefferson's lists of the classical orders for both the university and for Monticello, he distinguished between the "variety" orders, rather than between ancient/classical and modern/neoclassical. As Lasala writes, "For example, he [Jefferson] indicates that there are three varieties of Doric order (at least within his personal inventory of the finest examples). These are Doric without mutules (Palladio), Doric with mutules (Temple of Albano), and Doric with dentils (Baths of Diocletian). When he later repeats these same examples of the Doric order at the university, he once again differentiates them by their 'variety of style' on his list," which Lasala calls the "Rosetta Stone" of the Lawn. Lasala, personal communication, 30 June 2020.

34. Louis P. Nelson and Maurie D. McInnis, "The Landscape of Slavery," in McInnis and Nelson, eds., *Educated in Tyranny*, p. 69.

35. TJ to George Ticknor, 24 Dec. 1819, *PTJRS*, vol. 15, p. 302.

36. *The Autobiographical Ana of Robley Dunglison*, p. 23; Elizabeth Chew, "Inhabiting the Great Man's House: Women and Space at Monticello," in *Structures and Sub-jectivity: Attending to Early Modern Women*, ed. Joan E. Hartman and Adele Seefe (Newark: University of Delaware Press, 2007), pp. 223–53.

37. Bledstein, *The Culture of Professionalism*, p. 230.

38. "Minutes of Central College Board of Visitors," 7 Oct. 1817, *PTJRS*, vol. 12, p. 76.

39. Swift, "Thomas Jefferson, John Holt Rice and Education in Virginia," p. 50; Robert F. Pace, *Halls of Honor: College Men in the Old South* (Baton Rouge: Louisiana State University Press, 2004), p. 45.

40. TJ to Joseph Cabell, 24 Oct. 1817, *PTJRS*, vol. 12, pp. 133–34.

41. Edwin M. Betts, "Goundplan and Prints of the University of Virginia, 1822–1826," *Proceedings of the American Philosophical Society* 90, no. 2 (May 1946): 81–90.

42. TJ to Charles Yancey, 23 July 1821, Founders Online, https://founders.archives.gov/documents/Jefferson/98-01-02-2194.

43. TJ to Benjamin Latrobe, 11 May 1815, *PTJRS*, vol. 8, p. 479.

44. William B. O'Neal, "The Workmen at the University of Virginia 1817–1826," *Maga-zine of the Albemarle Country History* 17 (1958–59): 12.

45. Grizzard, "Documentary History of the Construction of the Buildings at the Uni-versity of Virginia," p. 68.

46. William L. Beiswanger, "Jefferson and the Art of Roofing," *Chronicle of the Early American Industries Association* 58, no. 1 (Mar. 2005): 18–25; Robert Self, "Thomas Jefferson's Plank-Kilns," *Chronicle of the Early American Industries Association* 58, no. 1 (Mar. 2005): 26–30.

47. Robert Self and Lucia Stanton, "'Memdm of Carpenter's Tools': Woodworking at

Monticello," *Chronicle of the Early American Industries Association* 58, no. 1 (Mar. 2005): 12–14; See also Robert Self, "Recreating Jefferson's Tool List: A Collector's Challenge," *Chronicle of the Early American Industries Association* 58, no. 1 (Mar. 2005): 14–18. Jefferson compiled a list of Dinsmore's tools; see "James Dinsmore's List of Thomas Jefferson's Tools," 15 Apr. 1809, *PTJRS*, vol. 1, p. 135.

48. "Memoirs of a Monticello Slave," p. 18.

49. Gordon-Reed and Onuf, *"Most Blessed of the Patriarchs,"* p. 74.

50. Chastellux, "A Conversation Always Varied and Interesting," p. 2.

51. Thompson, "Talking with Jefferson," p. 135.

52. TJ to Absalom H. Brooks, 28 July 1822, Founders Online, https://founders.archives .gov/documents/Jefferson/98-01-02-2972.

53. Moore, *Albemarle*, pp. 100, 122–23.

54. Arthur Brockenbrough to John Hartwell Cocke, 7, 13 Apr. 1825, Grizzard, "Documentary History of the Construction of the Buildings at the University of Virginia," p. 134.

55. David Watson to John Hartwell Cocke, 8 Mar. 1819, Cocke Family Papers, Albert and Shirley Small Special Collections Library.

56. William Short to John H. Cocke, 8 July 1828, John Hartwell Cocke Papers.

57. TJ to James Madison, 7 Apr. 1826, Founders Online, https://founders.archives.gov /documents/Madison/99-02-02-0654.

58. TJ to William Short, 17 Oct. 1822, Founders Online, https://founders.archives.gov /documents/Jefferson/98-01-02-3103.

59. TJ to Joseph Cabell, 28 Dec. 1822, Founders Online, https://founders.archives.gov /documents/Jefferson/98-01-02-3238.

60. TJ to Albert Gallatin, 29 Oct. 1822, Founders Online, https://founders.archives.gov /documents/Jefferson/98-01-02-3123.

61. Joseph Cabell to TJ, 23 Dec. 1822, Founders Online, https://founders.archives.gov /documents/Jefferson/98-01-02-3230.

62. Chapman Johnson to John Hartwell Cocke, 30 Mar. 1823, Grizzard, "Documentary History of the Construction of the Buildings at the University of Virginia," pp. 53–54. See also Joseph Cabell to TJ, 10 Mar. 1822, Founders Online, https://founders .archives.gov/documents/Jefferson/98-01-02-2707.

63. Bruce, *History of the University of Virginia*, vol. 1, p. 287; Grizzard, "Documentary History of the Construction of the Buildings at the University of Virginia," pp. 107–8.

64. Alexander Garrett to John H. Cocke, 18 Feb. 1823, John Hartwell Cocke Papers; Grizzard, "Documentary History of the Construction of the Buildings at the University of Virginia," p. 112.

65. Joseph Michael Lasala, "A Forensic Look at Thomas Jefferson's Architectural Drawings," *Palladiana* 10, no. 2 (Spring 2016): 2–5.

66. Boucher, "Palladio in a Cold Climate," p. 177.

67. Richard Guy Wilson, "Jefferson's Lawn: Perceptions, Interpretations, Meanings," in Wilson, ed., *Thomas Jefferson's Academical Village*, p. 71.

68. TJ to James Madison, 24 Sept. 1824, Founders Online, https://founders.archives .gov/documents/Madison/04-03-02-0385. See Endrina Tay, "Forming a Body of a

Library Based on the 'Illimitable Freedom of the Human Mind,'" in Ragosta, Onuf, and O'Shaughnessy, eds., *The Founding of Thomas Jefferson's University*, pp. 208–23. Tay notes that the original desiderata list and subsequent revisions do not survive, which she suggests may have resulted from their being given to the university and destroyed in the Rotunda fire of 1896 (221n34). However, we do have a fair copy of Jefferson's desiderata list compiled by Nicholas P. Trist, dated 2 June 1815.

69. TJ to William Hilliard, 31 Aug. 1825, Founders Online, https://founders.archives .gov/documents/Jefferson/98-01-02-5504.

70. Moore, *Albemarle*, p. 137. At Princeton, the library contained seven thousand volumes in 1816 and did not increase significantly again until the mid-nineteenth century. See James McLachlan, "The *Choice of Hercules*: American Student Societies in the Early 19th Century," in *The University in Society*, ed. Lawrence Stone, 3 vols. (Princeton, N.J.: Princeton University Press, 1974), vol. 2, p. 470.

71. Henry Clemons, *University of Virginia Library, 1825–1950: Story of a Jeffersonian Foundation* (Charlottesville: University of Virginia Press, 1954), pp. 5–6.

72. TJ to William Wertenbaker, 30 Jan. 1826, Founders Online, https://founders .archives.gov/documents/Jefferson/98-01-02-5868.

73. Clemons, *University of Virginia Library*, p. 91; Bruce, *History of the University of Virginia*, vol. 3, p. 105; Michael O'Brien, *Intellectual Life and the American South, 1820–1860* (Chapel Hill: University of North Carolina Press, 2010), p. 123.

74. The idea is discussed in Harnsberger, "Elevating Jefferson's High Flying Visions for His Last Delorme Dome Project," pp. 115–25.

75. Arthur Brockenbrough to TJ, 6 June 1825, Founders Online, https://founders .archives.gov/documents/Jefferson/98-01-02-5283.

76. Martha Jefferson Randolph to Nicholas P. W. Trist, 4 Apr. 1824, Grizzard, "Documentary History of the Construction of the Buildings at the University of Virginia," p. 121.

77. Levasseur, *Lafayette in America*, p. 240.

78. Jane Blair Cary Smith, "'The Carysbrook Memoir': The Carys of Virginia," ca. 1864, 69–78, accession no. 1378, Albert and Shirley Small Special Collections Library; *Central Gazette* (Richmond, Va.), 10 Nov. 1824, reprinted in *Richmond Enquirer*, 16 Nov. 1824.

79. Randolph, *The Domestic Life of Thomas Jefferson*, pp. 390–91; Thomas Jefferson Randolph's Memoirs, Randolph Family Papers, Accession no. 8937, Albert and Shirley Small Special Collections Library; *Central Gazette*, 10 Nov. 1824, reprinted in *Richmond Enquirer*, 16 Nov. 1824.

80. Peter Fossett, "ONCE THE SLAVE OF THOMAS JEFFERSON—The Rev. Mr. Fossett, of Cincinnati, Recalls the Days When Men Came from the Ends of the Earth to Consult 'the Sage of Monticello,'" *New York World*, 30 Jan. 1898.

81. Stanton, *"Those Who Labor for My Happiness,"* p. 33.

82. Levasseur, *Lafayette in America*, p. 241.

83. Thomas Jefferson, Address at the University of Virginia, 5 Nov. 1824, Rotunda Collections, University of Virginia Press, https://rotunda.upress.virginia.edu/founders /default.xqy?keys=FOEA-print-04-02-02-4662.

84. Levasseur, *Lafayette in America*, p. 241.

85. TJ to John Wayles Eppes, 30 June 1820, *PTJRS*, vol. 16, p. 67.

86. TJ to William Short, 24 Nov. 1821, Founders Online, https://founders.archives.gov /documents/Jefferson/98-01-02-2445.

87. Edward Stanley, *Journal of a Tour in America, 1824–25* (N.p., 1930), p. 153.

88. Margaret Bayard Smith to Anna Boyd and Jane Bayard Kirkpatrick, 12 Aug. 1828, Margaret Bayard Smith Papers, Library of Congress, Washington, D.C.; Grizzard, "Documentary History of the Construction of the Buildings at the University of Virginia," p. 165.

89. TJ to Joseph Cabell, 28 Dec. 1822, Founders Online, https://founders.archives.gov /documents/Jefferson/98-01-02-3238.

6. Useful Knowledge

1. George Long to Francis Walker Gilmer, 25 Jan. 1825, Fitzhugh, ed., *Letters of George Long*, p. 22.

2. George Long to Henry Tutwiler, 30 May 1875, ibid., p. 22; *The Autobiographical Ana of Robley Dunglison*, p. 20.

3. George Long to Francis Walker Gilmer, 24 Aug. 1824, Fitzhugh, ed., *Letters of George Long*, pp. 12–15.

4. George Long to Francis Walker Gilmer, 2 Sept. 1824, ibid., pp. 17–18.

5. George Long to Henry Tutwiler, 30 May 1875, ibid., p. 23.

6. TJ to Joseph Cabell, 22 Dec. 1824, Founders Online, https://founders.archives.gov /documents/Jefferson/98-01-02-4804.

7. George Long to Francis Walker Gilmer, 25 Jan. 1825, Fitzhugh, ed., *Letters of George Long*, pp. 22–23.

8. George Long to Henry Tutwiler, 30 May 1875, ibid., pp. 24, 25; Long to Tutwiler, 29 Apr. 1875, ibid., p. 60.

9. *Alumni Bulletin of the University of Virginia* 1, no. 1 (May 1894): 1.

10. Editor's review of "The History of the University of Virginia," *Alumni Bulletin of the University of Virginia*, 3rd ser., 16, no. 1 (January 1923): 69.

11. The biographical information on George Long in this and subsequent paragraphs comes from W. W. Wroth, revised by D. W. Martin, "George Long 1800 to 1879," *Oxford Dictionary of National Biography* (Oxford: Oxford University Press, 2004), https://www.oxforddnb.com/view/10.1093/ref:odnb/9780198614128.001.0001 /odnb-9780198614128-e-16967.

12. *Encyclopaedia Britannica*, 9th edition (1875–89), s.v., "Long, George."

13. George Long to Henry Tutwiler, 29 Apr. 1875, Fitzhugh, ed., *Letters of George Long*, p. 60.

14. George Long to Henry Tutwiler, 30 May 1875, ibid., pp. 21, 28.

15. George Long to Francis Walker Gilmer, 25 Jan. 1825, ibid., p. 22.

16. *The Autobiographical Ana of Robley Dunglison*, p. 21. See also Ellen Hickman, "Robley Dunglison (1798–1869), Encyclopedia Virginia: Virginia Humanities, https://www.encyclopediavirginia.org/Dunglison_Robley_1798–1869.

17. *The Autobiographical Ana of Robley Dunglison*, p. 22.

18. Ibid.

19. Ibid., pp. 28, 25.

20. Chad Wellmon, *Organizing Enlightenment: Information Overload and the Invention of the Modern Research University* (Baltimore: Johns Hopkins University Press, 2016), pp. 221–22.

21. TJ to Joseph Cabell, 3 Feb. 1824, Founders Online, https://founders.archives.gov /documents/Jefferson/98-01-02-4018.

22. Cheyney, *History of the University of Pennsylvania*, pp. 214–15. Cheyney believed that Jefferson's view of the University of Pennsylvania was connected with the appointment of a university trustee to the faculty of medicine.

23. TJ to Joseph Cabell, 3 Feb. 1824, Founders Online, https://founders.archives.gov /documents/Jefferson/98-01-02-4018.

24. *The Autobiographical Ana of Robley Dunglison*, p. 62.

25. Bledstein, *The Culture of Professionalism*, pp. 170, 269.

26. Lieve Gevers and Louis Vox, "Student Movements," in *A History of the University in Europe*, ed. H. De Ridder-Symoens, 4 vols. (Cambridge: Cambridge University Press, 1996), vol. 2, p. 279. For the emergence of an academic culture, see Margaret Sumner, *Collegiate Republic: Cultivating an Ideal Society in Early America* (Charlottesville: University of Virginia Press, 2014).

27. Morison, *Three Centuries of Harvard*, p. 42; McCaughey, *Stand Columbia*, pp. 58–59.

28. Bledstein, *The Culture of Professionalism*, p. 274.

29. Crotty, *Jefferson's Legacy*, pp. 42–43.

30. George Tucker, "Education in Virginia," *Quarterly Journal* 4 (1832): 58, 59.

31. TJ to Joseph Priestley, 18 Jan. 1800, *PTJ*, vol. 31, pp. 319–22.

32. TJ to Benjamin Latrobe, 12 June 1817, *PTJRS*, vol. 11, p. 432.

33. TJ to John Adams, 9 July 1819, *PTJRS*, vol. 14, p. 525.

34. John Adams to TJ, 22 Jan. 1825, Founders Online, https://founders.archives.gov /documents/Adams/99-02-02-7939.

35. Axtell, *Wisdom's Workshop*, p. 181.

36. Kelley, *Yale*, pp. 129, 136–37.

37. TJ to Richard Rush, 26 Apr. 1824, Founders Online, https://founders.archives.gov /documents/Jefferson/98-01-02-4218.

38. Taylor, *Thomas Jefferson's Education*, pp. 48–49, 131.

39. Tipton R. Snavely, *The Department of Economics at the University of Virginia, 1825–1956* (Charlottesville: University Press of Virginia, 1967), p. 20; Robert Colin McLean, *George Tucker: Moral Philosopher and Man of Letters* (Chapel Hill: University of North Carolina Press, 1961), p. 95.

40. Fieser, ed., *Life of George Tucker*, pp. 71, 65.

41. Jefferson used the word "school" for a department and the word "department" for what we would now regard as a school or college within the university.

42. McCaughey, *Stand Columbia*, pp. 63, 127.

43. TJ to Thomas Cooper, 7 Oct. 1814, *PTJRS*, vol. 8, p. 12.

44. [Everett], "Proceedings and Report of the Commissioners for the University of Virginia," pp. 120, 124.

45. TJ to Littleton Waller Tazewell, 5 Jan. 1805, Founders Online, https://founders .archives.gov/documents/Jefferson/99-01-02-0958.

46. Rudolph, *Curriculum*, p. 104.

47. TJ to Andrew Kean, 11 Nov. 1818, *PTJRS*, vol. 13, p. 388.

48. TJ to Robley Dunglison, 26 Nov. 1825, Founders Online, https://founders.archives.gov /documents/Jefferson/98-01-02-5687; TJ to Dr. Caspar Wistar, 21 June 1807, Founders Online, https://founders.archives.gov/documents/Jefferson/99-01-02-5789.

49. TJ to Andrew Kean, 11 Nov. 1818, *PTJRS*, vol. 13, p. 388.

50. TJ to William Green Munford, 18 June 1799, *PTJ*, vol. 31, p. 128.

51. He described his philosophy in most detail in TJ to Vine Utley, 21 Mar. 1819, *PTJRS*, vol. 14, pp. 156–58.

52. *The Autobiographical Ana of Robley Dunglison*, p. 26.

53. *The Jefferson-Dunglison Letters*, ed. John Dorsey (Charlottesville: University Press of Virginia, 1960), p. 78.

54. McCaughey, *Stand Columbia*, p. 63.

55. Dorsey, ed., *The Jefferson-Dunglison Letters*, p. 4.

56. Robert S. Gibson, "Medical Education in the Nineteenth Century: Jefferson and Flexner Revisited," in Ragosta, Onuf, and O'Shaughnessy, eds., *The Founding of Thomas Jefferson's University*, pp. 151–90. Thanks to the research of Professor Robert H. S. Gibson, the early history of the medical school is the best studied of any department at the university. He has a book manuscript in progress, which he kindly shared with the author.

57. John Bernard, "Recollections of President Jefferson" (1828), in Hayes, ed., *Jefferson in His Own Time*, p. 112.

58. TJ to Dr. John Emmet, 2 May 1826, Founders Online, https://founders.archives.gov /documents/Jefferson/98-01-02-6087.

59. Jefferson, *Notes on the State of Virginia*, pp. 147–48.

60. TJ to George Ticknor, 16 June 1823, Founders Online, https://founders.archives.gov /documents/Jefferson/98-01-02-3575.

61. Peter Thompson, "'Judicious Neology': The Imperative of Paternalism in Thomas Jefferson's Linguistic Studies," *Early American Studies* 1, no. 2 (Fall 2003): 187–224; Adams, *Thomas Jefferson and the University of Virginia*, pp. 43, 113. For a discussion of the racial overtones, see Reginald Horsman, "Origins of Racial Anglo-Saxonism in Britain before 1850," *Journal of the History of Ideas* 37, no. 3 (July–Sept. 1976): 387–410.

62. TJ to John Brazer, 24 Aug. 1819, *PTJRS*, vol. 14, pp. 629–31.

63. TJ to Joseph Priestley, 27 Jan. 1800, *PTJ*, vol. 31, pp. 339–41.

64. TJ to John Brazer, 24 Aug. 1819, *PTJRS*, vol. 14, p. 629.

65. Robert David Anderson, *British Universities: Past and Present* (London: Hambledon Continuum, 2006), p. 4.

66. "Jefferson's Hints to Americans Travelling in Europe," 16 June 1788, *PTJ*, vol. 13, p. 269.

67. Geiger, *History of American Higher Education*, pp. 26–28.

68. Fieser, ed., *Life of George Tucker*, p. 72.

69. L. W. B. Brockliss, "The European University in the Age of Revolution, 1789–1850,"

in *The History of the University of Oxford*, ed. M. G. Brock and M. C. Curthoys, 8 vols. (Oxford: Oxford University Press, 1997), vol. 6, p. 108.

70. Mark Wenger, "Thomas Jefferson, the College of William and Mary, and the University of Virginia," *Virginia Magazine of History and Biography* 103 (July 1995): 352, 368.

71. [Robley Dunglison], "College Instruction and Discipline," *American Quarterly Review* 9 (June 1831): 292.

72. Cheyney, *History of the University of Pennsylvania*, pp. 34, 177. Penn had a provost but the role of the office was very similar to that of the chairman of the faculty at the University of Virginia.

73. TJ to William Roscoe, 27 Dec. 1820, *PTJRS*, vol. 16, p. 499.

74. Richard Hofstadter, *Anti-Intellectualism in American Life* (1963; reprint New York: Vintage Books, 2012), pp. 240–41.

75. TJ to James Madison, 17 Feb. 1826, *PJMRS*, vol. 3, p. 687.

76. *Autobiography of Thomas Jefferson*, p. 58.

77. TJ to John Tyler, 26 May 1810, *PTJRS*, vol. 2, p. 420.

78. TJ to James Madison, 1 Feb. 1825, *PJMRS*, vol. 3, p. 47.

79. James P. Ambuske and Randall Flaherty, "Reading Law in the Early Republic: Legal Education in the Age of Jefferson," in Ragosta, Onuf, and O'Shaughnessy, eds., *The Founding of Thomas Jefferson's University*, pp. 225, 226, 234, 237–44.

80. TJ to James Madison, 17 Feb. 1826, *PJMRS*, vol. 3, p. 687.

81. TJ to Judge John Tyler, 17 June 1812, *PTJRS*, vol. 5, p. 136; TJ to Horatio G. Spafford, 17 Mar. 1814, *PTJRS*, vol. 7, p. 249.

82. TJ to John Minor, 30 Aug. 1814, *PTJRS*, vol. 7, pp. 625–31; TJ to John Garland Jefferson, 11 June 1790, *PTJ*, vol. 16, p. 480.

83. TJ to James Madison, 15 Oct. 1810, *PTJRS*, vol. 3, p. 165; TJ to Madison, 1 Feb. 1825, *PJMRS*, vol. 3, p. 47.

84. James Mercer Garnett, Paul Brandon Barringer, and Rosewall Page, eds., *University of Virginia; Its History, Influence, Equipment and Characteristics, with Biographical Sketches and Portraits of Founders, Benefactors, Officers and Alumni*, 2 vols. (New York: Lewis, 1904), vol. 1, p. 348.

85. Richard E. Dixon, "Mr. Jefferson's Law School," *Journal of Thomas Jefferson's Life and Times* 1, no. 2 (Fall 2017): 56.

86. Fieser, ed., *Life of George Tucker*, p. 64.

87. McLean, *George Tucker*, p. 23.

88. Jordan, *Political Leadership in Jefferson's Virginia*, p. 83.

89. As a professor at the University of Virginia, George Tucker also wrote *Jeffersonia; Hume's Political Principles* (1829), *Premises and Conclusions—Cause and Effect* (1829), *Contemporary Fame* (1830), *Metaphysics and the Metaphysics of Language* (1830), *Etymology* (1830), *Natural Language* (1830), *The Principle of Imitation* (1830), *The Theatre and of the Pleasure Derived from Tragedy* (1830), *Discourse on the Progress of Philosophy* (1835), and *Discourse on American Literature* (1837).

90. Eugene D. Genovese, *The Slaveholders' Dilemma: Freedom and Progress in Southern Conservative Thought, 1820–1860* (Columbia: University of South Carolina Press, 1992), p. 16.

91. Fieser, ed., *Life of George Tucker*, p. 70; Christine Coalwell McDonald and Robert M. S. McDonald, "'More Loved . . . and More Hated': George Tucker on Thomas Jefferson," in McDonald, ed., *Thomas Jefferson's Lives*, pp. 47–62.

92. Fieser, ed., *Life of George Tucker*, pp. 35, 71, 70.

93. James Madison to TJ, 8 Feb. 1825, *PJMRS*, vol. 3, p. 471.

94. TJ to Joseph Cabell, 3 Feb. 1825, Founders Online, https://founders.archives.gov /documents/Jefferson/98-01-02-4932.

95. Jennings Wagoner, *Jefferson and Education* (Chapel Hill: University of North Carolina Press, 2004), p. 138.

96. Fieser, ed., *Life of George Tucker*, p. xiii.

97. Robson, "College Founding in the New Republic," p. 327.

98. Battle, *History of the University of North Carolina*, p. 158.

99. Anderson, *European Universities from the Enlightenment to 1914*, pp. 45–46.

100. Fieser, ed., *Life of George Tucker*, p. 83.

101. Long, *Thomas Jefferson and George Ticknor*, p. 17.

7. A Wall of Separation

1. TJ to JA, 12 Oct. 1813, *PTJRS*, vol. 6, p. 546.

2. TJ to Benjamin Rush, 21 Apr. 1803, *PTJ*, vol. 40, p. 252. The letter enclosed "The Syllabus of an Estimate of the Merit of the Doctrines of Jesus, Compared with Those of Others," *PTJ*, vol. 40, pp. 253–55.

3. TJ to Joseph Priestley, 29 Jan. 1804, *PTJ*, vol. 42, p. 368.

4. TJ to William Short, 31 Oct. 1819, *PTJ*, vol. 15, p. 164.

5. TJ to John Adams, 12 Oct. 1813, *PTJRS*, vol. 6, p. 549.

6. TJ to William Short, 31 Oct. 1819, *PTJRS*, vol. 15, p. 164.

7. TJ to Francis Adrian Van der Kamp, 25 Apr. 1816, *PTJRS*, vol. 9, p. 703; Rubenstein and Smith, "History of the Jefferson Bible," p. 28.

8. Rubenstein and Smith, "History of the Jefferson Bible," p. 34. During the restoration and subsequent exhibition of the volume in 2011, the Smithsonian produced a collectible facsimile edition with essays by staff members. The original remains in the collection of the Smithsonian's National Museum of American History.

9. TJ to Ezra Stiles Ely, 25 June 1819, *PTJRS*, vol. 14, p. 471.

10. TJ to JA, 15 June 1813, *PTJRS*, vol. 6, p. 193; Robert M. Healey, *Jefferson on Religion in Public Education* (New Haven, Conn.: Yale University Press, 1962), pp. 25, 26.

11. TJ to Peter Carr, 10 Aug. 1787, *PTJ*, vol. 14, p. 14.

12. TJ to Alexander Smyth, 17 Jan. 1825, *Jefferson's Extracts from the Gospels: The Philosophy of Jesus and the Life and Morals of Jesus*, ed. Dickinson W. Adams and Ruth W. Lester (Princeton, N.J.: Princeton University Press, 1983), p. 416.

13. TJ to John Adams, 11 Jan. 1817, *PTJRS*, vol. 10, p. 658. For the personal beliefs and religious life of Jefferson, see Gordon-Reed and Onuf. *"Most Blessed of the Patriarchs,"* pp. 278–79; Eugene R. Sheridan, *Jefferson and Religion* (Charlottesville, Va.: Thomas Jefferson Memorial Foundation, 1998); and Edwin S. Gaustad, *Sworn on*

the Altar of God: A Religious Biography of Thomas Jefferson (Grand Rapids, Mich.: Eerdmans, 1996).

14. Dickens, *Like an Evening Gone*, pp. 71, 75. My thanks for information about the stool to Bob Self, who is the former Robert H. Smith Director of Restoration at Monticello.

15. Gordon-Reed and Onuf, *"Most Blessed of the Patriarchs,"* p. 292.

16. William M. Wilson, "The Myth of Jefferson's Deism," in *The Elusive Thomas Jefferson: Essays on the Man behind the Myths*, ed. M. Andrew Holowchak and Brian W. Dotts (Jefferson, N.C.: McFarland, 2017), pp. 118–30.

17. TJ to Benjamin Rush, 21 May 1803, *PTJ*, vol. 40, p. 251.

18. John Adams to TJ, 22 July 1813, *PTJ*, vol. 6, p. 299.

19. TJ to John Adams, April 11, 1823, Adams and Lester, eds., *Jefferson's Extracts from the Gospels*, p. 412.

20. TJ to William Short, 13 Apr. 1820, *PTJRS*, vol. 15, p. 539.

21. TJ to John Adams, 12 Oct. 1813, *PTJRS*, vol. 6, p. 540.

22. Gaustad, *Sworn on the Altar of God*, p. 23.

23. For an excellent discussion of the limitations of his scholarship and the contradictions in his religious views, see Paul K. Conkin, "The Religious Pilgrimage of Thomas Jefferson," in Onuf, ed., *Jeffersonian Legacies*, pp. 19–50. For Jefferson's selectivity, contradictions, and uncritical reading of Priestley, see especially pp. 33, 35, 38.

24. John Ragosta, *Religious Freedom: Jefferson's Legacy, America's Creed* (Charlottesville: University of Virginia Press, 2013).

25. *Autobiography of Thomas Jefferson*, pp. 58–59.

26. O'Brien, *Intellectual Life and the American South*, p. 279.

27. TJ to the Danbury Baptist Association, 1 Jan. 1802, *PTJ*, vol. 36, p. 258; Danbury Baptist Association to TJ, 7 Oct. 1801, *PTJ*, vol. 35, pp. 407–8; Thomas, *The Founders and the Idea of a National University*, p. 148.

28. David Barton, *Jefferson Lies: Exposing the Myths You've Always Believed about Thomas Jefferson* (Nashville, Tenn.: Thomas Nelson, 2012); Chris Rodda, *Debunking David Barton's "Jefferson Lies": The Chapter That Barton Calls "Lie #2" Jefferson Founded a Secular University* (N.p., 2012).

29. James Madison to Edward Everett, 19 Mar. 1823, *PJMRS*, vol. 3, p. 15.

30. Jefferson, *Notes on the State of Virginia*, p. 166.

31. TJ to William Plumer, 21 July 1816, *PTJRS*, vol. 10, p. 260.

32. TJ to Benjamin Rush, 22 Oct. 1800, *PTJ*, vol. 32, p. 168.

33. TJ to Jacob de la Motta, 1 Sept. 1820, *PTJRS*, vol. 16, p. 235.

34. TJ to James Fishback, 27 Oct. 1809 (draft), *PTJRS*, vol. 1, p. 564. TJ discreetly omitted this text from the final version sent to the recipient.

35. TJ to John Adams, 22 Jan. 1821, *PTJRS*, vol. 16, p. 563.

36. TJ to John Adams, 11 Apr. 1823, Adams and Lester, eds., *Jefferson's Extracts from the Gospels*, p. 412.

37. Winterer, *American Enlightenments*, pp. 66, 69.

38. TJ to James Smith, 8 Dec. 1822, Adams and Lester, eds., *Jefferson's Extracts from the Gospels*, p. 409.

39. TJ to Benjamin Waterhouse, 19 July 1822, ibid., p. 407.

40. TJ to John Adams, 12 Oct. 1813, *PTJRS*, vol. 6, p. 550.

41. TJ to Thomas Cooper, 2 Nov. 1822, Founders Online, https://founders.archives.gov/documents/Jefferson/98-01-02-3137/.

42. Jefferson, *Notes on the State of Virginia*, p. 165.

43. John Henry Newman, *The Idea of a University*, ed. Frank M. Turner (New Haven, Conn.: Yale University Press, 1996), pp. 26, 25, 39, 29–30. The book was first published as lectures in 1852 and under a different title in 1873.

44. Rush, "A Plan for the Establishment of Public Schools and the Diffusion of Knowledge in Pennsylvania," p. 10.

45. Newman, *The Idea of a University*, p. 105.

46. A. J. Engel, *From Clergyman to Don: The Rise of the Academic Profession in Nineteenth-Century Oxford* (Oxford: Oxford University Press, 1983), pp. 4, 48, 56, 77, 107, 280. Unlike Oxford, some Cambridge colleges made exceptions for married faculty (dons). Founded in 1800, Downing College, Cambridge University, was an exception, requiring only that two fellows be unmarried and having a predominance of laymen on its faculty of sixteen fellows. Caius College at Cambridge University abolished the requirement that their fellows not marry in 1860. Some students circumvented the religious tests by attending the university but not graduating.

47. Daniel Walker Howe, "Church, State, and Education in the Young Republic," *Journal of the Early Republic* 22, no. 1 (Spring 2002): 18.

48. Geiger, *History of American Higher Education*, pp. 159–60.

49. Bledstein, *The Culture of Professionalism*, p. 208.

50. Howe, "Church, State, and Education in the Young Republic," pp. 14–15; Wenger, "Thomas Jefferson, the College of William and Mary, and the University of Virginia," p. 346.

51. Kelley, *Yale*, pp. 123, 209; Stephan Thernstrom, "'Poor but Hopefull Scholars,'" in Bailyn et al., eds., *Glimpses of the Harvard Past*, p. 120; Woodburn, "An Historical Investigation of the Opposition to Jefferson's Educational Proposals," p. 171; Hofstadter, *Academic Freedom in the Age of the College*, p. 115; Bledstein, *The Culture of Professionalism*, 198.

52. Rudolph, *Curriculum*, p. 65; Axtell, *Wisdom's Workshop*, p. 127; Geiger, *History of American Higher Education*, p. 136.

53. Thomas, *The Founders and the Idea of a National University*, p. 134; McCaughey, *Stand Columbia*, pp. 74, 81.

54. Thomas, *The Founders and the Idea of a National University*, p. 134.

55. Rudolph, *Curriculum*, p. 20.

56. Joseph F. Kett, *Meritocracy: The History of a Founding Ideal from the American Revolution to the 21st Century* (Ithaca, N.Y.: Cornell University Press, 2013), p. 168.

57. Battle, *History of the University of North Carolina*, pp. 145, 201, 222, 230.

58. Wright, *Transylvania*, pp. 8, 12, 14, 15, 30, 48, 53, 58–60, 63.

59. Thernstrom, "'Poor but Hopefull Scholars,'" p. 120.

60. "The Rockfish Gap Report of the University of Virginia Commissioners," 4 Aug. 1818, *PTJRS*, vol. 13, pp. 217–18, 191, 203n, 211.

61. TJ to Thomas Cooper, 2 Nov. 1822, Founders Online, https://founders.archives.gov/documents/Jefferson/98-01-02-3137.

62. TJ to Arthur Brockenbrough, 21 Apr. 1825, Founders Online, https://founders .archives.gov/documents/Jefferson/98-01-02-5152.

63. James Madison to TJ, 24 Sept. 1824, *PJMRS*, vol. 3, p. 373.

64. Healey, *Jefferson on Religion in Public Education*, pp. 225–26, 244, 245, 253.

65. Jean M. Yarbrough, "The Moral Sense, Character Formation, and Virtue," in *Reason and Republicanism: Thomas Jefferson's Legacy of Liberty*, ed. Gary L. McDowell and Sharon L. Noble (Lanham, Md.: Rowman and Littlefield, 1997), pp. 271–305.

66. TJ to Ezra Stiles Ely, 25 June 1819, *PTJRS*, vol. 14, p. 471.

67. Harry Y. Gamble, *God on the Grounds: A History of Religion at Thomas Jefferson's University* (Charlottesville: University of Virginia Press, 2020), p. 24.

68. Tutwiler, *Early History of the University of Virginia*, p. 6.

69. Gamble, *God on the Grounds*, p. 52.

70. Rex Bowman and Carlos Santos, *Rot, Riot and Rebellion: Mr. Jefferson's Struggle to Save the University That Changed America* (Charlottesville: University of Virginia Press, 2013), pp. 37–38.

71. Gamble, *God on the Grounds*, pp. 57, 49.

72. Bruce, *History of the University of Virginia*, vol. 3, pp. 6–7.

73. Addis, *Jefferson's Vision for Education*, p. 133.

74. [George Tucker], *Defence of the Character of Thomas Jefferson, against a Writer in New-York Review and Quarterly Journal* (New York: W. Osborn, 1838), p. 24.

75. Bruce, *History of the University of Virginia*, vol. 3, p. 107; Peterson, *The Jefferson Image in the American Mind*, p. 129.

76. Addis, *Jefferson's Vision for Education*, pp. 133, 129.

77. Chapman Johnson to James Madison, 21 Apr. 1828, Founders Online, https:// founders.archives.gov/documents/Madison/99-02-02-1386.

78. Addis, *Jefferson's Vision for Education*, p. 133.

79. Harriet Martineau, *Retrospect of Western Travel* (1838), ed. Daniel Feller (New York: M. E. Sharpe, 2000), pp. 82–84.

80. Gamble, *God on the Grounds*, p. 63.

81. Peterson, *The Jefferson Image in the American Mind*, p. 114.

82. Gamble, *God on the Grounds*, p. 96.

83. McLean, *George Tucker*, p. 40. Henry St. George Tucker was the son of George Tucker's younger cousin St. George Tucker.

84. [Tucker], *Defence of the Character of Thomas Jefferson*, p. 27.

85. Bruce, *History of the University of Virginia*, vol. 3, p. 134. Judah Monis was a Jewish instructor of Hebrew at Harvard where he was appointed in 1722. However, unlike Sylvester, he outwardly converted. His case is discussed in Michal Hoberman, *New Israel/New England: Jews and Puritans in Early America* (Amherst: University of Massachusetts Press, 2011). My thanks for this reference to Jonathon Derek Awtrey.

86. Lewis S. Feuer, "America's First Jewish Professor: James Joseph Sylvester at the University of Virginia," *American Jewish Archives* 36 (1984): 152.

87. Bruce, *History of the University of Virginia*, vol. 3, pp. 132, 37.

88. *Watchmen of the South*, 5 Aug. 1841.

89. Emma Rogers, ed., *Life and Letters of William Barton Rogers*, 2 vols. (Boston: Houghton, Mifflin, 1896), vol. 1, p. 192.

90. Ibid., vol. 1, p. 165.

91. Virginius Dabney, *Mr. Jefferson's University: A History* (Charlottesville: University Press of Virginia, 1988), p. 78.

92. Uriah Levy to John Coulter, Nov. 1832, quoted in Donovan Fitzpatrick and Saul Saphire, *Navy Maverick: Uriah Phillips Levy* (Garden City, N.Y.: Doubleday, 1963), p. 128.

93. [Everett], "Proceedings and Report of the Commissioners for the University of Virginia," p. 130.

94. Lauren Jones, "Let Freedom Ring: U.VA. Professor Rediscovers Sacred Story behind Jefferson Statue," *UVA Today*, 2 July 2014, https://news.virginia.edu/content /let-freedom-ring-uva-professor-rediscovers-sacred-story-behind-jefferson-statue. My thanks to Scott Harrop.

8. This Deplorable Entanglement

1. Benjamin Banneker to TJ, 19 Aug. 1791, *PTJ*, vol. 22, p. 49.

2. Ibid., vol. 22, pp. 50–51.

3. Ibid., vol. 22, p. 51.

4. Ibid., vol. 22, pp. 51–52.

5. "On Negro Slavery and the Slave Trade, an Extract from the Columbian Magazine," in Benjamin Banneker, *Pennsylvania, Delaware, Maryland and Virginia Almanack and Emphemeris for the Year of Our Lord 1792* (Baltimore: William Goddard and James Angel, 1791), p. 93.

6. Charles A. Cerami, *Benjamin Banneker: Surveyor, Astronomer, Publisher, Patriot* (New York: Wiley, 2002), p. 150.

7. TJ to Benjamin Banneker, 30 Aug. 1791, *PTJ*, vol. 22, pp. 97–98.

8. TJ to the Marquis de Condorcet, 30 Aug. 1791, *PTJ*, vol. 22, pp. 98–99.

9. TJ to Joel Barlow, 8 Oct. 1809, *PTJRS*, vol. 1, pp. 588–89.

10. Peterson, *The Jefferson Image in the American Mind*, pp. 164–226.

11. Roger Wilkins, *Jefferson's Pillow: The Founding Fathers and the Dilemma of Black Patriotism* (Boston: Beacon Press, 2001), p. 134.

12. Martineau, *Retrospect of Western Travel*, p. 86.

13. Birle and Francavilla, eds., *Thomas Jefferson's Granddaughter in Queen Victoria's England*, p. 22.

14. Stanton, *"Those Who Labor for My Happiness,"* pp. 140, 24.

15. Nelson and McInnis, "Landscape of Slavery," p. 56.

16. Henry Martin, Letter to the Editor, *College Topics* (Charlottesville, Va.), 29 Jan. 1890; "Faithful Janitor Dead at 89," *Daily Progress* (Charlottesville), 6 Oct. 1915; "Funeral of Henry Martin," *Daily Progress*, 9 Oct. 1915; *President's Commission on Slavery and the University*, pp. 30–31.

17. Haulman, *Virginia and the Panic of 1819*, pp. 17, 65.

18. *President's Commission on Slavery and the University*, p. 28.

19. Bruce, *History of the University of Virginia*, vol. 2, pp. 56–57, 289.

20. Stanton, *"Those Who Labor for My Happiness,"* p. 25.

21. Bruce, *History of the University of Virginia*, vol. 2, p. 291; Elvin L. Jordan Jr., "'Chas-

tising a Servant for His Insolence': The Case of the Butter Bully," in Ragosta, Onuf, and O'Shaughnessy, eds., *The Founding of Thomas Jefferson's University*, pp. 70–85.

22. Jordan, "'Chastising a Servant for His Insolence,'" p. 80.

23. *President's Commission on Slavery and the University*, p. 23.

24. Faculty Minutes, 2 Mar. 1839, session 15; Chairman's Journals, 25 Feb. 1839, session 15, Jefferson's University: The Early Life, http://juel.iath.virginia.edu/resources.

25. *President's Commission on Slavery and the University*, p. 23.

26. Samuel Johnson, *Taxation No Tyranny* (1775), in *Political Writings: Samuel Johnson*, ed. Donald J. Greene, 23 vols. (New Haven, Conn.: Yale University Press, 2000), vol. 10, p. 454.

27. Jack P. Greene, *Evaluating Empire and Confronting Colonialism in Eighteenth-Century Britain* (Cambridge: Cambridge University Press, 2013); Christopher Leslie Brown, *Moral Capital: Foundations of British Abolitionism* (Chapel Hill: University of North Carolina Press, 2006).

28. Edmund Burke, "Speech on Conciliation with the America, 22 March, 1775," in *The Writings and Speeches of Edmund Burke*, ed. Paul Langford, Warren M. Elofson, and John A. Woods, 9 vols. (Oxford: Oxford University Press, 1996), vol. 3, pp. 122–23.

29. Gutzman, *Virginia's American Revolution*, p. 57; Cooper, *Liberty and Slavery*, p. 23.

30. Edmund S. Morgan, "Slavery and Freedom: The American Paradox," *Journal of American History* 59, no. 1 (June 1972): 2. He developed the argument in his book *American Slavery, American Freedom: The Ordeal of Colonial Virginia* (New York: Norton, 1975).

31. TJ to Jean Nicolas Démeunier, 26 June 1786, *PTJ*, vol. 10, p. 63.

32. TJ to William Short, 8 Sept. 1823, Founders Online, https://founders.archives.gov /documents/Jefferson/98-01-02-3750; TJ to Thomas Cooper, 10 Sept. 1814, *PTJRS*, vol. 7, p. 652.

33. TJ to Edward Coles, 25 Aug. 1814, *PTJRS*, vol. 7, p. 603.

34. Paul Finkelman, *Slavery and the Founders: Race and Liberty in the Age of Jefferson* (Armonk, N.Y.: M. E. Sharpe, 2001), p. 202; David T. Konig, "Whig Lawyering in the Legal Education of Thomas Jefferson," in Baron and Wright, eds., *The Libraries, Leadership, and Legacy of John Adams and Thomas Jefferson*, p. 108; Konig, "Thomas Jefferson, Slavery and the Law," paper presented at the University of Virginia Legal Workshop, Charlottesville, 30 Mar. 2015.

35. Thomas Jefferson, *A Summary View of the Rights of British America* (1774), in Ford, ed., *The Writings of Thomas Jefferson*, vol. 1, p. 440; Stanton, *"Those Who Labor for My Happiness,"* p. 108.

36. "Observations on Jean Nicolas Démeunier's Article on the United States Prepared for the *Encyclopédie Méthodique*," 24 Jan. 1786, *PTJ*, vol. 10, p. 58.

37. *Autobiography of Thomas Jefferson*, pp. 21, 62.

38. In the 1785 French edition of the *Notes*, he claimed that he had written an emancipation bill that was still pending before the state legislature. In the 1787 English edition, he wrote that his emancipation bill was not included in the revision of state laws proposed to the Virginia Assembly. In his autobiography, he also made an unsubstantiated claim that he had introduced an emancipation bill in the late 1770s.

See Gordon S. Barker, "Unravelling the Strange History of Jefferson's *Observations sur la Virginie*," *Virginia Magazine of History and Biography* 112, no. 2 (2004): 146–47.

39. Jefferson, *Notes on the State of Virginia*, p. 169.

40. Peterson, *The Jefferson Image in the American Mind*, p. 190.

41. TJ to Richard Price, 7 Aug. 1785, *PTJ*, vol. 8, p. 357.

42. Chad Vanderford, *Legacy of St. George Tucker: College Professors in Virginia Confront Slavery and the Rights of States, 1771–1897* (Knoxville: University of Tennessee Press, 2015), p. 91.

43. President's Annual Message, 2 Dec. 1806, *The Debates and Proceedings of the Congress of the United States, Ninth Congress, Second Session, Book 1851* (Washington, D.C.: Gales and Seaton, 1852), p. 14.

44. Padraig Riley, *Slavery and the Democratic Conscience: Political Life in Jeffersonian America* (Philadelphia: University of Pennsylvania Press, 2016), p. 124.

45. William W. Freehling, "The Founding Fathers and Slavery," *American Historical Review* 77 (1972): 81–93, makes the case for taking Jefferson's antislavery views seriously and arguing that he had a significant impact.

46. Issac Briggs's "Account of a Visit to Monticello," 2–4 Nov. 1820, *PTJRS*, vol. 16, p. 387; Stanton, "Perfecting Slavery," pp. 62, 65, 67–69, 74, 78, 79; Stanton, "*Those Who Labor for My Happiness*," pp. 19, 84, 100. For a broader treatment of his concept of amelioration, see Christa Dierksheide, *Amelioration and Empire: Progress and Slavery in the Plantation Americas* (Charlottesville: University of Virginia Press, 2014).

47. Cooper, *Liberty and Slavery*, p. 97; Steele, *Thomas Jefferson and American Nationhood*, p. 183; Dumas Malone, *Jefferson and the Ordeal of Liberty* (Boston: Little Brown, 1962; reprint Charlottesville: University of Virginia Press, 2006), p. 480.

48. Wood, *Friends Divided*, p. 347.

49. Jefferson, *Notes on the State of Virginia*, p. 145.

50. Vanderford, *Legacy of St. George Tucker*, p. 22; Philip Hamilton, *The Making and Unmaking of a Revolutionary Family: The Tuckers of Virginia, 1752–1830* (Charlottesville: University of Virginia Press, 2003), pp. 154–55.

51. Cooper, *Liberty and Slavery*, p. 33.

52. Ellen Coolidge to TJ, 1 Aug. 1825, Founders Online, https://founders.archives.gov/documents/Jefferson/98-01-02-5424; TJ to Coolidge, 27 Aug. 1825, Founders Online, https://founders.archives.gov/documents/Jefferson/98-01-02-5493.

53. TJ to Edward Coles, 25 Aug. 1814, *PTJRS*, vol. 7, p. 604.

54. TJ to St. George Tucker, 28 Aug. 1797, *PTJ*, vol. 29, p. 519.

55. TJ to John Holmes, 22 Apr. 1820, *PTJRS*, vol. 15, p. 550.

56. TJ to Lydia Howard Huntley Sigourney, 18 July 1824, Founders Online, https://founders.archives.gov/documents/Jefferson/98-01-02-1234.

57. TJ to John Holmes, 22 Apr. 1820, *PTJRS*, vol. 15, p. 550.

58. TJ to Lydia Howard Huntley Sigourney, 18 July 1824, Founders Online, https://founders.archives.gov/documents/Jefferson/98-01-02-1234.

59. Riley, *Slavery and the Democratic Conscience*, p. 92.

60. Taylor, *Thomas Jefferson's Education*, p. 132.

61. TJ to Edward Coles, 25 Aug. 1814, *PTJRS*, vol. 7, pp. 603–4.

62. TJ to George Logan, 11 May 1805, Founders Online, https://founders.archives.gov /documents/Jefferson/99-01-02-1709.

63. TJ to Jean Nicolas Démeunier, [26 June 1786], *PTJ*, vol. 19, pp. 61–64.

64. TJ to Walter Jones, 31 Mar. 1801, *PTJ*, vol. 33, p. 506.

65. Kierner, *Martha Jefferson Randolph*, pp. 60, 87, 186–87, 249, 250–51, 256–57.

66. Birle and Francavilla, eds., *Thomas Jefferson's Granddaughter in Queen Victoria's England*, pp. 328, 223; Kierner, *Martha Jefferson Randolph*, p. 265; Genovese, *The Slaveholders' Dilemma*, p. 61.

67. Birle and Francavilla, eds., *Thomas Jefferson's Granddaughter in Queen Victoria's England*, p. 223.

68. Fieser, ed., *Life of George Tucker*, pp 16–17; McLean, *George Tucker*, pp. 63, 68, 182; Vanderford, *Legacy of St. George Tucker*, p. 39.

69. Vanderford, *Legacy of St. George Tucker*, p. xvi; McLean, *George Tucker*, pp. 176–77, 181, 186, 193, 198, 199.

70. Andrew Burstein and Nancy Isenberg, *Madison and Jefferson* (New York: Random House, 2013), p. 20.

71. For a good summary of Madison's attempts to refute nullification and cession, see James Morton Smith's discussion in *The Republic of Letters: The Correspondence between Thomas Jefferson and James Madison, 1776–1826*, ed. James Morton Smith, 3 vols. (New York: Norton, 1995), vol. 3, pp. 1972–2003.

72. Thomas Howard and Alfred Brophy, "Proslavery Thought," in McInnis and Nelson, eds., *Educated in Tyranny*, p. 146.

73. Bruce, *History of the University of Virginia*, vol. 3, p. 137; Jennifer Bridges Oast, "Negotiating the Honor Culture: Students and Slaves at Three Virginia Colleges," in Harris, Campbell, and Brophy, eds., *Slavery and the University*, p. 95.

74. Howard and Brophy, "Proslavery Thought," pp. 152–53.

75. McLean, *George Tucker*, p. 200.

76. [Charles B. Shaw], *Is Slavery a Blessing? A Reply to Prof. Bledsoe's Essay on Liberty and Slavery: With Remarks on Slavery as It Is* (Boston: John P. Jewett, 1857), p. 25.

77. Howard and Brophy, "Proslavery Thought," p. 153; Bruce, *History of the University of Virginia*, vol. 3, p. 177.

78. Winthrop D. Jordan, *White over Black: American Attitudes toward the Negro, 1550–1812* (Chapel Hill: University of North Carolina Press, 1968; reprint Baltimore: Penguin, 1968), p. xii.

79. Jefferson, *Notes on the State of Virginia*, pp. 150, 146, 147. He compared himself to an orangutan in letters to both Maria Cosway and William Short; see TJ to Maria Cosway, 14 Jan. 1789, *PTJ*, vol. 14, p. 446.

80. Jefferson, *Notes on the State of Virginia*, pp. 147, 149, 150.

81. Douglas L. Wilson, "The Evolution of Jefferson's *Notes on the State of Virginia*," *Virginia Magazine of History and Biography* 112, no. 2 (2004): 124–25.

82. Douglas Sloan, *The Scottish Enlightenment and the American College Ideal* (New York: Teachers College Press, 1971), pp. 150, 151, 159.

83. James Oakes, "Why Slaves Can't Read: The Political Significance of Jefferson's Racism," in Gilreath, ed., *Thomas Jefferson and the Education of a Citizen*, p. 177; Eric

Foner, "Lincoln and Colonization," in Cooper and Knock, eds., *Jefferson, Lincoln and Wilson*, p. 114.

84. Robert A. Ferguson, *The American Enlightenment, 1750–1820* (Cambridge, Mass.: Harvard University Press, 1997), p. 25.

85. Immanuel Kant, *Observations on Feeling of the Beautiful and the Sublime* (1764), in *The Cambridge Edition of the Works of Immanuel Kant*, ed. Paul Guyer and Paul W. Wood, 15 vols. (Cambridge: Cambridge University Press, 1988), vol. 2, p. 253.

86. David Hume, "Of National Characters," in *Essays and Treatises on Several Subjects*, 2 vols. (London: A Millar, 1777), vol. 1, p. 207n10.

87. TJ to Abbé Henri Jean-Baptiste Grégoire, 25 Feb. 1809, Founders Online, https://founders.archives.gov/documents/Jefferson/99-01-02-9893.

88. TJ to Joel Barlow, 8 Oct. 1809, *PTJRS*, vol. 1, p. 589.

89. Joseph Easton, "The Election of 1796 and the Contest over American Nationalism," paper presented at the Robert H. Smith International Center for Jefferson Studies, Charlottesville, 22 Jan. 2019.

90. Gordon-Reed and Onuf, *"Most Blessed of the Patriarchs,"* p. 167.

91. TJ to Marquis de Chastellux, 7 June 1785, *PTJ*, vol. 8, p. 186.

92. TJ to Abbé Henri Jean-Baptiste Grégoire, 25 Feb. 1809, Founders Online, https://founders.archives.gov/documents/Jefferson/99-01-02-9893.

93. Arthur Sherr, "An Honest, Intelligent Man: Thomas Jefferson, the Free Black Patrick Henry, and the Founder's Racial Views in His Last Years," *Virginia Magazine of History and Biography* 127, no. 4 (2019): 301–39.

94. Stanley, *Journal of a Tour in America*, pp. 174–76. Stanley met with several statesmen in the United States, including John Adams and John Quincy Adams. He observed the 1824 election in Washington. He broke off his tour to return to England to get married but his companions continued to Monticello where they met Jefferson and visited the University of Virginia. His fellow travelers were John Evelyn Denison, Viscount Ossington, and James Archibald Stuart Wortley-Mackenzie, 1st Baron Wharncliffe. Denison afterward sent four books for the library of the university. Adam Hodgson, a leading merchant in Liverpool, wrote to Jefferson saying that he hoped he would meet Stanley. Hodgson to TJ, 13 Sept. 1824, Founders Online, https://founders.archives.gov/documents/Jefferson/98-01-02-4544.

95. Stanley, *Journal of a Tour in America*, pp. 174–76.

96. Riley, *Slavery and the Democratic Conscience*, pp. 247, 248, 254.

97. See Ari Helo and Peter S. Onuf, "Jefferson, Morality, and the Problem of Slavery," *William and Mary Quarterly*, 3rd ser., vol. 60, no. 3 (July 2003): 585.

98. Morris, "Southern Enlightenment," pp. 168–69.

99. Jefferson, *Notes on the State of Virginia*, p. 169.

100. Foner, "Lincoln and Colonization," pp. 107–9, 119.

101. Jefferson, *Notes on the State of Virginia*, pp. 144–45.

102. Terry L. Meyers, "Jefferson on Black Education," *ANQ: A Quarterly Journal of Short Articles, Notes and Reviews* 32, no. 3 (2019): 161.

103. TJ to Robert Pleasants, 1 June 1796, *PTJ*, vol. 29, p. 120.

104. TJ to Robert Pleasants, 27 Aug. 1796, *PTJ*, vol. 29, p. 177.

105. TJ to Robert Pleasants, 8 Feb. 1797, *PTJ*, vol. 29, p. 287.

106. Stanton, *"Those Who Labor for My Happiness,"* pp. 22, 164.

107. "The Memoirs of Madison Hemings."

108. Stanton, *"Those Who Labor for My Happiness,"* p. 164.

109. John and James Hemmings spelled their surname with two m's.

110. "James Hemmings's 'Inventory of Kitchen Utensils,'" 20 Feb. 1796, *PTJRS*, vol. 25, pp. 610–11.

111. "Hannah" to TJ, 15 Nov. 1818, *PTJRS*, vol. 13, pp. 393–94.

112. Stanton, *"Those Who Labor for My Happiness,"* p. 165.

113. Moore, *Albemarle*, p. 146. For the population of slaves and free Blacks in Albemarle County between 1790 and 1860, see Kirt von Daacke, *Freedom Has a Face: Race, Identity, and Community in Jefferson's Virginia* (Charlottesville: University of Virginia Press, 2012), p. 9.

114. Von Daacke, *Freedom Has a Face*, p. 9. These are the counterintuitive but well-substantiated findings of Kirk von Daake

115. Lorraine Smith Pangle and Thomas L. Pangle, *The Liberty of Learning: The Educational Ideas of American Founders* (Lawrence: University of Kansas Press, 1993), p. 95.

116. The attempts are described in an illuminating article by Kabria Baumgartner, "Towers of Intellect: The Struggle for African American Higher Education in Antebellum New England," in Harris, Campbell, and Brophy, eds., *Slavery and the University*, pp. 179–92.

117. Andrew Delbanco, *College: What It Was, Is, and Should Be* (Princeton, N.J.: Princeton University Press, 2012), p. 147.

118. Malone, *The Public Life of Thomas Cooper*, pp. 20, 281, 285, 307, 310, 328, 331, 335; O'Brien, *Intellectual Life and the American South*, pp. 202–3.

119. Fitzhugh, ed., *Letters of George Long*, pp. 27, 47, 48, 52, 58, 63.

120. Kirt von Daacke, "Free People of Color," in McInnis and Nelson, eds., *Educated in Tyranny*, p. 208.

121. Addis, *Jefferson's Vision for Education*, p. 114.

122. McLean, *George Tucker*, pp. 8, 183, 201; Bruce, *History of the University of Virginia*, vol. 3, pp. 71–72.

123. Hofstadter, *Academic Freedom in the Age of the College*, p. 246.

124. Craig B. Hollander and Martha A. Sandweiss, "Princeton and Slavery," in Harris, Campbell, and Brophy, eds., *Slavery and the University*, p. 54.

125. Beckert et al., "Harvard a Short History," pp. 233–34, 235, 236, 239–40.

126. Finkelman, *Slavery and the Founders*, pp. 221, 245.

127. Annette Gordon-Reed, "Thomas Jefferson's Vision of Equality Was Not All-Inclusive. But It Was Transformative," *Time*, 2 Mar. 2020, p. 46.

128. "Remarks by the Honorable John Charles Thomas at the 'Getting Word' Gathering," 28 June 1997, Jefferson Library manuscript collection, Thomas Jefferson Foundation, Monticello, Charlottesville, Va.

129. Stanton, *"Those Who Labor for My Happiness,"* pp. 289, 290, 291, 297, 299.

130. Philip Foner, *We, the Other People: Alternative Declarations of Independence by Labor*

Groups, Farmers, Woman's Rights Advocates, Socialists, and Blacks, 1829–1975 (Urbana: University of Illinois Press, 1976).

9. IDLE RAMBLERS INCAPABLE OF APPLICATION

1. Tutwiler, *Early History of the University of Virginia*, p. 10; Hunt, ed., *The First Forty Years of Washington Society*, p. 229.
2. Minutes of the University of Virginia Board of Visitors, 3, 6 Oct. 1825, Jefferson's University: The Early Life, http://juel.iath.virginia.edu/resources.
3. Tucker, *The Life of Thomas Jefferson*, vol. 2, p. 480.
4. Martha Jefferson Randolph to Ellen W. Randolph Coolidge, 13 Oct. 1825, Ellen Wayles Randolph Coolidge Correspondence, box 1, Alderman Library Special Collections, University of Virginia.
5. TJ to William Short, 14 Oct. 1825, Founders Online, https://founders.archives.gov/documents/Jefferson/98-01-02-5596; TJ to Joseph Coolidge, 6 Oct. 1825, Founders Online, https://founders.archives.gov/documents/Jefferson/98-01-02-5437; "Autobiography of George Tucker," *Bermuda Historical Quarterly* 18, nos. 3–4 (1961): 137–38.
6. Faculty Minutes, 5 Oct. 1825.
7. Ibid., 2 Oct. 1825.
8. TJ to Joseph Coolidge, 13 Oct. 1825, Founders Online, https://founders.archives.gov/documents/Jefferson/98-01-02-5596; Lewis, *The Pursuit of Happiness*, p. 125.
9. Martha Jefferson Randolph to Ellen W. Randolph Coolidge, 13 Oct. 1825, Ellen Wayles Randolph Coolidge Correspondence, box 1.
10. Faculty Minutes, 2 Oct. 1825.
11. Thomas H. Key and George Long to University of Virginia Board of Visitors, 6 Oct. 1825, Founders Online, https://founders.archives.gov/documents/Jefferson/98-01-02-5602.
12. TJ to James Madison, 18 Oct. 1825, Founders Online, https://founders.archives.gov/documents/Jefferson/98-01-02-5602.
13. TJ to Samuel Smith, 22 Oct. 1825, Founders Online, https://founders.archives.gov/documents/Jefferson/98-01-02-5611.
14. TJ to Joseph Coolidge, 13 Oct. 1825, Founders Online, https://founders.archives.gov/documents/Jefferson/98-01-02-5596.
15. Martha Jefferson to Ellen W. Randolph Coolidge, 13 Oct. 1825, Ellen Wayles Randolph Coolidge Correspondence, box 1. For a transcription, see Jefferson Quotes and Family Letters, Monticello, http://tjrs.monticello.org/letter/1010.
16. TJ to James Madison, 18 Oct. 1825, Founders Online, https://founders.archives.gov/documents/Jefferson/98-01-02-5602; Virginia J. Randolph Trist to Ellen W. Randolph Coolidge, 16 Oct. 1825, Ellen Wayles Randolph Coolidge Correspondence, box 1; David Meschutt, "'A Perfect Likeness': John H. I. Browere's Life Mask of Jefferson," *American Art Journal* 21, no. 4 (Winter 1989): 4–25.
17. Faculty Minutes, 18 June; 20, 22, 26 Sept. 1825.
18. William Short to TJ, 4 Oct. 1825, Founders Online, https://founders.archives.gov/documents/Jefferson/98-01-02-5570.

19. Taylor, *Thomas Jefferson's Education*, p. 275.

20. TJ Thomas Cooper, 2 Nov. 1822, Founders Online, https://founders.archives.gov /documents/Jefferson/98-01-02-3137.

21. TJ to George Ticknor, 16 July 1823, Founders Online, https://founders.archives.gov /documents/Jefferson/98-01-02-3639.

22. Steven J. Novak, *The Rights of Youth: American Colleges and Student Revolt, 1798– 1815* (Cambridge, Mass.: Harvard University Press, 1977), pp. 103, 104.

23. *The Autobiographical Ana of Robley Dunglison*, p. 22.

24. TJ to Robley Dunglison, 29 June 1825, Dorsey, ed., *The Jefferson-Dunglison Letters*, p. 33.

25. TJ to Vine Utley, 21 Mar. 1819, *PTJRS*, vol. 14, p. 187.

26. Wenger, "Thomas Jefferson, the College of William and Mary, and the University of Virginia," p. 357.

27. TJ to Peter Carr, 19 Aug. 1785, *PTJ*, vol. 8, p. 405.

28. TJ to Thomas Jefferson Randolph, 24 Nov. 1808, Founders Online, https://founders .archives.gov/documents/Jefferson/99-01-02-9151.

29. Bruce, *History of the University of Virginia*, vol. 2, pp. 81–82.

30. Kelley, *Yale*, p. 217.

31. Jefferson, *Notes on the State of Virginia*, p. 168.

32. Taylor, *Thomas Jefferson's Education*, p. 97.

33. Bertram Wyatt-Brown, *Southern Honor: Ethics and Behavior in the Old South* (New York: Oxford University Press, 2008), p. 22. See also Jennings J. Wagoner Jr., "Honor and Dishonor at Mr. Jefferson's University: The Antebellum Years," *History of Education Quarterly* 26, no. 2 (Summer 1986): 155–79.

34. Walter Rüegg, *A History of the University in Europe*, 4 vols. (Cambridge: Cambridge University Press, 2004), vol. 3, pp. 260–372; Pace, *Halls of Honor*, p. 8. For the boorish, adolescent student behavior in Germany, see Konrad H. Jarausch, "The Sources of German Student Unrest, 1815–1848," in Stone, ed., *The University in Society*, vol. 2, pp. 538, 545, 553.

35. David F. Allmendinger Jr., "The Dangers of Antebellum Student Life," *Journal of Social History* 7, no. 1 (Autumn 1973): 75; Corydon Ireland, "Harvard's Long Ago Student Risings," *Harvard Gazette*, 19 Apr. 2012, https://news.harvard.edu/gazette /story/2012/04/harvards-long-ago-student-risings/.

36. Bailyn, "Why Kirkland Failed," p. 25.

37. Morison, *Three Centuries of Harvard*, pp. 210, 231.

38. Ibid., pp. 208–9.

39. Ibid., p. 201.

40. Bledstein, *The Culture of Professionalism*, p. 229.

41. Morison, *Three Centuries of Harvard*, pp. 51, 230.

42. Andrew Dickinson White, *Autobiography* (New York: Century, 1905), p. 248.

43. Kelley, *Yale*, p. 119; Novak, *The Rights of Youth*, pp. 164, 12.

44. Novak, *The Rights of Youth*, pp. 7–8.

45. Stanley, *Journal of a Tour in America*, p. 139.

46. O'Brien, *Intellectual Life and the American South*, pp. 77–79; Fisher, *Albion's Seed*, p. 305.

47. Fisher, *Albion's Seed*, p. 355.

48. Hugh Fairfax, *The Forgotten Story of America's Only Peerage, 1690–1960* (London: Fairfax Family, 2017).

49. "The Rockfish Gap Report of the University of Virginia Commissioners," 4 Aug. 1818, *PTJRS*, vol. 13, pp. 209–24.

50. TJ to Joseph Cabell, 24 Jan. 1816, *PTJRS*, vol. 9, p. 397.

51. *The Autobiographical Ana of Robley Dunglison*, p. 29. See also [Dunglison], "College Instruction and Discipline," pp. 283–314.

52. George Long to Henry Tutwiler, 30 May 1875, Fitzhugh, ed., *Letters of George Long*, p. 26.

53. TJ to James Madison, 26 Dec. 1824, *PJMRS*, vol. 3, p. 454; Clemons, *University of Virginia Library*, pp. 15, 99; McLean, *George Tucker*, p. 34.

54. *The Autobiographical Ana of Robley Dunglison*, p. 31.

55. Cornelia J. Randolph to Ellen W. Randolph Coolidge, 3 Aug. 1825, Jefferson Quotes and Family Letters, http://tjrs.monticello.org/letter/989.

56. Fieser, *Life of George Tucker*, p. 66.

57. TJ to Joseph Cabell, 25 Jan. 1822, Founders Online, https://founders.archives.gov /documents/Jefferson/98-01-02-2614.

58. Cheyney, *History of the University of Pennsylvania*, p. 179; Bailyn, "Why Kirkland Failed," p. 25; Morison, *Three Centuries of Harvard*, pp. 183–84.

59. Hofstadter, *Academic Freedom in the Age of the College*, p. 231.

60. Robert H. S. Gibson argues in his forthcoming book that the tuition costs in medicine were competitive in relation to other colleges.

61. [Dunglison], "College Instruction and Discipline," p. 305; Geiger, *History of American Higher Education*, p. 167.

62. Charles Coleman Wall Jr., "Students and Student Life at the University of Virginia, 1825–1861" (Ph.D. diss., University of Virginia, 1978), p. 66.

63. Moore, *Albemarle*, p. 134.

64. Bruce, *History of the University of Virginia*, vol. 3, pp. 98, 99–100, 184, 199.

65. Dabney, *Mr. Jefferson's University*, p. 24.

66. Wall, "Students and Student Life at the University of Virginia," p. 44.

67. Adams, *Thomas Jefferson and the University of Virginia*, p. 167.

68. Thernstrom, "'Poor but Hopefull Scholars,'" pp. 117, 118.

69. Kelley, *Yale*, p. 138.

70. TJ to Robley Dunglison, 29 June 1825, Founders Online, https://founders.archives .gov/documents/Jefferson/98-01-02-5343.

71. Faculty Minutes, 28 June 1825.

72. *Correspondence of Thomas Jefferson and Francis Walker Gilmer, 1814–1826*, ed. Richard Beale Davis (Columbia: University of South Carolina Press, 1946), p. 93.

73. Adams, *Thomas Jefferson and the University of Virginia*, p. 181.

74. [Dunglison], "College Instruction and Discipline," p. 301.

75. Brockliss, "The European University in the Age of Revolution," vol. 6, p. 90.

76. Anderson, *European Universities from the Enlightenment to 1914*, p. 99.

77. TJ to Francis Eppes, 13 Dec. 1820, *PTJRS*, vol. 16, p. 457.

78. Webster, *On the Education of Youth in America*, p. 54.

304 NOTES TO PAGES 227–233

79. Rudolph, *Curriculum*, p. 13.
80. [Everett], "Proceedings and Report of the Commissioners for the University of Virginia," p. 123.
81. Wellmon, *Organizing Enlightenment*, pp. 187, 195, 199.
82. [Dunglison], "College Instruction and Discipline," p. 291.
83. Bruce, *History of the University of Virginia*, vol. 2, p. 130.
84. Bailyn, "Why Kirkland Failed," p. 24.
85. Stanley, *Journal of a Tour in America*, p. 153.
86. George Tucker, *Memoir of the Life and Character of John P. Emmet, M.D.* (Philadelphia: C. Sherman, 1845), p. 10.
87. [Dunglison], "College Instruction and Discipline," p. 312.
88. Kett, *Meritocracy*, pp. 69–70, 80, 84.
89. Tucker, "Education in Virginia," p. 64.
90. Adams, *Thomas Jefferson and the University of Virginia*, p. 153.
91. [Dunglison], "College Instruction and Discipline," p. 291.
92. Tucker, "Education in Virginia," p. 64.
93. Bruce, *History of the University of Virginia*, vol. 3, p. 65.
94. McCaughey, *Stand Columbia*, p. 82. Richard Hofstadter claimed that the proportion of the population attending college declined during the antebellum period, but his claim is no longer accepted.
95. [Dunglison], "College Instruction and Discipline," p. 306.
96. McCaughey, *Stand Columbia*, pp. 83, 137.
97. Adams, *Thomas Jefferson and the University of Virginia*, p. 166; Wall, "Students and Student Life at the University of Virginia," p. 55.
98. Cheyney, *History of the University of Pennsylvania*, p. 208.
99. Adams, *Thomas Jefferson and the University of Virginia*, pp. 167–68.
100. Thomas L. Howard III and Owen W. Galloby, *Society Ties: The Jefferson Society and Student Life at the University of Virginia* (Charlottesville: University of Virginia Press, 2017), p. 1.
101. Patton, *Jefferson, Cabell and the University of Virginia*, pp. 234, 239, 240–41. There were strong similarities with Princeton; see J. Jefferson Looney, "Useful without Attracting Attention: The Cliosophic and American Whig Societies of the College of New Jersey, 1765–1896," *Princeton University Library Chronicle* 64, no. 3 (Spring 2003): 389–424.
102. Kelley, *Yale*, p. 223. For general discussion of such clubs, see McLachlan, "The Choice of Hercules," pp. 449–94.
103. Edgar Mason, John W. Brockenbrough, and Robert Saunders to TJ, 11 Aug. 1825, Founders Online, https://founders.archives.gov/documents/Jefferson/98-01-02-5463.
104. TJ to Edward Mason, John W. Brockenbrough, and Robert Saunders, 12 Aug. 1825, Founders Online, https://founders.archives.gov/documents/Jefferson/98-01-02-5466.
105. Bruce, *History of the University of Virginia*, vol. 3, p. 133.
106. Howard and Galloby, *Society Ties*, p. 14.

107. Andrew Burstein, *America's Jubilee: How in 1826 a Generation Remembered Fifty Years of Independence* (New York: Knopf Doubleday, 2007), p. 30.
108. For an illustration, see Fowler, ed., *Dining at Monticello*, p. 10.
109. *Alumni Bulletin of the University of Virginia* 6, no. 3 (Nov. 1899): 69.
110. C. P. Semtner, "Poe's Richmond and Richmond's Poe," in *Poe and His Place in History*, ed. Philip Edward Phillips (New York: Palgrave Macmillan, 2018), p. 52.
111. TJ to Robert Greenhow, 24 July 1825, Founders Online, https://founders.archives.gov/documents/Jefferson/98-01-02-5403.
112. TJ to Cummings, Hilliard & Co., 9 Apr. 1826, Founders Online, https://founders.archives.gov/documents/Jefferson/98-01-02-6033.
113. T. C. McCorvey, "Henry Tutwiler and the Influence of the University of Virginia on Education in Alabama," *Transactions of the Alabama Historical Society* 5 (1904): 90.
114. Ibid., pp. 92, 97.
115. Ibid., p. 88.
116. Ibid., p. 101.
117. George Long to Henry Tutwiler, 30 May 1875, Fitzhugh, ed., *Letters of George Long*, p. 26.
118. *The Autobiographical Ana of Robley Dunglison*, p. 24.
119. Stark, "Reminiscences," p. 1.
120. Clemons, *University of Virginia Library*, p. 14.
121. Thomas Howard and Alfred Brophy, "Proslavery Thought," in McInnis and Nelson, eds., *Educated in Tyranny*, p. 146.
122. Taylor, *Thomas Jefferson's Education*, p. 274.

10. THIS ATHENAEUM

1. *The Memoirs of John Quincy Adams*, ed. Charles Francis Adams, 12 vols. (Philadelphia: Lippincott, 1874–77), vol. 7, p. 133.
2. Burstein, *America's Jubilee*, pp. 268–69; Morison, *Three Centuries of Harvard*, p. 227.
3. *The Autobiographical Ana of Robley Dunglison*, p. 32.
4. Ibid.
5. Burstein, *America's Jubilee*, p. 264.
6. Quoted in Smith, ed., *The Republic of Letters*, vol. 3, pp. 1973–74.
7. *The Adams-Jefferson Letters: The Complete Correspondence between Thomas Jefferson and Abigail and John Adams*, ed. Lester J. Cappon (Chapel Hill: University of North Carolina Press, 1959), p. xxxii.
8. TJ to John Adams, 8 Apr. 1816, *PTJ*, vol. 9, p. 650.
9. John Adams to TJ, 3 May 1816, *PTJ*, vol. 10, p. 5.
10. TJ to John Adams, 1 Aug. 1816, *PTJ*, vol. 10, pp. 284–85.
11. TJ to John Adams, 1 June 1822, Founders Online, https://founders.archives.gov/documents/Jefferson/98-01-02-2840.
12. TJ to John Adams, 14 Oct. 1816, *PTJRS*, vol. 10, p. 458.
13. TJ to John Adams, 13 Nov. 1818, *PTJRS*, vol. 13, p. 392.

14. John Adams to TJ, 1 Dec. 1825, Founders Online, https://founders.archives.gov /documents/Jefferson/98-01-02-5702.

15. John Adams to TJ, 25 Feb. 1825, Founders Online, https://founders.archives.gov /documents/Adams/99-02-02-7962.

16. TJ to James Madison, 17 Feb. 1826, *PJMRS*, vol. 3, p. 687.

17. Randolph, *The Domestic Life of Thomas Jefferson*, pp. 397, 399, 401. Their view coincides with his own explanation of his debts; see TJ to Thomas J. Randolph, 8 Feb. 1826, Founders Online, https://founders.archives.gov/documents/Jefferson/98-01 -02-5893, and TJ to Joseph Fay, *PTJ*, vol. 25, p. 402.

18. Randolph, *The Domestic Life of Thomas Jefferson*, p. 408.

19. TJ to Joseph Cabell, 20 Jan. 1826, Founders Online, https://founders.archives.gov /documents/Jefferson/98-01-02-5843.

20. Lewis, *The Pursuit of Happiness*, p. 193.

21. Jane M. Carr to Dabney Carr, 27 Feb.1826, Carr-Cary Family Papers, box 2, Albert and Shirley Small Special Collections Library.

22. Tucker, *The Life of Thomas Jefferson*, vol. 2, pp. 550, 558.

23. Taylor, *Thomas Jefferson's Education*, pp. 291–92.

24. Fieser, ed., *Life of George Tucker*, pp. 67, 292; "Andrew K. Smith's Account of Thomas Jefferson's Funeral," 6 July 1826, Jefferson Quotes and Family Letters, http://tjrs .monticello.org/letter/38.

25. Randolph, *The Domestic Life of Thomas Jefferson*, pp. 429, 431.

26. I am grateful to J. Jefferson Looney, the Daniel P. Jordan Editor of *The Papers of Thomas Jefferson Retirement Series*, for an exact copy of the unpublished transcription made from the original document at the Library of Congress.

27. Ellen W. Randolph Coolidge to Henry S. Randall, 16 May 1857, Jefferson Quotes and Family Letters, http://tjrs.monticello.org/letter/466.

28. Thomas Jefferson's will is on deposit at the Thomas Jefferson Papers, Albert and Shirley Small Special Collections Library. It is also printed in Tucker, *The Life of Thomas Jefferson*, vol. 2, pp. 584–87.

29. Tucker, *The Life of Thomas Jefferson*, vol. 2, pp. 584–87.

30. Gordon-Reed and Onuf. *"Most Blessed of the Patriarchs,"* p. 326.

31. Stanton, *"Those Who Labor for My Happiness,"* p. 3.

32. Martha Randolph Jefferson to Ellen Randolph Coolidge, 2 Aug. 1825, Jefferson Quotes and Family Letters, http://tjrs.monticello.org/letter/988.

33. Stanton, *"Those Who Labor for My Happiness,"* pp. 310, 203, 3.

34. Ibid., p. 228.

35. Taylor, *Thomas Jefferson's Education*, p. 310.

36. Frank Grizzard, ed., "'Three Grand and Interesting Objects': An 1828 Visit to Monticello, the University and Montpelier," *Magazine of the Albemarle County History* 51 (1993): 124. The article reprints the account of Margaret Bayard Smith

37. This is based on unpublished research by Jodi Frederiksen, "Private Residence, Public Domain and Vandalism at Monticello," an unfinished draft paper presented at the Vernacular Architecture Forum and "Early Nineteenth Century Graffiti at Monticello," Robert H. Smith International Center for Jefferson Studies, Charlottesville, 16 Aug. 2006.

38. Taylor, *Thomas Jefferson's Education*, p. 311.

39. Virginia Jefferson Randolph Trist to Ellen Randolph Wayles Coolidge, 28 Mar. 1827, Ellen Wayles Randolph Coolidge Correspondence, box 2, Albert and Shirley Small Special Collections Library. For a transcription, see Jefferson Quotes and Family Letters, http://tjrs.monticello.org/letter/1087.

40. Bruce, *History of the University of Virginia*, vol. 3, p. 184.

41. Taylor, *Thomas Jefferson's Education*, p. 312.

42. Kierner, *Martha Jefferson Randolph*, pp. 206, 243–44.

43. Tutwiler, *Early History of the University of Virginia*, p. 10.

44. Alan Pell Crawford, *Twilight at Monticello: The Final Years of Thomas Jefferson* (New York: Random House, 2009), pp. 221–22.

45. Frederick Daniel, "Virginian Reminiscences of Jefferson," *Harper's Weekly*, 19 Nov. 1904, p. 1766.

46. Duke of Saxe-Wiemar-Eisenach, "From the University of Virginia" (1828), in Hayes, ed., *Jefferson in His Own Time*, p. 105.

47. [De Vere], "Mr. Jefferson's Pet," p. 826.

48. Daniel, "Virginian Reminiscences of Jefferson," p. 1768.

49. Based on an anecdote of William Wertenbaker in F. W., "Our Library," *Alumni Bulletin of the University of Virginia* 2, no. 3 (Nov. 1895): 80. The offending volume still survives.

50. Fieser, ed., *Life of George Tucker*, p. 67.

51. *Richmond Enquirer*, 11 July 1826.

52. Thomas Mann Randolph to the University of Virginia Board of Visitors, before 7 Oct. 1826, Jefferson Quotes and Family Letters, http://tjrs.monticello.org/letter /462.

53. Elizabeth V. Chew, "Jefferson's Indian Hall and the Founding of the University of Virginia," paper presented at "Education in the Early Republic and the Founding of the University of Virginia," Robert H. Smith International Center for Jefferson Studies, Montalto, 24 May 2018.

54. George Long to Francis Walker Gilmer, 30 May 1875, Fitzhugh, ed., *Letters of George Long*, p. 24.

55. TJ to James Madison, 17 Feb. 1826, *PJMRS*, vol. 3, p. 687.

56. Geiger, *History of American Higher Education*, p. 179.

57. Whitehead, *The Separation of College and State*, pp. 137–41.

58. Hofstadter, *Academic Freedom in the Age of the College*, p. 269.

59. Adams, *Thomas Jefferson and the University of Virginia*, p. 87.

60. Negely Harte, John North, and Georgina Brewis, *The World of UCL*, 4th edition (London: University College London Press, 2018), pp. 13, 16.

61. Adams, *Thomas Jefferson and the University of Virginia*, p. 155.

62. Cremin, *American Education, the National Experience*, p. 114.

63. Adams, *Thomas Jefferson and the University of Virginia*, p. 193.

64. Bruce, *History of the University of Virginia*, vol. 3, pp. 250–51.

65. Delbanco, *College*, p. 84.

66. Cremin, *American Education, the National Experience*, p. 161.

67. Mike Rashotte, "16 Years a Founder: Documenting How One of Thomas Jefferson's

308 NOTES TO PAGES 257-261

Grandsons Was Misidentified as the Founder of Florida State University (2002)—
And How It Was Corrected (2018)," unpublished paper, copy in author's possession.

68. Bruce, *History of the University of Virginia*, vol. 3, p. 254.

69. Morison, *Three Centuries of Harvard*, p. 233.

70. George Ticknor to James Madison, 21 Nov. 1825, *PJMRS*, vol. 3, p. 501.

71. Josiah Quincy to James Madison, 22 Feb. 1829, Founders Online, https://founders
.archives.gov/documents/Madison/99-02-02-1707.

72. James Madison to Joseph Cabell, 19 Mar. 1829, Founders Online, https://founders
.archives.gov/documents/Madison/99-02-02-1736.

73. Wagoner, *Jefferson and Education*, p. 139.

74. Wilson, "Jefferson's Lawn," p. 54.

75. James Bryant Conant, *Thomas Jefferson and the Development of American Public Ed-
ucation* (Berkeley: University of California Press, 1962), p. 29. See also Wayne J.
Urban, "James Bryan Conant: Twentieth Century Jeffersonian," in Holowchak and
Dotts, eds., *The Elusive Thomas Jefferson*, pp. 130–42.

76. Malone, *The Public Life of Thomas Cooper*, p. 366.

77. O'Brien, *Intellectual Life and the American South*, p. 34; Genovese, *The Slaveholders'
Dilemma*, p. 1.

78. Malone, *The Public Life of Thomas Cooper*, p. 219.

79. Genovese, *The Slaveholders' Dilemma*; Elizabeth Fox Genovese and Eugene D. Genovese, *The Mind of the Master Class: History and Faith in Southern Slaveholder's World-
view* (Cambridge: Cambridge University Press, 2005); O'Brien, *Intellectual Life and
the American South*.

80. Hofstadter, *Academic Freedom in the Age of the College*, p. 269.

81. [Shaw], *Is Slavery a Blessing?* p. 25. He was a professor at the university from 1854 to
1855.

82. At the University of Virginia, this decline occurred despite some progressive reforms in the aftermath of the Civil War. See James T. Moore, "The University and
the Readjusters," *Virginia Magazine of History and Biography* 78, no. 1 (Jan. 1970):
87–101. I am very grateful to James R. Sofka for this reference.

83. Hellenbrand, *Unfinished Revolution*, p. 17.

84. TJ to "Henry Hopkinson" (Samuel Kercheval), 12 July 1816, *PTRSJ*, vol. 10, p. 22.

85. TJ to Roger C. Weightman, 24 June 1826, Founders Online, https://founders
.archives.gov/documents/Jefferson/98-01-02-6179. The letter is often erroneously
described as his last letter. It was not. He wrote two other letters afterward, one of
which concerns the shipment of wine from France. See J. Jefferson Looney, "Thomas
Jefferson's Last Letter," *Virginia Magazine of History and Biography* 112, no. 2 (2004):
178–84.

86. TJ to the Marquis de Lafayette, 9 Oct. 1824, Founders Online, https://founders
.archives.gov/documents/Jefferson/98-01-02-4608.

87. TJ to Augustus B. Woodward, 3 Apr. 1825, Founders Online, https://founders
.archives.gov/documents/Jefferson/98-01-02-5105.

INDEX

Italicized page numbers refer to illustrations, page numbers followed by "t" indicate a table, and cp followed by a number denotes plates in the color gallery. The initials "TJ" denote Thomas Jefferson, and "UVA" denotes University of Virginia.

models for UVA, 25; and national university, 51, 52–53; and "natural aristocracy," 42–43; and Northwest Ordinance, 50–51; primary schools, 73–79; public libraries, 50; and religion, opposition to, 78–79; and republicanism, 39–43, 52–53, 58–59, 82–83, cp49; schools and education, readings on, 27; women's education, views on, 34–35, 47–48

— and religion: atheism, charges of by opponents, cp17; at College of William and Mary, 23; and empiricism, 161, 166; influences on, 163–64; Jefferson Bible, 158–61, cp43; major religions, comparison of, 159; and morality, 161–63, 174–75; and organized religion as tyranny, views on, 165–66; personal beliefs of, secretive about, 167–68; Qur'an of, 181; and religious freedom, 88; religious services, attendance of, 165; and republicanism, 181; secular education, influences on idea of, 172–73; separation of church and state in public university, 173–74; TJ and his popularity, 175–77; TJ as deist, myth of, 162. See also Presbyterians

— and slavery: antislavery views of, 19, 105–6, 107, 186, 191–94; antislavery views of kept secret, 167, 194–95, 197–98; Black inferiority, views on, 183, 201–3; and colonization, views on, 204–5; in Declaration of Independence, original draft of, 192; and enslaved people, education of, 205–7; enslaved people at dinner parties, 28–29; enslaved people at Monticello, descendants of, 210; enslaved people at Monticello, surveillance of, 25–26; enslaved people of, sale of after TJ death, 247–48; as enslaver, 15, 27, 131, 194, 195–96, 239, cp44; as enslaver, sale of enslaved, 187–88; and free Blacks, 193; and Hemingses, 31–32, 186, 195, 206; on manumission, 192; and Missouri Crisis and Compromise, 105–6, 107; and slave trade, international, 193–94; solution for, lack of, 186, 196–97; TJ as patriarch, 29–30; and westward expansion, 192–94

— and UVA: academic village and friends at Monticello, 118; and John Adams, 39–40; design and construction of, 101–2, 122–25, 130, 133; faculty, recruitment of, 141–44; and family as metaphor for, 30, 221; as legacy, 261; location of, 94–100; "Mr. Jefferson's University" nickname origins, 2; publicity for, 122–23,

123, 130–32, 255; and religion, opposition to, 14, 78, 90–94; and Rockfish Gap Commission and Report, 61–64, 79–81; and student behavior, 211–13, 215–16, 221–22, 234; vision for, 53, 57–58, 236–37; visits to, 250–51
Jefferson Memorial, 9, 166
Jefferson Society (Jefferson Literary and Debating Society), 200–201, 230–33, cp48
Jews, 159, 164, 171, 178–82, 253, 256
Johnson, Benjamin, 190
Johnson, Chapman, 71–72, 127, 176, 216, 253
Johnson, Samuel, 191
Johnson, Thomas, 148
Judge, Ona, 197
Jupiter (enslaved person), 192

Kames, Lord (Henry Home), 163
Kant, Immanuel, 202
Kettle, Tilly, cp8
Key, Thomas Hewitt: demeanor of, 222; as enslaver, 187, cp43; and examination system, 228–29; faculty, appointment to, 138, 143; faculty, resignation of, 215, 256; and Monticello dinner parties, 250–51; on student behavior, 213; and Sylvester, 178, 256
King, Martin Luther, Jr., 210
King, William, 85–87
Kirkland, John Thornton, 172, 263n2
Kneller, Godfrey, cp6
Knox, Samuel, 24, 91, 94, 141
Kosciusko, Thaddeus, 33
Kraitsir, Charles, 179

Lacey, John F., 161
Lafayette, marquis de (Gilbert du Motier), 130–32, 233
Latrobe, Benjamin Henry, 85, 113, 118–19, 128, cp33
Leake, Samuel, 61
Leake, Walter, 61
Lee, Henry, 239
Lee, Henry, Jr., 239
Lee, John, 233
Legrand, J. G., 113–16
Leitch, James, 64
Levasseur, Auguste, 16
Levy, Jefferson Monroe, 248
Levy, Uriah Phillips, 180–81, 249
Lewis and Clark expedition, 16, 17, 20
Library of Congress, 20, 27, 116, 118, 181

Lincoln, Abraham, 109, 205; on TJ, 9
Linn, William, 56
literacy rates, 43, 45, 169, 207
Literary Fund, 71, 73–75, 76–78, 102
Locke, John, 17–18, 79, *cp6*
Lomax, John Tayloe, 144, 154, 157
Long, George, *cp38*; arrival of UVA, 134–36; attack on by students, 211–13; career of, 136–37, 140–41, 143, 256; on Confederacy, 208; demeanor of, 222; departure from UVA, 215; and examination system, 228–29; family of, 136; on job security, 135, 156; and *Penny Cyclopedia*, editor of, 144; and Poe, 233–34; on student behavior, 213, 236; teaching responsibilities of, 145, 146; and TJ, relationship with, 135–36; on TJ and legacy at UVA, 252–53; and Tutwiler, 13, 136, 234

Madison, Bishop James, 24, 65, 97
Madison, Dolley, 25, 89, 131
Madison, James, *cp24*; on academic freedom, 155–56; as Board of Visitors member, 2; and Central College, 71–72, 73, 84, 85; and Dunglison, 147; on education and republicanism, 82, 88–89; and faculty interactions, 136; finances of, 110; and Jefferson Society, 232; and Lafayette, 131, 233; Montpelier design, 124; and national university, 51; on Quincy, 258; and religious freedom, 88, 164; and Rockfish Gap Commission, 61–62, 90; and slavery, views on, 196, 199–200; and TJ, relationship with, 88–89, 164, 246; on Tucker as faculty, 154–55; on UVA and religion, 165–66, 176; and UVA faculty, 140; and UVA law school, 153–54, 155–56; on UVA library, 129, 173–74; as UVA rector, 90, 253
Mann, Horace, 46
Marshall, John, 58, 108, 152–53
Martin, Henry, 188
Martineau, Harriet, 177, 186–87, 198–99, 208
Maury, James, 22
Maury, Reuben, 162
Maverick, Peter, 122–23, 123
McCulloch v. Maryland (1819), 108
McGuffey, William Holmes, 177
Meade, William, 175
medical schools, 148
Mercer, Charles Fenton, 73–78, 100, 108–9, 181, 197

Methodists, 93, 109, 167, 177
Minor, John B., 200
Minor, Warner W., 189–90
Missouri Crisis and Compromise of 1820, 103, 105–6, 197, 198
Molesworth, Robert, 172
Molinos, Jacques, 113
Monroe, James, *cp25*; and Central College, 71–72, 73, 84, 85, 122, *cp25*; and Dunglison, 147; and faculty interactions, 136; as Freemason, 85; and Jefferson Society, 232; and Lafayette, 131, 233; and public education, 90, *cp25*; and Rockfish Gap Commission, 61–62; and UVA, 90, 253
Montandon, James E., 190–91
Monticello: Cabinet, 21–22, 25–26, 245, *cp4*, *cp5*; construction of, 248–49; design of, 16–17, 116–17, 120, 124–25; dinner parties at, 11–12, 28–29, 233, 250–51, *cp52*; enslaved people at, descendants of, 210; Entrance Hall, *cp3*; exterior, *cp2*, *cp11*; gardens, *cp11*; location of, *cp30*; management of, 32; sale of, 247, 248–49; soil quality of, 32; TJ's intellectual influences, portraits of, *cp6*; and UVA students signing of, 249; view from, *cp31*; visitors to, 25–26, 32–33, 241
Moore, Clement Clark, 54
Moore, Jeremiah, 56
Moses, Ezekiel, 182
Mountain Top Inn, 60–61
Murray, James A., 143
Muslims, 164, 181

Neale, John, 208
Neilson, John, 123–24
Newman, John Henry, 167
Newton, Isaac, 17, *cp6*
Nicholas, Wilson Cary, 2, 65, 71, 98, 109–10, 241
Northwest Ordinance, 50–51, 192–94
Notes on the State of Virginia (1787), by TJ, 18–20; on architecture, 115–16; on education, 41, 45, 47; on entitlement and despotism among planter elites, 216–17; and religion, 167; on slavery, 19, 192, 201, 204–5
nullification crisis, 109, 198, 199–200

Obama, Barak, 9
Oldham, James, 124